ks should be
ks (not alrea
cation, by

te Due

orrowers' ticke

amage to or los

orrowers must

nes charged

Championship

Tactics

Championship Tactics

How Anyone Can
Sail Faster,
Smarter, and
Win Races

Gary Jobson,
Tom Whidden,
and Adam Loory

Illustrations by Bill King

Published by Nautical Books
an imprint of
A & C Black (Publishers) Ltd
35 Bedford Row, London WC1R 4JH

ISBN 0 7136 3342 5

Originally published in the United States by St. Martin's Press, New York.
Design by Chris Welch

A CIP catalogue record for this book is available from the British Library.

Contents

Foreword by Gary Jobson

Most winning sailors owe their success to good instincts during the heat of battle. Often split-second decisions are made based on years of experience. But for many sailors defining how to make the right decision consistently is even harder than the sailing itself. Writing *Championship Tactics* was an exercise in evaluating the whys and hows of our sport. While most tactical decisions just happen during the race, our coauthor, Adam Loory kept probing deeper and deeper in both my mind and Tom Whidden's during the year we spent writing this book.

I first became impressed by Adam Loory at the 1986 12-meter World Championship in Fremantle, Australia. There were over two hundred journalists from around the world covering the event in anticipation of the 1987 America's Cup. While most journalists lobbed cream puff questions at the competitors, Loory was able to ferret out what was really happening on the water. His techniques gained the attention of *USA Today* and he was hired as a feature writer for the 1986/87 America's Cup Trials and Cup. Sail America used Adam as a public relations writer during the 1988 America's Cup.

Unfortunately neither Tom nor I made Adam's job easy. The good news we told him was "you have the job helping to write this book." But the bad news, he later found out, was finding us.

Tom Whidden and I have been fierce rivals in many of the world's most prestigious events for the past fifteen years. I like racing against Tom because he rarely makes mistakes. It is a real challenge to be creative and come up with something new to fool him. A number of times I've found myself on slower boats. It takes really clever tactics to beat the other boat in a match race. And its been these races when I've learned my best stuff. In all this time Tom Whidden and I have never faced off in a protest room.

During one of our working sessions in Annapolis, the conversation actually got a little heated. Adam was the first to realize. that the best material was coming to the surface.

Our research brought to light many patterns on how races are won using tactics. But there are always exceptions to every rule and we've included our best techniques and most closely guarded secrets in this volume.

Every racing sailboat, regardless of size, has a better chance of winning when using one crew member as a tactician. All the best skippers in America like Ted Turner, Dennis Conner, Buddy Melges, and the late Tom Blackaller understand the need for tactical advice both on and off the water. Tom Whidden and I occasionally get to skipper but both our greatest victories have been as tacticians. It's the lessons learned from these victories as well as many painful defeats that we present here to help give you the edge.

—Gary Jobson
Annapolis, MD, 1990

Foreword by Tom Whidden

In 1979, Dennis Conner invited me to be trial skipper on *Enterprise* and sail against him on *Freedom* in preparation for the 1980 America's Cup. At the time, I considered it a good place to begin my overall goal to win an America's Cup as a crew member and then someday perhaps even skipper my own America's Cup defender or challenger. Looking back, I think I gave Dennis all the competition he needed while earning a spot on *Freedom* in the sail trimmers' cockpit and helping with some of the strategy.

After defending the Cup successfully that year, I realized that Dennis was on his way to becoming an America's Cup institution. It seemed to me that if I wanted to continue as an integral part of his well-engineered campaigns, I had better reorient my goals. I decided to learn to be the best match race *tactician* possible. This was, in retrospect, a wise decision: I went on to do three more America's Cups with Dennis in the tactician's cockpit. Dennis was the best teacher I could have had. He is one of the most aggressive and creative match racers in the world. And frankly, the skills that I have acquired as a tactician for Dennis, have opened other doors for me since, such as the one that led to my current role as president of North Sails.

I also have learned during my years as a tactician that strategy and good moves on the racecourse are not the only skills you need to win. A good tactician must fulfill many roles onboard. He or she must be the eyes and ears of a concentrating helmsman, the cheerleader and motivator for an entire crew, and of course, an effective communicator, to ensure that all members of the crew pull together. If you're afraid to make a quick decision or make a mistake you need not apply for the job.

The axioms and rules that we share with you in *Championship Tactics* have been developed to make our job easier and to maximize our chances for success. Of course you don't have to have the job of "tactician" to benefit from this book. *Every* racing sailor should know tactics and how it can affect the outcome of a race. The best boats that I have sailed on rely upon the knowledge and advice of the entire crew in order to win.

Over the years, Gary and I have been competitors more often than team members. The rivalry that has developed from this competition made writing this book all the more challenging. Sharing ideas with Gary made me realize why he is so hard to beat. In many cases we brought similar beliefs to the project, but he also had a bag of tricks of his own.

Between the two of us, we have been in many important races, both on the winning and losing sides. While re-examining and discussing each of these experiences, I think we've discussed the subtleties of racing tactics with unique thoroughness and breadth. This book, plus practice, should give you the confidence to win on the water.

—Tom Whidden
Essex, Connecticut, 1990

Acknowledgments

A book as detailed as this one could not be done without a little help from our friends. Over the years numerous articles have appeared by Gary Jobson and Tom Whidden in *Sailing World*, *Yachting World*, *Yachting*, and *Sail* magazines. Some of the ideas and text have been borrowed from these articles for this book. To the editors of these fine publications, we are most grateful. We'd also like to thank the editors of the *North U. Fast Course* and the *North U. Smart Course* for material we used.

A special thanks goes to Ockam Instrument's Jim Marshall who wrote Chapter 8 on Tactical Instruments. Instrumentation is one of the leading edges of the sport, and Ockam has been out there leading the way. Jim writes a column in *Sailing World* called "Instruments in Action," which is a must read for anyone interested in getting the most out of their instruments. Thanks to George Hazen and Peter Schenn of Design Systems in Annapolis, MD, which produced the polar diagrams for the Tactical Instruments chapter.

We thank the United States Yacht Racing Union for its cooperation. Dave Perry and Dave Dellenbaugh were invaluable as rules consultants. Both are USYRU Senior Certified Judges. Perry is the author of *Understanding the Yacht Racing Rules Through 1992*, which treats the subject in a clear and conversational manner. Dellenbaugh has put out a video called *Learn the Racing Rules*, which brings the rules to life.

For the section on weather we'd like to thank Peter Isler who took time out from his current America's Cup bid to read over, correct, and comment on the section; Walter Stubner let us incorporate the article he wrote for *Sailing World* on using Weather Service data to gain local knowledge better than the locals, and Rob Mairs, the meteorologist for the 1988 U.S. Olympic Yachting Team, looked over the section. Thanks also to Gordy Bowers for his article on lake winds.

We also thank the people who reported on the various sailing venues: Chuck Inglefield, Jud Smith, Chuck Gravengood, Susan and Scott Taylor, Michael Fortenbaugh, John Shadden, Paul Gingras, Mark Washeim, Amy Sheppard, Merle Hallet, Larry Leonard, Mike Toppa, Stu Argo, and John Kostecki.

Most of all we'd like to thank those who helped get the manuscript ready for publication. We are indebted to Shane Mitchell, a contributing editor at *Yachting*, who rescued this project around the holiday season by putting in long hours editing while all the other players went off around the globe to sail. We'd also like to thank our editor at St. Martin's Press, Michael Sagalyn and his assistant Ed Stackler, Gary's associate Kathy Thompson, along with Stuart Loory, Lee Corbin, Tom Newmann, Robert Miller, Katherine Holland, the late Tom Blackhaller—and Eva Loory who encouraged and coaxed her grandson through his first book.

chapter 1

What Is a Tactician?

Sailors love to steer sailboats. Not all sailors like to be tacticians, however, because calling tactics is harder to do well. Steering is a limelight position. On most boats the helmsman doesn't have to work as hard physically as the rest of the crew; he or she stays dry, develops a pleasant rapport with the wind and waves, and takes the credit when the boat finishes well. The tactician, on the other hand, is in a high-pressure position; he or she calls the shots that can mean the difference between winning and losing. The crew can be working well and the boat going fast, but if the tactician makes a bad call on which side of the course to play, the boat will finish poorly.

Yet, on the other hand, a fast boat always makes the tactician look brilliant. It's easy to win sailboat races when the boat simply pops off the starting line and sails faster than the competition. But most boats these days sail at the same speed or race in a narrow band of handicap rating where the boats are moving through the water at nearly the same speed. Therefore, to win races you need superior boat-handling and tactics.

By using better tactics, you'll have a shot at beating boats that are faster than yours. One such "tortoise and hare" example Gary Jobson remembers occurred when he raced the 130-foot J boats *Endeavor* and *Shamrock* V in 1989. "At the first regatta, in Newport, Rhode Island, *Endeavor* proved to be

the much faster yacht. But both Ted [Turner, whom Gary raced against] and I had our good moments when we steered the slower *Shamrock*. In the second race, Ted did a good job avoiding a hole that I sailed *Endeavor* into. Before I got going again, Turner had an eight-boatlength lead. On the second day I got my revenge and pushed Ted, this time sailing *Endeavor*, over the starting line early. Somehow there is an inner sense of accomplishment when you beat someone tactically because it means you have outsmarted them on the water.

There are two ways to get around the course. The first is the one that gets you around the course fastest—your strategy for playing the wind and current. The second gets you around the course ahead of all the other boats—your tactical plan. How you sail the course is a compromise between strategy and tactics. Most tacticians get into trouble by trying to make races too complicated. The highest priorities are keeping your boat going fast in the right direction as often as possible, and staying between your competition and the mark. It's hard to get into too much trouble if you keep those two priorities in sight.

In this chapter we'll start out by introducing you to the tools of the tactician's trade. We'll discuss the differences between being a tactician on a big boat, where your only job is to call tactics, and being a tactician on a double-handed dinghy, where the tactician is also the helmsman or the person hanging from a trapeze wire. We'll explain how to get the most from wind and current on the course, how to update your strategic plan by gathering information about the wind as the race progresses, how to check the performance of your boat against the competition, how to control the atmosphere on the boat, how to keep track of where the boat is in the regatta standings, and how to coach the helmsman if he or she needs it. As you can see, the tactician's mind is always busy during the race.

On any boat, it takes discipline for skippers to leave the management of the race to someone else. The skipper is giving up a great deal of control. Unfortunately, most skippers believe they should be the tactician too; some we know would probably sail the whole boat if they could clone themselves. But modern fin-keel boats have no natural feel to the helm, and planing dinghies are skittish. Steering them well takes a helmsman's fulltime efforts (see Chapter 7). So if you're a skipper, remember that winning can involve delegation of all tasks except steering the boat.

Twelve-meter racing in the America's Cup has demonstrated the value of having a separate tactician. Twelves steer like trucks; since they are so heavy and so slow to accelerate, they take great concentration to steer well. For that matter, light boats like J/24s or Schock 35s take just as much concentration because they don't track. Therefore, the tactician is the one who looks around outside the boat and becomes the skipper's eyes and ears.

Even a skipper like Dennis Conner, who's a creative tactician in his own right, can't look around long enough to develop tactics for the big picture, i.e., the rest of the leg. Tom Whidden says, "Dennis takes quick glances, but I think it's important to give him feedback continually on where boats are and what the options are. If he's doing his job well, he shouldn't have to worry too much about tactics. If I'm doing my job well, I'm giving him enough feedback so that he can make the ultimate decision."

Tools of the Tactician's Trade

There are six basic tools that will give you enough information to stay between the competition and the next mark: (1) the race's sailing instructions, (2) a chart of the racing area, (3) tide tables, (4) pencil and paper to take notes with, (5) a hand-bearing compass, and (6) a couple of sets of tacking lines to monitor the fleet.

You need to study the sailing instructions because they depict the different courses the race committee will choose from, describe the marks, list any special rules in effect, state the race time limit, and indicate race committee procedures. If a boat you are covering suddenly starts heading for a different mark, you'd better have a copy of the sailing instructions at hand, to know whether to follow or not. Many major events have been won because competitors have carefully studied the sailing instructions, and plenty of disasters have occurred because people have assumed that all races are run the same.

Gary painfully remembers the 1984 Liberty Cup, when there was a clause at the end of a long passage that gave the race committee the power to call for a sail-off (like a tie-breaker in tennis) to resolve ties. "With the possibility of a sail-off, it would have been better to be more conservative, because the regatta could still be won in 'overtime.' Instead, I took some major chances in races that I shouldn't have, missed my opportunities, and didn't make the finals as a result. I've learned that being cavalier with the racing instructions can be very expensive."

A chart of the course and tide tables are necessary for figuring out compass courses between the marks and knowing where you can go to get out of adverse current, and where to get the most from favorable current.

It won't take too long to learn the merits of having a pencil and paper in your pocket. Your notes should include the course, the compass courses between all the marks of the course, the boat's upwind headings, the time the tide changes, lists of things that need to be changed or fixed before the next race, and details of a protest.

Waterproof paper like WetNotes is best, though some people like to write on a piece of duct tape stuck to the deck. On a dinghy you can write with a grease pencil on a piece of Mylar taped to the deck, or you can write right on the fiberglass deck itself; just make sure you don't write with an indelible marker.

A hand-bearing compass is to a tactician what a calculator is to an accountant. The most popular kind are referred to as "hockey pucks," because of their round shape and black rubber protective coating. Recently, electronic handheld compasses have been developed. Both can be used in many ways that let you know how your boat is faring. The most common tactical use for a hand-bearing compass is judging how much distance you are gaining or losing against another boat. For example, look through a hand-bearing compass and take a reading on your competitor's bow. Wait a few minutes and then take another reading on the his bow. If you are sighting a boat to the left, you are gaining on him if the compass-bearing numbers are decreasing. If you are sighting a boat to the right, and the heading numbers increase, then you're passing him. (See figure 1.1.)

Figure 1.1 *Using a hand-bearing compass to determine gain or loss relative to another boat.*

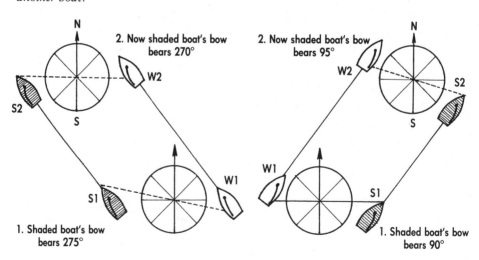

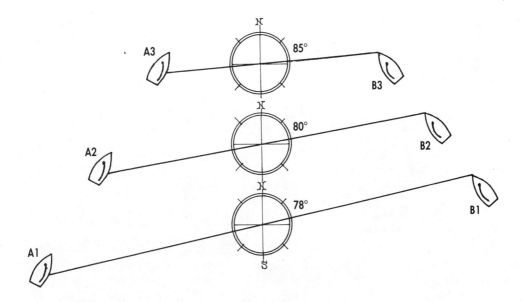

Figure 1.2 *A's skipper uses a hand-bearing compass to determine whether she can cross the starboard tack boat by taking three sights and noticing that her boat is gaining bearing steadily on Boat B. If the bearing between A and B did not change between sights, then the boats would be on a collision course.*

A hand-bearing compass can also be used to judge if you are going to cross in front of another boat or collide with it. Figure 1.2 shows how the skipper of a port-tack boat figures out that he is crossing a starboard tacker.

A hand-bearing compass can also determine whether you are gaining windward or leeward distance on a rival boat. Say that, sighting through the compass, you find the other boat is 4 degrees from the bow to the stern (figure 1.3). After sailing for two minutes, the boat to leeward measures 5½ degrees, while the bearing to the bow has remained constant. The explanation is that the boats have moved closer together laterally—provided the other boat has not altered course substantially.

Instead of worrying about gains and losses in feet and inches, the tactician can better serve the skipper by offering information on how he is gaining or losing. "I break down any change in position into two components," says Tom. "Think of your boat and the other boat on the rails of a railroad track. Except these aren't normal tracks; the distance between the rails can vary. Therefore, when the other boat is gaining, figure out if it's going farther down its rail, or if it is pointing higher, i.e., changing the course of its rail. What I call the

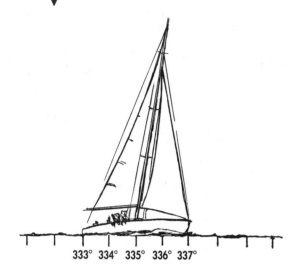

333° 334° 335° 336° 337°

Figure 1.3 *Using the degree scale on a hand-bearing compass to measure another boat.*

distance between the rails is gauge, and what I call going down the rail is range. That's important feedback to be able to give a skipper. When I tell Dennis a guy is gaining, he doesn't say, 'Okay.' He says, 'How's he gaining?' I've got to give him good feedback that will allow him to decide how to neutralize the threat."

You can even use your hand-bearing compass to judge whether you are gaining or losing ground on a boat ahead or behind you. This is a trick you can do only with non-digital hand-bearing compasses. Turn your hockey puck on its side and measure how many degrees tall the other boat's mast is. (See figure 1.4.) If you can't get the whole mast in, measure the distance from the spreaders to the deck. If the rig measures more degrees on a second reading, the boats have come closer together. The smaller the mast gets, the farther apart the boats are getting.

A dinghy sailor without a hand-bearing compass has several lower-tech methods available for judging his or her boat's performance. For instance, the compass secured to the deck can be used in the same way as a hand-bearing compass. Just sight another boat by looking over the top of the deck-mounted compass. Since you can't hold it up to your eye, it is less precise than a hand-bearing compass. (The only way you can use a non-gimbaled deck compass for measuring the height of another boat's rig is by capsizing your boat!)

Dinghy sailors don't have the luxury of using a hand-bearing compass to help them determine the performance of their boats, because the pace is so

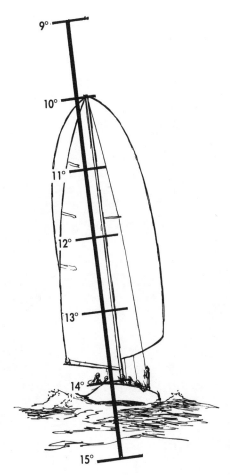

Figure 1.4 *Using a compass to measure another boat.*

much faster, and the crew are busy using their body weight to make the boat perform. But the tactician on a dinghy has one advantage over his counterpart on a big boat: The competition is closer together because the courses are shorter. With the boats close together, it's easier to use your eyes to determine how you are doing against others.

To judge your speed against boats inshore of you, take visual bearings on objects in the background. This is called "making trees." It's done by watching the other boat and the shoreline in the background at the same time. If the two of you seem to be advancing past objects on shore at the same rate, then both boats are going the same speed. The other boat is pulling away from you if objects, like trees, on shore seem to be coming out behind him. If you are "making trees" on the other boat, it will seem like the trees are coming from in front of its bow (figure 1.5).

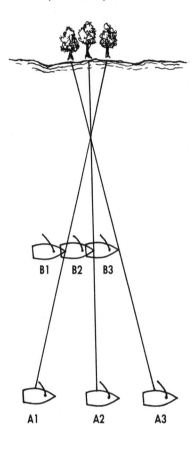

A1   A2   A3   Figure 1.5 *"Making trees."*

Another way to judge your performance against another boat without using a hand-bearing compass is to sight down your arm and use your thumb and your forefinger to measure how tall a boat's rig is, or to gauge the distance between its bow and stern. If you have to spread your fingers farther apart to make a second measurement, the other boat has gotten closer. To get a rough idea of how you are doing against another boat, line it up with something relative on your boat. If, on the first sighting, you see its bow in line with the leeward end of your traveler bar, and the next time you look its bow is behind your jib, then you know the boat is passing in front of you. Be careful, because if your boat changes course at all, you could get a false impression of loss or gain.

Tacking lines are the last basic tool a tactician uses to keep between the competition and the next mark. Drawn on the deck, tacking lines are a valuable reference for determining whether other boats are ahead or behind, or whether you can tack and lay a mark.

Tacking lines are three sets of angles drawn on the deck, used to sight other boats and laylines. Tacking lines should be drawn outboard on the deck on both sides of the boat. (See figure 1.6.) The longer the lines, the more accurate your sights will be.

To draw a set of tacking lines, you need to create a baseline that runs parallel to the boat's centerline. A boat's centerline can be found by running a string from the mast to the backstay. Next, use a protractor to draw in the angles that represent how close to the wind your boat can sail in light, moderate, and strong winds. As the breeze picks up, boats sail closer to the wind. For instance, a Schock 35 can sail 44 degrees to the wind in 8 knots, 41 degrees in 10 knots, and 38 degrees in 16 knots or more.

Figure 1.6 *Tacking lines are used three different ways: to determine if you can cross another boat, to determine when you've reached a layline to a windward mark, and to determine whether you are ahead or behind a boat on your windward quarter.*

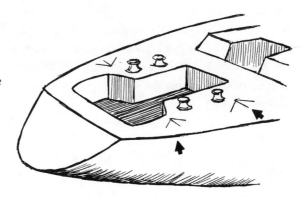
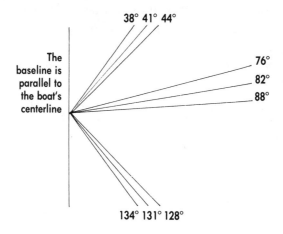

The next set of lines represents the angles that your boat tacks through in different wind strengths. Do this by doubling the angle of how close your boat can sail to the wind. For instance, if a Schock 35 can sail 41 degrees to the wind in 10 knots, it will tack through 82 degrees (figure 1.6). Thus, the boat's tacking angle in 10 knots wind is 82 degress. The lines representing your tacking angles are ones you'll sight to determine if you have reached a layline. Going back to the example of the Schock 35 in 10 knots of wind, you would know it was time to tack for the windward mark if you sighted along the 82-degree line and saw the mark on or behind an extension of that line. If the mark was in front of the 82-degree line, you'd be short of the layline.

The final set of lines point aft. To draw them, add 90 degrees to the first set of lines you drew, and draw in lines for the resulting sums, i.e., 128, 131, and 134 degrees. In addition to the baseline that parallels, the centerline of the boat, each set has nine lines. (See figure 1.6). Now duplicate all three sets in the corresponding place on the other side of the boat.

Now that you've got the tacking lines on your boat, let's go over their use, starting with the forward-pointing set of angles. The lines pointing forward are used in determining whether you can cross an approaching boat or whether you will need to duck. (See figure 1.7—Situation A.) Meeting another boat on the course like this is called a crossing situation; that is one boat is going to cross another.

Use the center set of lines to determine whether you are on the layline to a windward mark. As you approach the mark, sight up the line that indicates your tacking angle for the given wind strength. (See figure 1.7—Situation B.)

The rear-pointing set of lines indicate whether you are ahead of a boat to windward and behind you. Knowing if you are ahead is important when you are on starboard tack and want to tack to port. If you're ahead, you'll be able to tack to port and sail across the other boat's bow. (See figure 1.7—Situation C.)

To reduce confusion, it's wise to color-code the lines. Sticking with the Shock 35 example, the lines for heavy air—38 degrees, 76 degrees, and 128 degrees—could be red, with black for medium air, and blue for light air.

If you don't mind marking up the deck, it's a good idea to put the forward pointing component of the tacking lines by the jib trimmer's position. Since that person is usually to leeward trimming the jib, he will be the first to notice a boat approaching on the opposite tack. With the set of tacking lines, the trimmer can quickly determine whether the pending crossing situation is going to be close.

Situation A

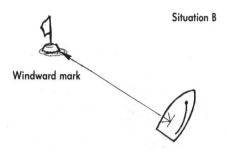

Situation B

Windward mark

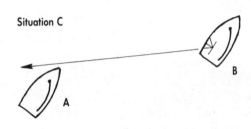

Situation C

Figure 1.7 *In Situation A, the tactician on Boat A—the port-tack boat—sights the forward facing line for the given wind strength to determine if he can cross Boat B—the starboard-tack boat. In this case, A can cross B since B is behind the sight line. In Situation B, the boat can tack and make the mark since the mark is in line with the tacking line that indicates the direction the boat will head on the opposite tack. Situation C shows that Boat A–ahead and to leeward—can tack and cross the boat behind and to windward.*

Both dinghy sailors and big-boat sailors can benefit from having lines marked on the deck. Once applied to the deck, they are a quick and easy way to pick laylines and judge crossing situations.

In dinghies, the best teams have separate individuals acting as helmsmen and tacticians. It's important to have the crew do the looking around and formulating tactics, while the person on the helm concentrates on speed. This is especially important when you are sailing an extremely short course. In races lasting less than 15 minutes, the skipper barely has enough time to concentrate on tacking well and getting the boat up to speed before it's time to tack again. Many times, skippers calling tactics for themselves concentrate so hard on tacking into a lee-bow position that they find themselves pinned out by a windward boat and forced to sail past the layline. (See figure 1.8.)

On the other hand, once the crew finishes the tack and trims the jib, he or she can keep track of what's happening outside the boat—while hiking. Having the crew call tactics is especially valuable when sailing in a pack of

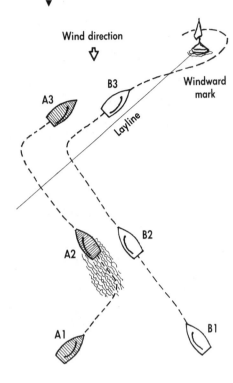

Figure 1.8 *Not being able to cross Boat B, Boat A tacks on B's leeward bow. If A can tack close enough to B, A can slow B with its backwind that goes to windward. But in this case, A tacks too far away from B and B is unaffected by A; therefore, B continues to sail at the same speed as A. Now A is "pinned out" since A can't tack until B chooses to tack.*

boats, as for example, at the starting line or approaching a mark—times when the helmsman needs to concentrate on keeping the boat's speed up to prevent getting passed and left in disturbed wind.

Even if you are sailing with an inexperienced pickup crew, you need to have the person take on some of the duties of a tactician. Even inexperienced crew can help out if you give them specific things to look for, such as, "Watch boats 2940 and 7077." Or ask them specific questions like, "Is there more wind on the left or the right side of the course? Look for where the boats are heeling over more or going faster."

"When I have a new crew," says Gary, "I try to talk through what I'm doing and how I'm interpreting what's happening on the course. That way my crew can get an idea of my thought process and what I'm looking for. Don't just say, 'Ready about, hard alee.' Instead, help your crew catch on by saying, 'We're tacking because we're in a major header,' or 'We are tacking because there is a bad set of waves coming,' or 'Let's tack to get out of the current. Didn't you see the current shear we just crossed?' or 'There are a lot of boats to the right, so let's tack and stay with the fleet.' "

Talking is an important part of the tactician's job. Silence often descends on a boat when things go wrong; boats that are doing poorly are usually very quiet. It's just as important to keep talking when the boat is doing poorly. If you get quiet because you're sensitive about being behind, crew morale will drop, and so will their level of intensity. When the boat does poorly, take the responsibility, and keep working—out loud—to gain back everything you lost.

Tacticians should try to keep their commentary and feedback even. Create a cadence. In other words, you can't be quiet for 20 minutes and talk for two. Keep presenting options. Look for wind, anticipate crossing situations, judge your performance by taking readings on other boats. Speak loud enough that the cockpit crew understands what is going on; don't just whisper to the skipper. When planning out the next move, like a spinnaker set or tack, the crew needs to hear your intentions so that they will be ready.

In addition to speaking continuously and loudly, "the tactician needs to be a soothing person to listen to," says Gary. "He must speak generally with an encouraging tone. He should predict what is going to happen, which makes the crew feel confident and at ease. Whatever happens, don't let panic show in your voice. And never, ever be sarcastic. Sarcasm destroys a crew. It's infectious, and pretty soon nobody likes anyone else."

Of course, speaking openly this way can put the tactician out on a limb, because everything he says is open to analysis and second-guessing by the rest of the crew. "My experiences on the 80-foot maxi boat *Matador* are some of the most fun and challenging that I've ever had," says Gary, "because there is a lot of pressure to make the right choices. There are 25 other crew members aboard who are all top sailors with their own ideas on how the race should be sailed."

Since the tactician is the person who talks the most on board, the job of controlling the emotional atmosphere usually falls on his shoulders. The crew needs some sort of emotional release along the way, because everyone develops a lot of adrenaline and pent-up excitement. Humor helps, but you have to be careful not to let it get out of control. You don't want everyone on the weather rail talking and yukking it up. Sometimes the tactician has to calm things down and get the crew concentrating again. It's important that you judge whether the pent-up emotion is helping or hurting. Don't quiet everyone down in the middle of an inspirational war chant.

In 1983, Gary was the tactician for Tom Blackaller on the 12-meter *Defender* during the America's Cup trials. "Blackaller and a bunch of the crew tormented

Dennis Conner by yelling mostly unprintable comments across the water," says Gary. "One day, to emphasize his point, Paul Cayard came out on the racecourse wielding a sledgehammer over his head. He looked like a cossack riding a horse into battle. I'm not sure whether Dennis was laughing at Cayard, or was upset by all the noise, but it had its effect—we won a lot of starts off of Dennis that summer." Gary said he kept quiet throughout the campaign of verbal assaults, because his style is not to talk with the other boat.

Every now and then the tactician needs a little boost when things are going poorly. Being surrounded by a loyal crew is a definite advantage. You've got to keep track of the longer-term goal. Races and protests will be lost, but there is a big future out there. "The way I get over that hump," says Gary, "is by reflecting on the past. I'll tell stories of other regattas where things started out badly, but worked out better. That helps to get people over the bad mood and reinvigorated.

"Your mood in a race is really important. Sometimes the smallest thing can help get me going. Going into *Sailing World* magazine's Hall of Fame Regatta in 1982, I hadn't been in any small-boat regattas all summer; I had been racing the 12-meter *Defender* instead. So I was wary of how I'd do racing Etchells 22s. But before the start I tuned up with some of the other boats, and found that I had good speed against Dave Ullman and Steve Benjamin. Knowing that we were as fast as the other boats, I got it in my mind that we could win the regatta. About 30 seconds before the start, I noticed the wind was shifting to the left. So I went to the port end of the line and was able to cross the whole fleet while on port tack. That little psychological edge, knowing that my boat had the same speed as some of the good guys, gave me the confidence to attempt a port-tack start when I recognized the wind shift.

"However, right after the start I found myself getting very nervous as Hank Stuart and Jud Smith, my crew, started talking about how we were doing compared to the competitors. It was the competitors' *names* that made me nervous. So at that moment I told my crew, 'For the rest of the regatta, forget about the names of these guys; I just want to know boat numbers.' That kept me from worrying about racing against all these *people*. By dealing with boat numbers, I could handle the situation unemotionally. That psychological tactic helped me win that regatta."

Gary was not the only one who got a little nervous at that start. The following is an excerpt from the *Sailing World* article "Hall of Fame Regatta: A Gathering of Legends," by Tom Linskey, who crewed for Dave Ullman:

With just 45 seconds remaining until the start of the first race, the high-powered company roaming the starting line is about as relaxed as a Steelers and Cowboys lineup before the snap. Aboard the Dave Ullman–skippered Etchells 22, we are on our final approach to the line, luffing slowly on starboard tack. It's my responsibility as middleman to feed Dave as much information as possible about the jockeying of the competition, but while gaping at the overkill of the legendary types around us, my throat tightens involuntarily and my mouth becomes parched.

" 'Okay . . . ah . . . well, there's Dennis Conner coming up fast from astern, and it looks like he'll try to dive underneath for luffing rights. Buddy Melges is heading at us on port and will probably tack on our lee bow. Lowell North, John Bertrand, Gary Jobson, and Steve Benjamin are reaching down the line from above. Stuart Walker and Bruce Kirby are fighting it out with Arthur Knapp and Hobie Alter at the committee boat, and there's one boat luffing everyone else up at the pin end. That looks like . . . Elvström. ELVSTRÖM!!' "

In our minds, Iain Murray deserves the ultimate award for lifting a crew's spirits. While getting swept by *Stars & Stripes* in the 1987 America's Cup, Murray came up with a deadpan line that provoked laughter from his crew and a flock of jaded reporters at the press conference. While *Kookaburra III* was trailing by almost two minutes on the last beat of the third race, her chase boat came up and yelled over that a bomb threat had been phoned in. Reflecting on the incident at a post-race press conference, Murray said, "Our immediate response was, 'Well, what's the bad news?' Then we thought, 'Well, this is our one chance to find out what life's all about after 12-meter racing.' Then we took the third option, which was to continue in the race. As we were well behind, we didn't think if a bomb went up it was going to affect the result of the race. There was one other option. If the bomb blew up, we could have appealed to race committee for an average of our points." Unfortunately, most of the press who heard the remarks weren't familiar enough with the sailing rules to pick up the humor of Murray's last option. *Kookaburra* lost the series 0–4, and an average of their points would have been zero.

Trust

No matter how much you know about tactics and strategy, you are not going to be used to the best of your abilities unless the skipper trusts you. There are times on the racecourse when an advantage can only be gained from an immediate maneuver. In those cases the tactician needs the authority to make calls without consulting the skipper, but few skippers will follow a stranger blindly. "Even with Dennis Conner," says Tom, "there are times when I'll take charge of a close situation and tell him, 'Tack now! Don't ask any questions!' In those cases he's got to believe in what I'm saying, and do what I say. Now that I've sailed so many America's Cups with Dennis, he doesn't question my calls. Maybe in 1980, when we sailed our first Cup together, he would have, but after years of sailing together, combined with my track record of calling enough moves correctly, Dennis trusts me. 'Enough' is the key word; no tactician can get every call right.

"The best way to earn a skipper's trust is to sail a lot and learn as much as you can about tactics and strategy. Accelerate your learning curve by sailing with better sailors. Then sail a lot with the person whose trust you are trying to gain. I've sailed so much that calling tactics has become second nature to me. Lately, for the first time in my career, I feel there are not many moves I make that are dead wrong. I'm afraid I've learned by making costly mistakes. It's no fun making mistakes, but that's how you learn.

"One of the great things that happens when you sail every day is that you get really good. That's what happens when you sail an America's Cup campaign. During the 1980 campaign, we were on the water 320 days out of the 365 before the trials started. In a situation like that, not only do you develop as a tactician, but time you spend working with the skipper cultivates a special relationship. Sailing on other boats is different, you slowly gain a reputation for being good or bad. If you're bad, you don't get asked back, and if you're good, you get invited all the time—more, sometimes, than you'd like to be invited.

"Jim Kilroy, the owner of the maxi boat *Kialoa*, is a good businessman, and he realizes that on big boats like maxis you'd better be able to delegate some of the responsibility. It's too big for one guy. After I sailed enough races to earn a permanent invitation onto the boat, Kilroy said to me, 'Look, you're going to make some calls that are wrong and you're going to make some that are good. We're hoping that you'll make more good than bad. So we're going to trust you, and if you say "tack," we'll tack.' "

One of the things Gary does to earn a crew's confidence and trust is to predict events. Sailing a wind shift right and passing a pack of boats makes your stock soar. But even a less glamorous call, such as slowing a competitor down by causing him to make two extra tacks before getting to a layline will earn the crew's respect and trust.

Like a baseball player, you can build a strong batting average, but no one gets a hit every trip to the plate. Instead of being quiet and trying to avoid the blame for a bad call, admit your mistake and try to avoid doing the same thing in the future. "Since Dennis is so intense all the time," says Tom, "I try to keep him and the crew from getting down by making light of a bad call. I'll say things like, 'I guess I can't charge you for that one,' or 'That wasn't too good an idea; I'm glad you thought of it instead of me. It was you, wasn't it?' That usually brightens up a bad situation."

As crews get more proficient, there is actually more pressure on the tactician, because fewer boat-handling mistakes mean that the tactician is the one who lost the race. The tactician is the one person who can lose the race at any time.

Of course, when sailing with inexperienced crew, there is still pressure on the tactician. Tom says that the pressure comes from within, rather than from the crew. "Less knowledgeable crews don't necessarily have the same high expectations as does a 12-meter crew, but you try to inspire them by showing them what a few good moves can do.

"Making a mistake while sailing with Dennis and the top crews he puts together is tough," says Tom. "If you make a mistake, you get kidded forever. Dennis introduces me as the only American tactician to lose the America's Cup. The call that I get the most grief for is how we played the run of the last race of the 1983 America's Cup. I defend what we did, not because I'm sensitive about it, but because if I was put in the same situation, I would do the same thing again."

The Big Picture

A common fault of too many tacticians is that they lose sight of the big picture. Many regattas are lost because the competitive urges of the tactician make him or her take a chance on winning a race, when all the boat had to do was finish in the top five to win the regatta. Top sailors are not always immune to this temporary blindness.

Your daily strategy includes going over the standings and knowing whom to beat and by how much, whom to cover and whom to let go. Don't let the skipper sail a grudge match against an old foe while a boat close in the standings goes by freely. This isn't too much of a problem in big regattas, but you should be especially aware of it in local races.

Races between similar boats within large fleets are self-destructive. Often, when popular one-designs sail in a handicap class with other boats, the one-designs finish worse then you'd expect. What happens is that they race against themselves and slow each other, instead of trying to be first in fleet. You've got to remember that you are racing against the whole fleet, not just your sister ships—unless, of course, there is a more important trophy for your one-design group.

"A big-picture lesson that college sailing taught me was to sail for an average," says Gary. "Going for the gold in race after race can be very costly. Two DSQs will wipe out a string of firsts. In fact, at the collegiate sailing national championship, often a 4.0 average will win the regatta. I remember one year at the Timme Angsten, a collegiate regatta sailed in Chicago in late November, it was really hard to do consistently well, as the wind seemed to splash down randomly on the water after careening through the buildings on Chicago's lakefront. By not taking chances like starting at the pin or splitting with the fleet, I was able to keep averaging fifth, and that policy worked out well. After about 20 races, our N.Y. Maritime team had an unbeatable lead going into the last race. Our coach that year, Dick Cheesebrough, said, 'Okay, Gary, I want you to go for a win now that the series is all wrapped up.' In that last race I got a lucky puff that pulled me out of oblivion, setting me down a leg ahead of the fleet. I remember there was a young freshman from Yale watching the races, who overheard my conversation with Cheese, and after the race the tall, thin, long-haired kid came up to me and asked why I had been holding back through the whole regatta. But later on, David Perry learned that consistency is the best policy."

Coaching

"If you are in a position where you have to coach the helmsman on how to steer well, one thing I usually do is enlist the help of a sail trimmer," says Tom. "To be an effective tactician, you can't limit your focus to coaching the helmsman; you have to keep your eyes outside of the boat. A trimmer's job is to create boatspeed. Therefore, I try to involve him to the point where he helps the helmsman, so that I can keep my mind on the big picture."

Gary says you have to be careful about coaching the sail trimmers too much. "A lot of sail trimmers have problems with tacticians, because tacticians will tell them what to do. Therefore, don't tell the guy to ease the jib because he's not trimming it right. Tell him to ease it because there is a bad set of waves coming and the boat needs speed to get through them, or tell him to ease the sheet three inches because the boat's in a big lift. As the tactician, you see things before the sail trimmer, because he has his eyes locked on the sail. Remember to be tactful."

"I find that when I've sailed poorly as a tactician, I've forced my boat to do too much," says Gary. "Classic errors that have cost me range from trying to cover another boat incessantly, to tacking on all the shifts no matter how small, to jibing too much, to forcing overlaps that don't exist—all of which only tangle the crew and slow the boat. I've found the surest way to lose races is to lack a game plan and, as a result, try to sail both sides of the course.

"When I've sailed well, it's generally been a patient, well-thought-out race. Of course, you have to stay flexible and adjust your game plan when something occurs."

A good tactician, whether he is sailing with a novice or the best sailor in the world, besides being the skipper's eyes and ears, is also the strategist. A strategy can be formed long before the race or just before the start. But at some point you've got to have a strategy to try to win a race. If you just walk on the boat and sail out to the racecourse, whether in a fleet race or a match race, without a plan of what you are going to do, your chance of performing to your highest potential is not very good. The following chapter is all about how to make a plan for success.

◄ c h a p t e r   2 ►

Creating a
Game Plan

$\mathbf{S}$trategy is how you'd sail the racecourse if there were no other boats in your way, and you were racing against the clock. Tactics govern the way one handles the competition on the course. The best tactics are based on knowing how the wind will shift in direction and change in speed, and what the current is doing on the course. Therefore, the first half of this chapter is an introduction to weather forecasting. The discussion will then turn to creating a strategy for sailing in current, followed by the final step of creating a strategic plan: collecting data on the water before the start. By the ten-minute gun, you'll be able to sift through all the data and create a strategy for the first leg. Your strategic plan can be the same for a whole race, but if the wind keeps changing, you'll have to update your strategic plan as you gather more information about the wind and current during the race.

Weather Forecasting

Knowing how the wind will shift and change in strength is the key to developing a strategic edge over the rest of the fleet. The best race-day forecast tells you when and where the wind will shift, as well as when and how the wind strength will vary over the course. Is that asking for too much? It depends on whom you ask. If you read the newspaper or watch the television, you'll get a forecast that's often too general. These forecasts are only specific enough to help you decide whether to spend the day outside, lawn bowling, or whether to spend the day inside, at the bowling alley. A better source is the continuous updated marine forecast from the National Oceanic and Atmospheric Administration, but even the NOAA radio forecasts don't give you the micro-forecast for the tiny part of the earth's surface that you will be racing on.

The following is the kind of forecast a racing sailor needs, but will never find on TV or in the newspaper: "And now the forecast for those sailing in the Soling North Americans on the Chesapeake Bay at the mouth of Annapolis Harbor. Shortly after the 1:00 P.M. start, expect the sea breeze to build from eight knots to 15 knots. Until the breeze builds to 15 knots, expect the wind to oscillate between 180 and 210 degrees. Watch for stronger puffs coming from due south as the wind channels up the Bay. After 2:00 P.M., when the breeze is at its maximum strength, the wind will persistently shift toward the west at a rate of 15 degrees an hour."

Unless you have a private meteorologist on your team, as on the Olympic sailing team and America's Cup contenders, you'll have to create your own race-day racecourse forecast. It's not as difficult as you think, especially since there is an 85-percent chance that the general weather pattern won't change from one two-hour period to the next. That makes figuring out the micro-forecast much easier.

The only way to make a micro-forecast is to collect your own weather data and analyze it yourself. Begin by collecting the newspaper weather maps for the area you'll be racing in, starting two days before your race. These are good for general frontal and air-mass movements, but weak on local weather.

Weather maps provide a framework for you to interpret the information you collect on the racecourse. Before we go into how to use this framework, let's go over the different parts of a weather map. A bold H indicates the center of a high-pressure system, while a bold L marks the center of a low-pressure system. In the northern hemisphere, the wind flows clockwise around the center of a high-pressure system and counterclockwise around the center of a low-pressure system.

The leading edge of a weather system is called a *front*. To a sailor, the approach of a front means a significant weather change. A *cold front*, indicating an oncoming mass of cold air, is marked on the map as a bold line with sharp spikes on its leading edge, pointing toward the general direction in which the front is moving. (The spikes are drawn perpendicular to the front, pointing to within 45 degrees of the front's direction.) A warm front is marked with round semicircles on its leading edge.

The concentric curves on a weather map are called *isobars,* and form a contour map of air pressure. Points of equal pressure are connected like contour lines of equal elevation on a topographic map. Think of high-pressure systems as "hills" and low pressure systems as "valleys." Each isobar is labeled with the last two digits of its pressure in *millibars* (mb); thus, 88 means 988 mb, and 12 means 1,012 mb. Average sea-level pressure is 996 mb. Wind velocity is determined by the rate of pressure change, which is indicated by the distance between isobars. The closer together the isobars are, the steeper the "hill" and the stronger the wind. Isobars are spaced more closely around lows than around highs, indicating that low-pressure systems bring more wind than high-pressure systems.

In the middle latitudes of the northern hemisphere, the weather systems move to the east or northeast. When comparing the weather charts for the two days prior to race day, note the movement of the systems from one chart to the next. Then note where the center of the weather system is, relative to your racing area. If you're sailing in the northern hemisphere and the center of a low-pressure system is to the south of you, expect the wind to back—to shift counterclockwise. The weather-system winds are only one of the factors that coalesce to create the wind over your racecourse. Other factors are thermal breezes created as the land heats under the sun, the friction of the spinning earth on the wind, upper-air systems like the jet streams, and the steering effects of topography around the racecourse. Therefore, weather maps are only one tool used in creating a race-day forecast.

On the day of the race, make sure you listen to the marine weather forecast from NOAA. The NOAA forecasts are updated every two to three hours on VHF frequencies 162.40, 162.475, and 162.55 MHz. One-design sailors who don't have VHF radios aboard can buy inexpensive weather radios dedicated to these channels, which are sold at electronics stores.

By observing the clouds, you'll be able to fine-tune the NOAA forecast for the racecourse area. One thing to remember when interpreting the clouds: Do not draw a forecast from a single cloud pattern; to make a prediction, you must note the *change* from one cloud type to another. Let's go through the different types of clouds, from highest to lowest.

Cirrus clouds, which form at the highest altitudes, appear as delicate filaments, sometimes called "mares' tails." These are among the best natural long-range weather forecasters; they appear ahead of approaching warm fronts and their attendant depressions. If the sky starts to fill in with clouds after cirrus clouds appear, get ready for a storm to pass through in the next 12 to 36 hours. If the cirrus clouds dissolve, look for the weather to improve.

Contrails are formed when aircraft fly in the deck of the atmosphere that we normally associate with cirrus clouds.* Sailors can use contrails as weather vanes in the upper atmosphere. If they shred sideways, the wind at their level is directed across them. If they do not shred, but instead intensify by growing small, turretlike tops along their length, the upper wind is running lengthwise along the trail. To get a good look at contrails, use binoculars.

When the contrails grow turrets, indicating that the upper-altitude winds and surface winds are both blowing in the same direction, you can anticipate no great change in the weather for several hours. If the upper wind is *backed*, i.e., shifted counterclockwise to the wind on the earth's surface, you can probably expect a high-pressure system and quiet sailing days, but if the upper wind is *veered*, or shifted clockwise, from the surface wind, expect a low-pressure system and more wind.

In temperate latitudes of the northern hemisphere, if you stand with your back to the surface wind, and cirrus clouds or contrails move from your left to your right, the weather will deteriorate; near or full gale is likely. In the southern hemisphere, stand facing the wind. This test may give you as much as 18 to 24 hours' warning.

Stratus or "layer" clouds are caused by the widespread lifting of stable air, as when the warm air of an approaching warm front lifts over the trailing edge of a cold air mass. (See figure 2.1.) Once you can identify this family of clouds, you will be able to forecast the onset of a warm front. (This generally applies to the East Coast.) As a warm front approaches, you will first see cirrus clouds, followed a few hours later by cirrostratus, a very thin haze that shows up as a halo around the sun. When cirrostratus clouds follow cirrus clouds, expect the weather to deteriorate. The larger the ring around the sun, the sooner the bad weather will be upon you. The haze is caused by the refraction of sunlight inside the ice crystals in the air.

When the haze thickens at a lower altitude, leaving the sun barely visible, then the cloud is called an *altostratus*. The increased density of the haze is the result of more ice crystals in the air. The ice particles are formed when

---

*Contrails are long white streams of condensed water vapor. They form as a result of the accelerated air flow from the exits of jet engines and from wing-tip vortices. The accelerated air creates low pressure, which holds less moisture then the surrounding air. Thus contrails are lines of ice crystals.

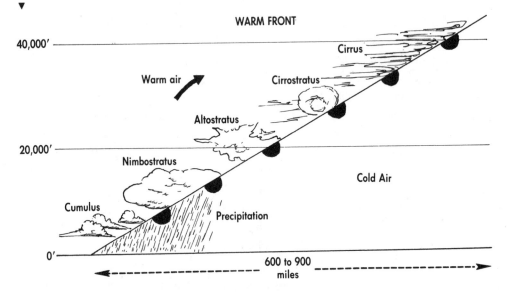

WARM FRONT

Figure 2.1 *This is a sectional view of warm front moving from the left to the right. As the warm front overtakes the denser cold air, the warm air overrides the cold air. As the leading edge of the front rises over the trailing edge of the cold air mass, it forms an extensive layer of clouds at steadily increasing altitudes. Warm fronts move slowly—less than 15 knots.*

the moist air from a warm front comes in contact with the cold, dry air of a cold front. Warm air can hold more water vapor than can cold air; therefore, when the warm, moist air is cooled, the moisture in the air precipitates out.

In general, stratus clouds indicate vertical stability and little intermixing. Surface winds tend to be weak and slow-shifting. Vertical stability and persistent shifts go together. Where stratus clouds indicate the approach of a warm front, be prepared for a persistent shift to the right. *Cumulus* clouds are cottony in appearance. When they are young and growing, their edges are sharply defined and cauliflower-like in appearance. Growing clouds have strong updrafts of warm air, or *thermals*, underneath them, and exert a correspondingly stronger influence on the direction and velocity of the local wind. Often, you'll find stronger winds under the cloud edges, where the downdrafts are sucking air into the clouds. Where land borders on water, which doesn't heat as rapidly as the land, the rising thermals overland create sea breezes as they pull in cold air from over the water.

The thermals that cause cumulus clouds promote vertical intermixing in the atmosphere, in which the upper winds dive to the surface and mix with the low-velocity surface winds. Vertical intermixing causes oscillating shifts. It's important during pre-race analysis to determine which way the upper, stronger winds will shift. Usually these downdraft puffs are right-hand shifts, but keep your eyes open and watch the compass to determine this before every race sailed in puffy winds.

Cumulus clouds die when they are deprived of solar energy at the end of the day, or when higher-level clouds prevent the land from being heated. A dying cumulus cloud exhibits poorly defined, ragged edges caused by ice particles. As a thermal weakens, its effect on the resultant wind weakens.

The lowest type of cloud you'll run into, literally, is fog. Fog is usually a cloud at sea level. There are two types of fog. Sea smoke, which evaporates, is minor and never accumulates more that several feet above the water's surface. The second type of fog, *advection* fog, can be thick, widespread, and persistent. It forms when warm, moist air flows over a cold surface such as a cold ocean current. In fact, it can last for hours or even days, endangering boats and forcing cancellation of races.

Cold Fronts

A cold front can move faster and more violently than a warm front. The towering cumulus clouds along its leading edge will, however, be visible for up to 50 miles. The winds along the front can be violent and squally. The barometric pressure rises steeply after the frontal passage, as the cold, dense air establishes itself.

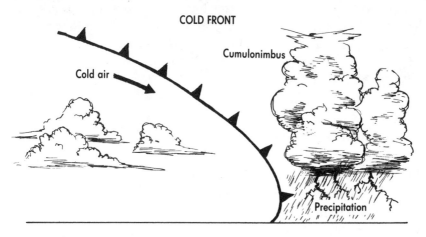

Figure 2.2 *This figure is a sectional view of the leading edge of a cold front.*

The sectional view in figure 2.2 shows how the cold air drives a wedge under the less-dense warm air as it races in from the west or northwest at 15 to 40 knots. Surface friction tends to slow the advance of the bottom of the wedge, curling behind the lower part of the leading edge, near the ground. In advance of the front, the sky is usually overcast with low stratus clouds. The front line is marked by active and growing *cumulonimbus* clouds—thunderstorm clouds. Behind the front, the weather will brighten. Hours after the frontal passage, scattered cumulus clouds usually appear as the land heats up pockets of polar air.

If the cold air forms over land (as it does in the United States before hitting most sailing venues east of the Rocky Mountains), its humidity and dew point will be very low. In fact, during the summer, sometimes the only way to identify a cold front is by the low humidity and clear visibility of the polar air mass; the usual temperature difference is obscured by the midday sun.

Putting It All Together

Now it's time to create a race-day weather forecast. The following conditions, observable on the local level, are often missed by the NOAA weather forecasts. Thus you'll have to fine-tune those forecasts with your own observations of what's happening over the racecourse. While you're at the dock or sailing out to the course, look around, because your forecast will have to include such factors as what the clouds are telling you, and whether the winds are being steered by surface friction or other geographical features; if there is a calm, you'll have to figure out what is causing it. It's up to you to identify and interpret these signs, and plan your strategy accordingly.

Sea Breezes

The most common summer breeze coastal sailors should look for is the *sea breeze*, which is indicated by growing cumulus clouds over the land. A sea breeze (figure 2.3) is caused by thermals, rising columns of hot air over sun-heated land. As the air rises, it is replaced by cooler air from over the water, which is in turn heated by the land and uplifted. (Sea breezes are called *onshore winds* because they blow from the water onto the land.) As the thermals cool

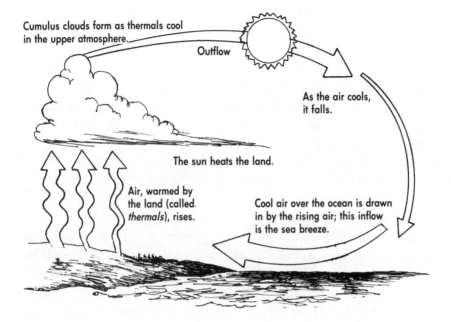

Cumulus clouds form as thermals cool in the upper atmosphere.

Outflow

As the air cools, it falls.

The sun heats the land.

Air, warmed by the land (called *thermals*), rises.

Cool air over the ocean is drawn in by the rising air; this inflow is the sea breeze.

Figure 2.3 *The anatomy of a sea breeze.*

in the upper atmosphere, they form cumulus clouds. The clouds form as the moisture in the cooling air precipitates out. A strong sea breeze is sustained by a light wind aloft that blows in the opposite direction of the onshore sea breeze. As the air flows over the water, it falls as it cools, only to be sucked back in over the hot land.

If the wind is flowing out to sea in the morning, a period of calm may occur before the onset of the sea breeze. The sea breeze will fill in first offshore, and then move toward land as a mini-front with a clearly discernible breeze line (although it can also build from the shore outward in a much more dramatic fashion). Calms can last from a few minutes to all day. Keep your eyes open for the new wind. If the old wind seems to be receding, you can bet the sea breeze is starting to fill in. If the old breeze dies and then comes back, it will be a long time until the sea breeze moves in, if it does so at all.

The strongest sea breezes are generated by a great contrast of temperatures between water and land. They are also encouraged by an offshore pressure system flow. The strongest sea breezes commonly form on warm spring days, or on hot summer days in areas where the water doesn't warm much. This is

▼

the case with one of the most famous sea breezes known to sailors—the "Fremantle Doctor." The proximity of the Antarctic-cooled Indian Ocean and the blistering desert of Western Australia produces a stiff breeze nine out of ten days during the Australian summer. The 12-meters that fought it out for the America's Cup in 1986–87 were bashed daily by the 18-to-25-knot sea breeze. The wind gets its name from the local landlubbers, who appreciate the strong breeze that lowers the temperature 10 to 15 degrees and blows away the incessant summer flies.

A lake should theoretically have a thermal breeze blowing onto all of its shores. Actually, the northern and western shores usually develop stronger thermals, because their slopes face the morning and midday sun.

Once the sea breeze is established (from about 10:30 A.M. to 2:30 P.M.), it will generally start to veer because of the Coriolis force; this motion will tend to be clockwise in the northern hemisphere. The Coriolis force is created by the rotation of the earth, which deflects moving objects to the right in the northern hemisphere and to the left in the southern hemisphere. In many areas the sea breeze frequently appears about the same time each day, since the land takes the same time to heat up. Of course, there are variables that will delay or accelerate the development of the sea breeze, such as cloud cover and air-flow strength and direction.

So, if you're in an area where the sea breeze commonly blows, look for cumulus clouds rising over the land. They are a sure sign that the sea breeze is on its way. Remember to keep an eye on those clouds throughout the day. Moving cumulus clouds are a sure sign that the weather-system wind is overpowering the thermal.

The Effect of Friction on Wind Direction

The earth's friction also has an effect on the surface winds. First, the surface wind is slowed, compared to the wind aloft; secondly, its direction is altered by the Coriolis force.

Difference in direction and speed between the higher-altitude winds and the surface winds can be confirmed by calling an airport and requesting the strength and direction of the winds at 3,000 feet. On some days, especially behind a cold front, the upper winds will be backed, so it's important to check. The strategic importance of the difference depends upon three factors: (1) the amount of directional difference between the upper-level wind and the surface wind, (2) the strength of the upper wind, and (3) the amount of vertical intermixing on that day. A high degree of any of these factors will heighten the importance.

For instance, consider a morning when the 3,000-foot wind is veered by 30 degrees and is twice as strong the surface wind. There are fair-weather cumulus clouds everywhere, indicating plenty of vertical intermixing. Hence, you would expect the surface winds to be gusty, with most of the gusts being veers (starboard tack lifts). As the day progresses, you would expect the surface wind to increase and veer as it is steered by the upper winds.

Geographic Effects

Topographic features around the course channel the wind, which follows the path of least resistance, e.g., down a river valley, along the long axis of a lake, between gaps in hills, and around islands and points of land. To understand these effects, plot your estimation of the wind's path on a local chart, being sure to locate the racecourse accurately on it. If you try to do this exercise without a chart, you'll be deceived by perspective.

If possible, another good method for assessing the effect of land and structures surrounding the racing area is to look down on the water from the top of a hill, or from a window of a shoreside building. Watch for patterns as the puffs blow across the racing area.

An obstruction such as an island may or may not blanket the water to leeward, depending upon the amount of vertical intermixing. If the air is vertically unstable as it flows over the island, it will kick up off the island into thermals and cumulus clouds. If the higher-altitude winds are strong, then the surface winds will be strong and gusty to leeward of the island. If the air is vertically stable, it will flow around the obstruction, causing bending shifts to windward and leeward. In an island chain, the wind will be squeezed and accelerated between the islands.

Two indicators of vertical stability are cloud forms and visibility. Vertically unstable air will produce cumulus clouds and good visibility because the particles in the air will be dispersed. Vertically stable air will create stratus clouds and haze, smog, or poor visibility, because the air particles are accumulating in layers.

There will be a local calm to windward of a high obstruction, where the air lifts off the surface to flow over it. In fact, the "blanket zone" to windward of an island can be worse than the one to leeward. This is true not only of islands, but of buildings, big ships, boathouses, tall piers, and tightly grouped packs of boats. An example of the last is a large fleet on a starting line. In that case, it can pay to be at an end of the line so that you can get away from the fleet as quickly as possible.

Calms

Calms are common in the center of highs, where pressure variations are minimal. Midsummer calms associated with highs are persistent; they break only when the high moves. Calms also indicate the collision of opposing air flows—for instance, thermal winds versus weather-system winds. This type of calm lasts from 30 minutes to a few hours, and it is important to watch closely. One of the colliding air flows will eventually overpower the other, and the breeze will fill in from that direction. When the wind shifts radically for a short while, and then goes back to its original direction, it is a clue that two weather systems are fighting each other.

The Fast Track to Local Knowledge

Most racing sailors assimilate knowledge of predominant winds and shifts through years of sailing in a local area. But if you're racing in a given venue for the first time, a little background work can help you catch up with the locals in predicting the wind.

The U.S. Weather Bureau records wind direction and strength at more than 100 stations in the United States (many near yachting centers), at three-hour intervals throughout the day. (This doesn't help all the time, unfortunately. The Olympic Yachting Committee of USYRU miscalculated its 1988 Olympic trial site selection by using data from a wind instrument located behind a hill!) Historical records can be obtained and examined to identify primary wind directions and frequency of their occurrence, as well as their strength. Tabulating and organizing this historical information will help you define certain local wind conditions that occur fairly regularly.

To illustrate how this can be done, we have employed data from the Bridgeport, Connecticut, airport, located on Long Island Sound. Weather histories were examined for the month of July, and to obtain a sample size that qualifies as statistically significant, the data was analyzed for the same time period each day of that month over three successive years, producing 93 samples.

A convenient method of presenting the prevailing wind statistics is to put together a Wind Direction Frequency Distribution graph. (See figure 2.4.) Such a graph shows how often the wind blows steadily from every direction, and is constructed by tabulating the percentage of time that the wind blows from a direction defined by a 20-degree band width. A width of 20 degrees was found to be optimum because most steady breezes have periodic shifts of over 5 degrees. Furthermore, a 20-degree band filters out very slow wind shifts, i.e., those that change less than 20 degrees in a three-hour period. (For example, figure 2.4 shows that the wind blew from a direction between 200 and 220 degrees 13 percent of the time during the month of July.)

The most obvious conclusion we can draw from the graph is that the dominant wind direction is the south sector. (The wind blows from this sector, between 140 and 240 degrees, over 41 percent of the time.) This is the well-known sea breeze. Notice, however, that there are two likely occurrences, or two types of sea breeze. The "classic" one is represented by the peak around 220 degrees, and a second peak occurs around 160 degrees. The wind is not likely to remain steady from the intermediate direction—due south—as we see from its low percentage of occurrence. During the development of the

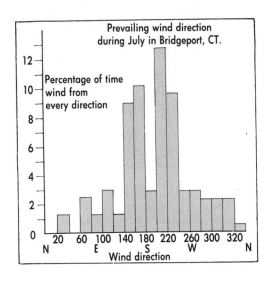

Figure 2.4 *This graph of the July winds in Bridgeport, Connecticut, shows that there are two sea breezes. One blows between 140 to 180 degrees and the other between 200 and 240 degrees.*

afternoon see breeze, winds will home in on one of the two "peaks." Meteorological conditions will dictate which of the two types of sea breeze will predominate.

The Weather Bureau data sheets record the weather conditions as well, and careful study of the daily reports will reveal weather patterns associated with specific wind directions. Further analysis of our July information shows that these breezes tend to be light. The Wind Strength Frequency Distribution graph (figure 2.5) shows the average strength of winds from the south sector. The data for days on which the wind blew from the south was analyzed into two-knot velocity increments. This analysis indicates that the most likely sea-breeze strength is between 8.5 and 10.5 knots, and that this occurs about 45 percent of the time.

Weather Bureau reports are quite detailed. For more information on obtaining these reports, contact the National Climatic Center, Federal Building, Asheville, North Carolina 28801.

America's Cup navigator Peter Isler remembers when he sailed aboard *Locura* in the 1983 Boca Grande race of the SORC when the historical sea breeze had a slight twist. "A classic sea breeze predominated for the start of the race, and as the fleet headed south toward the turning mark, 50 miles away, most boats favored port tack, sailing toward an "expected" right-hand shift forecasted by the NOAA weather radio. However, a last-minute phone call to a local meteorologist indicated that the oncoming cold front had stalled.

"Consulting with crew members Tom Whidden and Mark Soverel, I decided we should take the starboard tack toward the beach, counting on the sea breeze

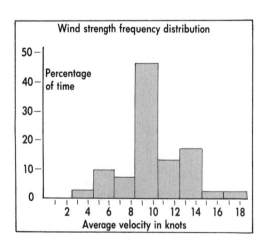

Figure 2.5 *This graph shows that the average strength of the sea breeze in Bridgeport, Connecticut, is between 9 and 11 knots.*

to be replaced at nightfall by a light offshore land breeze. The tactic worked famously. In the early evening hours, *Locura* got the maximum benefit of the land breeze shift to the left, and reached up the beach less than half a mile from the shore while the fleet remained becalmed offshore. *Locura* dominated the race, finishing first in both class and fleet. Obviously, it pays to get the most recent and accurate information available before leaving the dock."

Lake-Sailing Wind Predictions

Unlike large bodies of water, which are often characterized by stationary or slow-moving wind systems, a small lake presents a faster-moving, less predictable wind pattern. To be successful on a shifty lake, any plan of attack must be open to revision if your eyes tell you something unexpected is about to happen.

If you are on a hill overlooking a lake, the black-and-white patterns of a northeasterly's puffs and lulls are easy enough to spot. However, problems arise when you are in a sailboat on the water's surface and can no longer see the puffs from a bird's-eye perspective, since foreshortening has the effect of blending the contrasts. So when you are in doubt as to what you are actually seeing on the water, *the trick is to stand up*. This helps improve your angle of vision. (See figure 2.6.)

Figure 2.6 *If you could view the lake from above, tracking puffs would not be difficult. However, since a sailor's perspective is usually only a few feet above the water, the ripple patterns tend to blend together in the same way squares of a checkerboard distort when the board is brought to eye level.*

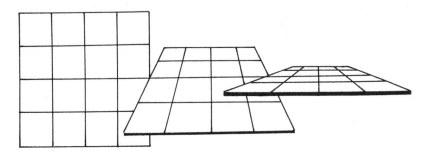

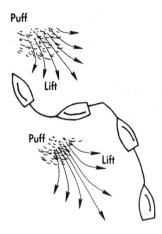

Puff

Lift

Puff

Lift

Figure 2.7 *When a puff hits the water it fans out so that boats sailing along the puff's back side get lifted.*

Before the start of a race, it's a good idea to sail part of the weather leg on your feet, so that you can better study how the wind influences your boat. With the knowledge you gain from this sort of pre-race analysis, you'll have a better understanding of what you are seeing while sitting on your duff during the race.

The best basic rule, in an environment so fickle that most rules are broken several times on a single weather leg, is to go for the puffs. Even if the direction doesn't change, a greater amount of wind will enable you to sail faster, increasing your apparent wind and thus allowing you to point higher. So, when in doubt about what direction the wind will take, sail for the dark ripples.

However, this dictum can be refined once one understands the structure of a puff. A gust's fanlike shape means that the changes in wind direction at its edges provide a lift for a boat sailing along the puff's back edge (see figure 2.7). When confronted with several gusts coming down the lake, try to sail a series of back edges so as to profit from both the fanning effect and the added wind strength. (See figure 2.7.)

To help find those crucial puffs, it pays to establish specific reference points on the course that keep you in touch with the shifting wind patterns across the lake. When sailing a weather leg, keep three areas in constant visual contact: the two corners and the center of the course. By limiting the horizon to three specific checkpoints for monitoring the lake's ever-changing wind pattern, the amount of time spent staring off into space is reduced.

When racing close to shore, breaks in topography can facilitate this process of assessing what shifts will be coming down the lake. Bays and dips in the treeline allow the wind to break out onto the water faster. When scouting the weather shoreline for puffs, clue in on such areas for some advance warning.

Downwind is no time to stop using these same techniques of observation. While reaching and running, many skippers seem to forget where the wind is coming from, and insist on looking only forward. Although the range of things you can do on an offwind leg is necessarily limited, knowing where the wind is coming from is just as critical. Turn your head around and look for the puffs coming down from behind you.

Since the wind can shift so quickly on an inland lake, judging laylines often becomes a process of approximation. However, anticipating what the wind will do when you make your final approach to the mark can help you decide when to tack. If, as you approach the starboard layline (assuming a port rounding), you see that it's going to be light around the mark, it will probably pay to continue a bit past the layline. This will position you above the general traffic at the mark, allowing you to pass the boats that won't be able to lay the mark in the subsequent lull. On the other hand, if you see a good puff coming down the lake, you can tack somewhat short of the layline with the knowledge that the change in velocity will enable you to point higher. This preplanning will help you decide whether to duck a group of boats on the starboard layline (which you should probably do if a lull is imminent), or tack ahead and to leeward of them (if a puff is in the works). (See figure 2.8.)

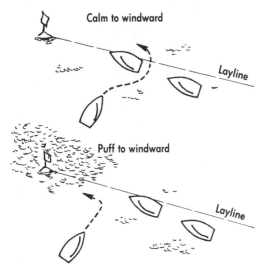

Figure 2.8 *When approaching a layline on a lake, try to determine if a puff or a lull is coming before you decide where to tack. If a lull is imminent, don't tack until you are above the layline—even if it means taking some transoms. If a puff is due to arrive before you round, tack below the layline because you'll be able to sail higher in the increased wind velocity.*

Figure 2.9

Land Lessons

The presence of land vastly complicates the wind patterns on an inland lake. Although land masses carve up the wind, they often do so in a predictable way. The following are a few guidelines.

Generally leeward shores are good places to avoid, because the wind wants to rise off the water in order to go over the trees on the shoreline—a phenomenon which begins at a distance that is three or four times the tree-height from the shore. (See figure 2.9.)

If the weather shore is at an angle to the prevailing breeze, the wind will be pulled in a direction perpendicular to the shoreline. (See figure 2.10.) Although this shift can benefit a boat sailing up the shore, the wind is lighter near the land—consequently, you can get in too far. The trick is to be close enough to get the shift, but not so close that you lose any wind strength.

Wind will often fan out of a bay, enabling you catch a lift just outside the bay's edge. But at the edges of the opening, the wind will be lighter and shift against you for the tack toward the center from both sides. However, if the wind shifts slightly to the right, the wind flowing off the right shore will be pulled perpendicular to the shoreline creating a sizeable starboard tack lift. (See figure 2.11.)

On narrow bodies of water, the wind will travel along the river or lake's long axis. If the narrow body of water twists, the wind will be strongest along the outside of the curves. (See figure 2.12.)

Figure 2.10

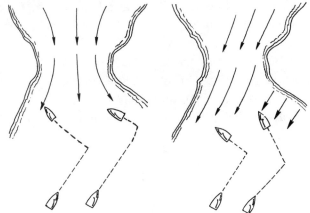

Figure 2.12

Figure 2.11

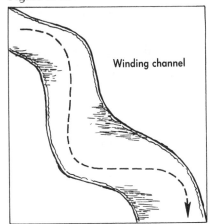

Winding channel

Sailing in Current

Just as you wouldn't go to a major regatta without gathering weather information, you shouldn't do so without gathering information on the course's currents. Tools needed to predict current flows are a chart, a tide table, and a current chart covering the racing area. Charts depict the underwater contours, which indicate the strength of currents you'll encounter; generally speaking, the deeper the water, the stronger the current. Tide tables disclose the times of high and low tides, as well as indicating the height of the tides' rise and fall. The greater the range between high and low tide, the stronger the currents you encounter. The third tool for forecasting course currents is a current chart. These charts are usually not detailed enough for one-design sailors sailing on triangular courses, but for those sailing point-to-point races, current charts show how the currents bend as tidal flows empty out of rivers and inlets into a central current. A current chart also indicates the relative strengths of the different flows.

If the current chart is not detailed enough for your small venue, you can take your own current readings before the race by observing the water rushing past buoys, boats, fishing floats, and anything else anchored to the bottom. You can take current readings around the course with a "current stick."

Making and Using a Current Stick

A current stick is used to measure the speed and direction of the current. Drop it in the water next to a buoy or some other reference point that's anchored to the bottom, and then note the direction your stick traveled, and the distance in feet per second (fps). The current's speed is calculated with the formula: $0.6 \times$ (fps) = knots. If you don't have a calculator aboard, remember that an object going one knot moves 100 feet in a minute, or 50 feet in 30 seconds, or 25 feet in 15 seconds.

A current stick can be something as simple as a banana peel or a sponge, or it can be something as elaborate as a broomstick with a weight bolted to one end and a piece of Styrofoam attached to the other. If your measuring device is constructed to reach below the surface, you won't be reading only the wind-driven current on the surface.

If you are having a hard time estimating exact distances, you can use the length of the committee boat to measure the current's speed, by dropping your current stick in the water by the committee boat's bow, and then timing how long your stick takes to drift to the boat's stern. Then multiply the committee boat's length in feet times 0.6, and divide that sum by the number of seconds it took the current stick to drift by the committee boat. For example, if the committee boat is 30 feet long and it took your current stick ten seconds to drift from bow to stern, then the current's rate is a hefty 1.8 knots.

Take readings at the weather mark, at the starting line, and at the layline corners, if you have time. If you're very serious, you can enlist a friend with a motorboat to take readings around the course for you; just make sure he or she gives you the results before the five-minute gun.

"In the Liberty Cup, I've had good success over the years because I've been able to accurately anticipate the different currents and wind shifts on New York Harbor," says Gary. "The way you learn what the current is up to is to test what's happening before the race. The more thoroughly you test, the more accurate your results will be. I try to sail a good part of the windward leg when testing the current. If I see a boat offshore, I'll go inshore to measure my performance against him current-wise. Testing will give you a little bit of an edge."

Using the Tide Tables

To avoid saddling sailors with a set of volumes equal to an encyclopedia, a tide-table book does not contain the predicted times and heights of the high and low tides for each day of the year at every town, cove, and river in the world. Instead, the book is kept manageable by reporting the times and heights of tides at key areas along the coast, designated as "reference stations." Be careful not to use local newspapers or recorded weather announcements, as they may not accurately pinpoint your area. To calculate approximate times and heights of tides at many other points along the coast—subordinate stations—the user is directed to appropriate tables. Use the book's index to find the station closest to your venue.

When using the tide tables, be sure to note what times they are using. Some use Greenwich mean time (GMT) while others use local standard time. If your tables use standard time, remember to add one hour during the summer, when your clocks are set for daylight savings time. If Greenwich time is used, you'll have to look up in your book how many hours to add or subtract to get local time. On the East Coast of the United States, you would add five hours to GMT to find local time; on the West Coast add eight hours.

Check not only the time of the tide change, but also the difference in height between high and low tide. In some areas of the world, the height difference of the tides differs little in one part of the month, but is much greater at another. The greater the difference, the stronger the currents you'll encounter.

The key to sailing in current is to sail in the fastest current when it is going the same direction you are, and to sail in the weakest current when it is heading in an adverse direction.

When the current moves at the same speed over the whole course, all boats, no matter what tack they are on, are affected equally by the current. To see this, imagine a fleet of boats on a table cloth. As you pull the table cloth across the table, all the boats move toward the edge of the table at the same rate, no matter at what angle they are pointed. So forget about the lee bow effect; it doesn't exist. You will not do better on one tack than on the other because of the current.

Figure 2.13 Situation 1 *shows the fair current's effect on two boats approaching a windward mark. Boat A tacked low of the layline and allowed the current to push it up to the mark, while B tacked on the layline and ended up overstanding.* Situation 2 *shows the effect of a foul current on two boats approaching a windward mark. Boat X factors in the current on its approach to the mark by sailing past the layline. After sailing to the mark, the current has pushed X to the mark.*

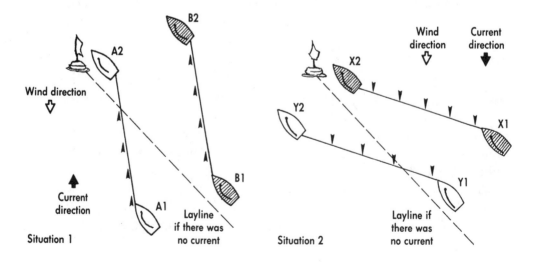

Also, when the current is equal over the course, it should not be a factor in determining which side of the course to sail. But you will have to factor current into your tactical game when approaching the starting line or rounding marks. While rounding a mark in adverse (opposing) currents, you will have to go beyond the normal laylines to avoid getting swept into the mark. With a favorable current, tack early so that the current does not make you overstand. (See figure 2.13.)

Current can have a dramatic effect on apparent wind, too. For example, if you are sailing downwind in a strong current going in your direction at 3 knots, and the wind is blowing 10 knots, you have very little apparent wind because not only are you moving forward at, say, 4 knots, but with the current, which is 3 knots. It's only 3 knots of apparent wind. With so little wind, it becomes hard to fill your sails. However, going upwind with the current, if you are sailing at 6 knots, and you have 3 knots of current with you, then you are going through the wind at 9 knots. Also, the wind you're getting at 10 knots is 19 over the deck and only 10 knots of breeze. You might find yourself depowering the sails in this situation.

A Sample Race in Current

To examine how current affects your strategic game plan, let's run through a sample windward/leeward race. (See figure 2.14.) Before sailing out to the racecourse, your tide tables indicate that high tide will be at noon. Since the start of the race is at 11:30 A.M., the best plan is to sail up the middle of the course to ride the final stages of the flood—the incoming tide. On the second half of the first beat, keep an eye on lobster pots or other objects anchored to the bottom. You're looking to see if the wakes coming off them indicate whether the tide is still coming in, whether it has gone slack, or whether the ebb tide—the outgoing tide—has started. The current over the whole course does not change simultaneously, and at most places on the course, the tide does not change right at the time you'll find in the tide tables.

The current should be slack, or just starting to turn, as you go around the windward mark at 12:15 P.M. To play things safe, overstand the mark so that you don't get swept into it in case the current has started to ebb. As you round the mark, make sure someone aboard checks to see what the current is doing.

If the tide has just started to go out and flow down the course, your best bet is to head into the shallower water, where the current changes direction

▼

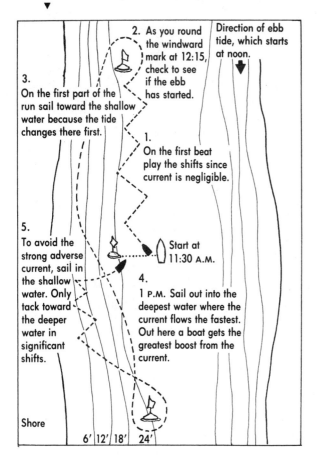

2. As you round the windward mark at 12:15, check to see if the ebb has started.

Direction of ebb tide, which starts at noon.

3.
On the first part of the run sail toward the shallow water because the tide changes there first.

1.
On the first beat play the shifts since current is negligible.

5.
To avoid the strong adverse current, sail in the shallow water. Only tack toward the deeper water in significant shifts.

Start at 11:30 A.M.

4.
1 P.M. Sail out into the deepest water where the current flows the fastest. Out here a boat gets the greatest boost from the current.

Shore

6' 12' 18' 24'

Figure 2.14 *Anatomy of a sample race.*

first. Once you know where the adverse current is, avoid it. Spectators in the San Francisco Big Boats Series get a great view of the action as 50 or more boats short-tack up the San Francisco City Front to stay clear of the currents roaring up to 4 knots in the deeper parts of San Francisco Bay. Scores of boats ranging from 80-foot maxis to IOR One Tonners tack back and forth in an area the size of a large drainage canal to avoid the powerful currents just offshore.

If crews racing 50-footers and maxis can do all that maneuvering, just think how many times a one-design can tack, gaining valuable ground, following a riverbank. If you are sailing a centerboard boat and the bottom is soft, don't be afraid of getting so close to the shore that you bump the bottom. Do the "bump and run"; as soon as you hit the bottom, pull up the board a bit and tack. Once you have tacked, lower the board, but don't go too far out into the current before tacking back. You'll gain a lot of distance by staying out of the faster current as long as the wind is equal over the course.

When you see that the current is flowing out quickly—check by looking at a buoy, pot, or anchored boat—jibe and head out into the deeper water, where the current runs fastest. Take advantage of the swift current to carry you down to the leeward mark.

At the leeward mark, start your turn early so that you don't get swept downwind of the mark. Once around the mark, make a long tack in toward the shallow water to avoid the strongest flow of the foul current. Ignore minor wind shifts that would bring you out into the deeper water, unless you get headed more than 15–20 degrees. Sail past the layline, since the current will carry you down the course.

In lighter winds, keep an eye on anchored ships. Generally, one knot of current will affect the set of a ship the same as 10 knots of wind. If the current is 2 knots and the wind is blowing 10 knots in the opposite direction, the ship will lay to the current. A dead giveaway that you'll have to deal with current is if the race committee boat is not pointing into the wind. Such an obvious sign should warn you to do a little more research about the current before the start. Finally, don't let the current sweep you into the committee boat before the start.

The wind has an effect on current. If the wind is with the current, it can delay the time the current changes direction. Also, if the wind is against the tide, the current will be slowed, but a short chop that is hard to sail through will result.

Anchoring on the Course

Fighting an adverse current can be a losing proposition when the wind drops down to a faint zephyr. To keep from losing ground, Racing Rule 53 allows you to drop your anchor while racing. In fact, by getting your anchor down stealthily, you'll pull ahead of your competitors. While you're standing still, they'll be swept backwards.

A classic example of a case in which anchoring during a race paid off occurred during 1989 Block Island Race Week. The around-the-island race was sailed in light winds, shifty currents, and dense fog. An ebbing tide made

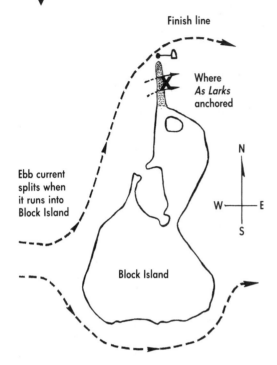

Finish line

Where
As Larks
anchored

Ebb current
splits when
it runs into
Block Island

N

W——E

S

Block Island

Figure 2.15 As Larks Harmoniously *won by anchoring until the wind filled in.*

it hard for the fleet to cross the finish line, set north of the reef at the north end of the island. As the fleet sailed north along the east side of the island, it was sheltered from the easterly-flowing current. The last 300 yards to the finish line were the toughest for the fleet, since it got hit with the strong easterly current that kept it away from the finish line. (See figure 2.15.)

As Larks Harmoniously, a 38-foot Bill Tripp design, solved the problem by sailing over the reef, where the adverse current was weaker than in the deeper water. When the wind lightened and the current started pushing the boat away from the line, her crew anchored in 11 feet of water. By setting the anchor stealthily, *As Larks Harmoniously* stayed ahead of the boats around her. While anchored, *As Larks'* speedometer read over three knots! After *As Larks* had spent 20 minutes on the hook, a 44-footer ghosted past, indicating that the wind had picked up slightly. When the bigger boat made it across the reef into the northerly-flowing current *As Larks* pulled up her anchor and inched across the reef into the favorable current. *As Larks* won her class, and finished with 15 minutes left in the five-hour time limit.

Before dropping the anchor, make sure you are indeed moving backwards, by taking bearings on points on land or on objects anchored to the bottom. A story has been circulating about a boat sailing in the Admiral's Cup in England, on which every line was tied together, including spare halyard tails, spinnaker sheets, and guys, to create an anchor rode to reach the bottom of the English Channel, 500 feet below. After patting themselves on the back for getting the anchor down, the crew found out why no one else had matched their efforts; the current was carrying the fleet to the next mark instead of away from the mark. Retrieving all the line was allegedly difficult, since the rode was covered with jellyfish tentacles.

Race-Day Prep

Here is a race-day checklist that you can follow from before you leave the dock through to the ten-minute warning gun. In this section we'll go over how to collect empirical data before the race, how to prepare the crew, and how to form a game plan for the race.

As the tactician, you need to be in the racing mode before the boat even leaves the dock. You should collect all the weather information, including weather maps from the newspaper and weather reports from the radio. You'll have to figure out the tide situation for the hours that you'll be racing, and you'll have to make sure you have all the equipment you'll need, such as a chart, paper and pencil, a hand-bearing compass, binoculars, and the sailing instructions. Discuss the experience level of the crew with the skipper to figure out whether your tactics should be more or less aggressive. For instance, if you're sailing with a green crew, you'll have to plan your spinnaker takedowns early, instead of leaving the chute to the last minute in an effort to grab an inside overlap.

To get to the course early enough to create a good game plan, the skipper and the tactician should see that the boat is rigged, provisioned, and launched before the skippers' meeting. Avoid getting stuck in crowds by using the bathroom and filling the water jug before the skippers' meeting. If there is no skipper's meeting, have your crew arrive at the dock early; avoid last-minute delays that can result from crowded launches or lines at the launching ramp or hoist. You need to get out on the course so that you have at least an hour to sail it before the ten-minute warning. The longer you are on the course, the more accurate your game plan will be; gauge current, test changes in wind direction and strength, and if your crew hasn't worked together before, practice spinnaker sets, jibes, and takedowns.

On your way out to the racecourse, don't relax; constantly gather information. As you sail to the course, keep track of the wind, even if it's a long sail to the racing area. The earlier you start detecting shifts, the better you can decide what the wind-shift pattern is. Your best information can be gathered if you have to beat out to the course. Utilize such a golden opportunity to track the wind by writing down your compass headings and observations about wind shifts. Write the headings, wind strength, and time on a piece of paper, or, on a one-design, use a grease pencil on a piece of Mylar taped to the deck, write on a piece of duct tape, or just write on the deck. By writing down the times of your observations, you'll be able to discern a pattern to the shifts.

If it's a reach out to the starting area, set your sails and cleat them. Then note the course changes you have to make to keep the sails flying properly. If you are motoring out to the course, keep an eye on the instruments monitoring true wind, if you have them, to get an idea of the wind shifts.

You might want to get the crew to stretch so that they'll loosen up their muscles, which are probably tight after sleeping on the way out to the course, or from not sleeping enough the night before. If the racecourse is close to the dock, have everyone stretch on the dock or the yacht-club lawn. If you've got a long tow or a long way to motor to the course, it's easiest to limber up before the sails are raised, because the boat will remain level. Making stretching a group exercise will help instill camaraderie and start the crew working together.

Once you get out to the course, start thinking about where the windward mark will be laid, and try to determine whether the shore will have an effect on either side of the course. Figure out whether you'll get more or less velocity, a lift, or a header as you get in toward shore. Test your hypothesis as you sail up the course before the start. When you're sailing on a lake, test both shores. Sail past the mouths of coves or rivers and around protruding points to sample their effect on the wind. Or, for your first regatta, consult local knowledge. The wind often varies dramatically from the starting line to the windward mark. The windward mark is near the shore, where the wind is generally much lighter. Also, there could be big variations in direction and velocity.

As you sail toward the windward mark, it is very important to note where the wind is coming from, so that you are sailing in an area of strong breeze when you make your final approach for the mark.

If there is a point of land, the wind usually goes around it at an angle adjacent to the land itself. Directly behind the point of land or on the downwind side, the wind is often very light.

As you sail up the course, gather information on the wind, practice tacking, and then practice spinnaker sets and jibes while going downwind. If you're racing a dinghy, make sure your crew hikes to keep the boat flat while taking your wind readings. This will loosen them up, as well as improving the accuracy of your observations.

If there is any question as to what sail to use for the wind conditions, try both sails that you're considering. The sail change will give you solid numbers to compare, and the change is good practice for the crew.

Many sailors determine the wind direction by luffing into the wind frequently. But since you can't luff head-to-wind while racing, you won't be able to compare your pre-race data with the data you collect while racing. Instead, write down your headings on both tacks, and then figure out the true wind direction from your compass log by adding the average port and starboard readings together and then dividing by two. For example, if your average compass heading on port tack is 160 degrees and the average compass reading on starboard tack is 250 degrees, then the true wind direction is 205 degrees.

As you sail the course before the start, look for current shears, which are marked by long lines of foam and flotsam on the water. Current shears indicate the changes in current flow. Floating debris gets caught in the eddies formed by the friction between the two different water flows. When you find a shear, take readings on both sides of the shear with a current stick to determine on which side the current is running faster. If you cross a shear while you're racing, keep an eye on the performance of boats on the other side of the shear, to make sure that you didn't sail into unfavorable current.

"When I raced in the 1989 Columbus Cup Regatta in Baltimore," says Gary, "we were racing in an area that I had never sailed in before. I had some interesting problems because there was a deep channel right in the middle of the course, and we found that the current was heading in one direction in the channel, while it was slack on either side. So the question was to figure out which side of the channel to sail on to reach the windward mark. What made it more interesting was that we would be match-racing, and the difference would be measured in only one or two boatlengths. So we found a current line on the edge of the channel. This was a line where the current was running on one side and slack on the other. As it turned out, going downwind against the crew from Denmark, we were able to use our starboard advantage, forcing them on the current side of the shear, which was taking them away from the mark. Just as they crossed the line, I was able to jibe away, stay out of the current, and gain a boatlength as we headed for the mark. That length was just enough to get an inside overlap later, and establish a lead that we did not relinquish."

Reading the Wind on the Water

Once on the course, start looking for wind on the water's surface. To see the wind on the water, get your eyes as high off the water as possible. Stand on a halyard winch or the bow pulpit, and if time and sea conditions permit, go up the mast in a bosun's chair. In one-designs as small as a Thistle or a Lightning, you can stand on the boom at the gooseneck, or on the spinnaker pole ring on the mast. If sailing a Sunfish or a Snipe, stand on your tiptoes. As figure 2.6 showed, the higher you get, the more accurate will be your reading of the wind on the water. The better perspective you get from being higher above the water is comparable to the better view of traffic you get driving a van or a truck, as compared to driving a low-slung sports car.

In watching the water for wind variations, you'll be more effective, for a longer time, if your eyes are relaxed. So use both eyes to watch the water, and don't squint. Wearing sunglasses will help you decipher the surface of the water. The polarizing filter will get rid of glare and the tint will add contrast. Check for any differences in the intensity of the ripples. You're looking for dark patches on the water, which are cat's-paws. If a cat's-paw comes straight at your bow, you'll get a knock. If it comes from your windward side, you'll get a lift. Look for streaks of wind, or if you are expecting a sea breeze to fill in, look for a wind line coming in from offshore.

It would be a lot easier to read the wind if you could actually see the wind molecules flowing through the air, as you can see water flowing down a rocky stream. Since the wind remains invisible, you have to track it as you would an animal in the forest. The tracks of the wind are not only cat's-paws and wind lines on the water's surface. Other clues to where the wind is and how it's blowing are provided by some boats heeling over more than others; by some boats moving faster than others; by boats on the same tack heading at different angles; and by flags, smokestacks, and trees on shore, pennants on the marks, and even smells coming off the shore.

In very light winds, it is important to head for the new wind. For example, if you see a puff coming from 70 degrees off your bow, so that the course you are sailing may not get to that breeze, it is better to make a tack and head for a puff. Don't wait. Maneuver and go to new wind any time you see it coming. Be careful not to sail parallel to a breeze line, but sail toward it, get into it, and use it to your advantage.

"In one Laser regatta, I was having trouble figuring out which way the first wind shift would go," says Gary. "And I noticed that because there were so many boats (over eighty in our fleet), I could not really see the wind on the water. I sailed about fifteen boatlengths to windward of the starting line—a risky move, because we were within about six minutes of the start—where I could see a good strong puff coming in from the port side of the course. So I went back down the starting line to the port end of the line, and went for the new wind. It worked, and I was among the top five boats at the first mark. The lesson: If you are having trouble reading the wind, sail to where you are away from other sailboats, and you may be able to see the wind a bit more clearly."

Checklist for Creating a Game Plan

Before the race, sail for an hour to determine whether the wind is steady, oscillating, or persistently shifting in one direction. If it is oscillating, play the middle of the course. If it is persistently shifting, sail toward the new wind first on the persistent header. If the wind is steady, look for other factors, such as more wind on the other side of the course, or more favorable or less adverse current, that could favor one side or the other.

Next, notice whether there is more wind on one side of the course. Do the puffs fill in from a particular side? If so, those are good reasons to favor that side.

Is the windward mark close enough to shore that the land will bend the breeze, or will the land block the breeze? What other effects will the land have on the wind over the course? For example, are there low spots between hills, where the wind will accelerate as it channels through? Do points stick out from the shore, from which you'll get lifts? Assess such geographic effects by sailing up to the land and noting what happens to the wind.

Are you expecting a sea breeze to fill in? Look for cumulus clouds over the land, then head offshore to get the new wind first. Your plan might thereby have a contingency, such as to stay inshore, playing the lifts off the land, and then go offshore just before the sea breeze fills in, so that you can greet the new wind before any other boats in the fleet.

You'll also have to consider differences in current when picking which side of the course is favored—that is, unless the current is equal across the course.

Crew Meeting

When you get back to the line, after creating a strategy for how to play the wind and current on the first beat, and after the spinnaker has been repacked, get the crew together for a meeting. "Before every race I sail, I give a pep talk," says Gary. "This should include why it's important to do well in the race. Also, when you go over crew assignments, include specifics such as, 'I'm going to give you more time to set up the spinnaker, but once it's set up, I want you to come back off the bow. We're going to try to set the chute up when we're in very flat water on port tack. What we don't want is people on the bow on starboard tack, because we'll be taking the waves on the nose then.' I never berate an individual during the pep talk. The time for correcting a person's past problems is in private. End your crew meeting with a rabble-rousing conclusion, and then get on with the race. Remember to give your pep talk as close as you can to the ten-minute gun. A psych-up speech loses its effect if everyone goes to sleep for a half hour after hearing it."

Gary says that during his pep talks he tries to get a crew ready for psychological let downs: "I mentally prepare my crew for some weirdness—some bizarre, unpredictable event that can happen during a regatta, such as a barge coming through the fleet, costing us the lead. But if you get your crew mentally prepared for adversity, they won't quit, even if the second spinnaker shreds. They'll know they're still in the race if they can quickly get the last spinnaker rigged right. Many crews fall apart and never recover from problems.

"If there is a postponement before the start because of light air, I don't like to mill around with the other boats. I find that throwing Frisbees and water balloons distracts my crew. So I like to sail away from other boats to avoid distractions. Most of the boats that get caught up in games and socializing end up being late in preparing for the start.

"The 1988 12-Meter Worlds in Sweden was a case where we couldn't sail around, figuring out the wind before the start, because we had an hour-and-a-half tow to the course, and then we usually had to wait another two hours for the sea breeze to fill in. The first day we hung around with the other boats, and we ended up by not sailing as well as we could because we weren't prepared. After that day, I sailed the boat away from the others during the wait for the breeze, so that everyone could sleep; one person kept a lookout so that we wouldn't miss anything. Then, when it came time to race, we got everyone up, stretching and tuning together."

After you've created a game plan for the first beat, and held your crew meeting, you'll have a chance to check your game plan if other fleets start before yours. Watch the boats that start first, and try to figure out who is ahead, and where they sailed to get ahead. Also, look at the angles they are sailing, so that you can figure out where the shifts are. See if one side of the course has more wind than the other; your clue, as mentioned earlier, will be if some boats are heeled over more than others.

Marblehead, Massachusetts

During the summer months, June through September, the prevailing wind direction is south 150 to 210 degrees. The June and July sea breeze is stronger (5 to 15 knots) because of temperature difference between land and ocean. The August and September sea breeze is even lighter (3 to 12 knots).

Typically as the sea breeze fills in it starts out at 150 degrees and as it develops can be very shifty in 10 to 30 degree oscillations. Generally the left-hand side of the course pays off early because the sea breeze is stronger further from shore and farther to the east. Once it develops, it slowly veers to the right, often to 180 degrees or as far as 210 degrees. In the afternoon the right-hand side of the course generally pays off unless the velocity drops near shore.

During the summer Marblehead weather is affected by one low pressure system after another moving toward the northeast. Generally this is the typical pattern: as the cold front approaches, the breeze picks up from the southwest, 10 to 20 knots, for up to 24 hours before the front. Marblehead does not usually get squally conditions with a frontal passage. Maybe one or two 30-knot squalls occur during the whole summer. The worst weather generally passes to the south of Boston or north to the Merimac Valley to Portmouth, New Hampshire.

Once the front passes, perhaps with just a brief shower, there is almost no wind until the sky begins to clear. The northwest gradient begins to build *only* when the clouds are on the horizon. The northwest gradient is typically 10 to 20 knots with gusts and shifty. The second day after a frontal passage is, "depending on the gradient," weaker, or is defeated by the sea breeze.

June and July are the best months for sailing. August and September are often either too light or too stormy.

The current floods toward the southwest at less than ½ knot. The ebb is not evident on the surface. Naturally the flood is strongest in a northeaster. Otherwise the current is not a big factor offshore.

The cable weather channel is a good weather information source.

Just like any sea breeze area, the amount of cumulus clouds that develop over the land will help you predict when the sea breeze will fill in and help predict the velocity to expect. The local sea breeze dies late after sunset. Then the regional weather gradients effect the wind at night.

Chicago, Illinois

South to westerly's at 8 to 15 knots are normal. Checking the wind's direction on Lake Michigan when leaving the harbor on the way to a race course (usually about 4 miles out) will give information for the knock or lift in shore. Direction, wind speed, temperature and time of day dictate where and when to go inshore. More often than not along the Chicago shoreline, in high 70- to 90-degree range, there is a much stronger breeze 0 to 1 mile offshore. When breeze is more southerly, it should be a knock; when more westerly, it should be a lift.

When a front arrives, it gets cold and wet. Fronts often come very fast and leave no wind. A more normal northerly will stay in area for two to three days, blow 10 to 20 knots and slowly overnight, move from east to south and stay at prevailing southwest to west. Sometimes there is current but for general sailing it does not mean much.

The best sailing is in late spring–early summer because of stronger breezes, and in fall because the water is warmer than the land. Sometimes the warmest place to be is offshore Chicago.

There is a NOAA station here which is a good weather information source. The weather is fairly predictable around here. If you have lived and sailed here for a while you recognize the regular cycles.

People always think the "Windy City" is named for naturally windy conditions. Wrong. The Windy City actually has light to moderate sailing area as far as wind speed goes. The "Windy" comes from the windy politicians in Chicago's stormy politics.

From 5:30 to 6:30 P.M., the wind dies 90 percent of time. It comes back slowly and often is light until about 2:00 A.M. to 4:00 A.M. If the wind does not return by 4:00 A.M. you won't have any till about 10:00 A.M.

Newport, Rhode Island

Southwesterly

In the summertime the standard weather is a thermal arriving late in the morning. The closer you are to land from Point Judith to Beavertail Point, the more important it is to sail on the right side of the course in a southwester. However, if you head toward the old America's Cup buoy on the east side of Block Island Sound and then experience a filling southerly, it often pays to stay on the left side of the course. But generally the wind will fill from 180 degrees and bend as the afternoon wears on as far as 250 degrees to the right.

Northwesterly

Several times each month throughout the summer in Newport, Rhode Island, a northwesterly front will arrive from Canada. The wind is very strong and can often last as long as three days. The breeze tends to shift back and forth between 320 and 005 degrees. It pays to be patient and wait for the wind to shift back on longer windward legs because it almost always does.

On the second or third day of a northwester, depending on the strength of the front, this wind will eventually die out. In a dying northwester you always want to sail to the right side of the course going upwind and the left side of the course when sailing downwind.

Easterly

Easterlies in Newport generally mean rain. However if there is a clear southeast breeze, one of the little-known tricks is to head off to the left side of the course. There is generally more wind to the left than to the right.

I find the sailing to be best in Newport in June through September.

There is about a half a knot of current, consistently across Block Island Sound but the current is consistent and not often a factor in the outcome of the races.

There are a lot of great sources of weather information ranging from the

Newport Daily News and the *Providence Journal*. The National Weather Service has good, reliable information. Sometimes you can get cooperation from the Coast Guard stations. For example, Point Judith Coast Guard can relay information on what is going to happen next before it happens in Newport with a filling southerly. With Block Island, Martha's Vineyard, and Montauk Point between 20 and 30 miles away, you can get a good handle on when the sea breeze is going to come in.

Of all the places I've sailed, Newport, Rhode Island in the summertime offers the greatest variety of conditions, although the windshifts within each general wind direction are fairly predictable.

The most important instrument in Newport is the compass. Your compass tells you what your course is and gives you a good feeling of changes in weather pattern.

At night time in Newport the wind often dies and then comes in from the west or northwest. It can get pretty strong and blow in a generally westerly direction in the morning, but this will die out as the day warms up.

Robbie Doyle always used to say that you can tell how strong the wind is in Newport in the morning by how much dew is on the grass. The more dew, the stronger the wind, and his lore generally works out.

Annapolis, Maryland

The Chesapeake Bay off of Annapolis, Maryland, is a very challenging place to sail. In the summer there is often a southerly late in the day and in the spring and fall there are frequent northwesterly fronts.

The current in the channel in the middle of the Bay can often be very strong. You can watch the current by the direction anchored ships spin. Keep in mind it takes about 10 knots of breeze to overcome about one knot of current so in light wind you often find the ship's stern facing the breeze.

When the wind is southeast, it is better to play the eastern shore. While the wind is southwest it is better to play the western shore. I often find that sailing in the middle of the course pays the least dividends while sailing on the edges give the greatest rewards. The trick is to get in phase with the windshifts and watch the boats in other classes around you. There are generally hundreds of boats sailing on the Chesapeake Bay and it is easy to watch them to see what is going to happen next.

The prevailing wind direction is SSW; the average speed is 8 to 10 knots true.

Flood tide—Shipping channel runs up the Eastern Shore of the Bay, 120 feet of water. Stay to the west for less current. New sea breeze will start from the south to southwest and go to south to southeast as it builds.

Ebb tide—go to the east for better current and for the slow oscillation to the east.

Storms come from the south and can be very harsh on Chesapeake Bay. They come up quickly and can be violent particularly late in the afternoon or early evening in the summertime when you get frequent thunder squalls due to the heat.

There is often a prevailing westerly, light winds in the evening and although the Chesapeake Bay has a reputation for very light winds in the summer, the fact is many regattas have sailed in very good breezes.

As the front goes through, wind will clock to the west until it reaches northwest, which is the prevailing cold front direction. Depending on the strength of the front, winds will blow from the northwest at 20–25 true for two to three days, slowly clocking to northeast and dying. Wind will reappear from the southerly direction as a new sea breeze is generated.

The Chesapeake, I think, is at its best in the months of April and May and then again in October and November. This is when we like to sail here the most.

The current flow is tidal and flows north and south in the Bay. It's also heavily influenced by influx of many rivers and the fact that prevailing winds are north and south.

Many races on the bay are attacked by big strong ebb or flood tides. Published tables are *not* accurate. We depend on local signs of what is happening such as crab pots or tankers laying with anchor.

Use NOAA weather radio, National headquarters in Washington, D.C., BWI Airport, and U.S. Coast Guard at the Thomas Point Light.

Pay strict attention to wind patterns during a dying northerly. Wind will remain from the north on the western shore of the bay while the new sea breeze has already started on the Eastern Shore. Knowing the predominant weather pattern will help you decide which direction will prevail up the first beat. Sailors should be prepared to sail in chop in Annapolis created by traffic on weekends.

Wind will get lighter and swing to the west at night.

New York Harbor, New York

New York Harbor is one of the toughest places in the world to sail. It is fed by a large tidal basin along the Jersey shore and throughout the Narrows. Much of the water is shallow and yet a lot is deep thanks to the Ice Age, which created deep trenches and the natural harbor of New York.

The wind generally either flows up or down the Hudson River or in from Verrazano Narrows. When the wind comes from the side, whether it is east or west, is very difficult sailing in New York Harbor because of the effect from the buildings.

On the New Jersey side of the bay the land is generally low and you sometimes get good breeze. Thermals come in but generally not until noon. In the Liberty Cup regatta, which I have raced in New York Harbor five times, we find that we often lose one day of sailing due to no wind. But most of the other racing is in strong breezes of at least 15 to 18 knots from the southerly or from northwesterly fronts.

Prevailing wind direction is south-southeast in the spring, summer, and fall; northwest in the winter. Wind speed averages around 12 knots. The farther down the harbor you go (i.e. toward the ocean) the stronger the SSE breeze. New York Harbor has much better breezes than Long Island Sound during the summer. Sea breezes come in particularly every day.

Fronts come from the west generally. You will find great views of the clouds. Thunder storms usually approach from the west-southwest during the summer. Sometimes a front passes over from west to east, then stalls off the coast and comes back, bringing in a hard northeasterly wind (this happened during 1988 International Yacht Club Challenge).

Sailing is best in the afternoon from 3 to 7 P.M. Winds usually begin to diminish after 7 P.M. The conditions are very similar throughout the summer months (May through October). You can't really pick a best time because they are good so often. The only problems occur during summer days when a high gets stuck over the sea. But when New York Harbor has no wind, no one has any wind, not even along the Jersey shore.

The thing that makes New York Harbor so tricky is the currents. The East River is focal point between all of Long Island Sound and the Atlantic Ocean. Then you have the complication of the Hudson River. It is important to look at the tide charts and a tidal current prediction table. These are very accurate and they need to be for all the commercial traffic that passes through New York Harbor.

The current changes frequently and the best thing to do is to watch the buoys and to stay in touch. When you race in New York Harbor, have a tide book on deck at all times and keep trying to update the information about every 30 minutes.

There is usually less current along the Jersey shore, in case you are sailing against it. Current can reach 3 knots in the Hudson River during the ebb, about 2 knots during flood.

Listen to the radio weather channel or one of the TV weathermen.

New York Harbor has become remarkably clean in the past three years since the Manhattan Yacht Club was formed. This is largely due to the huge new treatment plant just south of the George Washington Bridge. Watch out for the cruise ships; they are impressive sights, but don't like to get out of the sailboat's way. We have not had any accidents with commercial traffic in three years of operation so it's a lot safer here than crowded places like Long Island Sound where power boats zoom back and forth.

Racing in New York Harbor at night is beautiful because of all the twinkling lights of the cityscape but it is actually treacherous because there is rarely wind and there is a lot of traffic. The best thing to do is to enjoy the night life ashore and not be out on the water after dark.

If you are out on the water, we recommend anchoring just west of the Statue of Liberty and enjoying the great statue and skyline with a cocktail.

Newport Beach/Long Beach, California

On a typical summer day, in the morning the wind begins to build from the south at 170 to 180 degrees; it shifts right throughout the day stabilizing at 220 to 230 degrees. Thus the right-hand side is favored as the day progresses.

The morning starts with a light southerly flow, we call it the Catalina Eddy, which can last all day depending on the weather conditions. The southerly flow is associated with low visibility, a smoggy hazy condition, as the skies clear begin to look for the westerly filling in and the breeze going right.

Fronts depend on the time of year. The fronts move slowly here and are visible many days before they arrive. Fronts are out of the south or north. Sail toward the beach. July and August are the best months for sailing.

Current flow is very little. It is usually wind swept current flowing north to south. Newport Beach can develop a strong current along the beach heading south depending on conditions.

I get my weather information on the evening news and when I look out the window in the morning.

You don't always go right in Southern California! The morning race is usually in a southerly so watch the left side, but the second you see the skies clearing start favoring the right.

If you sail at night, in the summertime you can get a strong warm offshore breeze 280-plus degrees. It only goes out 1 to 2 miles then dies. A normal occurrence is for the wind to die at sunset. A light onshore or offshore breeze develops depending on the time of the year and the air temperature in the Los Angeles basin. The best rule is to stay onshore or close to it!

Palm Beach, Florida

Here's how normal, prevailing winds work: April through October wind southeast at 8 to 12 knots. November through March wind east-northeast at 12 to 15 knots. The right side of course is favored.

When a front comes through, the wind is south at 15 to 20 knots for a day; then west to northwest for a day at 10 to 20 knots; then north 15 to 20 knots the next day; and northeast to east on day four or five at 10 to 20 knots.

February and March are the best sailing months, though January is also very good. These are the windiest months and the temperatures are moderate. April through October can be very warm and there is less wind.

The Gulf Stream is only one mile offshore and flows north at a speed averaging 3 knots. Tide is not a factor here. The location and strength of the Gulf Stream is all important. Sometimes there is a countercurrent running south along the beach inside the stream.

In the winter, if there is a high pressure system over Cape Hatteras, the wind will be from the east about 15 knots during the day but will increase to 20 knots at night and decrease again at daylight.

In the summer, southeast wind prevails all night, dying off and shifting to west around 3:00 to 6:00 A.M.

NOAA weather radio is the best weather information source.

Long Island Sound, New York

Often, the wind will come from anywhere, at a speed of 0 to 12 knots. Which way do you go? Home!

But when there is wind it is from the southwest at about 4 to 8 knots, building in the afternoon to about 12 knots. If there are any cover clouds over Long Island and you have a fairly early start (before 1:30 P.M.) then it is best to go south. The wind will build strongest from off of Long Island and tend to back a little in the process. If there are no clouds over Long Island and just thermals over Connecticut, I like to stay more north of the fleet. As the thermal builds through the day, it tends to knock down the thermal breaking effect of Long Island. This effect causes the breeze to touch down from north to south.

In any event, the current, time of day, and length of the leg weigh heavily on determining a strategy. The current is always a large consideration especially when it's the only means of propulsion.

Usually a front will be a very shifty northerly at about 18 to 22 knots.

Sailing is best in October and November, regardless of how cold it gets.

Listen to NOAA to "explore the possibilities" but *never* count on it. Look for clouds (thermal, fronts, cover, . . .) flags, smoke stacks, cruising boats, etc. . . . Anything could happen.

In a distance race it usually pays to stay to the Connecticut side. The southerly almost always fills there first and if you get a northerly it's usually stronger closer to Connecticut.

Cleveland, Ohio

On Lake Erie prevailing wind is from the southwest around 7 knots. General weather systems will move the wind to the right 95 percent of the time. Playing the right side of the course upwind will pay off most of the time. In superlight wind conditions, playing the thermals near shore in the evening and staying outside of the fleet (farther offshore) can be important in distance races.

Fronts generally approach from the southwest and flow northwest. The front is usually in the form of a squall, with high gusty winds (upper range reported 40 to 70 knots), waves, rain and lightning. Because of Lake Erie's shallow depth, the passage of the front can generate steep waves (6 to 10 feet), very short in frequency, and very hard to steer through.

Sailing is best during the periods of May/June and September/October. During those periods, temperature differences between the land and water are greatest, generating some of the steadiest breezes.

There is a minute current through the lake, from ½ to 2 knots depending on the lake water level, running from west to east. Effects are noticeable only in dead calm conditions.

The best source of weather information for the area is the Federal Aviation Administration Pilot's One-call Briefing, (216) 267–3700, which provides air pilots weather briefings. NOAA weather reports (VHF WX1) provides marine forecasts, but are frequently inaccurate with their forecasts, and delinquent with storm warnings, which usually come after you've been caught in a squall. Plus you have to listen through numerous farm reports in this area.

Keep a sharp eye out for low dark clouds on the horizon (indicating a frontal system). You will generally have enough time to prepare for inclement weather.

Here are a couple of tips. Warm summer water temperatures (low to mid 70s) encourage rapid algae growth. Recent invasions of the tiny zebra mussels are causing many problems because of their adhesion to boat bottoms and props. Checking a boat's bottom for these hazards before a race has become essential for success.

The backside of strong frontal systems generally create winds from the northeast. The rule of thumb is that if it blows from the northeast, the wind and weather will hold for three days straight.

During the summer and early fall months, there is an evening offshore breeze that comes up when daytime onshore temperatures rise above 80 degrees, usually appearing around 10:00 P.M. This is generated by heat retained by the land mass, while on-the-water temperatures cool. The breeze can be substantially stronger directly offshore of the major metropolitan areas. Daytime onshore winds can decrease to dead calm immediately after sunset during the summer months until the offshore breeze comes in.

Seattle, Washington

The prevailing wind direction on Puget Sound is north/south. It's more northerly in the summer and more southerly in the winter. Summer speeds range from 7 to 10 knots; winter speeds 10 to 20 knots. Generally spring and fall frontal systems can be devastating with winds to 65-plus knots. Most winter/

summer fronts are more benign and are accompanied by normal wind shift patterns. One should note considerable orographic influence is prevalent throughout Puget Sound and races of any distance can encounter truly dramatic wind differences. At night generally the wind dies to zero.

Sailing is generally best in spring and fall. Sailing is done year-round on Puget Sound but April and October are the best months.

Dramatic current and tidal flow can reach current speeds of 4 or more knots. The bottom contour and where two currents meet can bring about current differences of plus or minus 4 knots within 50 yards of each other.

The best weather source is NOAA (National Oceanic and Atmospheric Administration). This has an extremely well-equipped weather forecasting center in the Puget Sound area. Also, very cooperative.

Gulf of Maine

Normally, the prevailing wind is southwest, 8 to 9 knots. It's best to go right. When a warm front with low clouds, drizzle, and fog comes in, the winds are usually from the south to southeast. Behind the front the wind clocks to the southwest.

Sailing is best in August and September. There are fewer foggy days, more dependable winds from the southwest at an average speed of 9 knots.

The tide floods offshore to the east and ebbs to the west. Inlets and harbor entrance floods north, ebbs south approximate.

When sailing in offshore races, the rule of thumb is "when in doubt go out." Inshore, go for lifts off the land, and—within limits!—seek shallow water, where there is less current.

At night the wind becomes light. Sometimes it's stronger offshore.

San Diego, California

The prevailing wind is 260 to 280 degrees. Typical speeds in the summertime are 10 knots, and in wintertime 12 knots.

Go right if close to Silver Strand area near Coronado—offshore it is less right-hand biased.

Most fronts come from the southerly direction. South wind often brings rain. April and May are the months for the best wind and weather. The weather station at the airport provides the best weather information. There is some current north and south, but it's not a worry in the Coronado Roade.

Bring a kelp stick and keep foils clean. Learn to go fast in swells in San Diego.

Typically the wind goes away at night. Some offshore breeze remains when it's very warm.

Gulf Coast of Florida

Normal prevailing wind direction on the Gulf Coast is southeast. The velocity is fairly light, 5 to 10 knots and is often overcome by an equally light westerly sea breeze in the summer. Both wind directions battle each other so the result is light air from the direction that prevails. The east coast has the same prevailing wind direction and the sea breeze fortifies this, so there is generally more wind there.

In the summer months, fronts are blown out before they get this far south, so their effects are minimal. Late October to early April is when we see frontal affected weather. There's a strong southerly as wind is sucked into the leading edge. Then the wind shifts into the northwest and blows hard. As the front passes south, the wind shifts slowly into the east and dies.

The best sailing months are October to April because the air temperature is in the 65- to 85-degree range and there is generally consistent wind. Summer sailing months are accompanied by 90- to 100-degree air temps, very little wind and violent afternoon squalls with heavy rain. My vote for the two best sailing months would be January and February.

Tidal current flow parallels the coast with the change of the tides. There is also flooding and ebbing in and out of the various inlets. Tampa Bay has strong tides that are affected by spoil banks and shallows. Oceanographers have just started a new tidal study of Tampa Bay due to the changes in bottom topography caused by frequent dredging.

The best sources of weather information are NOAA radio, weather maps, and local airport meteorologists.

Unlike in places I've lived, like Newport and Annapolis, I don't know of any gospel rules to follow when racing on the Gulf coast other than to anticipate the dying of the land breeze and approach of the sea breeze. If you're racing along the coast and get too close to shore, squeezing the last of the land breeze, you'll be the last one to get the new sea breeze.

Typical evening wind is easterly off the land.

Lake St. Clair

The prevailing wind direction is east-northeast to south-southeast at 6 to 12 knots. When the wind flows off the Canadian shore, it generally tries to bend to flow perpendicular to the land. This makes the right side of the course the favored way to go. Occasionally, there will be more velocity just left of center on the course, which you need to watch out for, but 90 percent of the time the last shift will be to the right.

There are usually two types of fronts that affect the normal pattern of Lake St. Clair. Warm fronts flowing up from the Plains states will generally clock the "easterly" breezes around to the southwest and strengthen to 15 to 20 knots with gusts. Cold fronts that flow down from the Canadian Northwest will drop the present breeze to near zero for several hours and then bang in from the northwest at 10 to sometimes 35 to 40 knots depending on the pressure differences.

The best times for sailing are late May–early June and the month of September. July and August are usually hot, humid, and have very little breeze like Long Island Sound or the Chesapeake. October can make for some great fall sailing if you don't mind adding extra clothes.

Lake St. Clair is in the middle of two significant rivers, the St. Clair River flowing out of Lake Huron and the Detroit River flowing into Lake Erie. As you get closer to either end of the lake you can receive a south to southwest push 6 miles out into the lake ranging from ¼ of a knot to as much as 2.5 knots. There is also a current increase as you get closer to the shipping channel that is dredged to 36 feet as opposed to the average 14 feet depth of the lake.

The best source of weather information is still local knowledge on the dock. Regional airports are also a good form of information for a 24-hour picture in all directions. Detroit has several sources where you can get a marine forecast, just call information. Cloud formations are also a good indicator of incoming weather conditions. The weather fax, the weather map in the local paper, and the weather person on local TV and radio may also assist you in formulating your race game plan.

Spring and early summer tend to present a lot of wind shear on Lake St. Clair so it is important to make sure your sail trim matches accordingly, especially on those light to moderate days. Don't be concerned if your trim is way off from side to side. Navigationally, the lake is very shallow around the edges and there is a dumping ground at the southern end of the lake just west of the channel which is well marked with unlit cans. It's best to have a chart on board and to review it often. Most of the range lights have submerged parts so make sure you give them a minimal 6 foot berth.

The wind tends to die at night unless there is an incoming front that will have the same characteristics of a daytime front.

San Francisco, California

Berkeley Olympic Circle is the best place to race. In the morning, the wind is 200 to 215 degrees then slowly shifts to 230 degrees by the end of the day. The left side pays in the morning and the right side in the afternoon.

The wind shifts to the south 140 to 180 degrees when a front comes through.

September and October are the best months to sail because the wind is 15 to 20 knots, it is warm, and there is no fog.

The best source for weather information is VHF radio.

Countdown

Your game plan, or strategy, does not take into account the other boats in the fleet; it's solely a blueprint for how to use the wind and current to get around the racecourse as fast as possible. Since creating a game plan for each race requires calculating myriad details, we'll borrow an organizing technique from the space program: the countdown. In creating a game plan, the countdown clock starts two days before the first race of a regatta.

T Minus Two Days:

By collecting newspaper weather maps that show the locations of high- and low-pressure systems and frontal zones, you can get an idea of how the weather systems are moving. Since wind flows around a high-pressure system in a clockwise direction, and around a low-pressure system in a counterclockwise direction, try to figure out the general weather-system wind flow.

Check your sailing notebook for what happened the last time you sailed at the venue. (See Chapter 9.)

If you are not sailing on a lake, and current will be a factor, obtain a chart of the sailing area and get access to a tide table.

Check times of high and low tides. Determine when to expect slack tide. Use a chart of the race area to determine where the current will be strongest. Figure out where you can sail to avoid an adverse current.

T Minus Four Hours

Listen to the NOAA weather forecast on your VHF radio or on an inexpensive "weather radio" of the kind available from electronics stores such as Radio Shack.

Keep your eye on changes in the cloud cover, and note the wind direction and strength.

Get the boat rigged, top off the fuel tank, take ashore any sails that you won't be using, fill the water bottles, put lunch aboard, and stow foul weather gear. If your boat is dry-sailed, get it in the water before the skippers' meeting. Do whatever you can so that you can leave the dock right after the skippers' meeting. Even go to the bathroom before the meeting, to avoid the lines.

T Minus One and a Half Hours

Attend the skippers' meeting. Make sure you understand the course, and the signals the committee will use. Find out whether the one-minute rule will be in effect. Can you sail through the finish line if you are not finishing? Is an alternate penalty system in effect? What will the turning marks look like?

Ask for changes in instructions, when and where protests will be heard, and clarify any points not clear in the instructions.

Leave the dock.

T Minus One Hour

If it's a long sail to the course, take wind readings along the way. Note the development and movement of clouds. When you get to the starting line, sail upwind, recording wind strength and your compass readings on both tacks. Try to get readings on both sides of the course. Check the direction and strength of the current by looking at the water as it flows past objects anchored to the bottom. On the way back to the starting line, practice a few spinnaker jibes. Get back to the line early enough so that the crew can repack the chute while the "brain trust" comes up with a game plan. Solicit input from all the crew. When everyone is finished, hold a crew meeting to discuss specific maneuvers the crew should be ready for.

T Minus 10 Minutes

Plan your start. For information on how to do just that, turn to the next chapter.

Starting

R aces are often won in the period two minutes before the gun until the first wind shift emerges. In this chapter you'll learn why. Winning the start doesn't guarantee that you'll win the race, of course, but it helps. When you start poorly in sailing, your situation is comparable to that of a team that begins a football game 14 points behind. Good teams can overcome early deficits, but it's not easy. Getting a good start also gives you a psychological lift that helps your crew work harder for the rest of the race. Once you're out in front of the fleet, you'll find that the rich simply get richer. With clear air, you'll have superior boatspeed along with the opportunity to respond to any wind shift without having to sail through the bad air. As the rest of the boats in the pack battle it out with each other for clear air, the leaders pull away, playing the wind shifts.

During long-distance handicapped races, some skippers don't start aggressively enough, because they don't want to quibble over a good position on the line when the race will take hours to sail, and the intrinsic speed of each unique boat will be factored into the final standings of the fleet. The justification of a mediocre start asks why it's worth fighting on the line when everyone will get clear air as soon as the fleet separates—something that's bound to happen as the different boats sail to their respective potentials. This philosophy is self-defeating, for many races have been lost by a precious few seconds. Getting a good start in a 600-mile distance race may not seem important, since on the second night you may well be alone on the ocean, wondering about the rest of the fleet's location, but a good start creates a psychological lift for the crew, which motivates them to push the boat harder throughout the race.

In this chapter we'll cover the starting techniques that will get you ahead of the pack, whether you are racing a one-design dinghy, a Performance Handicap Racing Formula (PHRF) cruiser/racer, or an IOR racing machine. We'll finish the chapter with how to get back in the game if you stumble at the start.

Starting Strategies

The most important questions when planning your start are where along the starting line you want to be when the gun sounds, and where you want to go afterwards. Most people make their first mistake of the race by simply sailing out to the course, and then determining which end of the line is favored— that is, which end is farthest upwind. Usually they do the latter by luffing head-to-wind in the middle of the starting line. Then they try to start on starboard tack at the favored end. But don't forget that when the starting gun goes off, you want to be in a controlling position on the line, and you'll subsequently want to keep control during the race. One sailboat controls another by blocking an opponent that wants to tack to a more favored side of the course, or, for example, through aggressive application of rights under the racing rules.

Therefore, the first part of the chapter will deal with starting strategies. In the second half of the chapter we'll look at how to control the boats around you, once you've chosen which side of the course and which side of the line you want to start on.

Anatomy of a Racecourse

Let's define some terms relating to starting lines. As we go along, refer to figure 3.1, which labels these parts of the starting line.

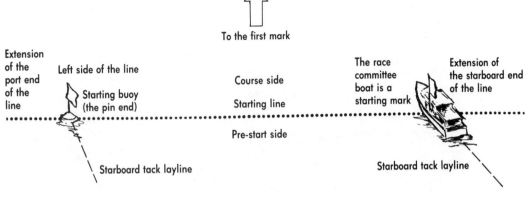

Figure 3.1 *The starting line.*

Most races start upwind, because windward legs spread fleets out. Upwind starts practically demand that competitors start on starboard tack, because of the right-of-way benefits that starboard tackers enjoy. When the marks are to be rounded to port, the committee boat will be on the right side of the line. That way you'll pass *all* the marks to port—including the starting line buoy.

People sometimes inaccurately call the committee boat's side of the line the "windward end," and the pin (buoy) side the "leeward end" of the line. These labels are derived from sailboat racing's most common approach to the starting line—close-hauled on starboard tack. In this common situation, when you're crossing the line the committee boat is always on the windward side. But the pin end (normally the left end of the starting line) can be favored too. Thus, "windward end" should refer only to the side of the line that is farthest upwind. To keep yourself and your crew from being confused, only call the right side of the line the windward end when the wind favors it.

The starting line is an invisible line between a specified position on the committee boat, such as a flagpole, and the starting buoy. The line has a course side and a pre-start side. The extensions of the starting line constitute the path the line would take if extended past either of its ends. Eight key variables affect the all-important decision as to where to start:

1. Which side of the line is farther to windward, and whether that is indeed the favored end.

2. Which shift pattern the wind is in.

3. Wind strength.

4. Direction and strength of current.

5. Your boatspeed, compared to others starting with you.

6. Whether you'll have to sail on one tack more than the other during the beat.

7. Where the bulk of the fleet will be starting.

8. The penalties that the race committee has instituted (via the racing instructions) for premature starts.

Let's go through the above list of considerations in order.

The Favored End and the Windward End: Not Always the Same

No matter what kind of starting line you have—whether it's to be crossed sailing to windward or to leeward—there is always a favored end of the line. Just don't get fooled as to which end it is. Determining the favored end should involve much more than just luffing head-to-wind and noting which end of the line is closer to the direction in which your bow points. Get out to the course early and figure out what the wind is doing over the course.

Long Beach

A perfect example of how the end of the line that is farthest upwind may not be the best place to start occurs in the waters off Long Beach, California. Race committees there favor the left end of the line by moving it a couple of boatlengths to windward. This is because when the line is set square to the wind, fleets bunch up at the committee boat end of the line to get to the persistent veer (clockwise shift) that occurs with regularity in that area. So, when races start at a customary time, the best tactical decision in 90 percent of the contests is to start next to the committee boat, tack to port right after the gun goes off, and then tack back to starboard once you're headed by the right shift that Long Beach sailors know they can expect. (See figure 3.2.)

In the above case, the tactician must calculate whether he·should take an immediate gain at the end of the line farthest upwind, or get to the shift before

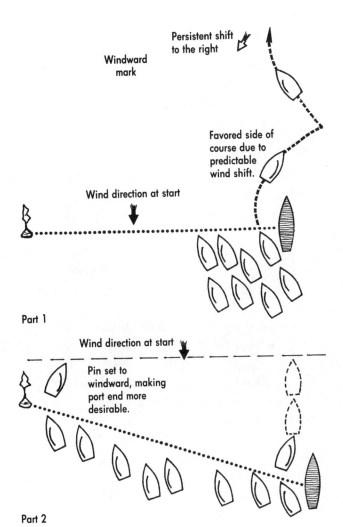

Persistent shift
to the right

Windward
mark

Favored side of
course due to
predictable
wind shift.

Wind direction at start

Part 1

Wind direction at start

Pin set to
windward, making
port end more
desirable.

Part 2

Figure 3.2 *Race committees at
Long Beach, CA, usually favor the
left end of the starting line to
avoid fleets bunching up on the
right side. Because of the usual
persistent shift to the right,
competitors converge at the right
side of the line so that they can get
to the right side of the course
quickly (Part 1). But when the left
side of the line is purposely favored
by several boatlengths (Part 2), the
fleet is more likely to spread out as
some skippers elect to take the
initial gain at the port end of the
line. Part 2 shows that a boat at
the favored end of the line has a
two-boatlength lead at the start
of the race.*

other competitors. "Remember," Tom says, "it doesn't matter where you are
at the start—it's where you are at the finish."

Miami and Fort Lauderdale

That the end of the line that is farthest upwind isn't necessarily the place
to cross the line is also illustrated at the start of most long-distance races off
Miami or Fort Lauderdale, Florida. In the first part of such races, it's important

to get into the Gulf Stream as fast as possible, which flows to the north at three knots, a mile and a half offshore. So the key is to start at whichever end of the line gets you to the Gulf Stream first. This means you don't want to end up to leeward of boats that may luff you. In that case it might even be worth starting late and a boatlength to leeward of those boats, so that you can bear off and head toward the Gulf Stream.

San Francisco

On San Francisco Bay, you don't simply start at the windward end of the line. Because of the strong currents, you have to fight for a position on the line that will allow you to get out of adverse current or get into a favorable current quickly.

The above three examples are meant to encourage the tactician in you not to *assume* that you should always start at the upwind end of the starting line. Nonetheless, the windward end must always be determined before a race, and in many if not most situations, a start at the windward end will give you an advantage over other boats.

The simplest and most often used method is to sail to the middle of the starting line and then luff straight into the wind. Whichever end of the line your bow points to is the farthest upwind, i.e., the favored end. This isn't very exact, but it's quick and easy. Remember that if you are not right in the middle of the line, perspective will throw off your perception of which end is favored. Furthermore, once the countdown to the start begins, you probably won't have another opportunity to luff head-to-wind. Thus you won't be able to compare that initial reading to subsequent readings taken in the same way. If you are using this method and your boat has an overlapping genoa, take your reading from your masthead fly. On dinghies, your boat is dead into the wind when the boom is luffing over the centerline of the boat.

Another quick method, and one that is more reliable, is to sail head-to-wind at one end of the line. Then sight across an athwartship part of your boat, like the traveler or the back edge of the cabin, toward the other end of the line. If your line of sight is to windward of the far end of the line, then the near end is favored, and vice versa. With this method you can get a rough idea of the extent to which one end is favored. When sighting, notice how many boats at the other end of the line fit between your line of sight athwartship and the starting line. (See figure 3.3.)

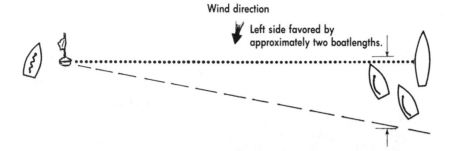

Figure 3.3 *By sighting over an athwartship part of the boat, like the traveler or across the back of the deck house, when the boat is luffing head to wind, you can tell more than just which end of the line is favored. To determine how many boatlengths the line is skewed, observe how many boats fit between the mark at other end of the line and your sight.*

The best way to determine the windward end is to sail down the line and note your compass course. Then luff up into the wind and take a compass reading for the wind direction. Compare the two readings; the line is square if the angle between the two is 90 degrees. The end of the line that makes an angle smaller than 90 degrees to the wind is the favored end. For example, imagine that you luff up and find that the wind is blowing from a direction of 105 degrees. Then you sail down the line to the pin and find you're on a compass course of 10 degrees. By subtracting 10 from 105 you get an answer of 95; thus the right side of the line is 95 degrees from the wind. That means that the left is side of the line is favored by five degrees since it is 85 degrees off the wind. (See figure 3.4.)

The longer the line, the more variables you'll have to weigh in working out which end of the line is favored. To simplify the complex problem of weighing different wind and current strengths and determining which end is farther upwind, use the buddy system. After sailing to windward with a friend to get your boatspeed tuned, go back to the line, and at a prearranged time cross the line at opposite ends and sail to windward toward each other. Whoever is ahead when you meet started at the favored end. This is much more accurate than trying to figure out which side has more or less wind, which side has more or less adverse current, and which side is farther upwind. The buddy system gives you an empirically derived solution to a tough problem.

After using the buddy system to test the starting line at the 1974 Laser North America's in Toronto, Gary found that the port end was favored enough to enable him to port-tack the fleet of 90 Lasers. "Although it appeared that the

Figure 3.4(A) *If the wind is not perpendicular to the line, the side of the line that makes the smaller angle to the wind is the furthest upwind. In this case Angle X is smaller than Angle Y; therefore, the right side of the line is further upwind.*

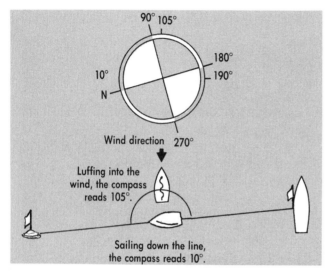

Figure 3.4(B) *To figure out which end of the line is favored, sail from the left side of the line to the right side and note your compass course. Next luff into the wind, and then subtract the heading of the wind from the bearing on the line. If the difference is less than 90 the right side is favored. If the difference is more than 90, the left side is favored. In this case the right side is favored by five degrees (190 − 105 = 85).*

starboard end was favored, when I tested the line by crossing it on port from the leeward end, I was able to cross my buddy, who crossed the line at the same time on starboard from the committee boat end by six boatlengths. The test showed that starting at the port end was favored because of the current and waves. It was one of the greatest highs I've ever had in sailing when I successfully port-tacked the fleet and crossed 90 Lasers by five boatlengths. I went on to win that race."

Recognizing and Using Wind Shifts

Sailing in clear air with the ability to tack on the first shift is crucial. Getting the first shift can affect your decision as to where you'll want to start. Racers who catch the first shift correctly, and are able to tack on it while staying in clear air, will usually be the leaders at the windward mark. To be able to take advantage of the first wind shift after the start, you need to start at the end of the line that gets you to the initial shift before anyone else. As we saw in the example of Long Beach, California, that favored end may not necessarily be the end that is farthest to windward.

The Timing of Shifts

Look for a last-minute shift that could change the favored end of the line. If you already know the bearing of the starting line, you can determine which end of the line is farthest upwind, should such a shift occur.

If you've kept a good log of your wind readings, you should have an idea when to expect the next shift. But don't get overconfident; keep checking the wind direction as late as you can. On a shifty day, postpone your decision as to which end is farthest upwind until the last possible moment.

Consider the sort of wind-shift pattern that is affecting the course. In open water the wind will either be persistently shifting in one direction, oscillating between a veer (clockwise shift) and a back (counter-clockwise), or there will

Figure 3.5 *Sometimes it pays to cross the line at the unfavored end of the line. Even though Boat A was a boatlength behind those that started at the favored committee boat end, A is able to cross those boats when the wind shifts to the left shortly after the starting signal because it is on the inside of the lift.*

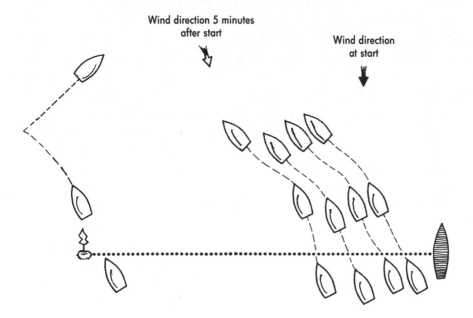

Wind direction 5 minutes
after start

Wind direction
at start

be a combination of a persistent and an oscillating shift. When part of the course is close to land, expect the wind to bend around the land. If you are expecting a persistent shift, or if your pre-race compass readings indicate that you are in the midst of a persistent shift, the favored side of the line is usually the one that allows you to sail toward the new wind first.

In oscillating winds, you need to know the timing of the shifts in order to pick the favored position on the starting line. For example, if you know that port tack will be lifted within minutes after the start, cross the line at the left end, even if the right end is favored when the gun goes off. When the shift comes, all the boats on starboard will be headed, enabling you to tack and cross the competitors that started at the "favored end." (See figure 3.5.)

Wind Strength and Turbulence

In light winds of less than 8 knots, the favored end is anyplace on the line where you will be able to foot off and sail in clear air. In these conditions, boats' backwind and blanket areas are felt much farther away then in heavy air. Therefore, if everyone gathers at the committee-boat end, it may well be better to start to leeward of the pack. Or if everyone starts at the leeward end, you can play it safe by starting 10 to 15 boatlengths to windward of the bulk of the fleet. Boatspeed is king in light air, so forget about trying to point. It's good to have at least a three-boatlength-wide hole to leeward of you on the starting line so that you can foot for speed after the gun goes off. Later in this chapter we will discuss maneuvering techniques for achieving this goal.

Around the starting area, every time a boat sails through the wind, it creates turbulence. As boats crisscross behind the line, they chop up both the wind and the water's surface. In the ten minutes before the start, an oval-shaped area of chopped-up wind hangs over the starting area like a cloud. Even if you are to windward of a group, you will be slowed, since what wind there is will be deflected over the pack. (See figure 3.6.) Most of the wind bends around and rises over the fleet, which lessens the wind on the starting line. The wind starts to bend and lift at a distance equal to roughly twice the height of an object in its path. (The wind treats a tightly packed fleet as a single object.) Therefore, if the average height of a mast in your fleet is 50 feet, the wind will start to rise above the water 100 feet in front of the line. This is called

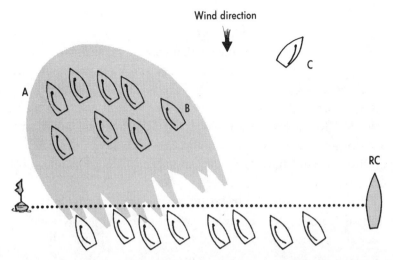

Figure 3.6 *Even though boats A & B are not in a particular boat's wind shadow, they are in disturbed wind since the wind backs up to windward of a tightly packed group of boats. Boat C is the only boat with truly clear air.*

the "snow fence" effect. The lighter the wind, the more you'll feel the effect; therefore, the farther you are from the fleet, the more accurate your wind readings will be. The "snow fence" phenomenon makes luffing head-to-wind at the line somewhat unreliable. So if you like to luff head-to-wind to determine the wind direction, it's best to do so at least four boatlengths in front of the line, or ten boatlengths from either side of the line.

Until the fleet breaks up, a cloud of backwind, before and behind the fleet, travels with the group of boats like the dust cloud that hovers over the "Peanuts" cartoon character Pig Pen. Therefore, even the boats in the front row are going slower than they would if there were no other boats around. That's why, in a big or tightly packed fleet, you will make big gains by separating with packs of boats by at least five boatlengths.

The decrease in the strength of wind as it collides with a fleet of boats explains why a port-tack start works so well when the boat on port tack can get across the fleet. The farther a boat goes as it crosses a fleet of starboard tackers, the farther it will be getting away from the cloud of disturbed air created by the fleet. In a big fleet, separating from the masses can be beneficial enough to justify tacking to port and ducking the sterns of many starboard tackers.

One of the biggest mistakes many sailors make is to be afraid to tack to port early to get clear air. It's very difficult, early on in a race, to admit that you are behind, and ducking another boat means that you are behind, but dipping one or two sterns doesn't give away much distance, and the greatest concern you should have is getting clear air and getting the correct side of the course.

If you are the second fleet to start, beware of the cloud of disturbed air in the wake of the fleet that started before you. The bigger the fleet that went before you, the longer it will take for the chopped-up wind to dissipate. In light air especially, you will have to amend your game plan to avoid sailing downwind of packs of boats from the preceding fleet.

Finally, as the wind is chopped up by boats maneuvering behind the starting line, the wind will seem lighter. Therefore, when considering sail selection for the start aboard a big boat, keep in mind that the wind will most likely be stronger 100 yards to weather.

Current

Current is another factor that you have to judge when planning where to start. Since most sailors ignore or misjudge the effect of current while starting, you can gain quite an advantage by anticipating and identifying the current's effect on the fleet. In an adverse current, i.e., one that flows against the direction in which one wishes to sail, fleets tend to be late crossing the line. Therefore, during the countdown you'll want to stay closer to the line. How close you stay to the line depends on the strength of both wind and current. The only way to get your timing right is to time yourself from an anchored object to the line.

In a favorable current—one pushing you over the line—it's best to hang back so that you can make a full-speed charge, while those who misjudged their starts will be trying to slow down. One of the worst starting situations is to drift over the line early in light air, when the current is flowing toward the first mark. In this nightmare, you'll have to fight the current to get back across the line, while the rest of the fleet is being whisked to the mark by the same current that you are cursing.

At the match-racing series after the 1985 maxi boat regatta in Newport, Rhode Island, Dennis Conner was skippering *Kialoa* with Tom calling tactics when just this sort of disaster occurred. According to Gary, the competitive juices were flowing as the crews of *Kialoa* and *Matador* went head-to-head, since both boats had sailed a keenly fought series of races earlier in the week. Gary, who called tactics on *Matador*, recalls what happened:

"Being early, *Kialoa* was in a slowing-down mode, which left the 80-footer vulnerable. We jumped on them by getting *Matador* up to full speed to leeward of them, and then luffed *Kialoa* over the line. It was one of the few times Dennis misjudged his distance to the line; maybe it was because of the current pushing both boats toward the line." That nonfeasance cost *Kialoa* the race. By the time Conner got back behind the line after fighting the current without a spinnaker up, *Kialoa* was 20 lengths behind and never had a chance of catching up.

"The other place where I've done well sailing in current is at the Liberty

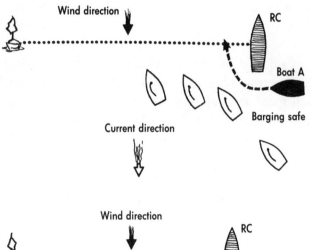

Figure 3.7 *The skipper of Boat A is insured of being on the line at the start since she is staying near the line and is able to reach in with a lot of speed. Those approaching the line on a close-hauled course are slowed by the current, which increases the chance that Boat A will find a hole to sneak into behind the committee boat.*

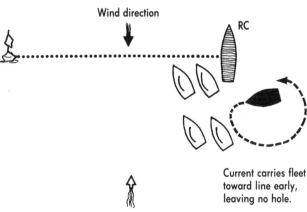

Figure 3.8 *When the current is pushing the fleet toward the line, there will be no space behind the committee boat for barging boats.*

Cup, sailed in the swirling currents of New York Harbor off the Statue of Liberty," Gary says. "When the current is pushing you across the line, it's important to hang back and not push the line hard. I've won a lot of races by having a better handle on the current. To read the current, I watch my progress relative to either end of the line against the shoreline. This gives me a good feeling of the rate at which I'm being swept toward the line."

Barging on starboard tack can be a preferable starting technique when the current washes the fleet back from the line. By staying on an extension of the line, you avoid not being able to get back up to the starting line. Also, the chances of getting picked off for barging are minimized, since the boat approaching the line on a close-hauled course will most likely be late, with the current slowing its progress. (See figure 3.7.) On the other hand, barging is the worst approach you can make to the line when the current is pushing the fleet across the line. (See figure 3.8.) When the current moves across the line from right to left, you will have a better chance of barging at the committee-boat end of the line, because those trying to close you out will be swept toward the leeward end of the line by the current. This is the one time when starting a few seconds late can pay off. If the first group of boats is not up to speed, the current will carry them to leeward, giving you a chance to come around the committee boat at full speed and pop into the hole they left. (See figure 3.9.) Be careful of trying to start at the leeward pin when the current is moving from the committee boat to the pin. The actual starboard layline will be much farther up than you think.

If the current flows from the pin to the committee boat (figure 3.10), don't even think of barging. Depending on the speed of the current and the lightness

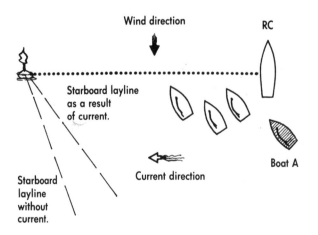

Wind direction

RC

Starboard layline as a result of current.

Current direction

Boat A

Starboard layline without current.

Figure 3.9 *The laylines to the starting marks change when the current sweeps from one side of the line to the other. In figure 3.9, the pack of boats approached the line on what they thought was the layline, but they misjudged the current and were swept to the left of the committee boat allowing Boat A room to reach the starting line.*

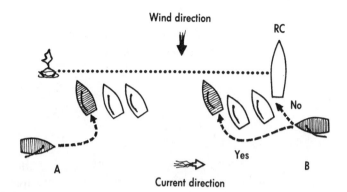

Wind direction

RC

No

Yes

A

B

Current direction

Figure 3.10 *With the current flowing from the left side of the starting line to the right side, Boat A makes a good start by approaching the line on port tack. At the other end of the line Boat B's best option is to duck behind the two boats and start to leeward of them.*

of the wind, you'll be able make your approach to the line from below the starboard layline (if there is no current), and still be able to squeeze out the boats above you for barging. It will also be easier to get the perfect pin-end start because you will be able to tack to leeward of the boats already set up on the line. Even though you might not be laying the pin, if you luff the boats above you, the current will carry everyone down the line toward the committee boat, so that you will make it around the pin.

This is the main point to remember about starting in current: The lighter the wind strength, the greater effect the current will have. In light air, be especially attentive to the slightest bit of current.

Comparative Boatspeed

If you are not sailing in a one-design event, your starting plan will have to take into account the speed capabilities of the other boats in your fleet or division. If you're sailing a J/24 in a Wednesday-night race where boats of all sizes ranging up to 40-footers start together, avoid the perfect pin-end start. Getting the best start in the fleet will only be a Pyrrhic victory, since soon after the start the bigger boats will sail by you to windward, leaving you gasping for air. Instead, start to windward of the bigger boats to keep from getting smothered as they move ahead.

Being the fastest boat in the fleet may guarantee you the first-to-finish award, but if you don't push your boat hard from start to finish, you won't save your time on the rest of the fleet. As scratch boat, use your speed to grab the optimal start. Our friends racing *Shillelagh*, a Schock 35, were able to port-tack the whole fleet during one of their yacht-club races because they were scratch boat. They didn't plan to port-tack the fleet, but when the port jib sheet became fouled and had to be cut, they had no other option. Since then, they've added the port-tack start to their arsenal of starting procedures for their club races, where, for now, they are the fastest boat in the fleet.

Favored Tack on the First Beat

The next strategic consideration you have to weigh when figuring where to start is whether you will have to sail on one tack more than the other during the beat to the first mark. For example, if you're going to have to spend a lot of time on starboard, you'd better figure out a way to make sure your air is going to be clear on starboard. So if you start next to a slightly faster boat, you'll have a hard time keeping your wind clear. The point is, if you are going to spend a lot of time on one tack, make sure that your position is a good one.

Where Will the Fleet Start?

The next two considerations as to where to start are based on how the fleet and your closest competitors in the rankings are positioned. After determining the favored end of the starting line, visualize how the bulk of the boats are going to start, so that you can create a starting plan. You'll want to think about how you can put yourself in a decent position despite all the traffic around you. Furthermore, you'll want to pay attention to the places with the most congestion, so as not to be trapped by other boats just when you're ready to break out toward better wind or advantageous current. As the starter's clock ticks down the final five minutes before the start, you will be able to confirm your hypothesis as to how the fleet is setting up. If your plan calls for playing the right side of the course, but you know that there will be a huge pack of boats at the committee-boat end of the line, don't try to be a hero by being the one boat in the fleet to start right next to the committee boat. Instead, play the better percentages and start behind the pack. Despite being in the turbulent wind that trails the fleet, you'll have clearer air and better speed than those close to the "favored position." Those fighting for the committee-boat start have a good chance of being over the line early in full view of the committee boat, and they risk being mired in a morass of boats and bad air.

If you plan to sail the middle of the beat, try to pick a place on the line where you'll have clear air and where there are roughly equal numbers of boats on either side of you. If it's clear that the left side of the course is favored, and you're racing in a big competitive fleet, it may actually be better not to fight to get the pin-end start that all boats vie for. By avoiding the traffic jam, you differentiate the superficially favored end from the tactically favored end.

When You Need to Beat Another Boat

If you're racing in a series, and if you need to finish ahead of one other boat in the fleet, you'll tend to adopt match-racing tactics vis-à-vis your special opponent; such tactics are discussed later in this chapter. However, while you are aggressively seeking control, other factors deserve your attention. In particular, even if traffic prevents you from getting to a close controlling position at the start, you can still obtain an advantage if you get the first wind shift before your opponent does. Or you can try to position yourself so that you'll gain if the first shift reaches both of you at the same time. Therefore, if you both start on starboard tack and you expect the first shift to be a header, start to leeward of your opponent. If you expect the first shift to be a lift, start to windward of him. When you're not sure what the wind is going to do, stay close to your competitor to minimize possible losses. (See "Leverage," page 140.) Also start to starboard of him, so that at least you know you'll have the starboard tack advantage on him when you come together in a crossing situation.

When starting with the goal of beating one other boat, you have to take into account whether he points or foots. Due to differences among helmsmen, these can be considerations even in one-design racing. Tom says: "When *Stars & Stripes '87* was racing against *Kookaburra III* in Fremantle, Australia, we thought we could foot faster than they could. I don't think it's common knowledge, but I'll say it now. We were convinced that in a straight pointing contest, *Kookaburra* could have beaten *Stars & Stripes*. We always started to leeward of them, because if they'd been to leeward and started to point better, we'd either have had to pinch up and lose speed, or else be forced to tack away when we fell down toward them and suffered from their backwind. We reaped an extra bonus from this tactic, since the left side of the course was usually favored due to the persistent backing of the sea breeze.

"The danger of starting to leeward of someone is that you might never be able to cross him. In a match race, you might get trapped going all the way to the layline if your boatspeed is equal. Against *Kookaburra* we had the confidence that we could get in front of them in time. This is a perfect example of why you have to know which is the short layline to the windward mark."

One is often advised to "sail the long tack first." Here's one reason why: If the course is skewed so that you have to sail much less time on starboard tack than on port, and you start to leeward of a starboard tacker, you might not be able to get far enough in front of the windward boat to cross him before getting to the port-tack layline. You'd end up trapped, having to sail the whole windward leg with a boat to windward that might not afford you room to tack.

When concentrating on beating one other boat, use all the weapons at your disposal. A cute trick you can use to leave a competitor behind involves positioning yourself near the starting line three or four boats to leeward of your prey. Then start luffing the boat above you. This will create a chain reaction in which all the boats in the pack to windward of you luff up and slow down. They'll also get packed closer together around your competitor, making it nearly impossible for him to get clear air after the gun goes off. You'll leave him, and the boats around him, behind as long as you have a hole to leeward

Figure 3.11 *Needing to beat the shadowed boat by more than one place, Boat A lines up several boats to the left of its prey. With a large hole to leeward, Boat A luffs the boat to windward which causes a chain reaction up the line. This way the shadowed boat is still luffing as Boat A is back up to speed.*

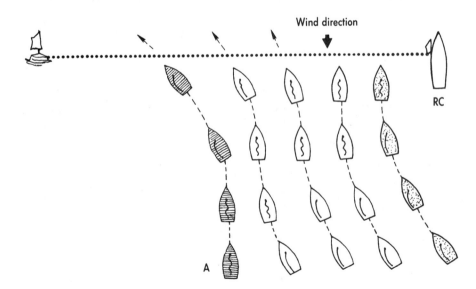

to fall off into. By creating a traffic jam that slows many boats, you'll be sure to slow the one boat you're after. (See figure 3.11.)

Consider the Penalties for an Improper Start

The last criterion for figuring out where to start on the starting line is what penalties are in effect for starting early. The two procedural rules that limit your starting options are the "one minute" and "black flag" rules. When in effect, the one-minute rule (Rule 51.1[c]) requires that when any part of a boat or its equipment or crew is on the course side of the starting line within a minute of the start, that boat must return to the pre-start side of the line by going around one of the ends of the line. Most race committees call for the one-minute rule to take effect after the first general recall. At other times, race committees will tame overanxious fleets by writing into the sailing instructions that the one-minute rule is in effect for all starts.

With the one-minute rule in effect, you'll want to start near an end of the line if you think there is a slightest chance you'll be pushed over the line within a minute of the start. In some cases, you might as well sail back to the dock if you are over the line early, for instance, if you're in the middle of a long starting line. Think about it. In a big fleet you won't be able to sail for an end until the fleet has passed by, and then you might have to sail a quarter of a mile to the nearest end of the line, if the line is half a mile long.

The black-flag rule is the deadliest weapon a race committee can use to tame a fleet plagued by numerous recalls. Under the black-flag rule, if you're over the line within a minute before the start, you are disqualified from the race. Once you are disqualified, you are out of the race for good, even if there are more recalls after you've been sent back to the dock. The rule is designed as a last resort to winnow out those who are drawing the fleet over the line early, or to intimidate the more aggressive starters in the fleet. The black-flag rule is not in the rule book, but it is a provision that race committees can write into the sailing instructions. Without the black-flag rule, skippers who go over early can avoid starting last by pulling enough boats over the line to provoke a recall. As soon as premature starters begin to block the view of the committee boat and the leeward pin, the rest of the fleet wanders over the line.

Be careful here, since Rule 51.1(d) makes it the responsibility of each skipper to start correctly. Therefore, if you know you are over, even if you know the race committee can't see you, you must go back and restart anyway. Even so, many sailors go through a lot of effort to avoid standing out on the starting line. When buying a boat, some make sure that their boat will be the same color as most of the boats in the fleet.

Starting Tactics

It took time, but at last you've finally figured out where you want to start. When the gun goes off, you hope to be at your planned position on the line at full speed, in control of the boats around you, with clear air to windward and leeward, heading for the favored side of the course when the gun goes off.

Sighting the Line

To ensure that you hit the line at full speed at the gun, you can follow one of three methods. You can sight the line with a third object on an extension of the line; you can put a crewman on the bow to visually check how far from the line you are; or you can use your compass. To sight the line, sail over to one end and sight through both ends to a stationary point of reference. This

Figure 3.12 *In position 1, luffing on an extension of the line, the skipper takes a line sight. Compensating for sitting aft in the boat, she creates a small fudge factor by sighting through the pin to an object just to windward of the one she sighted when she lined up both ends of the starting line.*

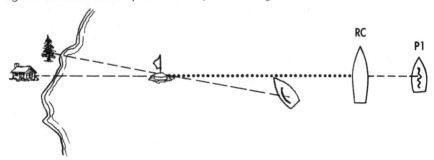

way, if you are in the middle of the line, you'll only have to sight through one end of the line to your point of reference to figure out whether or not you are on the line. Your point of reference could be on land, such as a house, a water tower, or a clump of trees, or it could be on the water, like an anchored boat, a buoy, or a rock pile. (See figure 3.12.)

When the skipper or the tactician sights the line, he has to take into account how many feet in front of his eye the bow of the boat is. On a small dinghy like a Snipe or an Optimist, the correction is negligible. But on an 80-foot maxi boat, your bow could be half a boatlength over the line, while the tactician, back in the cockpit, is 40 feet shy of the line. If you want to be a little conservative, build in a fudge factor by picking a point of reference slightly in front of the extension of the starting line.

Sighting the starting line is the best way for small-boat sailors to be right on the line when the starting gun goes off. On a big boat you can afford to have a crew member stand on the bow, judging how far from the line you are. Using a line site on a big boat is more difficult that it is on a dinghy, because there is more boat in front of you. Even if you have a crewman on the bow, checking how close your boat is to the line, the helmsman or the tactician should still make the major decision as to where you are on the line. The bowman should be used as a tool, but in the frenzy of trying to get a good start, it's hard to listen to your bowman.

To use your bowman efficiently, work out a system of hand signals for distance to the line, measured in half-boatlengths. Also have signals for "come

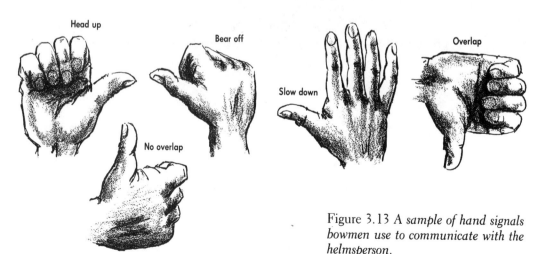

Figure 3.13 A *sample of hand signals bowmen use to communicate with the helmsperson.*

up," "fall off," "duck below," "slow down," "speed up," and "go for it." (See figure 3.13.) Make sure the rest of the crew members stay low, so that they don't get between the helmsman's eyes and the bowman's signals. Using hand signals is faster, more reliable, and tactically more sound than having the bowman shout back to the helmsman. Words get lost in the wind, time is lost repeating the call, and, worst of all, close competitors will know exactly what you are doing.

Small-boat sailors can use their compasses to determine whether they're over the starting line when there is no land or third object to line-sight on. To do this, sail down the line with the committee boat at your stern and the leeward pin on your bow. Note the compass heading. For this example, the pin bears 270 degrees. As you approach the line to start, make a quick turn and point your bow at the pin. You'll know you're past the line when the bearing to the mark is less than 270, and you're behind the line when your bearing to the pin is greater than 270. (See figure 3.14.) To fall off quickly, without losing much distance to leeward, luff your main and trim your jib before you bear off, and point for the pin.

A hand-bearing compass eliminates the need to swing the bow of the boat around to the mark when checking whether you're on the line or not. Memorize the course to the pin, and its reciprocal bearing. As you approach the line to start, sight the pin with your hand-bearing compass. Your boat is on the line when the pin is at the same bearing as when you were sailing down the line. If you can't see the pin because other boats are blocking it, sight the committee

Figure 3.14 *Without a hand-bearing compass or objects on the shore to get a sight on, dinghy sailors can use their boat's compass to figure out their relative position to the starting line.*

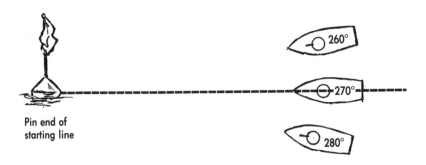

Pin end of
starting line

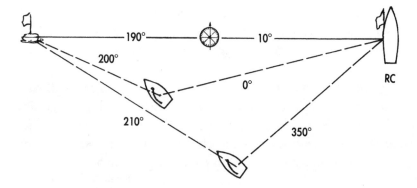

Figure 3.15 *Using a hand-bearing compass to know if you're on the line is simple. In this case Boat A knows that she is on the line when the bearing to the pin is 190 degrees. If the pin is not visible, sight the committee boat with the compass. Boat A is on the line when committee boat bears 10 degrees—the reciprocal of 190.*

boat. You're on the line when the committee boat bears the reciprocal of the course to the pin. (See figure 3.15.)

In the middle of a long starting line, you'll often find that boats misjudge how far they are from the line, and end up some distance behind it. The fleet tends to sag below the line because their crews haven't bothered to sight the line. Also, conservative skippers, unable see the ends of the line, usually hold back. The longer the starting line, the more common this mid-line sag will be. By getting a good sight on the line, you can gain a phenomenal two-boatlength lead over the sagging fleet. A two-boatlength lead puts you in clear air, gives you the opportunity to tack whenever you want, and allows you to bear off for speed whenever you need to, without having to worry about falling into another boat's backwind. In short, do everything short of selling your soul to get a two-boatlength lead.

Making and Protecting a Hole

Whatever approach you take to getting to the line, one of the first skills you have to master is creating and protecting a hole to leeward, so that when the gun goes off, no boat will be slowing you with backwind. Having a hole below also allows you to bear off slightly and accelerate to get away from the pack as you cross the line. To create space to leeward while on a crowded line, simply luff up the boat to windward of you (hailing "Head up!" repeatedly, as the rules require). As you do this, the boats to leeward will keep sailing down the line.

Boats will swarm like locusts toward the hole you've created, so you'll have to fight to protect it by heading back down before the gap is filled. Boats tacking below you on port will most likely be looking for clear space into which they can tack; the same is true of boats on the same tack that are overtaking you from behind. These fellow starboard tackers coming up behind you will create the most problems since, according to the rules, they will have rights over you as soon as they establish an overlap to leeward. Once a boat gets a leeward overlap, its skipper is free to luff you, and you will not be able to fall off unless he does. Act early when defending against starboard tackers coming from behind; if you need to slow down or change course significantly, it will take time for you to regain a good position. The best defense against having an overlap established from behind is to have enough speed so that you can prevent the overlap from being established or so that you can break an overlap once it exists. The more you fall off, the sooner the starboard tacker will establish an overlap. (See figure 3.16.) If you fall off before an approaching boat establishes an overlap, sail down the line, leaving a hole in the line where you were. With any luck, the approaching starboard tacker will head up into it. If the approaching boat takes your old spot on the line, you'll be to leeward of it and in the controlling position. (See figure 3.17.)

To discourage a port tacker from trying to tack into the hole to leeward of you, head right at the boat to force its skipper to tack early or, better yet, to sail past you in search of a different hole. (See figure 3.18.) You don't want

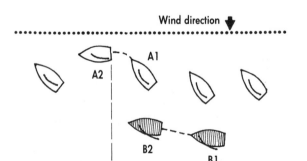

Figure 3.16 *When you bear off to prevent a boat from sailing into the space you created on the starting line, remember that your transom swings around enabling the trailing boat to establish an overlap sooner.*

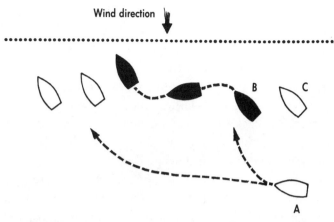

Figure 3.17 *To protect its space to leeward, Boat B falls off as much as it can without hitting Boat C. Boat A is left with two choices: Sail into the space to windward of A, or fall off and look for another hole in the line.*

to abandon your hole, of course, and you'll want to keep clear of the backwind of the next boat to leeward of you.

Beware of port tackers that come in and tack on your lee bow. When they are stealing the space you created, it is in their interest to tack as close to you as possible, since they gain their own bit of room to leeward. To make a port tacker tack earlier than it wants to, bear off and head directly at it. Since there is no such thing as a proper course before the start, you are free to change your course. Only when the port tacker starts to tack does the Rule 35 require you to hold a proper course.

If the port tacker does tack closely, don't let it start luffing you until it has completed its tack. The port tacker has not completed its tack until its bow

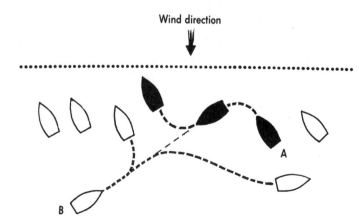

Figure 3.18 *To defend its space, A bears off and aims right at B. This forces B to tack early, which will maximize the separation between the two boats. Some times this technique persuades the port tacker to give up and keep sailing up the line.*

has gone through the eye of the wind and then fallen off to a closehauled course on starboard. Beware of boats that start luffing before they've fallen off to a closehauled course.

In a dinghy, keep your boat heeled before the start. Heeling the boat will help you protect your hole to leeward, since your mast will occupy space to leeward, which will keep approaching boats farther from you. Boats approaching from port will be forced to tack early because their mast will hit yours before the two hulls collide. Keep an eye on your mast tip once the other boat tacks, though; as a windward boat, you must keep all of your boat clear of a leeward boat. If you see a boat approaching from behind you, fend him off not only by heeling your boat to leeward, but by easing your boom out so that you occupy even more space to leeward of your hull. Thus, if a boat that approaches from behind establishes an overlap and luffs you up, you can pull in your main and flatten the boat out to get away from him before you have to resort to heading up.

Another advantage of keeping your boat heeled to leeward before the start is that it helps the sails take shape. You'll then want to get the boat back on its lines to get up to speed. When the boat is too flat, it's hard to accelerate, and if you're heeled too far, you'll go too slowly. The 1989–92 IYRU rules make a common starting practice of prior years illegal. You can no longer heel the boat to leeward and then flatten the boat out and trim your sails in to get a burst of speed.

Speed Control at the Start

To keep your tactical options open around the starting line, you must learn how to be in control of your boatspeed at all times. In many instances, the more speed you have, the more aggressive you can be. You can sail through the lee of slower boats, reposition your boat in response to wind shifts, or bail out of your position on the line and get another spot if a boat unexpectedly takes your wind. Furthermore, when the presence of other boats prevents you from heading to port or starboard, frequently the only defense you have against attack is to increase or decrease your speed.

The greater your ability to slow down, the more flexibility you have to modify your start to suit rapidly changing conditions. The most common way to slow down is to let your sails out. Luff the jib first, and then the main if necessary. If you luff the main and not the jib, your boat will be forced to leeward. Other ways to slow down are to make sharp turns quickly by jamming the rudder from one side to the other. Your boat will slow down by skidding through the water. It's best to warn your crew before you do it. If you've got the manpower, you can slow the boat by pushing the boom out to leeward. Try to avoid slowing your boat by heading into the wind, because if you slow down too much you will have a hard time speeding up again. You may even get into irons.

To accelerate as fast as possible, ease your sails slightly and fall off to a close reach. Sculpt your sails for speed by easing the outhaul, cunningham, backstay, and halyards to get fuller and more powerful sails. After you're up to speed, you can shift gears to the pointing mode by tightening up everything you eased.

Those who luff on the line a minute before the start are the most vulnerable to boats that prowl around at full speed under the line, looking for a big hole that someone has carved out. If you're the boat that's carved out a hole, your best defense against fast-moving scavengers is to keep your speed up so that you can react and scare them away. If a boat tacks to leeward of you, cash in some of your speed by pinching to windward to get away from him. You'll be able to pull away from him, since he'll lose a lot of speed while tacking.

In big dinghy fleets, a multitude of boats will be dead in the water during the final seconds, luffing on the line. A dramatic start you can pull off involves bursting through a hole barely wide enough for your boat. By making a well-timed run at full speed, you'll be able to break through the wall of disturbed wind from all those sails luffing on the line—with enough speed left over to break away from the stalled fleet. We'll call this "the Sherman start," after the Civil War general who scorched a wide swath through the Confederacy. Leaving the fleet wallowing while you pop through into a commanding lead will have the same psychological effect on the other skippers as Sherman's "March to the Sea" had on the people of the South—they'll be devastated.

Divide the Starting Line into Thirds

Think of the starting line in terms of thirds of its length, not only of its ends. If the boat end is favored, chances are the right side of the line will be crowded. You can avoid the bulk of the mess by starting a third of the way down the line from the committee boat. If the pin is favored, avoid the crowd attempting to get the pin-end start by lining up to windward of the pack of boats at the pin. By starting a third of the way up the line from the pin, you'll get most of the advantages of starting next to the pin without risking a foul or getting stuck in bad air.

Starting at the starboard end of the line is a safe bet, since you can tack away if you get in trouble. On starboard tack at the right end of the line, you'll have a commanding view of the fleet as it sets up for the start. If you change your mind and decide to start elsewhere, you can easily reach down the line to a better location. If the right side of the course is favored, you are free to tack onto port and hustle over there. The disadvantage is the crowds it attracts.

Middle-of-the-line starts have their advantages also. Usually the middle of the line is less crowded, which gives you a better chance to start in clear air. Also, if there is a bit of mid-line sag, you'll be able to get a head start on the boats around you. The disadvantages of a mid-line start are: (1) the exact location of the line is hard to determine; (2) you'll have a hard time hearing the race committee announce premature starters; and (3) the wind tends to be lighter and the surface of the water more chopped up in the middle of the line in a big fleet. Finally, if you do go over the line early, the race instructions may require you to reach all the way to one of the ends and jibe around in order to restart from below the line.

Starting at the pin or port end is very difficult, but offers high rewards when done well. You can either drive off to leeward, or pinch to start a chain reaction of heading-up that diminishes the speed of boats to windward. If the left side of the course is favored, you'll get there first. Disadvantages are that (1) if you are early, you will have to jibe out of the front row and try to start on port tack; and (2) after the start, you run the risk of being pinned on starboard tack for a long time. If you don't get a perfect start, a boat to leeward may lee-bow you and so force you into a second row start. A poor start at the leeward end will surely lead to disaster.

Even if you are sailing a slow boat, you can make consistently good starts if you master one of several starting techniques. Let's go through some starts to windward for big and small boats, and then go through some offwind starts for big boats.

Starboard Approach

Approaching the starting line on starboard tack from the windward side of the line is the safest and most common start in sailboat racing. The starboard approach gives you a lot of options—even in a crowded fleet. Most sailors approach the line on a reach from the area to the right of the committee boat, which can be barging.

If a boat establishes an overlap and tries to push you up to the line early, build speed and break the overlap so that he loses his luffing rights. The problem with this approach is that you could end up too far down the line if you have to keep accelerating to get away from boats to leeward of you. To avoid this problem, approach the line on a close reach instead of a beam reach. This way you'll be to leeward of the fleet and will not have to worry about a lot of boats establishing overlaps. You'll be the one forcing boats to squirm across your bow or to head up and risk being pushed over the line early.

Don't let everyone reach across your bow unless you know they're going to be early. When deciding whether to let a boat pass to windward of you, consider how much time is left until the start, and how close you are to the line. If there is little time left (under a minute) and a boat crosses you, you may find yourself in his backwind if he chooses to head up to the line.

If you're positive that you're less than a boatlength away from the line, and there's more than a minute left, go ahead and let a boat reaching down the line cross in front of you. As long as you are close to the line, you won't hear from him again at the start. If he does try to jump into the hole you've created to leeward, he'll have to make a sharp turn to leeward and then a sharp turn

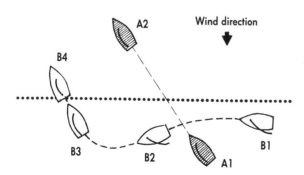

Figure 3.19 *Being close to the line before the start, Boat A can safely let Boat B reach by. To start, Boat B must fall off before she can head up to the line to avoid starting prematurely. The two sharp turns will slow B greatly.*

▼

to windward in order to avoid being over early. The two sharp turns will practically stop him, allowing you to sail by. (See figure 3.19.)

If the hole to leeward of you is a boatlength wide or less, you can let a boat go over you, since he will not have enough maneuvering room to get into your hole. As discussed earlier, if the hole is wider, you're inviting boats to drive in.

When you don't want a boat going over you, squeeze up underneath him, keeping your mast in front of his bow. Overtrimming the main not only helps you point, but it blasts a boat to windward with backwind. (See figure 3.20.) In a dinghy, you can suffocate a boat to windward by heeling your boat to windward. When pinching off a boat above you by heeling your boat to windward, or by overtrimming your main, make sure you are going at least two-thirds speed, since both moves will slow you significantly. You can't overtrim your main and heel your boat to windward long, because it will start slipping to leeward as the centerboard or keel stalls out. When you slow another boat, remember that you also slow your own boat. So if you slow someone, do it prior to the last 20 seconds so that you'll have time to accelerate back up to full speed.

If you are close to the line and can't keep your bow in front of his, luff him over the line early. Even if he doesn't start prematurely, you'll have clear air once you both fall back to a close-hauled course. (Figure 3.21 shows how, when two boats pivot, the windward boat falls back into the disturbed air to windward of the leeward boat.)

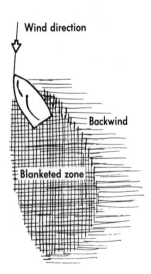

Wind direction

Backwind

Blanketed zone

Figure 3.20 *Sailboats cast part of their wind shadow to windward; therefore, to slow a foe to windward, increase the area of backwind by over-trimming your main to hook the battens to windward. If you are sailing a dinghy, heel your boat to windward also.*

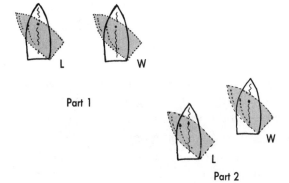

Part 1

Part 2

Figure 3.21 *In Part 1, boats L and W luff head-to-wind and bow-to-bow. When the boats fall off to a close-hauled course the windward boat is sailing in disturbed wind of the leeward boat. In Part 2, W is ahead of L when the boats luff head-to-wind. Even so, when the boats fall off to closehauled, L still has clear air.*

Another advantage of coming in on a close reach is that you'll have a good view of how the fleet is setting up on the line. If the exact position you chose has no space for you, you'll be able to change your mind and reach off below the crowd to another spot in that third of the line.

Avoid stacks of boats on the starting line. Such stacks are formed when a boat sits luffing on the line, usually in a favored position, and a second boat sails to leeward of it and luffs. The process is repeated until a stack of ten or more boats is formed on the line. In the pile-up you lose your ability to maneuver, to say nothing of the disturbed air you'll be in the midst of. So even if you're not at the favored end, few in the bunch at the better end will be able to profit from it.

On crowded starting lines, where masses of boats are stacked up on the line gunwale-to-gunwale a few rows deep, you'll have no choice but to join the fray. Here are a few suggestions:

1. When luffing on the line, never let your boat go slower than your competition. Gary: "On *Courageous*, we never let the boat slow down below 4.5 knots. Anytime we found ourselves slower than that, we accelerated so that we could still maneuver easily." Tom: "A 12-meter moving below 4.5 knots is painfully slow to accelerate because the boat's sail-area-to-hull-dis-placement ratio is quite low. The boats don't have a lot of power for their weight. The only thing that makes the 12-meter a fairly high-performance boat is its narrow, efficient hull shape. Therefore, the danger when luffing on the line, particularly in a heavier boat, lies in slowing down relative to the boats around you; they'll be able to roll right over you into a controlling position. Another danger to watch out for when sailing a big, heavy boat is that if you

slow down so much that you almost have no maneuverability, than you are vulnerable to fouling out. Save space to leeward that you can fall off into, then accelerate to full speed when the gun goes off."

2. Keep your boat on the course that you will be sailing after the start so that you will not have to bear off to accelerate. In a dinghy, it helps to keep your boat heeled slightly to leeward. As you trim your sails and flatten out the boat, you create wind in your sails, which gives you quick acceleration. If a boat is heeling to windward, it sideslips, and you have to bear off and heel the boat to leeward before you can begin making headway. If you get luffed by another boat and you end up going so slowly that your rudder is giving minimal control, backwind your jib to enable you to fall off. Avoid trimming the jib until you get some way on, or else the helmsman will have to jam the rudder over leeward to keep the boat from falling off excessively under the influence of the tightly sheeted jib. With the rudder hard over (in an attempt to head up) and the jib too tight, the boat won't go anywhere but sideways, fast.

3. Always fight to be in the first row of boats, so that you will encounter the least disturbed wind. To work your way up through the crowd, try "crabbing" to windward. Crabbing is a technique in which at half-speed, you continually luff into the wind and then fall back to a close-hauled course to take bites to windward. Work your way into a hole that a boat has created, and then luff him up to create a hole to leeward for yourself.

4. When a fleet of aggressive boats is jammed three rows deep onto a starting line, competitors will sit on the line luffing as early as two or three minutes before the starting gun. The result is many general recalls. In this case, one of three things usually happens: (1) the committee lengthens the starting line to reduce the number of boats pushing those in the front row over early, (2) the committee institutes the black-flag rule, which disqualifies any boat over the line within a minute before the start, or (3) out of frustration the committee lets the fleet start, and only penalizes the boats farthest over the line with a PMS (premature start).

5. Hiding behind other boats on a crowded starting line is a good hedge against being called over early. But don't depend on this tactic, because if the

boat you are hiding behind is not on the line, you are guaranteeing yourself
a bad start.

Dealing tactically with large, aggressive fleets is a difficult problem, but not
an impossible one. The second-best spots on the line are found either just to
windward or just to leeward of a stack of boats at the favored end of the line.
Only a few will come out of the stack at the favored end with great starts,
while the rest in the pack will be trapped in each other's bad air. The best
way to avoid getting caught in a stack without room to maneuver is to approach
the group on port tack. This way, holes in the line are easy to find. This brings
us to our next starting technique, the port approach.

Port Approach

To avoid getting trapped in a lockstep with the masses on starboard tack
migrating down the line, you can start "against the grain" by approaching the
starting line on port tack. On port, you are free to sail under the fleet and
then tack into a hole in the favored third of the line. In this method, you're
adopting the role of those port-tacking aggressors against whom we warned you
earlier. Make your approach at least two boatlengths below the fleet, so that
when you find your hole, you can head up and sail to the line on a close
reach before tacking to starboard. On a reach you'll build up a lot of speed,
and if you make a sweeping turn when tacking from port to starboard instead
of a sharp turn, you'll have a good head of steam coming out of the tack. That
speed will be needed so that you can immediately start luffing the starboard

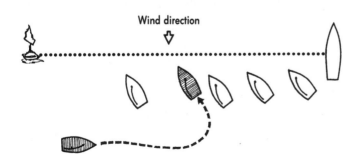

Figure 3.22 *When tacking
into an open space during a
port approach, keep as close
as possible to the windward
boat to maximize your hole
to leeward.*

tacker to windward. Remember that you must fall off onto a close-hauled course, which completes your tack to starboard, before luffing another boat.

When you make your tack for the line, it is important that you end up close to the boat to windward and at least two or three boatlengths to windward of a boat to leeward. (See figure 3.22.) If the line is crowded and you have to settle for a marginal hole, you can work to enlarge the space to leeward of you by luffing the boat to windward.

The placement of your boat after the tack is crucial. Position yourself ahead and to leeward of the boat you are keying on. If you fall behind, you'll be blanketed. If you tack too far ahead, he can drive under you and luff you over the line.

Look for a hole where the boats have been luffing for a while. Without speed, those boats will be unable to maneuver to protect themselves. Just as lions attack the sick and elderly zebras, so you can tack under a boat that you know is slower than yours, or under a "marshmallow"—a nonaggressive sailor. Proximity to these sorts of players will diminish the odds of having a windward boat ride over you. On the other hand, tacking under a hotshot will usually result in his gaining a position to windward, blanketing your sails, and causing you to lose speed and gain leeway.

If you use a port approach to get the pin-end start, note how much time remains as you pass below the left end of the line on port tack. If half the time to the start goes by before you tack, you know that you will be able to tack, trim in, and hit the pin at full speed. However, if you see seven or eight boats on starboard that are going to stack up by the pin, sail beneath them on port, and don't tack to starboard until you are up the line from the mess.

The port approach is least effective when the starboard end is favored. As everyone tries to start at the favored end, the fleet will be stacked several rows deep, leaving you no chance to find a hole in the first row. But even if there wasn't a convention of beer drinkers at the committee-boat end, on a starboard-favored line, every boat to leeward of another is already behind and about to get blanketed.(See figure 3.23.)

But if the fleet stacks up at the windward end of the line, and the line is square, approach the mass on port and then tack to leeward of the tangled throng.

Every now and then you'll get the opportunity to port-tack the fleet at the start. When you do it, you get a tremendous psychological lift—and you'll demoralize your competitors. One of these maneuvers that stands out in Gary's

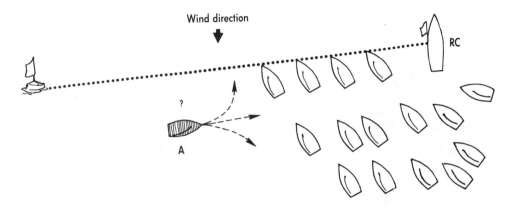

Figure 3.23 *The port approach is not a good starting technique when the starboard side of the starting line is favored. Boat A's best option is to tack to leeward of the fleet. Boat A should tack to starboard early and gain speed well before the start to gain clear wind.*

mind happened during the first race of the 1984 SORC. "I was skippering *Jubilation* [a 54-foot German Frers design] in her first regatta ever when we port-tacked our class at the start of the St. Petersburg–Fort Lauderdale Race. It gave all of us a real lift except Jack James, the owner, who didn't like the idea of putting his new baby in the sights of the 23 other guns in our class."

Timed Run

Properly executed, a timed run (also known as the Vanderbilt start) brings you to the starting line with speed as the race begins. It works well because a sailboat goes the same speed close-hauled as it does on a broad reach. Therefore, if you find the point on the line you'd like to start from, and broad-reach for one minute away from it, it will take you one minute to return to that spot (not counting the time it takes to tack or jibe around). As a rule, set up your timed run so that you are maneuvering when no one else is. Instead of the standard two- or four-minute timed run, which most sailors use because it is easy to calculate, try a run of a minute and 35 seconds, or two minutes and 15 seconds. (See figure 3.24.) If you still encounter congestion, such as a stack of boats, don't take any unnecessary risks by starting in their vicinity. You

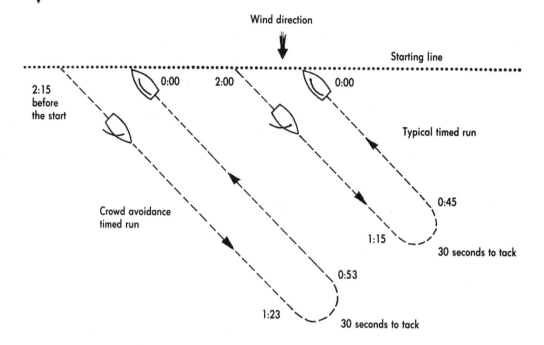

Figure 3.24 *When many boats make timed runs to the line, groups of boats end up tacking and jibing close together since a typical timed run is based on leaving the line with exactly one or two minutes before the start. To avoid mixing it up with a crowd, don't sail away from the line with whole minutes to go.*

might decide to start a bit farther down the line of the stack, where you will be assured of clear air.

To figure out the timing for a Vanderbilt start, you have to know how long it is going to take your boat to tack or jibe in the conditions you are sailing in. When changing tacks to turn back to the line for your approach, remember that a tack takes longer than a jibe, but, unlike a jibe, a tack usually gains you distance to windward. A jibe is quicker, but is riskier in heavy air, and moves you to leeward. Choose the maneuver that helps you fine-tune your position for the approach.

As you sail away from your chosen spot on the starting line, note how much time is remaining before the gun. Add the number of seconds it will take you to tack, and then divide that sum by two. Begin your turn at this time. Don't forget to convert minutes to seconds when making your calculations. Also, if the starting area is crowded, add some time for some evasive action.

When making your final close-hauled approach on a timed run, be aware of boats reaching down over you. Warn any boat sailing down toward you early to keep clear. After all, they are windward boats and must keep clear. Make sure the skipper of a windward boat knows that you are not luffing him. The definition of *luffing* is "altering course to the wind." If you do luff the windward boat, Rule 40 requires leeward boats to luff slowly so that the windward boat has an opportunity to keep clear. Hence, the sooner you start hailing the windward boat, the less chance he'll have of saying you luffed him without due warning.

Under the rules, there is no proper course before the start, so you may maneuver at will. "Of all my starts, the timed run is my most reliable," says Gary. "It gives me an accurate judge of how far I am from the line. And by using a timed run, I've got a reference as to how long it will take me to get up to full speed. I credit my old coach, Graham Hall, with teaching me this."

Our experience shows that the timed run helps the most on bigger boats, because they are harder to maneuver to kill time. Since you can speed up and slow down a dinghy so easily, there is not as much need to depend on a timed run. On keelboats, ranging from Shields and Solings up to maxi boats, the timed run works well because it takes a long time for these boats to build up speed, so the momentum you generate during a properly executed timed run is a great advantage.

The best timed start Tom remembers was in the fourth race of the 1983 America's Cup. "That start was a beautifully timed start that allowed *Liberty* to cross *Australia II*'s bow while on port tack. It was a case of pure timing. They missed on their timing, and we made ours. It's inexcusable when anybody crosses your bow on port tack at the start of a match race. There is nobody in the world who times a start better than Dennis Conner; he's got a sixth sense for it."

The perfectly timed run that stands out in Gary's memory was the Class A start of the 1984 Bermuda race. "I was skippering *Jubilation*. At 54 feet long, she was the smallest boat in Class A, but that didn't stop us from nailing the start. The windward end of the starting line was favored by a good 15 degrees, and the 19 boats in our class were spread out along the line instead of bunched at the favored end. I simply did a three-minute timed run at the windward end, and our timing was perfect. We sailed away from the committee boat on a broad reach for one minute and 15 seconds; I used 30 seconds to tack, and then I had one minute and 15 seconds to get up to full speed. We were at the favored end of the line at the gun, going full speed. Everyone else was sitting and luffing before the start, while we jutted ahead of the fleet. It took 20 minutes for *Boomerang*, an 80-foot maxi, to catch up."

Keep your boat moving, reaching as much as possible, so that you have more speed than the boats around you, and you will be able to pop into clear air when you hit the line. If you have the option of passing to leeward or to windward of a given boat, don't pass to leeward unless you are absolutely certain of breaking through. If, for example, the boat ahead is moving at two-thirds speed with its sails full, it is better to pass to windward. If the boat ahead is practically dead in the water, with both sails luffing, then passing to leeward can work.

Triangle Starts

There are three triangular methods of starting that we find effective. In the first, which works well in a dinghy or a keel boat that turns and accelerates quickly, pick a point on the starting line to starboard of where you want to be when the gun goes off. Sail directly downwind, harden up to a starboard beat, and approach the line at full speed. This start tends to clear out a space on the starting line. Peter Commette used this start successfully in qualifying for the 1976 Olympics in Finns. When starting with this method, remember that for every boatlength you sail dead-downwind off the line, you will end up that many boatlengths to port of the point where you left the line. (Remember the

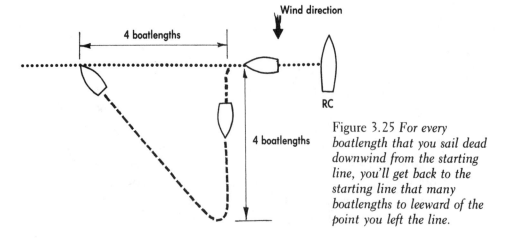

Figure 3.25 *For every boatlength that you sail dead downwind from the starting line, you'll get back to the starting line that many boatlengths to leeward of the point you left the line.*

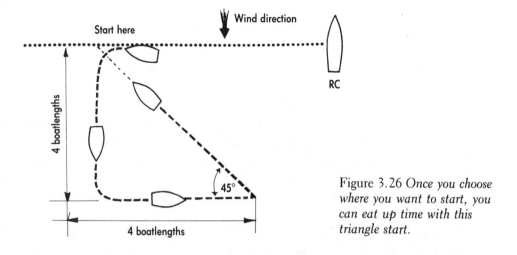

Figure 3.26 *Once you choose where you want to start, you can eat up time with this triangle start.*

properties of the 45-45-90 triangle from high school geometry? See figure 3.25.)

The second triangular approach simply involves starting on the line, sailing downwind, jibing onto port, and sailing abeam of the line before tacking over to starboard to make your final approach. (See figure 3.26.) This technique is a modified port approach that helps you start at a particular point on the line while clearing a zone for you to sail into when you make your final approach. In using both of these techniques, your aim is to be close-hauled and at full speed when the race begins.

Gary used this start while sailing aboard *Matador* at the 1988 Kenwood Cup in Hawaii. "I would start the triangle maneuver on the line at the point where I wanted to be when the gun went off. Next we sailed the 80-foot maxi straight downwind for one minute, jibed to port, and sailed on a broad reach for another minute, and then tacked and sailed close-hauled back to the starting point. I used this maneuver with the windward end of the line as the point to which I planned to return. It helped me to figure out where the layline was."

To sum up, the triangle start does not take you too far from the line, it helps you stay away from the boats that reach back and forth behind the line, and it lets you stay somewhat out of sight of those setting up on the line. When you swoop in toward a hole, you may catch your competitors unawares.

Match-Racing Moves

When you are concerned about only one other boat, such as when you are match-racing or when it's late in a regatta or a series and you have to beat another boat, you want to do anything legal you can to make your opponent's start worse than yours. Ideally, you'll start right on his wind, but since that is hard to do, you can fall back on other options. The two most severe options are to chase the other boat away from the line so that he can't return until after you have, and the second—the more effective, when done right—is to pin the other boat across the line so that he has to circle around to cross the line after you've started.

This was the case in a match in which Tom steered the 80-foot maxi *Kialoa* against Peter Gilmour, who helmed the Australian maxi *Sovereign*. The two had a bit of a score to settle, since Gilmour was the aggressive starting helmsman on *Kookaburra III* during the 1987 America's Cup. "It was sweet, pushing Peter over the line early during the maxi boat match-racing series after the 1988 Big Boat Series. He had us on the hook early in the starting maneuvers, but at about six minutes to go, the tide changed. Then we got on his tail and continually forced him up to the line. We kept him from sailing away from the line by luffing him when he tried to bear off, and we tacked below him and luffed him again when he tacked. With a two-knot current pushing us toward the line and only a light ten-knot breeze to maneuver in, we managed to get Peter pinned between us and the committee boat. Both of us were just a little bit early, and since he was pinned between us and the committee, he had to continue past the committee boat entirely before he could turn around and come back. Because the current was so strong and he didn't have a spinnaker up, it took him a full minute to get back to the start." By winning the start, *Kialoa* won the race, since the strong tide flowing toward the windward mark made getting to the leeward side of the line painfully slow for *Sovereign*.

As you will recall, mast abeam does not apply until after the starting gun; therefore, a leeward boat can luff a windward boat all the way to close-hauled with the smallest of overlaps.

The way to force another skipper away from the line is to get behind him to prevent your opponent from tacking or jibing.

When he falls off and tries to jibe, go down inside of him. When he heads up and tries to tack, go up with him. To do this, you must stay close enough

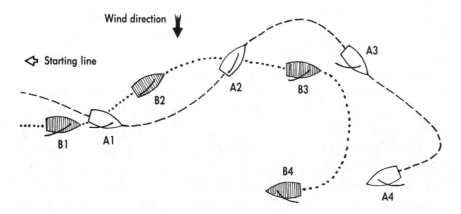

Figure 3.27 *Being behind, Boat B is in the controlling position. In position 1, A cannot fall off without fouling B. In position 2, A attempts to head up to tack, but B cuts inside to prevent it. In position 3, B sails back to the line after the starting gun has sounded or when B can sail back for the line at full speed and not be early.*

that he could easily foul you by tacking or jibing too close. If you are too far away, he will be able to start his tack or jibe, and then the rules prevent you from making any maneuver that prevents him from keeping clear. (See figure 3.27.) There is a fine line between fouling and blocking.

If the other boat in a match-racing situation does get back to the line, you still have options. Get under him and force him over the line so that he has to restart while you're sailing the first leg of the race—a technique that works in fleet racing as well. Unless the one-minute or black-flag rule is in effect, the rules allow both of you to go over the line if you are back behind the line before the starting gun goes off. Your goal here is to have a good sight on the line, so that you can get back before the gun while he is still above the line.

The best-known feature of a match-racing start is the sight of two boats chasing each other in circles. In circling, each skipper tries to get his boat behind the other boat so that he'll be in the controlling position. But many top skippers shy away from circling because it is hard on equipment and it risks a foul too easily.

At the finals of the 1987 America's Cup in Australia, there was much speculation that the aggressive crew on *Kookaburra III* would get the best of *Stars & Stripes '87* at the start. But, as in the 1983 Cup finals, when Dennis Conner faced a more maneuverable boat, he was able to neutralize the turning advantage by controlling the start without getting into a circling battle. How did he do it? "That's an easy question to answer," says Tom. "We just did a timed run and made sure that when we tacked or jibed to the start, we were on starboard tack. There is virtually nothing the other guy can do. Since this technique is defensive in nature, the starts were always close. In exchange for not hammering the other guy, you are assured of an even start. It pays to be defensive if you know you are fast and don't want to take any chances of fouling out. In Australia, we knew *Stars & Stripes* didn't circle as well as *Kookaburra*, and we were afraid of fouling out."

"The big mistake that *Kookaburra* made was that they always went to the windward position at the start," says Gary. "What they needed to do was get to leeward of *Stars & Stripes* so that they could luff and slow *Stars & Stripes* down. Instead, they let Dennis control the timing."

"Let me tell you," Tom adds, "that start is no fun to defend against. What do you do? If we were a little early, they should have gone behind us and pushed toward the line to make us even earlier. And if we were late, they should have tacked ahead and below us to gas us. But since our timing was so good, they had a hard time deciding where they wanted to be when they approached us. It's not that easy. The Kookas weren't too bad until the last race [of the 1987 America's Cup]—in that last race I think they could have done better."

Our final match-racing move for starting is a slick trick you can use while racing lightweight boats. One of the first rules you learn while boating is that an overtaking boat must keep clear. Well, here's a new twist on that old rule. Who must keep clear of whom when one boat is stopped and the other boat is sailing backwards? The answer is contained in Rule 37.2, which states that a boat clear astern must keep clear of a boat clear ahead. Therefore, you can gain the controlling position over a boat that has been controlling you by backing down on him. If you hit his bow with your transom, he is a boat clear astern that failed to keep clear. If you hit his leeward forward quarter with your stern, he is not only a boat clear astern that did not keep clear, but he is also a windward boat that failed to keep clear. You are most likely to succeed in this maneuver if you keep your bow pointing on the same compass course. It's the bearing straight off the bow that counts, not the actual course you're making rearward.

Downwind Starts

Unlike dinghy races, in which the first leg is a beat from a starting line that's square to the wind, big-boat starts run the gamut from upwind to dead down-wind, because instead of setting buoys for a 25-mile race, race committees typically send fleets around government marks.

The need for good timing is paramount in downwind starts. During an upwind approach to a starting line it's easy to slow down, though getting back up to speed can be difficult. However, when approaching the line on a down-wind course, a quick stall is nearly impossible. Because of this, it is important to take current into account, especially if it's strong and moving with the wind; otherwise you may get caught over the line at the gun. Beating back against the tide to clear yourself while others swoop down the course is not fun, especially if you have to take your chute down first. If you are starting on a run or a broad reach, make several timed runs (close-hauled away from the line, broad-reaching toward it). On your final run, concentrate on keeping speed up so that you can maneuver to keep your air clear. Don't set the spinnaker until you are certain you will not be over early, but then again, don't dawdle in getting it flying when the moment arrives. A boatlength gained here can often mean the difference between clear air and getting smothered just after the race begins.

Finding clear air is often the most important task during a downwind start. One proven method is to take a good range sight on the line prior to your start. Then, if there is too much traffic at the favored end, start toward the middle of the line. With a good range sight, you can have the confidence to be right on the line at the gun. You won't have to give up distance to those starting at the ends, and you will probably find yourself with a good jump on those around you who are hanging back with no way of judging the line.

On reaching starts, most committees set the starting line perpendicular to the course to the first mark. If they do, you have no choice but to start at the windward end of the line. The windward-end boats get the puffs first, and have clear air. The leeward-end boats have a slightly better (higher) reaching angle, but they are in danger of being blanketed and overrun by the boats to windward.

A great way to get the windward start with clear air and leave the fleet in shambles is to fool the fleet by running downwind toward the leeward pin.

▼

About three or four boatlengths from the line, head up and sail toward the committee boat at the windward end. As leeward boat, you'll be able to force everyone to head up where they will tangle with each other. If you timed your approach correctly, you should be at the committee boat when the gun goes off. At the gun, you fall off and head to the mark gunwale-to-gunwale with the committee boat, so that there is no room for anyone to get above you.

If you are late and don't reach the committee boat before the start, Rule 42.4 (the anti-barging rule) does not allow you to deprive a windward boat room at the starting mark after the gun goes off by sailing above the course to the next mark. You still have your rights as a leeward boat to luff at will under Rule 38.1, but you can't exercise those rights until your luff won't make the other boat collide with the windward end of the starting line.

The windward end is not always the place to start during a reaching start. Race committees can bias the leeward end by setting it closer to the next mark. A fair line has a bias of about 15 degrees toward the leeward end. Favoring the pin end helps to prevent the boats to windward from smothering the boats to leeward. With the leeward end closer to the windward mark, the competitors have to calculate the risk-to-reward ratio of where to start.

Reaching starts are tough for smaller or slower boats. Slower boats are forced to start at the windward end in order to keep from getting blanketed by the bigger and faster boats. If the bigger boats choose the windward end also, you'll be better off delaying your start to follow them across the starting line. The advantage of following them is that you will be able to catch a tow—without a grappling hook—by riding the stern waves of the bigger boats. You can only catch a tow when the wind is strong enough to push the bigger boat to its hull speed. (For more information on catching a tow, or drafting, turn to page 199.)

Starting Speed Tips

To get off the line quickly and get away from the fleet, never pinch right after the start—sail for full speed. Out in front, you will be able to play the shifts and bear off for speed to go through waves without other boats hampering your strategic decisions. If you pinch, others will leave you behind, wallowing in their bad air. Therefore, if you worked hard to create a hole to leeward of you on the starting line, the time to cash in on it is just before the start. Only through practice will you know how long and how much distance it takes to get up to speed. For instance, if you were sailing a standard 35-to-40-foot boat in 12 knots of wind with moderate chop, it will take you about 15 seconds to accelerate from 3.5 knots to 6.2 knots. Incorporate this test in your pre-start data collection. If you are early, slow down soon enough that you'll have room to get back up to full speed by the start.

Communication before the start is critical to attaining the ideal pre-start speed. Within the last five minutes before the start, the only crew members talking should be the tactician and skipper. The bowman should be communicating with hand signals. This doesn't mean the tactician and skipper only mutter between themselves; they should talk loudly enough about what they are planning that the crew can listen in and anticipate their responsibilities.

Only one person should make decisions at the start. As tactician, talk to your skipper before the race and determine who will call all the shots. Generally, you should set up one-quarter of a boatlength ahead of the boats on either side, so that you have clear air. The person in charge needs to call sail trim to maintain the position he wants. To minimize pre-start confusion, the person who's calling the pre-start maneuvers should tell the trimmers always to trim for speed unless told otherwise. That way they won't second-guess him and slow the boat down when he is timing an approach to the line.

The tactician is in charge of putting the boat on the line at the gun with full speed on, regardless of the fleet's position. Before the start, he memorizes the line range or hand-held compass bearing. During the approach, he yells out the time and the number of boatlengths to the line, i.e., "Forty seconds, eight lengths to go!" If the boat has been luffing slowly to the line, he will give the "Trim and go!" command as well. If he has to wait to less than 15 seconds before the gun to give the "go" command, the boat absolutely will not be up to speed for the start.

Warn your crew before making a radical turn, so that sails can be trimmed accordingly. If you find that your start is working out according to plan, and you know that you're going to be early or get luffed to the wrong side of the committee boat, the time to bail out is right away. Turn your boat quickly, before you're trapped by the other boats packing closer and closer together as the clock ticks down. The faster you exit a bad situation, the better your chance of finding a new hole in the line.

To avoid collisions, look constantly to leeward, or, on big boats, have the bowman stand in the bow pulpit and call the position of nearby boats as well as the distance from the line. Don't sail around wishing everyone good luck; nice guys like that finish last. The time to be aggressive at the start is when the warning signal goes off. If you see a difficult situation developing with another boat, hail your intentions early, so that there is no misunderstanding. If you find yourself being tailed, shake off the other boat early, so that you don't end up in trouble. It is imperative to protect your lee bow on the starting line; don't allow boats to tack to leeward of you. Keep your options open during the starting sequence, and don't commit yourself to one side of the line or the other until you are absolutely sure which is better. If you think that one end is favored and all the other boats are at the wrong end, be a little sneaky and wait until the last minute to sail down to the favored end, so that no other boats follow you there. If you know that you can get away with a port-tack start, do not cross the line six or seven times on port; that only gives away your secret. Wait until the gun goes off to reveal it.

By understanding these starting techniques, you will know in a short time which boats are making good approaches to the line and which ones will have trouble. It is always a good idea to start near boats you think are slow, so that you'll pop into a valuable lead. By using one of these starting techniques and keeping these pointers in mind, in a short time you will be able to start consistently with clear air and speed, which will dramatically improve your racing performance.

Keeping an Open Mind

The greatest sailors, such as Buddy Melges, are good at being able to forsake their carefully laid plans at the last minute, should a sudden change in conditions require a new strategy for starting well. It's not unusual for Melges to change his game plan completely, seconds before the start, based on what's happening with the wind. Many sailors are so preoccupied by the desire to get a certain position on the starting line that they forget to look up the course to find out what's going to happen next.

Gary: "I'll never forget sailing with Buddy Melges in an A Scow regatta in 1985 in Madison, Wisconsin, when we got caught in a pack of these 38-footers with no room to accelerate at the start. With 10 seconds before the gun, Buddy tacked to port and sailed up the line to get away from the crowd. When we finally tacked back to starboard, we were 15 seconds late, but we had clear air while everyone else was still in a jam. The two quick tacks to get clear air was like an instinctive reaction—it was impressive."

Speed at the Line

To get off the line quickly, your sails should be shaped for power. Ease the outhaul, cunningham, backstay, and halyards to get fuller and more powerful sails. You can flatten them out for pointing after you get off the line and away from the fleet. Then ease your sheets slightly and bear off a few degrees into your hole to leeward.

Most boats are as much as 1½ knots slow at the start because they either don't know how far from the line they are, or they've misjudged their approach and are slowing to avoid being over early. This gives you the perfect chance to break out. By going faster than the boats around you, you open the door to all the advantages. You'll have clear air while boats to leeward will be blanketed and those to windward will be hurt by your backwind. After sailing for five to ten boatlengths, you'll slow the boats around you enough that they will tack away, giving you the opportunity to tack at will.

Always work out a line sight or a range bearing on the line so that you can do a full-speed charge at the line; that's certainly preferable to luffing in the middle of a pack. Having speed at the start is doubly important because if you start with clear air but are only going the same speed as the boats around you, your boat still won't be performing up to its potential. Because of the snow-fence effect described earlier, you will be sailing in lighter wind than would a boat sailing alone.

Picking Up the Pieces

How many times have you done your homework before a race, gotten out to the course early to test the wind, and created a game plan, only to find yourself buried in the midst of a host of boats as the race gets under way? You chastise yourself for failing to get clear air, for not heading toward the side of the course you know is favored. Do you escape the miasma by giving up your game plan and sailing on the opposite side of the course from the rest of the fleet, simply because there is no one to block your wind? And then, once you are out in the "wrong" side by yourself, do you start thinking, "Well, just one good shift and I'll cross in front of the whole fleet"? Sound familiar?

Just after the start, keeping your air clear is critical. You can tell if your air is being blanketed by observing the speed of the boats around you and by looking at wind indicators. If a boat to windward has its masthead fly pointing in your direction, you can be assured that you are being blanketed. Most sailors underestimate how far wind shadows are projected. For many boats the wind shadow extends between four and six mastlengths to leeward and behind.

A boat's sails also create disturbed air to windward. This backwind is not as severe as the blanketing effects of the wind shadow, but these vortices will effect your speed as well. Backwind extends four to six mastlengths to windward and behind a leeward boat. The farther you are from the source of backwind, the less you'll be affected. You will lose speed sailing in another boat's bad air, but that can be preferable to being forced to tack with no speed into a fleet of oncoming starboard-tack boats.

Tom: "My opinion on sailing in dirty air is that you trim the sails as if you weren't in dirty air. Dirty air does not mean that all of a sudden you don't have any wind. You have some; it's just disturbed. It doesn't have to be lighter, but typically it is. Trim for the point of sail that you're on. If you decide to reach off below a person who's blanketing you, though your wind is disturbed you should be trimmed.

"I think Stuart Walker's idea that you should twist your sails and move the draft forward for dirty air is only an interesting theory. I think understanding the subtleties of sailing in dirty air is not so important that you ought to have a general theme for how to set up your sails for it. The general rule is to try not to sail in dirty air."

You can't think of dirty air as a header, as some people do. It's not that simple, because it's wind that is chopped up. In undisturbed wind, the air molecules flow in neat lines, while in disturbed wind the air molecules spin in eddies or vortices created as the wind is deflected by another boat's sails or anything else chopping up the wind—like a building or an anchored ship. You sail the best you can until you get through.

Typically, it's better to head off a little when sailing in turbulent wind, not because you're headed, but because a boat is a little fast anyway when heading off. So, with what wind there is, you should be able to perform as well as or slightly better than the opponents upwind, until you get your chance to tack away.

Sailors who are slow coming off the starting line commonly err by making too many tacks. If, for any reason, you find yourself behind after the start, having missed a shift, having been at the wrong end of the line, or just having had a bad start, do not tack blindly to get clear air. Tack to clear your wind only if you can be sure of staying in clear air. A dinghy loses about one to one and a half boatlengths by tacking, and a big boat loses about two to four boatlengths per tack. If you make three tacks after starting and the competition does not tack at all, you may lose up to eight or ten boatlengths. Moreover, you'll be unlikely to regain this distance, since you'll probably be in bad air.

To avoid this needless loss, set up for one key tack after the start. When you do tack, increase your success on the new tack by using a blocker to clear a path for you. Do this by waiting until at least one or two boats behind you tack. When you are about five boatlengths to windward of them, tack. If a blocker is forced to tack by a starboard tacker, you will have at least five boatlengths of warning. More likely, the blocker will tack on the lee bow of the right-of-way boat, which will slow both boats down and enable you to cross.

If you aren't sure which way to go after the start, and there aren't specific boats that you feel you have to defeat, sail conservatively until a trend becomes apparent. Pick your way up the middle, watch what other boats are doing, and finally choose a side; it's almost inevitable that one side of the course will get you to the mark faster than the other. There aren't many areas where one boat sails the left and the other the right side of the course, and then come together at the windward mark. Ideally that provides the best racing, but it rarely happens because of wind shifts created by the weather system or geographical formations. Current, if it is not equal over the course, can create a favored side of a beat.

Rules at the Starting Line

Because the starting line is the most crowded area of the racecourse, there are many rules governing specific close-quarter situations.

When the Rules Take Effect: The Definition of Racing

The definition of racing states that you begin racing once the preparatory signal is raised. Since by definition you are not racing until the five-minute preparatory signal, you are allowed to use any means of propulsion and receive outside assistance until the preparatory signal. So if you realize you're going to arrive at the course late, you may motor, paddle, or be towed as long as you turn off your engine, stop paddling, or cast off the tow line at the preparatory signal.

When Penalties Take Effect, Rule 31

According to the preamble to the Right-of-Way Rules, those rules (Part IV of the rule book) apply from the time a boat intending to race begins sailing in the vicinity of the starting line until it leaves the vicinity of the course after dropping out or finishing the race. Before the preparatory signal, you are expected to respect the rules even though you can't be penalized under them. Penalties for infringing a right-of-way rule are meted out only after a boat starts racing, according to Rule 31.1, which states, "A yacht may be penalized for infringing a rule of Part IV only when the infringement occurs while she is racing." The one exception is Rule 31.2, which states that you can be penalized for a foul before you start or after you finish if you seriously hinder a boat that is racing.

Penalties at the Start

The racing rule (52.2[b]) that governs hitting a starting marker or fouling a boat before the start of the race states that if you hit a starting mark within the preparatory period, you can clear yourself by doing a 720-degree turn (two revolutions) as soon as possible. No longer do you have to wait until after you have started to make your penalty turn. Also, under Appendix 3 of the "720 rule," when you foul another boat before the start, you can do your 720 right away—before starting the race. It's wise for you and your crew to practice this maneuver occasionally.

General Recall, Rule 8.2(b)

This rule absolves you of any fouls committed between the preparatory signal and the starting signal of the recalled start. It states, "Rule infringements before the preparatory signal for the new start shall be disregarded for the purpose of competing in the race to be re-started." Once again, Rule 31.2 is noted in 8.2(b) as the only exception.

Luffing Before the Start, Rule 40

Under Rule 40, any boat that has not started or cleared the starting line is entitled to luff a windward yacht head-to-wind. Any luff that requires a windward boat to alter course to avoid a collision must be carried out "slowly and initially in such a way as to give a windward yacht room and opportunity to keep clear." This rule is why you hear so much loud yelling of "Up! Up! Up!" at the starting line. Leeward boats continuously yell to windward boats in order to establish that they warned, rewarned, and warned again that they are luffing. This way they can't be accused of luffing too quickly.

The provision covering "luffing slowly" applies until your boat, or the boat luffing you, has cleared the starting line. You do not get your normal luffing rights when the gun goes off. Every part of your boat, and the boat you are luffing, must be across the starting line before you can luff at will without any warning.

The only other limit placed on the leeward boat by Rule 40 has to do with one of the most misunderstood rules before the start: mast abeam. When the skipper of the windward boat, sighting abeam from his normal position, sights at *or forward of* the leeward boat's mast, the windward boat has "mast abeam." Before the start the mast-abeam rule does not require the leeward boat to stop luffing a windward boat; it only means that the leeward boat can't luff a windward boat passed close-hauled.

Limitations on Altering Course, Rule 35

This rule states, "When one yacht is required to keep clear of another, the right-of-way yacht shall not alter course so as to prevent the other yacht from keeping clear . . . except . . . when assuming a proper course to start, unless subject to Rule 40 or to the second part of Rule 44.1(b)." The first exception allows a starboard tacker sailing below the line to alter its course by heading up to a close-hauled course to start. Any port tacker in the way of the starboard tacker commits a foul, even if the port tacker could have crossed the starboard boat before it altered its course. The skipper of the port-tack boat must anticipate that the starboard boat will head up to cross the line when the starting signal is raised (figure 3.28). The second exception involves a boat returning to the line to restart. Rule 44.1(b) says that when a boat regains its rights after getting completely to the pre-start side of the line, it must give a properly starting boat room and opportunity to keep clear. (See figure 3.29.)

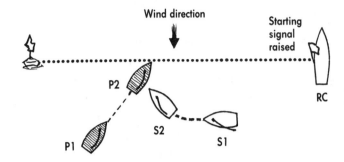

Figure 3.28 *Even though P is steering a course that keeps clear of S, Rule 35(b) allows S to head up to cross the starting line at the gun.*

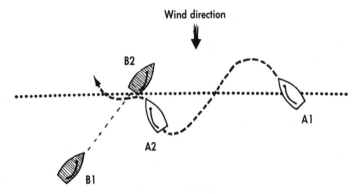

Figure 3.29 *Rule 44.1(b) states, "When she [a boat restarting] thereby acquires right of way over another yacht that is starting correctly, she shall allow that yacht ample room and opportunity to keep clear." Therefore, A must fall off and go behind B.*

Visual Starting Signals Govern, Rule 4.5

At the starting line, remember not to become dependent on starting your stopwatch to the race committee's audible signal—be it cannon, gun, or horn. Rule 4.5 states, "Times shall be taken from the visual starting signals, and a failure or mistiming of a gun or other sound signal calling attention to starting signals shall be disregarded."

Barging, Rule 42.4

Referred to as the "anti-barging rule," Rule 42.4 states: "When approaching the starting line to start, until clearing the starting marks after starting, a leeward yacht shall be under no obligation to give any windward yacht room to pass to leeward a starting mark surrounded by navigable water, including such a mark that is also an obstruction; but, after the starting signal, a leeward yacht shall not deprive a windward yacht room at such mark by sailing either (a) to windward of the compass bearing of the course to the next mark, or (b) above close-hauled." What this all says is that before the start, a leeward boat is free to luff under Rule 40 to prevent a windward boat from passing between itself and a starting mark. Once the start is signaled, the leeward boat must fall off to a close-hauled course, or, for a non-upwind start, the leeward boat must not head above the compass course to the next mark. If the leeward boat meets these requirements after the start is signaled, and there is still no room for the windward boat to sail between the leeward boat and the mark, then the windward boat is barging and is not entitled to room at the mark. (See figure 3.30 A-D.)

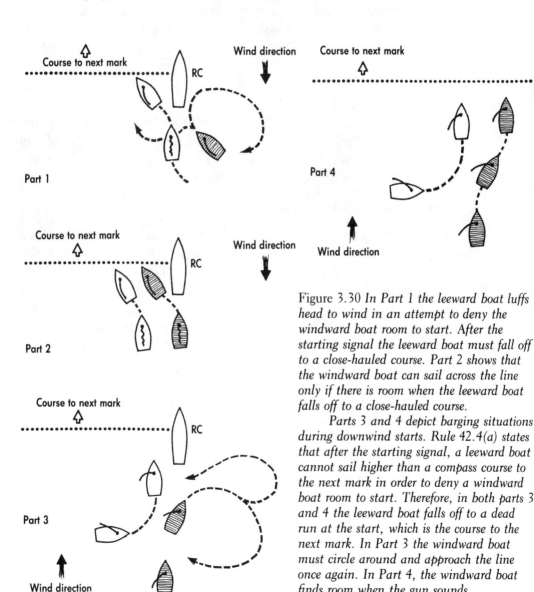

Figure 3.30 In Part 1 the leeward boat luffs head to wind in an attempt to deny the windward boat room to start. After the starting signal the leeward boat must fall off to a close-hauled course. Part 2 shows that the windward boat can sail across the line only if there is room when the leeward boat falls off to a close-hauled course.

Parts 3 and 4 depict barging situations during downwind starts. Rule 42.4(a) states that after the starting signal, a leeward boat cannot sail higher than a compass course to the next mark in order to deny a windward boat room to start. Therefore, in both parts 3 and 4 the leeward boat falls off to a dead run at the start, which is the course to the next mark. In Part 3 the windward boat must circle around and approach the line once again. In Part 4, the windward boat finds room when the gun sounds.

If you're reaching toward the committee boat on starboard tack, hoping to squeeze over the line at the last moment, you're at risk of fouling out, for, as explained above, that may be barging. To keep from getting closed out, you'll have to judge how the fleet is setting up, and watch the clock. Your only escape, if someone slams the door at the committee boat, is to fall off and go behind your competitor.

The first phrase of Rule 42.4 is the qualification, "When approaching the starting line to start." This means the anti-barging rule is only in effect when boats are coming up to the line to cross it at the gun. While boats are reaching back and forth under the line before the start, a leeward boat must give room to a windward boat to get below a starting mark, provided the windward boat meets the requirements of Rule 42, Buoy and Obstruction Room.

If the windward side of the line is the end of a dock, or an obstruction not surrounded by navigable water, then a leeward boat must give a windward boat room at the mark if the windward boat established an overlap in time, i.e., before the first boat reached the two-boatlength circle.

When a Starting Mark is an Obstruction, Rule 43.3(a)

This rule creates a "coffin corner" at the left or pin end of the line when the left end of the line is a boat. The rule states, "When an obstruction is a starting mark surrounded by navigable water, or the ground tackle of such a mark, and when approaching the starting line to start and after starting, the yacht clear ahead or the leeward yacht shall not be entitled to room to tack." In other words, a boat starting at the leeward end of the line is denied obstruction room to tack if it can't clear the leeward mark after crossing the starting line.

The One-Minute Rule, 51.1(c)

When in effect, the one-minute rule states, "When any part of a yacht's hull, equipment or crew is on the course side of the starting line or its extensions during the minute before her starting signal, she shall sail to the pre-start side of the line across one of its extensions and start." If you know that you are over the line while the one-minute rule is in effect, you don't have to wait until the start to sail around one of the ends to clear yourself. If you got pushed over near the pin at 59 seconds before your start, it would be easy to sail around the pin and be back below the line to start on time.

Starting Correctly, Rule 51.1(d)

Since sailing is still a gentleman's sport, this rule makes it each skipper's responsibility to start correctly. The rule states, "Failure of a yacht to see or hear her recall signal shall not relieve her of her obligation to start correctly." Be wary of other boats relaying the committee's call of who is over. During the confusion of the start, with heated hails crisscrossing the course, it's easy for a recalled boat's number to be transformed as it's relayed through the fleet!

Since it's your responsibility to make sure you're behind the line at the start, take every step to prove it to yourself. Have your bowman stand on the bow and look at both ends of the line. Use line sights so that you know whether you are over the line or not. Take compass bearings on the ends of the line. Gary remembers wasting a great start at the 1988 12-Meter Worlds because he lost his confidence and returned to the line unnecessarily: "When the committee signaled that a boat was over, I assumed it was us since we had the best start in the fleet. Yet I was sure that we weren't over. When my bowman told me he didn't know if we over or not, I lost my confidence and turned back. It turns out we wasted a great start. So take all the readings you can and have confidence in them."

Returning to the Start, Rule 44

This rule has three provisions: The first, 44.1(a), says that a premature starter returning to the pre-start side of the line has no rights and must keep clear of all boats that have started correctly until the boat is totally on the pre-start side of the line or one of its extensions. Included under this provision are any boats that are late getting to the starting line and that were not behind the line or its extensions before the starting signal.

The second provision, 44.1(b), states that once a premature starter sails to the pre-start side of the line, it regains all its rights. The second portion of this rule is an exception. It states, "But when she thereby acquires right-of-way over another yacht that is starting correctly, she shall allow that yacht ample room and opportunity to keep clear."

The third provision, 44.2, says that a premature starter does not lose its rights under the rules "until it is obvious that she is returning to start."

Anchoring at the Start, Rule 53.1

This rule clearly states that you can be anchored at the start, but you are not allowed to tie up to a dock or a mooring. The reason for allowing you to anchor and not to be moored is that you are required to pick up your anchor and carry it with you during the race. If the race committee is bound and determined to get off a start in light air against an adverse current, you are within your rights to motor up to the line before the preparatory signal, and anchor. While you are anchored, says Rule 46.1(b), boats that are still sailing must keep clear of you. Avoid dropping your anchor on the course side of the starting line, because both anchor and line count as the boat's equipment. The definition of starting requires *every part* of a boat to be behind the starting line when the start is signaled. When you're pulling up your anchor, know that if your boat goes faster than it would by sailing in those conditions, you're breaking Rule 54.1 by using an illegal means of propulsion.

Shifting Ballast, Rule 22.2

This is a rule that has received much attention on the IOR grand prix circuit after a few notable fouls. The rule states, "From 2100 on the day before the race until she is no longer racing, a yacht shall not ship, unship, or shift ballast, whether movable or fixed, or take in or discharge water, except for ordinary ship's use and the removal of bilge water." So if you're entering a point-to-point race and expect the wind to blow from one direction the whole race, you are allowed to shift all your extra sails, gear, and water to one side of the boat, as long as you leave it all in place after 9:00 P.M. the night before the race. But you're taking a gamble. If the wind shifts, you aren't allowed to shift the ballast while racing. Most of the competitors racing the 2,250-mile TransPac race from Los Angeles to Honolulu load all their water, food, beer, and spare parts on the starboard side of the boat, since the race is always starboard-tack broad reach. The boats look odd as they motor to the line with a noticeable list to starboard.

No matter how many rules are written governing starting, Gary thinks you can't get a fair start if there are more than 40 boats on the line. Gary says, "The best fleets, to my mind, contain between 20 and 40 boats. With more boats than that on the line, it gets to be a zoo. In huge fleets the committee can't call back the boats in the middle of the line, and can't see everyone who's over. I watched a fleet of 90 J/24s start at their Atlantic Coast Championships in Annapolis in 1988. The sight reminded me of the bumper cars at a carnival. It seemed you couldn't get them off the line without greasing their topsides first."

Upwind Tactics

Y our game plan for the beat should not be limited solely to what the wind and current are doing. There are other questions: How long is the leg? How much longer you expect to be on one tack compared to the other? Is there a geographical feature that will make one side of the course more favored than the other? You have to take into account your competition and whether it's early or late in the regatta. In this chapter we'll explore these questions, and then discuss how to get the lead and keep it.

Your strategy depends on what type of wind-shift pattern you are sailing in. In open water the wind could be persistently shifting in one direction, oscillating back and forth, or a combination of the two. When part of the course is close to land, expect the wind to shift as the result of geographic influences. Knowing the pattern in which you'll be racing only comes from doing your homework before the start; thus the importance of getting out on the course early and recording your compass headings on both tacks.

Strategy in an Oscillating Shift

In an oscillating wind shift, the wind direction jumps from left to right and then back again. By getting out on the course early enough, you will be able to time the periods between shifts and note their magnitudes and discern a pattern that will greatly benefit your racing strategy upwind and downwind.

Likely causes of oscillating shifts include the following:

Vertically unstable air. Often the strong upper-altitude wind blows in a slightly different direction from the weaker surface wind. Mixing brings high-altitude shifts and gusts down to the surface.

Thermal conditions. Cumulus clouds are caused by thermals, or rising columns of hot air, which create vertical mixing of the atmosphere.

Offshore breezes. Wind that has passed over sun-warmed land before flowing out over the water is likely to have oscillating shifts.

There are several keys to doing well in oscillating winds. The first is knowing when to tack. With the wind jumping around, you'll have to get a lot of readings on each tack and determine highest, lowest, and median compass headings for both port and starboard tack. On boats with more than two crew members, assign someone besides the skipper or tactician to watch the compass and call whether you are high, low, or at your average course. The tactician needs to be free to look up the course for new wind, figure out how the boat is performing, call crossing situations, plan mark roundings, and consult with the skipper, instead of keeping his eyes glued to the compass. The compass caller should provide the tactician with information on wind-shift trends. The tactician should write in a notebook what the headings (high, low, and average) for the leg were, along with the time between the shifts.

The job of calling the compass has been made easier and more precise by the development of the electronic digital compass, which indicates your exact heading in large, easy-to-read numbers. Any member of the crew can pick out one-degree changes in the boat's course, a vast improvement over the five-degree accuracy of standard analog compass cards. A digital compass allows you to check performance changes as the result of minute course adjustments.

The tactician should not only monitor the compass to detect shifts, but should use the rest of the fleet for this purpose. Use the fleet just as you would keep an eye out for brake lights on cars half a block ahead of you while driving in rush hour. Often, small shifts show up more clearly on the fleet than on the compass. Use the fleet to create a map of the wind across the course. Boats ahead and to windward will telegraph shifts that you should expect next. (See figure 4.1.)

The correct strategy for sailing in oscillating winds is to delay your tack until you are headed below the median compass reading. If you are sailing on a lift, do not tack when you first get headed. For example, if you were lifted 10

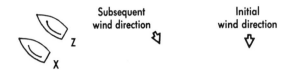

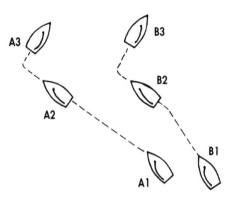

Figure 4.1 *If you see a header coming, by seeing boats ahead of you sailing a lower course, you should always sail to it faster by footing. The figure shows how Boat A makes great gains on Boat B by getting to the header first.*

degrees, you would not tack until you were knocked at least 15 degrees—5 degrees low of the median wind direction. (A *lift* is a wind shift that allows a boat to sail closer to its destination upwind, and a *knock* is a shift that makes you head away from your destination.) If the wind is jumping around quickly, don't even tack when knocked below the median. Sail into the header a few boatlengths to make sure it's not a short-lived knock.

In oscillating conditions you have to be on the lookout for temporary wind shifts that are created by a change in windspeed. These shifts are referred to as *velocity shifts*. As the wind loses strength, the boat doesn't slow down immediately, owing to its momentum. This excess speed for the lower wind strength will cause the apparent wind to go forward and your sails will luff, implying that you are in a header. Once the boat settles to its slower speed in the lull, the boat will return to the heading it was sailing before entering the lull. To understand this misunderstood concept, turn to the section on velocity shifts (page 130) to review the concepts of apparent wind and apparent wind angles. To guard against velocity headers, watch the compass. If you stay headed after sailing a couple of boatlengths, you are truly knocked, but if you come back to course after sailing a few boatlengths, you were experiencing a velocity header. Also keep your eyes outside of the boat and look at the boats ahead of you. If they start heeling less, you'll know that the wind is easing, so you can expect a short-term header. If you have a true-wind-direction instrument, you can watch that also.

Other times you'll find that the shifts are not short-lived at all. Sometimes the magnitude of the oscillations will change. In those cases you'll have to readjust your numbers to create new high, low, and average readings.

Knowing the timing between oscillations is important to your strategy. If you know when the next shift is coming, you'll know whether to tack on a competitor's lee bow or duck him in a crossing situation. Also, by knowing the timing of the next shift, you'll know whether to spend some of your windward advantage by footing to drive over a leeward boat, and you'll know where to set up for your final approach to the windward mark. For instance, if the wind is oscillating every ten minutes, and you estimate that you're 15 minutes from the mark, you need to set yourself up to take advantage of the final shift. Let's say you are lifted while on port tack as you're approaching the starboard layline. If you delay your tack to starboard until the wind oscillates

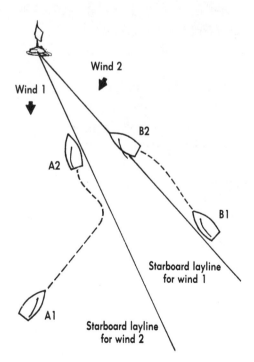

Figure 4.2 *With a rough timing on the wind's oscillations, Boat A tacks to starboard knowing that the wind is about to shift to position 2. When the wind shifts, A gets lifted to the mark. In the meantime, Boat B, which had sailed to the layline for the wind in position 1, ends up overstanding.*

to the right, you will overstand the starboard layline. So what do you do? Tack before the layline and before the wind oscillates to the right. In this position you'll be lifted to the mark when the shift comes. By expecting the shift and tacking before the layline, you'll gain or pass the boats that overstood because they went out to the layline that existed during the port lift. (See figure 4.2.)

On the other hand, if the wind is oscillating every ten minutes and you are less than ten minutes from the mark, you are no longer considered to be in an oscillating wind shift pattern, since you'll round the mark before the next oscillation. In this case you'll have to view the wind as steady.

Apparent Wind

A boat's movement through the water affects the direction and strength of the wind. The wind you feel while on the deck of a moving boat is called the *apparent wind*. The wind you feel when the boat is tied to the dock is the *true wind*. Both the true and apparent winds have two components—speed and direction. Therefore we will talk about true windspeed and true wind direction, and apparent windspeed and apparent wind direction.

To help understand this concept, let's get on a motorcycle with an anemometer to measure wind strength and a windvane to measure wind direction. On our first ride the wind is calm. As we accelerate, the windspeed instrument reads the same as the bike's speedometer, while the windvane indicates that the wind direction is straight ahead. While maintaining the same speed, we can turn in any direction and the readings will not change. In this example you can see how wind is created by movement.

When we drive at 55 mph into a 15-mph headwind, the apparent-windspeed instrument would read 70 mph—our speed plus the speed of the wind. If we turned around and drove 55 mph, with the 15-mph wind at our backs, the wind instrument would read 40 mph.

Now let's get off the motorcycle and back on the boat. Before we get into the math and the vector diagrams, let's draw some commonsense conclusions based on our motorcycle experiences. First, if your boat is going at an angle toward the wind—anywhere from dead into the wind to 89 degrees away from the wind—your apparent wind strength will be stronger than the true windspeed. Conversely, when sailing between 91 degrees and 180 degrees from the

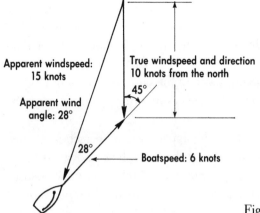

Apparent windspeed:
15 knots

Apparent wind
angle: 28°

True windspeed and direction
10 knots from the north

45°

28°

Boatspeed: 6 knots

Figure 4.3

wind, the apparent wind strength decreases the more downwind you sail. When you sail with the wind right on your beam, the apparent wind and true wind strength are the same.

Consider the following five figures. (Note: Vector diagrams are drawn with the arrowheads indicating the direction of motion, and the length of the arrows proportionally representing speed in knots.) Figure 4.3 shows a boat beating to windward at 6 knots. It is sailing 45 degrees to the true wind, which is blowing 10 knots. By vector subtraction, connecting the tails of the arrows

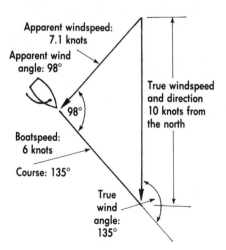

Apparent windspeed:
7.1 knots

Apparent wind
angle: 98°

98°

True windspeed
and direction
10 knots from
the north

Boatspeed:
6 knots

Course: 135°

True
wind
angle:
135°

Figure 4.4

representing boatspeed and windspeed, we get the apparent wind angle and speed. In this case, the crew would feel a 15-knot breeze coming from 28 degrees off the windward bow. Their apparent wind is 5 knots stronger than the actual wind.

Sailing downwind at the same 6-knot speed in the same 10-knot wind (figure 4.4), the crew would only feel a 7-knot breeze coming from 98 degrees off the windward bow.

A velocity shift is a temporary shift in the apparent wind direction created by a change in wind velocity or boatspeed. If the same boat shown in figure 4.4 picked up 2 knots of speed by surfing down a wave while the true windspeed and direction remained the same, the apparent direction would move forward to 85 degrees off the boat's bow (figure 4.5). Once the wave passed, the boat would slow back down to 6 knots, and the apparent wind would go back to being 98 degrees off the boat's bow. Because of this temporary header, it's a good idea during a long leg to rig a preventer to hold the boom in place, so that when the boat picks up speed while surfing, or the wind shifts in direction or strength, the boom won't be able to wander toward the center of the boat as the mainsail luffs. Even though you might slow down a bit from the mainsail backwinding, giving up that little speed is far better than having an out-of-control boom raking the deck.

Figures 4.6 and 4.7 illustrate how your boat can get lifted or headed during a puff or a lull. The temporary change in apparent wind angle is a result of

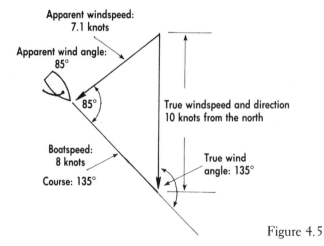

Figure 4.5

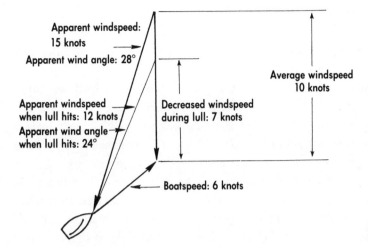

Apparent windspeed:
15 knots

Apparent wind angle: 28°

Apparent windspeed
when lull hits: 12 knots

Apparent wind angle
when lull hits: 24°

Decreased windspeed
during lull: 7 knots

Average windspeed
10 knots

Boatspeed: 6 knots

Figure 4.6

the boat's momentum. If the wind decreases in velocity as in figure 4.5, the boat will coast until it reaches its new slower speed. While coasting, boatspeed is a larger-than-normal component of apparent wind vector. Once your boatspeed matches the new wind strength, the apparent wind angle returns to nearly the same angle it was before the change in windspeed.

Therefore a tactician not only has to keep his eye on the compass but also on the fleet, the wind on the water, and the true-windspeed instrument. How

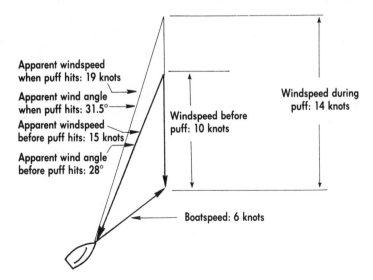

Apparent windspeed
when puff hits: 19 knots

Apparent wind angle
when puff hits: 31.5°

Apparent windspeed
before puff hits: 15 knots

Apparent wind angle
before puff hits: 28°

Windspeed before
puff: 10 knots

Windspeed during
puff: 14 knots

Boatspeed: 6 knots

Figure 4.7

many times have you been sailing on a lift, then gotten a knock, tacked, and then found yourself on another knock? It's not that the wind gods were playing with you—they were just testing you to see if you could tell the difference between a velocity shift and a real shift in the wind direction. The solution is to sail into a new windshift two or four lengths to see if your boat gets lifted back to its course before the shift. You have to be especially careful in oscillating winds when you are expecting the wind to shift. Thus, if you don't have a true-windspeed instrument, don't tack as soon as you get knocked. Keep sailing for a few boatlengths to see if your course comes back up to average.

The leading edge of a puff of wind is normally the strongest. Since puffs are usually short-lived, don't waste the wind by tacking or jibing. In smaller boats, it is best to sail well into a puff before tacking, to maximize the strength and new direction of the wind. On larger boats, particularly in lighter winds (under 5 knots), it is often better to make your tack before a puff reaches your boat. If you wait for the puff to hit, you may use all its energy in making the tack. By setting the boat up on the desired tack just before the puff, you will be able to accelerate as the puff hits.

If the new wind is approaching slowly from abeam, it is best to tack and sail toward it. If the wind appears to be coming from ahead, continue sailing until you are up to speed in the new wind. By being the first boat to reach the new wind, you'll gain a lot of distance on the fleet. Keep a good lookout for wind on the water before and during the race. If you're sailing a boat with more than two crew, have one person constantly looking aft on the runs for puffs coming down the course.

Strategy in a Persistent Shift

In a persistent shift, the wind gradually moves in one direction. Persistent shifts can be caused by moving weather systems, the ongoing development or decay of a sea breeze, or a shoreline effect on the breeze. When your compass readings indicate a shift in one direction, the correct strategy is to sail toward the new wind direction. To sail toward the new wind, you'll have to sail on a knocked course. Stay on the header until you are between the fleet and the new wind. Figure 4.8 shows why getting between the new wind and the fleet is called being "on the inside of the shift." Those choosing not to sail the

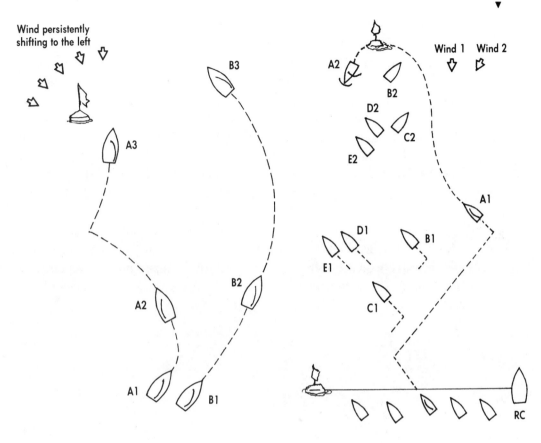

Figure 4.8 *Recognizing the persistent shift, A tacks and sails toward the new wind. Boat B, on the other hand, rides the lift. As the wind keeps shifting to the left, B sails the "great circle route" while A tacks back to port and gets lifted to the mark.*

Figure 4.9 *The correct strategy in a persistent shift is to sail to the side of the course where the wind is blowing from, or where it is expected to blow from.*

header toward the new wind during a persistent shift end up on what is called the "great circle route." They get lifted and lifted, but don't make much progress toward the mark. (See figure 4.9 for the correct strategy to sailing in a persistent shift.)

When you find yourself on the great circle route, all you can do is tack and sail into the header. You'll have a terrible angle as you sail to the other side of the course, and most likely you'll pass astern of a lot of boats. But every boat you pass astern of, you have a chance of passing because you'll be inside of them as the wind keeps shifting.

It takes courage to tack onto the headed tack—especially while you're currently on a lift. Many sailors feel a psychological prohibition against dipping other boats' sterns. But if you know that you are on a persistent shift, it pays in the long run to get to the inside as soon as you can. Gary remembers sailing at *Yachting* magazine's Block Island Race Week in 1986, on an S2 9.1. "We were well back in our class, but I recognized we were in a persistent lift, so I tacked off the lift away from the fleet to get to the inside of the boats in our class. We went from sixth place to well ahead by splitting with the fleet and sailing to the inside of the shift.

The key to victory in a persistent shift is early detection and firm conviction. Always keep an eye out for indications of a persistent shift. Watch your compass and keep an eye on the boats to windward. If your compass indicates a persistent shift, and the boats to windward are lifted compared to you, then tack. Even

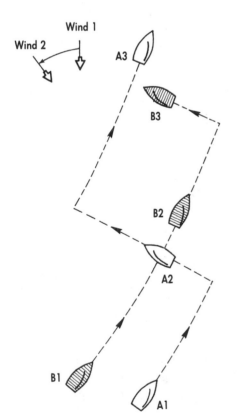

Figure 4.10 *Before the wind persistently shifts to the left, boats A and B are even. As the wind shifts, B pulls ahead since it is on the inside of the shift. Recognizing that it is on the outside of the shift, A tacks onto the header and takes B stern. A passes ahead of B in the next crossing situation because A moved to the inside of the persistent shift.*

though you'll be tacking onto a header, bite the bullet and tack. You'll be making money on those who remain on the great circle route. (See figure 4.10.)

If you get caught on the outside (to leeward) of the fleet in a persistent shift, make your mistake a short-lived one. Don't hang on hoping for a header, unless you believe that the wind will oscillate back. Perhaps you'd do well to copy that last sentence down on the deck where the whole crew can see it.

Be careful not to sail into the shift so far that you overstand the mark you are sailing for. As the wind keeps shifting, the layline will keep moving toward you. If you overstand, boats to leeward can lift up to the mark and pass by leeward. (See figure 4.11.)

In the first race of the 1982 Hall of Fame Regatta, Gary port-tacked the fleet and got a great start. "I knew the wind would be bending to the right at

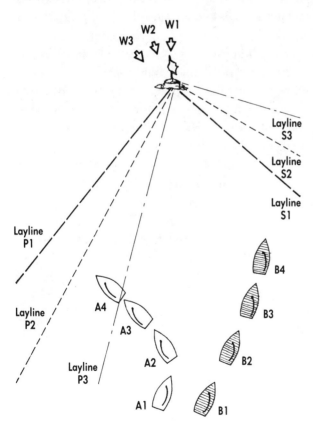

Figure 4.11 *When sailing toward a persistent shift, be careful not to overstand the mark. As Boat A sails on the headed tack toward the shift, the port tack layline moves toward it. However, the starboard layline keeps moving further away from Boat B.*

the windward mark, because it always did in that area of Narragansett Bay. But I was so nervous and hyped up, being ahead of all the best names in sailing, that I allowed myself to tack on the layline without figuring in the effect of the wind change. I ended up going from first to fourth as Buddy Melges, Dave Ullman, and Paul Elvström lifted up to the mark under me. But I never made that mistake again in the regatta, and went on to win the series."

The farther to leeward of a big fleet you are, the more you will lose in a persistent shift, and the harder it will be to get back in the race. When in doubt as to what wind-shift pattern you are sailing in, cut potential losses by not separating from the bulk of the fleet. If you do find yourself on the wrong side of a shift, you won't lose much distance on the fleet and you will be able to cut your losses early by tacking and footing to the favored side. (Footing is sailing lower than your best upwind course to pick up speed.) If someone tacks on your air while you are sailing across to the favored side, drive through his lee—don't tack away. The sooner you get to the inside of the shift, the sooner you will start making gains.

Nothing in life goes perfectly according to plan, and the wind is no different. So don't count on encountering evenly oscillating winds or perfectly persistent shifts. In most cases you will be sailing in a mix of oscillating and persistently shifting winds. When the wind is serving up a little of each pattern, those who got on the course earliest and took the most wind readings will often be able to make the best sense of the seemingly desultory shifts. When sailing in both persistent and oscillating winds, work the inside of the persistent shift and tack on the oscillations. This is the most common strategy for a windward leg— favoring one side of the course while tacking on the headers.

As has been stated before, races are won by minimizing mistakes. Sailboat racing is not really a game of brilliance; it's simply the elimination of errors. The boats that make the fewest mistakes are the ones that usually win. When you go for a brilliant move, often you are taking a big risk. You win by staying with the fleet and doing the better job of executing maneuvers and taking advantage of wind shifts, as well as concentrating on boatspeed. It's the little things that make the difference. The farther you are from another boat, the more distance you will gain or lose when the wind shifts.

Even if he is sure the fleet is going the wrong way, a smart sailor will stay near the competition, but on the favored side of the course. In exchange for giving up the chance to win big, the racer is insured against a catastrophic loss. If you're ahead, you'll never get into trouble by staying between your competition and the next mark. If there are eleven other boats within striking distance, and nine sail to the left side of the course and two go to the right, that's an indication you should probably go to the left.

Playing the middle of the course keeps your options open, allowing you to react to an unexpected shift. Sailing to one side of the course eliminates most of your options, giving you a small chance of getting to the mark first. Sometimes longshots pay off big, but no experienced gambler makes a living betting longshots. If you sail all the way over to one of the laylines, you are automatically in a no win situation. If you get a lift, you'll overstand the mark and boats below you will lift up to the mark under you. (See figure 4.12.) If you get a header you'll lose to all the boats to leeward since none of you will make the mark, but any boat to leeward will be able to tack and make the mark before you. (See figure 4.13.)

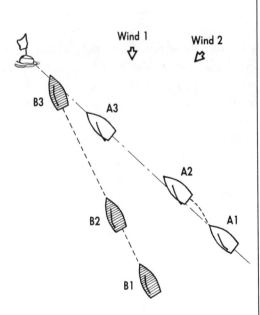

Figure 4.12 *If you get to the layline too soon, you can get passed by boats to leeward if the wind shifts and lifts.*

Figure 4.13 *Also, if you get to the layline too soon, you can get passed by boats to leeward if the wind shifts and heads you.*

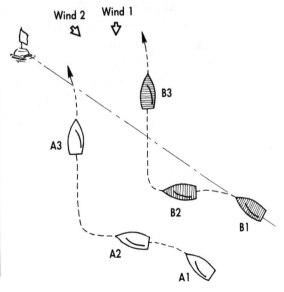

Consolidation

To help you stay out of corners, tack on small headers when you are sailing away from the middle of the course. When sailing back into the middle, ignore the small or temporary headers that would force you to the outside of the course. At the beginning of each beat, determine which is the longer layline. At the beginning of the leg tell the skipper the relative time you'll be sailing on port and starboard tacks. In this way, you can adjust your game plan so that you don't get out to a layline too soon.

Remember that the fleet determines where the course is—if the fleet goes to the left and you sail up the middle, then you're actually sailing on the right side of the course. Right and left are terms that are always relative to where the bulk of the fleet is. For example, if the fleet is on starboard tack and you are worried about the wind lifting, stay on the right side of the fleet even though the fleet is to the left of an imaginary line drawn from the windward mark to the middle of the starting line.

Another reason for tacking back to the middle of the course is to realize a gain from a header. If a header puts you into the lead, or you have made a substantial gain from a wind shift, then tack and cross the fleet to take the gain. It's better to take an early gain than to be greedy and wait for more. Often when you go for more, it all evaporates.

"In 1985 at the Maxi Worlds aboard *Matador*, we had a great start at the leeward end of the line," says Gary, "but the wind kept lifting us as we headed for Block Island. Eventually we were able to head right at the island, which put us in fifth place. After two hours we got a major 40-degree header. At this point we could have tacked and easily crossed ahead of the other maxis, but instead we waited for even more of a header so that we could get even farther ahead. That was a big mistake. Ten minutes later the wind went back and the golden opportunity to take the lead slipped away. The problem was that too many people were studying the radar and trends on computers without simply watching the other boats."

If you are ahead and to leeward of the fleet, you will not collect the gain from a header until you tack and cross the fleet that is on your windward hip. Until you cross the fleet, you will not have taken advantage of the shift. (See figure 4.14.) Figure 4.15 shows how windshifts produce "paper profits" only, unless you tack and take advantage of them.

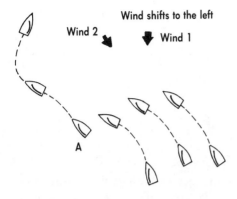

Wind shifts to the left

Wind 2   Wind 1

A

Figure 4.14 *Boat A does not realize the advantage of the header until it tacks and crosses in front of the other boats.*

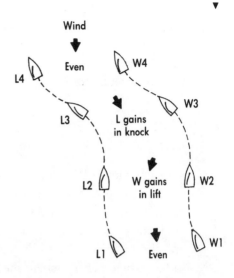

Wind

Even

L4

W4

L3

W3

L gains
in knock

L2

W gains
in lift

W2

L1   Even   W1

Figure 4.15 *The position between the boats does not change if the two boats sail through the wind shifts without tacking. In position 2, Boat W would be ahead if L tacked, and in position 3, L would be ahead if she tacked.*

If you are the boat that got hurt by a header, you can defend yourself from a boat that tacks to consolidate on you. Either tack before he does, or tack before he crosses you. On the new tack, you are trying to get to the next shift

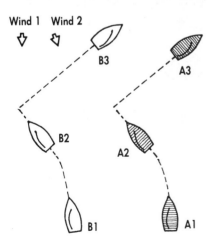

Wind 1   Wind 2

B3

A3

B2

A2

B1

A1

Figure 4.16 *Boat A demonstrates how to defend against a boat attempting to consolidate from a shift. Before the wind shifted to the left (Wind 1), the boats are even. The header (Wind 2) puts B ahead. Therefore, B tacks in an attempt to cross A and consolidate its lead. A defends by tacking. With both boats on port, A will be in the favored position if the wind oscillates back.*

before he does. The more distance you open up, the more of an advantage you'll have and greater the gain you'll realize when the wind oscillates. If you keep ahead of him, you'll get to the new shift first and gain the advantage from it. (See figure 4.16.)

Leverage

The separation between you and another boat is the stored energy for making a gain or a loss. The distance between your boat and others won't turn into passing power unless the wind shifts. The farther apart you are, the greater your gain—or loss—depending on which way the wind shifts. The closer you are, the more conservatively you're playing.

In triangle racing, where the fleet stays relatively close together, boats that are ahead don't want the boats behind to have much leverage. Let's say you are going into the last race of a five-race one-design national championship. You've sailed better than ever; going into the last race, you are in second place and there are seven points between you and the national champion's crown. If the leader decides to cover a group of boats instead of you, the distance between the boats affords you some leverage. But take into account how close the third-place boat is behind you in the standings. Perhaps by not covering with the leader you'll risk dropping to third place. Your thinking might go like this: "I've been second three years in a row, and I've never won the gold. I don't care if I end up third, but I'm taking a chance at winning it all." Or you might think, "I've never been up here before. Who knows if I'll ever get the chance again? Second is more than fine by me."

When to Risk Everything

"I think if you are behind someone you have to beat," says Tom, "you should do everything opposite, regardless of whether it makes sense or not. The other guy is ahead of you because he's either the same speed as you or better. Therefore, a game plan based on making small, incremental gains won't work. If you are willing to take the risk of losing a few places, separating with the boat ahead of you puts you in a position that allows you to be rewarded."

"In the 1984 Oxford Regatta on the Chesapeake Bay, I was over the line early and had to restart while steering a friend's 30-footer," Gary says. "Being behind, I split from the fleet and ended up sailing in even worse wind. On the next two legs I continued the pattern of splitting with the fleet, and only kept falling farther and farther behind. Finally, on the last leg, while well behind all the other boats, I tried a flier one last time—what did we have to lose? This time it worked, and we won the race. Fliers can pay off when you're in last place, doing badly, but the percentages aren't with you. Being very enthusiastic, I told the crew that if they hung in, we'd catch up by the end of the race. I made believers out of all them, but to tell the truth, I was just lucky."

"One of the reasons Ted Turner has won so many offshore championships," says Gary, "is that when he finds himself hopelessly out of it, he tries the most bizarre tactics. For example, if the whole fleet is on the Long Island shore of Long Island Sound, he'd split and go to the Connecticut shore. He would rather take a shot at first and lose than sail conservatively and take fourth place. It's all or nothing for Ted."

Another example of an occasion when you wouldn't care about losing second place in an effort to win it all is when you're racing in a large handicap fleet that includes a subset of your sister ships. Say that out of a fleet of 27 boats, five are Santana 30s. If the top Santana 30 qualifies for a regional championship, or if a more important separate trophy is awarded, then by all means take a gamble and get some leverage in an attempt to pass other Santanas. As long as the boats close behind you are not other Santana 30s, you've got nothing to lose by taking a gamble late in the race. If you don't get around the leader, you'll still be the first Santana 30, even if you finish third overall.

Your Bag of Tricks

"To keep another boat from keying (constantly covering or following) on me so that I can get away and take some leverage," says Gary, "I try to blend in. If every boat is white, you don't want a red one. One of the sneaky things I've done over the years in small boats is to change my clothes throughout the series. I bring several sets of different-colored foul-weather gear so that I can change my color scheme every couple of races, making me hard to focus in on. If the series is close, I'll definitely change my foul-weather gear so that when someone is looking to cover a guy in a white boat, wearing a red one-piece suit, he'll have a hard time noticing me in my white foul-weather gear. It's amazing how easy it is to blend in when you're sailing in a large fleet. I'll never forget a Penguin regatta I sailed against a guy who I had a hard time covering. I got confused trying to keep track of him because the port side of his boat was painted blue and the starboard side was painted white. I later asked the guy why in the world his boat was painted two different colors. He told me that he had no tactical goal in mind—it was just a case of not having enough blue paint to finish the whole boat. I ended up losing the regatta to him."

Monitoring the Fleet

If you are totally befuddled and can't figure out which side of the course is favored, you can (a) blindly follow the usual leaders in your class, or (b) sail conservatively in the middle of the fleet while monitoring how the boats on either side of you are doing. According to Tom, "Often the boats destined to lead the fleet know which way to go right away. In all the races I sail, I update my game plan by monitoring the performance of the boats on the extreme sides of the course." Reading the performance of the rest of the fleet is essential in figuring out which side of the beat is favored.

"My method for monitoring the fleet is very simple," Tom says. "All you do is take a compass bearing on another boat; the boat can be on your tack or the other tack. Now think of that bearing line as a starting line. To figure out who's ahead, you need to determine which boat is at the end of the line farthest upwind—the favored end. Before the start, you can figure out the favored end by luffing into the wind and looking to see toward which end of the line your bow points. During the race, you'll have to use a more mathematical method. First find the true wind direction. You can get the true wind direction from a deluxe instrument system, or you can figure it out by computing the average of your port and starboard headings. Your headings on each tack should be readily available, since a good tactician always writes them down.

"Now you have all the pieces of the puzzle; all you have to do is put them together. To find out if the other boat is ahead, subtract its bearing from the

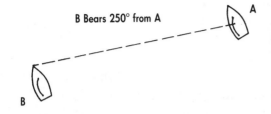

B Bears 250° from A

B

A

Figure 4.17 *Tom's method for determining who's ahead: First, take a compass bearing on the other boat; in this case B bears 250°. Think of that bearing line as a starting line.*

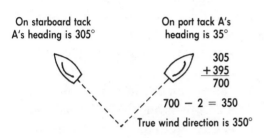

On starboard tack
A's heading is 305°

On port tack A's
heading is 35°

```
  305
+ 395
  700
```

700 − 2 = 350

True wind direction is 350°

Figure 4.18 *Second, find the true wind direction by reading an electronic instrument, or solving for the average of your port and starboard tack headings.*

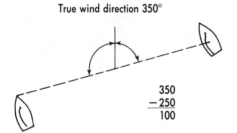

True wind direction 350°

```
  350
− 250
  100
```

Figure 4.19 *Third, subtract the other boat's bearing from the true wind direction. If the answer is less than 90 degrees, the other boat is ahead since it's at the upwind end of the line. If the answer is greater than 90 degrees, than you are ahead. If the answer is 90 degrees, than both boats are even.*

heading of the wind. If the answer is less than 90 degrees, the other boat is ahead, since it's at the upwind end of the line. If the answer is greater than 90 degrees, you are ahead. And of course, if the answer is 90 degrees, both boats are even, since you're behind a square starting line (See figures 4.17, 4.18, and 4.19).

"Not only can you figure out who's leading with this method, but you can determine in boatlengths how great the lead is. Look through your hand-bearing compass and notice how many degrees it is from bow to stern of the other boat. Say it's 5 degrees. If the wind is still coming from 100 degrees and you sight the other boat and notice that it bears 25 degrees, you know immediately that it's ahead (100 minus 25 equals 75). The angle is less than 90 degrees, so the other boat is at the favored end of the bearing line. If it was even with you, it would bear 10 degrees (100 minus 90 equals 10). Since you previously determined that 5 degrees equals one of its boatlengths, and you know that the other boat is 15 degrees ahead of a square starting line, you can conclude that the boat is three boatlengths ahead of you."

If the fleet is split, and you are on the right side of the beat, then monitor the performance of the other side of the course by taking bearings on another boat. For example, say your boat and the boat you need to beat to win the spring series both get good starts, but your competitor tacks to port right after the start. You don't tack to cover right away because there are too many boats around, and besides, you think you are going off in a lift. Both boats sail on opposite tacks for five minutes. Your tactician sights the other boat and says, "We've got a good lead. Even if we got headed 10 degrees, we'd be even." He can say this because if you were both about to start, he'd be 10 degrees behind a square starting line. (See figure 4.20.) By saying that you won't fall behind the other boat even if you get a 10-degree shift, the tactician is giving the skipper more useful information than he would by simply stating how many boatlengths you're leading by.

The only time you need to know the length of your lead is when you are considering crossing another boat or tacking in front of another boat. To tack dead ahead of another boat, you have to be one and a half boatlengths in front of him when you tack. If you don't tack that far ahead, you risk getting rolled while your boat is trying to accelerate.

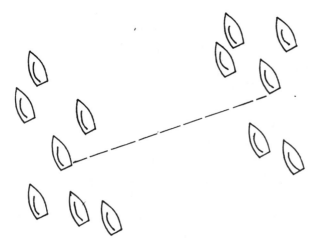

Figure 4.20 *When the fleet is split up, monitor the conditions on the other side of the course by taking bearings on a boat with similar speed characteristics.*

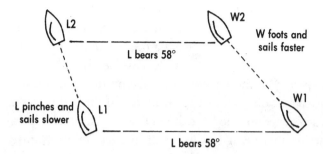

Figure 4.21 *In position 1, L and W are even. Though the two boats move through the water at different speeds, L and W are even in position 2 since the bearing between them hasn't changed.*

You can also use a hand-bearing compass for gauging your speed against another boat by assessing whether you're gaining or losing bearing. "When I'm going upwind," says Tom, "I like to keep it simple by thinking about the two boats being on the starting line at all times. Let's say you're even with another boat—that is, you've taken a bearing on him and the wind is perpendicular to the bearing line. If the other boat moves from being ten boatlengths away to five boatlengths away while the compass bearing to him has not changed, which boat has gained? The answer is neither. All you've done is moved closer together on the imaginary starting line. (See figure 4.21.) This could be the result of the boat to leeward pinching while the boat to windward could either have been sailing slower than it should have, or it could have been footing. In either case, the two boats are making progress upwind at the same rate.

If you've been sailing well and the boat on the other side of the course has gained, determine whether that boat benefited from the other side of the course, or whether it's just sailing faster. That's the hard judgment call. Start by checking your performance against the boats around you. If you are sailing as well as or better than the boats around you, while the boat across the course is doing better yet, it's a good indication that the other side of the course has better wind or better current. While crossing to the favored side of the course, foot off a bit to get there as quickly as possible.

Be careful when assessing why the other boat has gained. If the boat across the course is doing better than you are, don't automatically assume you're on the wrong side of the course. Make sure your progress is not being impeded by factors such as another boat sitting on your wind, bad steering by your helmsman, or a crew problem, such as a slow tack.

One side of the course could be favored by more wind, less adverse current, or a geographic shift. When deciding whether the other side of the course has more wind, look to see if boats over there are heeling more than those around you, if there are white caps over there, or if the water's surface is darker from more cat's-paws. The frequency of the readings you take on the boats on the other side of the course depends on how worried you are. "If I'm sailing with the whole fleet around me except for one boat, I don't worry too much," says Tom. "I'll accept that he is either going to win big or lose big, but the worse case is that I'll only lose to one boat. The odds are better if I stick with the bulk of the fleet."

Picking which side of the course is favored before the start is always hard. Therefore, Tom suggests that you delay committing your boat to a side of the course until you've had a chance to monitor the fleet to see which side of the course is paying off. It's ironic that many times good tacticians fail to believe what they see; instead, they see only what they want to see. For instance, say your game plan calls for going to the right, but after the start you notice that the boats on the left are pulling into the lead. In that case, you had better think of ways to get over to the left unless you have good reason to believe the right is going to pay. Also, if your fleet isn't the first to start, don't forget to study which boats did better in the fleet that started before you.

Other Ways to Monitor the Fleet

"Taking this all a step further," says Tom, "a good tactician should always base his tactics on whether his boat is gaining or losing. That's why, during all our America's Cup campaigns, we were such sticklers about how many boatlengths we were ahead or behind. We lived and died by the creed that if we were losing we'd do something different, and if we were winning we wouldn't change a thing.

"The only reason we had to be so exacting is that 12-meters are so close in speed. If one boat was going one-tenth of a knot faster, that was a significant difference. In most races you shouldn't waste too much effort in trying to figure out your lead in numbers of boatlengths. A tactician has plenty of other things to devote his attention to. In most cases you can make your tactical decisions solely on trends—is the other boat gaining or losing? Basic gaining or losing trends can be determined with several sights from a hand-bearing compass."

"One of the best gauges of how you're doing against other boats," says Gary, "is to sail over to where other boats are, so that you can measure your performance. That's a tactic that both Tom and I use frequently.

"I find that I do a better job of judging the performance of my boat if I stay in one place and look. For some strange reason, on a 12-meter, when I was right in front of the helmsman I could tell exactly how we were doing. But if I went anywhere else in the boat, I had trouble judging."

Four Ways to Measure Gains or Losses

1. Tom: "A lot of times, right after the start in a match race, Dennis will want to know who's ahead. Usually I won't have a clue, because for the last five minutes we've been locked in a maneuvering battle with the other boat. At the gun, the whole crew's adrenaline is surging, and I'm in the midst of grinding my running backstay. But since Dennis needs to know who's ahead right away, I've made removable cards with our tacking angles for every wind strength that fit around the compass. The cards can be read quicker than standard sets of tacking lines, which can be a jumble of color-coded lines representing a boat's tacking angles. With the cards, all I have to do is sight down one line and see if the other boat is ahead or behind it. If you don't have the card, then use the imagined starting line technique. It will just take a little longer."

2. "On *Stars & Stripes*, we used an instrument called a stadimeter, which precisely measures the triangulation of height to solve for distance," says Tom. "It's a World War II measuring device that's not hard to get in an army-navy store, but it's a little cumbersome to use in races. During the America's Cup we used it all the time. But you really don't need something so accurate." For the stadimeter to give you accurate results, you need to calibrate it by sighting something on the other boat whose height you know, e.g., the height of a boat's mast above the deck or the distance between its draft stripes. By calibrating the stadimeter, you can accurately measure how far away another boat is in feet or yards. If you don't have a measurement to calibrate the stadimeter by, you can use the instrument to tell you relative gains or losses.

3. If you want to measure the distance between your boat and another, you can use a sextant horizontally. Besides a sextant, you'll need a set of tables, a

calculator, and a crew member free to do all the math. In an ocean race this is good to do, because that one other boat in sight will be the only performance gauge you might have for days. But, just like a stadimeter, you can use your sextant without the tables and calculations to find out whether you are gaining or losing. You just won't know how many feet or yards you are gaining or losing. Both a stadimeter and a sextant will give you better readings the closer the competing boat is.

4. Big boats can use radar to figure out whether they are gaining or losing against other boats. The radar screen is set up like a bull's-eye, with your boat in the middle. By knowing the distance between the concentric circles on the screen, you can measure the distance to another boat's blip. By checking how far away his blip is, later you can find out how you are doing against him. Of course, the expense and the wind resistance of the radar dome tend to limit its use to large offshore racing yachts.

Exotic Gear for Monitoring the Fleet

When money is no object, Gary has come up with a shopping list of the latest high-tech gadgets for monitoring the fleet. Many of these were designed more for watching the Red Army than for racing boats.

"Gyro binoculars are the greatest thing I've seen on a sailboat for a tactician to use. They are available commercially to those willing to plunk down about $5,000—but then good standard binoculars are going to cost you nearly $1,000. Gyro binos are steadied by an internal gyroscope that runs off a battery; they'll stay fixed on an object being observed. The price of these will start falling soon.

"A night scope is a military device that you look through, which turns night into day. You can use it to identify boats, see who is on deck, and what sails they're flying—it's really wild.

"Next on the list is a laser rangefinder. It looks like a big pair of binoculars. It emits a laser beam that bounces back from the object being observed, and can be read by the rangefinder to tell you exactly how far away you are.

"High-tech stadimeters have an electronic hand-bearing compass built in. The readings from the two instruments are wired directly to a computer with a program that takes those readings and tells you whether you're ahead or behind. The program also uses the true wind direction from the instrument system. You can get the same results for less money by spending a few moments inputting the readings into a programmable calculator."

Controlling the Fleet

On the beat, gaining the "starboard tack advantage" is a powerful tactic for controlling your surrounding competitors. By being on the starboard side of a competitor, you ensure that whenever you come to a crossing situation with the other boat, you will have the right-of-way. Having the right-of-way puts you in a powerful position to slow your competitor. When he tacks to avoid you, he loses one to six boatlengths—depending on such factors as whether you are racing high-performance dinghies or heavy cruiser-racers, whether the wind is light or strong, and whether the water's surface is smooth or wavy. The beauty of the starboard tack advantage is that it lets you take the lead from the other boat. Even if you are slightly behind, and would not be able to cross the other boat, your competitor is required to tack to leeward of you or duck behind you to avoid risking a foul. If he is conservative, he might duck behind you, even though he could have crossed closely in front of you.

To avoid losing the starboard tack advantage after making a port tacker duck behind you, you'll have to tack to take his wind. When done right, not only are you on his wind, but he is also pinned so that he can't tack until he falls behind you. Tacking on your competitor as he tries to duck behind you is called a "slam-dunk." "It takes impeccable timing," says Tom. "You have to do it exactly right, because the defense against it is easy to master. You can lose your lead if you screw it up. The boat ducking you builds up a lot of speed when it falls off, and with that speed, it can go right through your lee if you don't come out of your tack with your speed up. If he gets through your lee, you'll be slowed by his backwind, leaving you no choice but to tack."

A slam-dunk is best attempted in flat seas with winds ranging from 10 to 18 knots. Start by bearing off slightly for speed. Tack when your competitor is pointing amidships about a boatlength away. With all the extra speed you've built, your boat will carry to windward during the tack, making it virtually impossible to foul for tacking too close (see figure 4.22.)

Wind direction

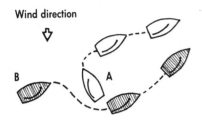

Figure 4.22 *To "Slam Dunk" Boat B, the crew of Boat A must tack well and not lose much speed. To develop speed, fall off slightly after the tack.*

If you don't feel comfortable doing a slam-dunk, you can protect your starboard tack advantage by delaying your tack for a boatlength or two after the port tacker ducks you. This way, while you are both going off on port tack, you will be close enough to prevent the other boat from tacking. If you misjudge your tack and wait too long, you can correct your mistake by cracking off your sails and driving down to your competitor. This move is especially handy when you get close to the starboard layline. Though, if you tack too far away while thinking you have pinned the other boat, you could be surprised if he tacks and hails "starboard."

One way you can control the fleet before the race even starts is to encourage boats to battle among themselves. Remind others how they are placed in the standings. If you're in fourth, and the boats in second and third are tied, sail over to them between races and say something like, "So you and Racer X are tied now. You guys are going to have a good race." It pays to take the standings out to the course, and then update them as races are completed. If you can get two boats to go after each other, they'll be less apt to pay attention to you.

Tacking Too Close

When you tack close to another boat, remember that you have the onus of proving to a protest committee that you did not tack *too* close. Rule 41 states that a boat either tacking or jibing must keep clear of a boat on a tack. Also, the boat on a tack does not have to begin altering its course to avoid you until you've completed your tack. When you're beating, you've completed your tack when you've borne away to a close-hauled course. Having your sails trimmed to the new course is not a requirement for completing your tack. If your boat and the protesting boat were on parallel courses before a protesting yacht began to alter its course, the rules could be on your side, since that suggests you had borne off all the way to a close-hauled course. Better yet, when you are given the chance to cross-examine the protesting skipper in a hearing, ask him to show the committee what position your boat and his were in just before he started altering his course. If he admits that the two boats were on a parallel course, he'll lose the case.

Ducking

Ducking a starboard tacker (also known as dipping) is an important moment in a race, because if you make a good dip, you can take the lead from the starboard tacker you go behind. When you come together the next time, he'll be on port and have to decide whether to duck you or not.

The common errors made while ducking another boat are postponing the decision too long, bearing off too much and too fast, or not easing the sails and then trimming them back again.

Here's how to avoid these errors and make a good duck. First, begin bearing off between three and five boatlengths away. Bearing off early is much better than bearing off late, because your course adjustment throughout the maneuver will be less; therefore, you won't lose much speed. The key to dipping well is not to lose speed, because if you slow down, you're asking to get slam-dunked. If you are roaring along from the speed you built up while reaching off to duck, the other skipper will find it harder to make the slam-dunk stick. To avoid oversteering, chase the stern of the other boat with your bow. If you head too low, your competitor has a better chance to tack on your wind. Don't forget to ease your sails out to increase your speed as you dip the other boat. By the time your bow passes behind its transom, your boat should be back up

Figure 4.23 *Make a minimal course change when dipping another boat by starting your turn early. Dipping at the last minute risks a collision with the other boat's mast.*

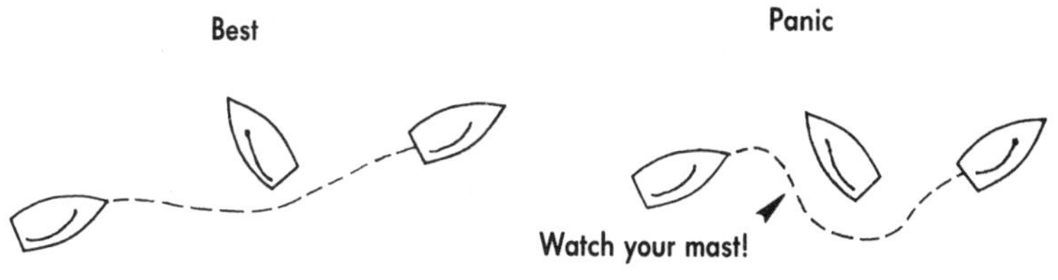

Best   Panic

Watch your mast!

▼

to a close-hauled course while only inches from the crossing boat's stern. If you're close enough and back on the wind as you pass behind the other boat, you can collect a bonus by taking advantage of the lift coming off the back of the crossing boat's mainsail. (See figure 4.23.)

One last piece of advice: Before making your final decision as to whether you are going to cross, tack, or duck, have your crew get the sheets out of the cleats and in somebody's hands. Too many collisions on the race course result from boats not being able to fall off because the mainsail hadn't been eased out or the running backstays weren't freed.

"Sailing 12-meters, Dennis and I worked out a system that produced ducks that were so close that we gave a lot of gray hairs to our competitors," Tom says. "I would go to leeward and call the situation. When it came time to duck, I'd steer with the leeward wheel. As the starboard tacker came into Dennis's view, he'd usually take over the steering duties with the windward wheel. A lot of times our bow missed the other boat by less than a yard. With Dennis being more aggressive than I, we'd usually get into a tug-of-war on the wheels while I was trying to bear off and Dennis was trying to head even closer to the other boat. We'd watch the videos of our races and not believe that there wasn't a collision."

Other defenses against getting tacked on when you duck a starboard tacker is to intimidate your opponent by hailing him not to tack too close. If he does tack, you have the right to tack simultaneously, and the rule book says that the boat on the left has to keep clear (Rule 41.4). The burden of keeping clear is on the boat tacking from starboard to port.

The bigger the boat you're sailing, the harder it will be to make a good dip, because you'll have a problem eyeballing distances. (Larger boats also travel at higher speeds.) A potentially dangerous situation occurs during a panic dip. Say you thought you could cross, but at the last minute you chickened out. Don't wait until the last minute to change your mind, or else you'll be committed to a collision one way or another. If you decide to dip at the last minute and make a radical turn, the two boats will be sailing almost gunwale-to-gunwale in opposite directions. In this case your mast could easily collide with the rig of the boat you are trying to duck. As you sail under him, you'll lose your wind and your boat will stand up straight, while the other boat, with clear air, will still be heeling. In a dinghy you can attempt to avoid this problem by using your crew weight to heel your boat to leeward. In most panic situations, your crew will not think quickly enough to jump to the leeward rail unless you've taught them what to do beforehand.

Corralling a Fleet

If you've sailed well and find yourself in the lead, here's how to draw up your insurance policy. Since it's impossible to cover boats on both sides of the course, your goal is to corral the fleet to one side of the course so that you get the same general shifts and velocity changes everyone else has. Let's say you come off the line on starboard to windward of a group of boats, where the right side of the course is favored. Because of human nature, the boats below you will be reluctant to tack and duck you, because that's an admission of being behind. Hence they won't tack until you do. Take advantage of their reluctance and drive them to the unfavored side of the course before tacking. Now when you tack, they'll all follow and you'll be in control.

A better way yet to corral the fleet is to force the group over to the long layline to the mark. (See figure 4.24.) The sooner you get them to the long

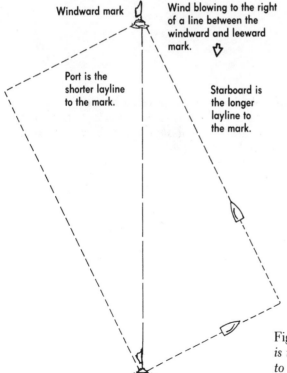

Windward mark

Wind blowing to the right of a line between the windward and leeward mark.

Port is the shorter layline to the mark.

Starboard is the longer layline to the mark.

Leeward mark

Figure 4.24 *When a windward mark is not perfectly upwind, you will have to spend more time sailing on one tack than the other.*

layline, the sooner you'll be in complete control. This is one of the few cases in sailboat racing in which it pays to get to the layline early. The leader of a race does not have sole proprietorship of the round-up method. You can employ this technique to stay ahead of a pack of boats around you, or just those that you need to beat to win the race or regatta.

To corral the fleet to one side of the course, you need to use loose and tight covers. Cover a boat loosely—not disturbing its wind—when the boat is going in the direction you want. (See figure 4.25.) Cover a boat tightly—slowing it down by disturbing or blocking its wind—when you want it to tack and sail in the opposite direction. (See figure 4.26.)

The proper way to implement a loose cover is to situate your boat anywhere from one to three boatlengths to windward of the lead boat in the group. Take care not to disturb his wind, or he will tack away in the direction you don't want him to. To ensure that you are not disturbing his wind, don't let your bow get in front of his mast. A loose cover is a strong weapon because it places you in an invincible position. With a loose cover you are leading the herd to

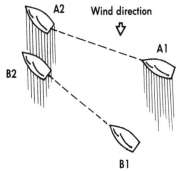

Figure 4.25 *Boat A has a loose cover on Boat B since it is not disturbing B's wind. If A decides to tack, it should reach across B's bow to slap on a tight cover, which would make B tack also.*

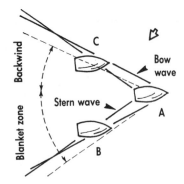

Figure 4.26 *A tight cover slows the trailing boat. Boat A is blanketing B and leebowing C, and both B and C are pitching in A's wake.*

the layline, where you will be firmly in control, and you are in a position to discipline any boat that gets out of line. If the wind shifts or if a boat to leeward gets going faster than you are, you can "slap him around some" by cracking off your sails and footing over the top of him. Once you block his wind with your sails, he'll slow down dramatically. If he tacks to get away, tack with him and hit him with another tight cover. When he tacks back, delay your tack so that you'll resume your loose cover. (See figure 4.27.)

The most damaging form of tight cover occurs when you blanket the other boat. Blanketing is positioning your boat to windward of another so that your sails block the wind from his. The closer together the two boats are, the less wind the leeward boat will get. If you're not sure you're blanketing the other boat, use your masthead fly or the direction in which your shroud telltales are streaming to check. When these gauges point directly at the boat to leeward, she's being blanketed. One of the things you have to ask yourself when trying to blanket someone is, "Am I actually slowing that boat down?" Know where your wind shadow is. Sailors often think they are on another boat's wind, but they're not.

Blanketing the other boat's wind is not the only way to apply a tight cover, even though it is the quickest way to force another boat to tack. A second way to slow a boat down and force it to tack is to use the backwind off your sails.

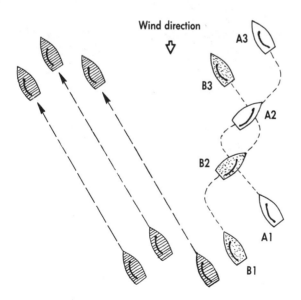

Figure 4.27 *Rounding up a stray: Boat A has a loose cover on the fleet to leeward. B attempts to escape, so A tacks to cover B tightly. Choking in A's blanket zone, B tacks back. To deny B a reason for trying to escape again, A tacks back to port in a position where it does not interfere with B's wind—a loose cover (position 3).*

You can gas another boat with backwind by camping on a boat's lee bow or by sailing directly in front of that boat. Your choice as to where to position your boat depends on your goals and the extent of your lead.

If blanketing another boat is the fastest way to force a boat to tack, tacking on an opponent's lee bow is the slowest. But to blanket a boat, you have to have a good lead so that you can cross the other boat, sail to windward of him, tack, and still have your stern ahead of his mast. If your lead is precarious while sailing on port tack, and you want a starboard tacker to keep away from the left side of the course, tack on his lee bow. If you are going to tack on someone's leeward bow, only tack in that position if you have a 100-percent chance of making the lee-bow work. If there is any chance that they'll sail over you, it's better to dip or tack early.

Once you've tacked into a lee-bow position, you'll have to work at forcing the windward boat to tack away. The starboard tacker will be able to sail in your backwind for quite a while unless you were able to tack within a boatlength of him. To maximize the effect of your bad air, pinch him off. (See figure 4.28) The first step to pinching off a boat is to get up to speed as quickly as possible by footing. When you are close-hauled at full speed, pick a time when you are sailing in relatively flat water, and head the boat up between 2 and 5 degrees above your optimal close-hauled course. When making this alteration of course, keep the boat flat and trim your sails as you head up. Keep heading high for one to three boatlengths—until you just begin to slow down. Then, never allowing your boat to go slower than your competitor's, head back down to your original course and re-trim your sails to build your speed back up. The

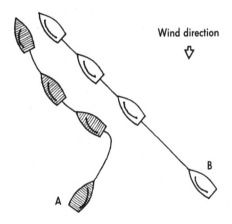

Wind direction

B

A

Figure 4.28 *When you can't tack on another boat's wind, use the backwind to windward to slow down a windward boat.*

heavier your boat, the more you will be able to head up with each bite to windward. Sailing higher than your optimum close-hauled course to make distance to windward, and then falling off lower than your optimum course to build your speed back is called "scalloping."

"When we sailed *Courageous*," says Gary, "we were able to alter our course from 3 to 10 degrees without losing more than one-tenth of a knot of speed. We would work our way up the windward leg, scalloping about one-half to one and one-half boatlengths at a bite, every two minutes. And I can say that Dennis Conner is the extreme in scalloping. Nobody scallops more than he does."

The windward boat's defense is to ease its sails and foot over the top of the leeward boat and blanket it. But the leeward boat has the advantage, since it picks the time it wants to "take a bite" to windward. If the crew loses its concentration and handles a wave poorly or mistrims the sails, the boat will slow down and the other boat will be able to take the offensive. This has been the real war of 12-meter sailing, and is one of the sterner tests of any two well-sailed, evenly matched boats.

If you want to tack on a boat's lee bow, but you're not sure you can do it without the other boat rolling over you, the conservative approach is to tack early—farther to leeward. If the other boat tries to roll over the top of you by falling off to gain speed, then fall off and match its course change and only come up when you are sailing as fast. Then you will be in a better position to pinch up toward the windward boat. Your backwind will eventually slow your competitor.

Once you get the boats you want corralled, your objective is to sail them over to the long layline to the mark. Once at the layline, they will only lose distance to you by sailing the rest of the leg in your backwind, or by making extra tacks to clear their air, which will make them lose distance while tacking, and lose time by overstanding the mark.

Covering vs. Wind-shift Phasing

Early on in a race or a series, you should be more concerned with getting ahead by playing the shifts than with covering specific boats. If you start covering someone before some of the major moves are made, it will inhibit your chance to make big gains. If you are covering someone, you could miss a big shift while making a covering tack. Also, if you are not paying attention and you tack on someone who is sailing in a header, all you'll do is force that boat over onto the lifted (i.e., advantageous) tack.

Even in a match race, you have to be careful not to tack on someone just for the sake of doing so. Understand the difference between wind-shift phasing and covering. Staying in phase means that you are always sailing on the tack that will get you closest to the mark. The boat that stays in phase the longest is the one that will get to the next mark the fastest. It's possible to tack on another boat all day while he gains on every tack because he's in phase more than you are.

A trailing boat can slowly but surely eat boatlengths out of a rival's lead by staying in phase and getting the leader out of phase. The final beat in the seventh race of the 1983 America's Cup is a perfect example. *Liberty* cut *Australia II*'s lead in half during that tacking duel. "They stopped paying attention to the wind shifts and just tried to tack on us," said Tom.

"I call this 'overcovering,' " says Gary, "but sometimes it's necessary. If you are making the final sprint toward the finish line, it is better to make extra tacks to maintain your position, even though you lose distance. Any other time on the racecourse, covering too closely usually spells disaster because you lose a lot of distance making all those tacks. At times like this, it's important to wait until your boat is sailing at full speed before executing a new tack.

"When this happens to me, I force myself to remember that the hardest thing to do in sailing is to pass another boat. While it's easy to catch up distance, it's hard to get around a boat. Therefore, pressure is on the boat behind."

The risk-to-reward ratio is the main theme in covering an opponent. When you are sailing against one other boat, either in a match race or where there is only one other boat you have to worry about in the standings, you'll cover it in almost any situation other than where you are on a good heading and you're crossing him. If the wind is oscillating and you're in phase, it's better to continue on. In such situations, it pays to have practiced the art of deducing leverage—that is, figuring out what kind of wind shift it would take to put the other boat ahead of you.

Inherent in knowing how to use leverage is knowing whether you are ahead or behind. "I go back to the starting-line idea," says Tom. "When the line is short, the other trailing boat is going to need a much bigger shift to pass you than if the boats were far apart. On a short line he might need a 20-degree shift to get by you, but if you let him get far away, he might only need a 1-degree shift. That's the best reason for covering."

There are many factors to take into account when deciding whether to tack on someone. You will need to know how much time you have to sail on each tack, whether you are in a lift or a header, how far behind he is, and whether the competition is gaining on you by tacking. If there is twice as much starboard tack to sail as port tack, then you should always tack on your competitor on the long tack to the mark, to maximize the amount of time you are on his wind.

A lift or a header also affects the decision to tack on another boat. Often you'll see the boat behind tack into a header in an attempt to draw the leader out of phase. Once the leader tacks on to the header, the trailing boat tacks back to the lifted tack. The leading boat will not tack before it gets up to speed, and may even delay for many boatlengths to avoid a tacking duel. The longer the leader stays on the knock, the less chance he has of remaining the leader. Therefore, when you're leading, and the trailing boat tacks into a header, don't tack immediately. Instead, stay on the lift. By delaying your covering tack, you'll stay in phase longer than the trailing boat. Your delay could also call his bluff; realizing you didn't fall for the bait, he might tack back and join you on the lift.

Be careful not to let him get too far to windward if you are sailing in a persistent shift, because his move to windward puts him on the inside of the shift. On the other hand, if you are sailing in an oscillating wind, by being ahead and to leeward you will get the next shift first and extend your lead greatly.

Another factor in deciding whether to tack on a boat is how far behind the other boat is, and how much of a shift he will need to get by you if you separate. If he needs a 50-degree shift to gain the lead, then it's not likely, but if he only needs a 3-degree shift, then it's not beyond the realm of possibility, so you should tack and stay with him.

The final factor is whether the other boat is gaining on you during the tacks. When one boat is gaining, you'll see the other boat break off and go to a loose cover to try to keep it's speed up.

Tacking Duels

A tacking duel occurs when a boat ahead decides it needs to cover, or when the boat behind needs to escape. Since tacking slows you down, don't get so wrapped up in beating one boat that you forget the rest of the fleet. If your lead is narrow, a tacking duel could drive both you and your competitor deep into the fleet. This may not matter if you need to finish ahead of a particular boat to win a regatta. But if you can't afford to lose to other boats, perhaps a better option would be to apply a loose cover on the one boat you are trying to control. This way you will stay between him and the wind, and since you won't be disturbing his wind, he will be less intent on trying to escape.

On the subject of waging a tacking duel, Tom says, "We learned in America's Cup sailing that if you're the trailing boat in a tacking duel, you can make a lot of distance by tacking in the leader's bad air. Instead of tacking immediately when somebody tacks on your wind, wait until his wind shadow actually gets to you. By so doing, you will be able to tack without losing as much distance, because you will cut down on the windage created as your boat goes through the eye of the wind with its sails luffing. As soon as you come out on the new tack, you are in clear air again. You'll want to avoid sailing into the other boat's wake, because sailing through his chopped-up water will slow you down."

When you're the lead boat in a tacking duel, you want to stay in phase with the other boat and with the wind. If you can be up to speed at the same moment when your opponent comes up to speed, and tack every time he does, while staying on his wind, then you are perfectly in phase. But if the boat behind tacks before the lead boat is up to speed, and the leading boat doesn't tack, then the leader is out of phase.

Remember that the boat behind is constantly trying to get the leader out of phase. The most obvious way for the trailing boat to get the leader out of phase is by tacking into a header. That way the leading boat tacks to cover and the trailing boat immediately tacks back. The leading boat usually will not tack until he's built up his speed a little. As the leading boat is building speed, the trailing boat is spending more time on the lifted tack. If the trailing boat keeps doing that, eventually he'll gain. Or maybe the leader won't realize he's tacked into a header, and he'll let the trailing boat go. So not only does the tactician have to stay ahead of the other boat through tacking, but he also has to do it by staying in phase with the wind shifts.

False Tacks

The false or fake tack is another move that can be used by the leading or trailing boat to get an opponent out of phase in a tacking duel. "A false tack is perhaps best used when you are ahead," Tom says. "To ensure that the other boat tacks while you're in the midst of your tack, come in and plant a tack right where you interfere with the other guy's wind. Tack slowly so that he finishes his tack before you do. Once he's falling off onto the new tack, fall off to your original tack, and you'll be right on top of your opponent. Now you're perfectly in phase. You are on the lifted tack, with your opponent pinned below you." (See figure 4.29.)

The trailing boat can use the false tack to get clear air. During your tacking duel, try to standardize all your moves so that you can persuade the other boat to react reflexively, like one of Pavlov's dogs. Advertise your pre-tacking moves. The time for your false tack is when the other boat starts tacking with you. When you are on the lifted tack and the other boat is on your wind, start to tack, but hold your boat into the wind or a little past head-to-wind in the middle of your tack. If you trained him well, he'll tack onto the knocked tack and you can fall back onto the lifted tack.

Since making a fake tack work is difficult, a simpler way to get the other boat out of phase or off your wind is to do a half-tack. When you start your tack, sail through the wind, fill your jib on the new tack, but don't bear all the way off onto your new course. Once your jib just fills on the new tack,

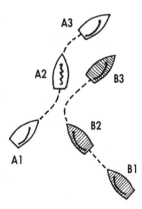

Figure 4.29 *In order to get on the same tack and cover Boat B, Boat A uses a fake tack.*

tack right back to your orginal course. The half-tack gets its name from the fact that you don't swing the boat all the way onto the new tack. For instance, say your boat normally tacks through 90 degrees; during a half-tack you'd only turn the boat through 70 degrees before tacking back to your original course.

The half-tack gets the leading boat out of phase with you, since, in a tacking duel, if the trailing boat tacks first, the leading boat will generally tack faster to catch up. By spinning faster, the leading boat will be forced to bear off more on the new tack to regain speed. Once the leading boat tacks to cover, start tacking back immediately. The advantage of a half-tack is that you don't lose as much distance as you would in a false tack, since you don't hold your boat into the wind with your sails luffing. Where the other boat may delay its covering to protect against a fake tack, the half-tack is a more convincing trick, since the the other boat will actually see your crew trimming the sails on the new tack. But as soon as the leader takes the bait and tacks to cover, tack back. (See figure 4.30.) The trick is not to fall off all the way onto the new tack, since you'll be tacking back right away. The less you have to turn the boat in this process, the less speed you'll lose. In comparison, if the leading boat tacks too fast, it will have to bear off more on the new tack to get up speed.

One of the basic ways to get free of a boat covering you is to avoid telegraphing your tack. The simplest way for your opponent to discern your plan is to watch your crew get in position. On a dinghy, the crew will come in off the trapeze or get up from hiking, and on big boats normally half the crew will get off the rail up to a minute before the tack. To keep the element of

Wind direction

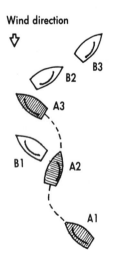

Figure 4.30 *Boats A and B are in a tacking duel. Boat A shakes free from Boat B by using the half tack. Notice the course difference between A and B in position 2 even though they are both on starboard tack. B is falling off to build speed after the tack, while A is ready to tack back to starboard.*

surprise, make sure your crew does not move a muscle until the helm swings to leeward. This way you will complete your tack and be up to speed by the time the other boat's crew is ready to tack. Keeping your crew on the rail not only masks your intentions, but is also a lot faster, since as soon as the crew stops hiking, the boat heels over and gains leeway.

If you want to tack, but are being pinned by a boat right on your windward quarter and haven't been able to pinch him off, then use your rights as the leeward boat and luff him head-to-wind and hold him there. Under the rules, when luffing another boat, you cannot go past head-to-wind. The windward boat must do whatever he can to keep clear. Nine times out of ten, if the boats are close together during a sharp luff, the windward boat will go past head-to-wind to keep clear. When that happens, the windward boats usually complete the tack instead of trying to fall back onto the previous tack. If the windward boat doesn't tack immediately, he'll tack when his speed starts to deteriorate, because he's responsible for keeping clear.

In the second race of the controversial 1988 America's Cup, the 132-foot *New Zealand* twice forced the 60-foot catamaran *Stars & Stripes* to tack by luffing head-to-wind. "They luffed us," says Tom, "and then their momentum allowed them to keep going into the wind. Our boat was much lighter and didn't have the momentum to keep going, so we had to tack off."

Just as a wise prison guard is always on the lookout for escape plans hatched by crafty prisoners, the leading boat has to be alert to tricks from a trailing boat. David Dellenbaugh, a champion sailor, admitted to coming close to getting fouled out by a boat faking a tack. "We were to leeward and ahead, but we couldn't tack onto a lift because we couldn't get across the starboard

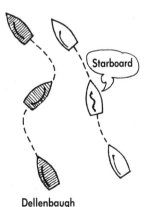

Dellenbaugh

Figure 4.31 *Impatient to get the better side of the course, champion sailor David Dellenbaugh tacked as soon as the other boat started to tack. But the other boat didn't tack, and instead surprised Dave by yelling "Starboard" forcing Dave to do a panic tack.*

tacker on our hip. I pinched as high as I could to force the other guy to tack. We were so intent on getting onto the lift that when he started to tack, we went with him. Our elation turned to panic when we heard a yell of 'Starboard!' He saw we were tacking, so he stopped turning before he got to head-to-wind. Only our best crash tack kept us out of a protest. He knew we wanted to get on that lift badly, so he tried to foul us out with a false tack. Now I'm searching for a situation to use it." (See figure 4.31.)

If you suspect that a competitor is going to do a false tack or a half-tack, or that there is a chance that a competitor is going to try to fake you out, make sure that the tactician of your boat keeps his eyes on the action aboard the other boat. What you want to avoid at all cost is a double or triple tack. Once you commit to making a maneuver—either way—it's better to follow through than to keep going back and forth.

When all else fails, you can use a tacking duel as a desperation tactic to force any number of errors or breakdowns on your competitor. In the heat of a frenetic tacking duel, sheets can get wrapped around winches, sails can rip after being yanked across the shrouds and mast, a skipper can drop the tiller, an override can develop on the running backstay winch, or the other crew can just tire of tacking and let you go.

Dennis Conner was desperate to get around *Australia II* on the final leg of the final race of the 1983 America's Cup. Conner wrote in his book *Comeback*, "After we both rounded the windward mark and bore upwind toward the finish line, we said, 'Right, we'll tack them down,' and we did. There were 47 tacks on that last leg, and a lot of times I went head-to-wind and got Bertrand all screwed up. At the end, I took him over into the spectator fleet. I thought I might get lucky and someone might run him down!"

Once you are in control of another boat, you can expand your lead by steering the other boat to the wrong side of the course or into other boats' bad air. Tom remembers how *Stars & Stripes '87* slowed *Kookaburra III* down with the slop-chop from the spectator fleet during the first race of the 1987 America's Cup. "It was the first race of the series, and there were thousands of boats on the course watching. Expectations ran high among the spectators, but the wind velocity was uncharacteristically low. Because of a 30-degree shift to the left, we had to sail farther to the right. Unfortunately for Iain Murray and the crew of *Kookaburra*, the spectator fleet did not shift; they and all the wash they kicked up were on the old starboard-tack layline, which meant they were on the course instead of clear to the side. If Murray tacked to starboard, we would have been on top of him with a tight cover, and if he kept going on port, he was slowed by the spectator boats. And that's just what happened. We ruthlessly sailed him into the wake of the spectator fleet, which killed him in the light air.

"Iain got even with us for that move two years later. A match-race series, referred to as a rematch between Dennis and Iain, was sailed in 12-meters in Sydney Harbor in January of 1989. Iain took the lead in the sixth race when we had to tack around Alan Bond's monster motor yacht, anchored in the middle of the first beat. He sailed us over toward Bond's boat, and we had to tack to get around it while he made it around the other side without tacking. Those two extra tacks cost us the lead."

One of the rules in the sailing instructions of the Congressional Cup match-racing series is that all spectator boats must stay stationary when they are in the vicinity of the starting area. This way, the spectator boats become obstructions that the starters can use as picks to scrape off a competitor. As long as there is room to maneuver, it doesn't matter where the spectator boats are. The competitors can deal with them as long as they can count on the spectator boats not moving.

Rule 43: Hailing for Room to Tack at Obstructions When Close-Hauled

The gist of Rule 43.1 is that when two boats are beating on the same tack, and the boat to leeward or clear ahead needs to tack to avoid an obstruction, but can't tack without hitting the boat to windward or clear astern, he can hail for room to tack. An obstruction could be a right-of-way boat, an anchored boat, a dock, a shoal, or a ship going through the course.

Rule 43.1 covers many scenarios. The most common of these occurs when two port tackers are on a collision course with a starboard tacker. The rule specifically decrees that the boat to leeward or clear ahead makes the decision on how to avoid the collision. Even though the windward boat might want to duck the starboard boat, the rule gives the choice to the leeward boat, which can decide to duck or tack. If the leeward boat ducks the starboard tacker, it has to bear off enough to give room to the windward boat to duck too.

A second scenario occurs when two close-hauled boats approach an anchored boat. If the leeward boat can pass the obstruction without making a substantial alteration of course, it cannot hail for room to tack. This is so even if the leeward boat must go below the anchored boat while the windward boat goes above it. USYRU Senior Certified Judge David Perry, in his book *Understanding the Yacht Racing Rules Through 1992*, interprets "a substantial alteration of course" to be a turn of 10 degrees or more. In his opinion, if the leeward boat has to bear off more than 10 degrees to clear the obstruction, it can hail for room to tack.

The skipper of the windward boat must tack if the leeward boat calls for room to tack, even if he feels the skipper of the leeward boat could go to leeward of the obstruction by making a minor alteration of course. Instead of denying the leeward boat room to tack, his only option is to protest the leeward boat.

A third scenario is provided by two close-hauled boats approaching an obstruction like a dock, a seawall, or a shoal. If the leeward boat can tack and then immediately dip the windward boat without hitting it, the leeward boat is not entitled to hail for obstruction room. (See figure 4.32.) The rule is only designed for safety, not for preserving or creating an advantage. Only when left with the choice of running aground or hitting the windward boat can the leeward boat hail for room.

Under Rule 43.2, the windward boat or the boat clear astern (the hailed boat) must tack as soon as it can, in which case the hailing boat must tack at the same time. (See figure 4.33A.) If the boat hailing for room delays its tack,

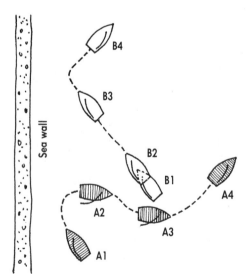

Figure 4.32 *Boat A is not entitled to obstruction room since she can tack and then duck Boat B.*

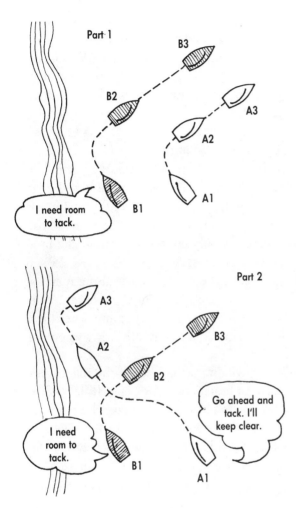

Figure 4.33 *When Boat B hails for room to tack, Boat A must tack (Part 1) or A can respond by telling B to tack. If A tells B to tack, then A must keep clear of B (Part 2).*

even for a moment, in an attempt to get clear air, it has infringed the rule and is subject to protest. The second option that the hailed boat has under Rule 43.2 is to respond to the hail by yelling back words to the effect of "You tack." After the hailed yacht responds with "You tack," the hailing boat must tack immediately and the hailed boat must give the hailing boat room to tack. (See figure 4.33B.) The new provision in this rule (43.2 [b] [iii]) states, "The onus of satisfying the protest committee that she gave sufficient room shall lie on the hailed yacht that replied 'You tack.' "

Burdened with the onus of proof, the skipper of a hailed boat is in a tough position even though Rule 42.1 states that a hailing boat is only entitled to obstruction room when it can't tack without colliding with the hailed boat. As long as there is no collision, the protest committee should rule in favor of the hailed boat. Even if the hailing boat testifies to the effect that, "When the outside boat yelled 'You tack,' I tacked, and I would have hit him if I hadn't radically altered my course and borne off." This testimony would prove that the hailing boat had room to tack and avoid a collision. But if there is a collision, the hailed boat had better have a witness to say that the hailing boat made no attempt to duck behind the hailed boat after it tacked.

Since the rule is intended to promote safety, the hailed boat must either tack or give room to the hailing boat to tack. The skipper of the hailed boat is not allowed to argue with the skipper of the hailing boat over the legitimacy of the call. If the skipper of the hailed boat feels strongly that the hailing boat called for room when it wasn't needed, his only option is to follow the procedures for filing a protest.

Rule 43.3 deals with room to tack when the obstruction is also a mark of the course. Rule 43.3(a) specifically denies tacking room to a leeward boat that can't make it around a starting mark that is an obstruction, when that mark is surrounded by navigable water. This situation usually arises when the leeward end of the line is a boat.

Rule 43.3(b) covers situations at the windward mark when the mark is an obstruction such as an anchored boat or a beacon on a rock pile. Rule 43.3(b) says that a leeward boat can not hail for room to tack to make the mark, if the windward boat is fetching the mark. (See figure 4.34.) In the name of safety, the rule goes on to say if the leeward boat gets pinned between the windward boat and the obstruction, the leeward boat can hail for room a second time, but at that point the leeward boat is committing a foul. As soon

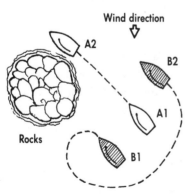

Figure 4.34 *Under Rule 43.3(b) if Boat A can make it around the obstruction without tacking, it does not have to give Boat B room to tack around the mark. B must circle around and try again.*

as the windward boat can, it must tack and give room, but "after receiving room, the hailing yacht shall either retire immediately or exonerate herself by accepting an alternative penalty when so prescribed in the sailing instructions," says Rule 43.3(b). (See figure 4.35.)

Rule 43.3(c) prescribes a penalty for a hailed windward boat that refuses to give a hailing boat room to tack around an obstruction. Rule 43.3(b) allows the hailed boat to ignore a hailing boat if the hailed boat is fetching the mark, which is also an obstruction. But 43.3(c) states, "When, after having refused to respond to a hail under rule 43.3(b), the hailed yacht fails to fetch, she shall retire immediately or exonerate herself by accepting an alternative penalty when so prescribed in the sailing instructions."

Crossing Situations

Whenever you cross or get crossed by another boat on the beat, you have a chance to make a gain. But before you decide how you'll react, you must think like a chess player and visualize the moves that will result from your choice. Those who simply strut down the course, yelling "Starboard!" at every port tacker that comes into view, or those port tackers who automatically tack on the lee bow of every starboard tacker they come across, are ignoring options that could give them the lead.

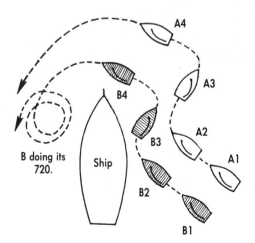

Figure 4.35 *In position 1, Boat B hails for room to tack around the windward mark, which is also an obstruction. Boat A refuses B's hail saying that it is fetching the mark. In position 2, B becomes pinned between the mark and Boat A. At this point A must tack and give room to B for safety's sake, but B has committed a foul.*

▼

In any crossing situation your goal should be to come out on the favored tack and to be between the other boat and the favored side of the course. The favored side is where the next wind shift will come from. Near the windward mark, the favored side is to the right of the the other boat, so that you will have the starboard tack advantage.

Now let's go through some crossing situations and examine how you can achieve your goal of getting control of the other boat. In the first situation, you are on starboard and want to keep going to the left because you're on a lift and you are expecting the wind to oscillate. A port tacker comes into view, but he's not far enough ahead to cross cleanly. If he tried to cross, you'd probably hit him toward his stern. In this case it's actually better to waive your starboard tack rights. By waiving him across, you will have clear air to pursue the next shift, and he will be sailing off to the wrong side of the course. If you forced him to tack, he'd be on your lee bow.

When yelling "Go ahead," or "You can make it," to another boat, make sure he understands you by waving your hand to indicate that he is clear to cross. To reduce the possibility of confusion, see that the tactician is the only person communicating with the other boat. The worst thing would be for some anxious crew member to yell "Starboard" when the tactician wanted the port tacker to cross.

"It's refreshing that at the highest level of the sport of sailing there is a strong code of honor, although this is not always true. Usually, in the grand prix circuit, close crossing situations are frequent. And if you want to tag someone out by bending your course, it is easy to do. One occasion when I was on port, crossing in front of a starboard tacker, stands out in my memory over all the rest. Paul Cayard was steering *Il Moro di Venezia* at a maxi regatta in St. Thomas in 1988, and I was calling tactics on *Matador*. We just made it across Cayard, and instead of yelling protest, he gave a wave and said, 'You made it.' Somehow you remember those situations and become more lenient as the regatta goes on. The moral of the story is that it is often better to give a little room instead of forcing an issue, to keep everyone out of the protest room."

If the port tacker looks as if it's going to lee-bow you, fall off and ease out your sails a touch. By heading toward it, you will force the boat to tack early. Once the port tacker tacks to starboard, trim in and head up to avoid his backwind.

Let's jump on the port-tacking boat for the next example. The port tacker's goal here is to force the starboard tacker to tack away to the unfavored right side of the course, or to tack early himself and beat the starboard tacker to the next oscillation.

As a port tacker, the move that will put you farthest ahead is to tack closely on the starboard tacker's lee bow, so that your backwind forces him to tack away. Even if you can cross the starboard tacker, it's in your interest to tack on the starboard tacker's wind so that you'll be heading toward the next shift, and he'll have to tack away. Don't be afraid to be a wolf in sheep's clothing. If a starboard tacker bears off to let you cross, take advantage of his generosity by slam-dunking him.

If you realize that you won't be able to cross the starboard boat and that he's too far ahead for you to tack on his lee bow and give him bad air, then it's best to tack three or four boatlengths to leeward of him. By tacking early, you will get to the next shift first, and if the shift doesn't materialize, you will have enough space to tack and duck the starboard tacker whenever you want to. If you tack any closer to him, you will be unable to tack until he does. (See figure 4.36.)

Now let's go to a second crossing situation. In this case you're on starboard and you want to protect the right side. Currently you're the most windward boat in the fleet, while the wind is persistently shifting to the right. Your goal is to remain on the inside of the shift.

Battle stations. A port tacker is approaching. If he doesn't tack when you yell "Starboard," fall off a little and aim at him so that he'll tack early. Once he tacks, head back up to course and re-trim your sails. With the extra speed gained from footing toward him, you should be able to ride over him if he tacks closely. As long as you stay clear of his backwind, you've got him in your control. He will not be able to tack back to port until you do.

If someone is able to tack on your lee bow, tack to port before he starts to

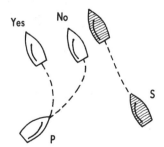

Figure 4.36 *A port tacker that can't slow a starboard boat by tacking on its leebow should preserve its tactical options by tacking two or three boatlengths to leeward of the starboard boat.*

slow you down with backwind. Even though he forced you to tack, you are retaining your starboard tack advantage for your next crossing situation with him, and you are sailing farther to the inside of the persistent shift.

If a port tacker ducks you and tries to get to the favored right side of the course, slam-dunk him and force him back to the left side of the course.

If the port tacker can cross you, then tack on his lee bow, or if he is too far ahead for you to hurt him with your backwind, tack before he crosses your course. By doing so, you will be in a position to gain, as port tack is persistently headed. (Remember, in this example you are protecting the right side because of a persistent shift to the right.) As both of you get headed, you will be in a better position to pinch him off. (See figure 4.37.)

Just as in playing chess against a computer, the difficulty level is set by how much time you give the computer to think of all the moves that can result from its choice, time is also the key to making the best decision in a crossing situation. The sooner you see a boat approaching, the more time you will have to consider the ramifications of each choice. Without time to think, you'll yell "Starboard" and end up getting lee-bowed and forced to the wrong

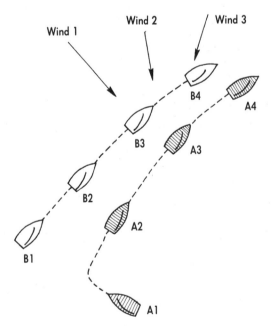

Figure 4.37 *Expecting a shift to the right, Boat A protects the right side of the course by tacking to leeward of B before B crosses. In position 1, B is clearly ahead of A, but as the wind shifts, A takes the lead by position 4.*

side of the course. Or you'll end up doing a panic tack, only to get pinned to the wrong side of the course by a starboard tacker who refuses to tack.

Comeback Tactics

You can never minimize your losses, but you can minimize further losses. Accept your trailing position and then figure out how to get back in the race. When behind, don't be overly concerned with the boats around you. Since you, as well as the boats nearby, are already behind the leaders, none of you has much to gain from jousting. All of you have to make up distance, and the way to do it is by concentrating on speed and on catching the next wind shift. Getting back in phase with the wind shifts is critical. At times, particularly in shifty air, it is better to sail on a lift and be in another boat's backwind than to tack off of a header in search of clear air.

The key element in a comeback is your attitude. If you're behind, make the rest of the race a game and, just for the fun of it, see how well you can do. If a trophy is out of the picture, turn the rest of the race into a learning experience. If you can't shake off your depression and grumpiness, you might as well sail off course instead of making life miserable for you and your crew. Now that you're starting a new race, hold a new crew meeting as you sail along. Go over your goals for the rest of the race; their spirits as well as yours will need rejuvenation. Falling behind happens to all of us, but the best sailors can work themselves out of a depression by relaxing and concentrating intently.

Sailboat races are often won by eliminating mistakes, so learn how not to do what you did wrong. If your strategy for the race was all wrong, look around and figure out why the leader's game plan worked. Was current more or less of a factor than you thought? How was the wind affected as it came over the shore? What wind-shift pattern is in? Is your boatspeed a problem? Have you checked your sail trim and settings? Once you've figured out a new strategic game plan for the rest of the beat, start the race over in your mind and see how well you can sail against the boats around you. If you are in last place by the time you get your wits back, see how many boats you can catch.

"If you haven't lost it all," says Tom, "but have only lost a few critical boats, the best advice is to learn patience. Instead of trying a low-percentage maneuver to regain the lead in one swoop, stalk your prey. Tire him out, force him to make a mistake, and collect all the crumbs he lets fall off the table. Most of the time you'll get your chance."

When you are forced to take chances, weigh the risk-to-reward factor carefully. Assess what it will mean to your standing in the regatta or series to be farther behind if your gamble doesn't pan out. How many boats can you afford to lose before you drop another place? If there are ten points between you and the third-place boat and only one point between you and the first-place boat, then it's clear you can take a pretty risky flier.

When crossing the course on one long tack, your potential for much gain is minimal. Minimize future losses by working to the favored side in small increments. For example, if you are stuck on the outside of a persistent shift on the right side of the course, tack off of starboard as soon as your compass heading goes down to a wind direction that is average or even sightly lifted. Once on port, don't tack to starboard unless your compass tells you that you've reached a new low heading.

Working back across a large fleet is more difficult. "When you're 'sailing in the muck,' as I call being caught in a fleet," says Tom, "you may not be able to sail the shifts the way you want. You will have to pick areas where you can tack with the least boats on your wind. When trying to get around a tightly packed group of boats, use the same strategy you would if the group were one boat—that is, tack ahead and to leeward of a group if you are expecting a header, or duck the group and tack to windward of them if you are expecting a lift. Be especially careful of tacking in bad wind around a clump, because you might be prevented by the other boats from tacking to clear your air."

When people are confident in their speed, they tend to accept their loss as soon as they realize that the other side is paying. So they'll tack and get over to that side and accept a three-boatlength loss. Those who think they are slow are more apt to continue in the same direction, even though they realize that the boats on the other side of the course have gained. They count on the wind shifting in their favor—or "catching the golden ring," as Halsey Herreshoff used to say.

Avoiding the Starboard-Tack Parade

In any kind of wind—oscillating, persistently shifting, or steady—getting to the laylines prematurely often creates a no-win situation. As soon as you get to a layline, shifts will only hurt you and help the boats not on the layline.

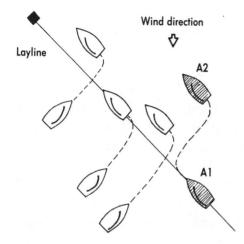

Wind direction

Layline

A2

A1

Figure 4.38 *Boat A got on the starboard layline early and as boats tack in front, A is forced to make extra tacks above the layline to get clear air.*

A header requires you to make another tack or two to get around the mark, and a lift makes you overstand while shortening the distance to the mark for your competition. If the wind is fairly steady and you are not the lead boat, others will tack in front of you and smother you with backwind—worst of all, they could blanket you and force you to make two more tacks. (See figure 4.38.) Even those two extra tacks past the layline give you no guarantee of clear air. The closer to the mark, the wider the layline gets as more boats pile into the same area. This line of boats is referred to as the "starboard-tack parade."

In big fleets, the starboard-tack parade becomes a wall of boats that creates some devastating effects on the wind and water. In the layline parade, you are slowed down because the water is choppy and confused from the boats' wakes, while backwind is practically unavoidable. Also, if the fleet is packed together, the wind will lift off the water and go over the parade.

Approaching the Windward Mark

When approaching a windward mark that is to be rounded to port, the fleet is generally organized on starboard tack, sailing the layline and bearing off as they round. With so many boats packed together and going slowly from each other's backwind and wakes, passing packs of boats is easy with a good approach to the mark. For the same reason, a bad approach can cost you many places. If you are not leading the fleet, avoiding the starboard-tack parade is tough.

"I commit to my final approach as late as possible," Tom says. "It adds a bit of risk, but if you have to duck a bunch of boats to get in the starboard-layline parade, it's like admitting guilt that you're back in the fleet. If I have to do it, I wait as long as I can." Gary, on the other hand, says, "Make your final tack onto the starboard layline 10 to 15 boatlengths from the mark. This way you will be close enough to the mark to judge the layline accurately, you will have time to set up for the spinnaker set, and even if you have to sail in backwind, it won't be for long. Use your tacking lines to know when to make the final tack."

In most cases it's better to make your final approach to the windward mark on starboard tack because you have the right-of-way; you do not have to give buoy room to boats trying to round on port tack; and your crew will have time to set up the spinnaker for a bear-away set.

Unless you are clearly in the lead or there are no other boats around, it pays to overstand the mark by one to one and a half boatlengths. For the little bit of extra distance you sail, you get a lot of insurance. Most sailors tend to undershoot the mark, hence they have to pinch to get around it. By overstanding, you'll be able to drive over the top of those who misjudged the layline. You'll also be insured against a wind shift. If an unexpected header appears, you will be able to bear off and still make the mark, and if an unexpected lift materializes, you will be able to reach down to the mark with speed and get over those who got lifted to the mark.

"One of the greatest moments using this trick came while racing the maxi boat *Matador* in 1987 during a regatta in Palma de Majorca," says Gary. "It had been a particularly close race between *Kialoa, Boomerang, Ondine,* and *Matador* approaching the windward mark. I had *Matador* make my standard final tack with one-half boatlength to spare over the layline. Two of the maxis had tacked earlier just to leeward, but both were in trouble because they were not fetching the mark. A third boat dipped behind these two and tacked just to windward of them, but to leeward of me. With two boatlengths to go before the mark, we had *Matador* sailing at 12 knots while the other boats were pinched up and only sailing about seven. We were able to roll over top, exit with a perfect spinnaker set, and ended up five boatlengths ahead of the crowd. It was a huge morale boost for our crew to be caught in the thick of a lot of traffic and end up comfortably in the lead. The strength behind the maneuver was sailing a few extra seconds before making the final tack on the layline."

In light air and adverse current, you must overstand not only to get out of bad air, but to ensure that you won't be swept into the mark. If there is a boat already hung up on the mark, overstand by at least two boatlengths.

Of course, the ideal position is to be the first boat on starboard, leading the fleet around the windward mark. If you're not, judging the right approach must be based on what oscillation the wind is in and how much of it there is, what the current is doing, how rough the surface of the water is, and whether you'll have a chance to shoot the mark from downwind of it. Ask yourself this question: Is it better to sail beyond the parade and go above the layline a bit to miss the bad air, or is it better to approach on port and try to find a spot to tack near the mark? Either way, you are avoiding turbulent wind from other boats' sails.

If the wind is oscillating, one of the criteria for deciding whether to tack above or below the parade is which shift you are in if the wind is oscillating. Always approach the mark on the favored tack, so that on your final approach you will gain distance over boats sailing on a header. If you are in a left shift—lifted on port tack—tack below the parade in hopes that the wind will go back to the right, so that when you tack onto starboard you may actually end up laying the mark. Don't do this too close to the mark, unless the wind shifts are coming in very frequently.

If you are in a right shift, sail to windward of the parade and tack. Even if the wind does not shift back, you will have clear air to the mark, because boats will tack below you instead of crossing in front of you. If the wind heads you while on starboard, you will be able to fall off and sail for the mark with speed, while those in the parade will probably be pinching and going slowly.

If an oscillation to the left occurs after many boats are already lined up in the starboard-tack parade, your best approach is on port tack. Most likely they did not anticipate the shift and many are going slowly, pinching to make the mark. Your faster speed will allow you to pick a hole to sail through or to tack into. The port approach to a windward mark of a port-triangle won't work when there are a lot of boats going down the reach. They will create a wall and block your wind.

The struggle between tacking away from the right direction and paying the price of sailing in dirty air in order to go the right direction is always a hard one for a tactician. When you are on a windward mark layline and in dirty air, you have to make a judgment based on how far from the mark you are. It's better to make two quick tacks to get some clear air when the boat in front of you has a large mainsail roach, which creates an inordinate amount of backwind to windward. It's also a good idea to tack away if a bigger boat is in front of you. Even if you overstand the mark after your two tacks, by reaching in to the mark with good speed, you'll save some of the time you lost.

Misjudged the Layline?

If you get a major header near the mark, you can shoot the mark—that is, luff into the wind and count on your momentum to carry you up to and around the mark. You can practice shooting into the wind before a race to get an idea how much carry your boat has. Generally, a centerboard boat will carry for a boatlength before losing so much speed that she will become unmaneuverable. Keel boats can go between two and four boatlengths into the wind. The heavier your boat, the more way it will carry when the sails are not drawing.

When practicing, you learn that your boat will shoot farther in smooth water. To increase the distance your boat will carry into the wind, make your turn slowly. When you jam your rudder over, your boat slows down. Also, let the jib sheet go altogether to prevent it from backwinding, which will push you backwards. If you know you are going to shoot the mark, try to get your boat up to full speed beforehand.

The don'ts of shooting a mark include the following: Don't plan to approach on port tack, and then luff around the mark; your boat will not have enough speed. Don't shoot in strong winds, because the wind resistance of the luffing sails will counteract the boat's momentum quickly. Don't try to shoot in adverse current or in waves; you'll lose far more by doing a 720 for hitting the mark than you would by making two extra tacks to get around the mark cleanly.

If you misjudge the mark and realize that you won't be able to get around, bail out and tack quickly. The only way to make the mark might involve ducking starboard tackers; if so, do it. The earlier you admit to the problem and correct it, the less traffic you'll have to pick your way through. If, on the other hand, you find yourself overstanding by too much, reach down to the layline immediately to prevent others from lee-bowing you. Once on the layline, you'll force port tackers to take your stern.

Other Approaches

If you've got a boat on your weather hip, you should do everything you can to squeeze him off and slow him down, since when you round the mark you won't want him within striking distance of your wind. To slow a boat to windward, overtrim your mainsail, hooking your battens to windward, which will channel disturbed air to windward. On a dinghy, you can heel your boat to windward for a short period to get even more backwind to windward. Be cautious when heeling to windward, because your boat will sideslip to leeward if you lose too much speed. Tom feels that hooking the leech on a high-aspect main is less effective than looking the leech on a low-aspect main at slowing a boat to windward, because the tall, narrow sail produces less vortices. If overtrimming doesn't work fast enough, work up and pinch him off. He probably won't tack away, no matter how much gas you give him, if both of you are above the layline already, but you will be able to make some serious distance on him. (See figure 4.39.)

If you're coming into the windward mark after overstanding and have a boat overlapped to windward, don't fall off and sail to the mark until you are one to two boatlengths away from the mark. Sail as high as possible to give the boat to windward as much bad air as you can. Then fall off and head for the mark. He'll be left behind, wallowing in bad air, allowing you to sail the next leg of the course without having to alter your course to fend off a boat that is trying to take your wind or pass you.

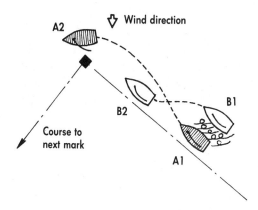

Figure 4.39 *For a good getaway after rounding the windward mark, keep boats from rounding with you. For example, Boat A slows B with backwind by overtrimming its mainsail. On a dinghy you can heel your boat to windward to channel even more backwind to windward.*

You'll also want to dispose of boats to leeward of you, to prevent them from claiming room at the mark. Drive off and use the extra speed gained from footing to get in a blanketing position. Go off until you are barely making the mark.

If you've tried everything and the boat to leeward is still hanging on to an overlap, then it's time to play dirty—that is, give him the dirtiest air possible. By flogging the mainsail on a masthead rig, or flogging the jib on a fractional rig, you will chop up the wind so well that he'll be out the back door in moments. Try not to catch too many bugs in your teeth as you grin back at your "friend."

One way to get in front of another boat is to resort to a little trickery. If you're not laying the mark while on starboard tack, and a port tacker crosses in front of you, make it appear that you are making the mark to induce him to tack on your lee bow. If he falls for the bait and tacks on your lee bow, you should immediately tack to port and sail over to the starboard layline. Tricking him into tacking shy of the layline will not only slow him down while he makes two extra tacks, but the next time you come together, you'll have the starboard tack advantage. To create the appearance that you are laying the mark, heel your boat slightly to make it look as if it's pointing higher than it actually is. Appear to be looking at the mark by staring to leeward and ahead. You might comment to your crew, "Prepare to ease off," or "Is our chute ready?" Again, don't let the other skipper see you make any sudden alteration in course. This trick can be used on a port tacker crossing under your stern. Most skippers look at those on starboard to judge where the layline is. If you get the port tacker to tack early, he'll forfeit the starboard tack advantage.

When you are overstanding the windward mark to pick up distance on a port tacker crossing behind you, bear off course before he looks your way, so that you appear to be undershooting the mark. If convinced, the other skipper should continue on past the layline—losing distance. When you bear off, there are several techniques you can use to make your bluff more convincing. Keep your sails trimmed tight, don't let the boat heel, don't look directly at the other boat, don't make a sudden course change, don't say anything to the other skipper, and wait until he has sailed past you and is looking away before you resume your original course.

Starboard Roundings

Race committees set courses with starboard windward mark roundings only when the wind direction does not allow them to set up a port rounding on the body of water they have to work with. As soon as they decide on the starboard rounding, they start thinking of how late the protest committee will be working that night. With a starboard rounding, one starboard tacker approaching on the starboard-tack layline can wreak havoc on a fleet of port tackers lined up for a bear-away rounding. (See figure 4.40.) Any boat on port tack must maneuver to get out of a starboard tacker's way.

In this situation, the goal of the port and starboard tackers is to get around the mark first. Obviously the starboard tackers have the high hand. On starboard, you can come in on the layline and tack around the mark whenever you like. You are within your rights in sailing as far as you want beyond the mark before tacking. This move is effective if a port tacker does not duck you, but instead tacks on your lee bow. After he tacks, go ahead and tack. You'll have slowed him down and made distance on him, since he will have made two tacks to your one.

If the port tacker ducks you, you'll have to pull off a perfect slam-dunk to slow him down. If you don't break the overlap before two boatlengths from the mark, he is entitled to room. Therefore, the only way a starboard tacker can lose at a starboard rounding is if the port tacker successfully ducks. Well, there is a devious way to defend against that. When you see a port tacker falling off to duck behind you, slow your boat down by luffing one or both sails so that he can't lay the mark after ducking your stern. (See figure 4.41.)

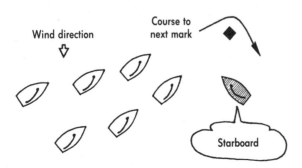

Figure 4.40 *This problem is endemic to starboard roundings of windward marks.*

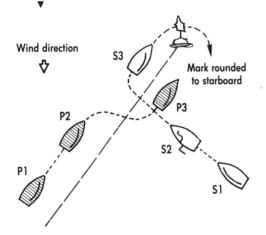

Wind direction

S3

Mark rounded
to starboard

P3

P2

P1

S2

S1

Figure 4.41 *The only way a starboard tacker can round behind a port tacker on a starboard rounding is when the port tacker dips behind the starboard tacker and gets buoy room. Boat S defends by slowing down without changing course (S2). When P ducks it will be surprised to find that it is not laying the mark (P3).*

If you are on starboard, make sure that you don't change your course, because he could protest you under Rule 35 for being a right-of-way boat preventing a give-way boat from keeping clear. Rule 35 only prevents a right-of-way boat from altering its course to prevent a burdened boat from keeping clear. Therefore, the right-of-way boat can slow down and not infringe Rule 35.

If you are the port tacker approaching a mark to be rounded to starboard, overstand the mark by one to two boatlengths. Thus, if you encounter starboard tackers, you will be able to dip their sterns, or you will have space to luff and wait for them to go by. Once they're out of your way, you will be able to fall off to build speed and not have to worry about laying the mark. When dipping, yell in a threatening voice, "Don't tack too close," to make them postpone their tack and thereby give you room to get around the mark. The worst thing you can do is tack to starboard to stay clear of the starboard-tack boat. Then you will be forced to tack again to port to round the mark, and you may find a second starboard tacker coming in, of whom you will have to stay clear.

Even though port tackers get abused by boats on starboard, most people set up on port because it gives them time to set up their spinnaker. Since many crews are not capable of performing a tack-set, their skippers line up for the slaughter. The only way to escape the wrath of the lions by becoming one is to practice, practice, practice.

Rules at the Windward Mark

When rounding a windward mark, there are situations in which Rule 42 (Buoy Room) applies, and others in which Rule 36 (Port/Starboard) takes precedence. The buoy-room rule only applies when boats are on the same tack. To rephrase: the buoy-room rule does not apply to boats on opposite tacks at the windward mark! A port tacker coming in to round the mark cannot claim room from a starboard-tack boat.

When two boats on starboard approach the windward mark overlapped, the outside boat must give room to the inside boat. (See Rule 42.1[b].) The leeward boat is entitled to room to shoot the mark if needed, but the leeward boat can't luff past head-to-wind to avoid hitting the mark. Once a boat goes beyond head-to-wind, by definition it's tacking and must keep clear. If the leeward boat can't round the mark without luffing past head-to-wind, it must fall off to leeward and attempt to round the mark again.

If the two boats approach the mark and there is no overlap when the boat clear ahead crosses the perimeter of the two-boatlength circle, then the boat clear astern must keep clear and round behind or outside of the leading boat (Rule 42.2).

If two overlapped port tackers approach a windward mark to be rounded to port, the outside boat must give room to the inside boat not only to round the mark, but to tack also. Rule 42.1(a) states that room "includes space to tack or jibe when either is an integral part of the rounding or passing maneuver."

In a situation where two non-overlapped port tackers approach a windward mark to be rounded to port, the boat clear ahead must keep clear of the boat clear astern when tacking to round the mark. According to Rule 42.2(c), when two boats are not overlapped, "a yacht clear ahead that tacks to round a mark is subject to Rule 41 (Changing Tacks)." Thus Rule 41, which states that a boat that tacks or jibes must keep clear of a boat on a tack, takes precedence over the buoy-room rule at windward marks. Yet the boat clear ahead is given some protection from the boat clear astern; Rule 42.2(b) states, "A yacht clear astern shall not luff above close-hauled so as to prevent a yacht clear ahead from tacking to round a mark."

Thus, a boat clear astern without buoy-room rights can get around a windward mark first if the leading boat cannot tack and clear the trailing boat. (See figure 4.42.) In effect, you'll get buoy room as long as the other boat cannot tack and get across your bow. If there are no other boats around, and you

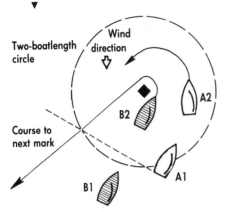

Figure 4.42 *Boat A is clear ahead of B as it enters the two-boatlength circle. Under the buoy room rule, B is not entitled to room at the mark. But in this case, B is able to round ahead of A anyway since Rule 42.2(c) states, "A yacht clear ahead that tacks to round a mark is subject to Rule 41 (Changing Tacks).*

want to increase your lead over the other boat, don't tack as soon as you can make the mark. Instead, drive past the layline, not tacking until you can approach the mark on a beam reach. This way the other boat will trail you into the mark and not have a chance to blanket your wind. (See figure 4.43.)

Now let's go through some other port-starboard cases at the windward mark. The first case involves a port- and a starboard-tack boat converging at a windward mark to be rounded to port. If the port tacker tacks to leeward of the starboard tacker before either boat crosses the perimeter of the two-boatlength circle, then the port tacker becomes a leeward boat governed by Rule 38 (Luffing Rights). Once one of the boats crosses the perimeter of the two-boatlength circle, the leeward boat is entitled to room at the mark.

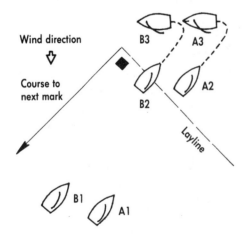

Figure 4.43 *A and B enter the two-boatlength circle overlapped on port tack. In an effort to expand its lead, B delays its tack so that A rounds the mark clear astern instead of with an overlap. Rule 42.1(e) only requires an inside boat to jibe at the first opportunity— not tack.*

On the other hand, if the port tacker tacks to leeward of a starboard tacker inside the two-boatlength circle, then it is automatically entitled to room— and not because of the buoy-room rule. This is purely a case of a windward boat having to keep clear of a leeward boat. The leeward boat, neé port tacker, is within its rights to luff as it pleases under Rule 38.1. The windward boat must keep clear under Rule 37.1. Even if the windward boat gets mast abeam, the leeward boat will still be able to luff to get around the mark. Rule 38.2 says that a leeward boat can sail no higher than its proper course when the windward boat has mast abeam, but luffing to get around the mark is the leeward boat's proper course.

What if a port tacker crosses in front of a starboard boat and ends up clear ahead after completing its tack inside the two-boatlength circle? Even though the starboard tacker has more speed up, it can not establish an inside overlap and claim room. The starboard boat must luff to get outside the boat that tacked in front. (See figure 4.44.)

But if a port tacker crossed a starboard tacker within the two-boatlength circle and then tacked to windward, the leeward boat is entitled to room. To avoid chaos, Rule 42.3(a)(ii) states that ". . . when a yacht completes a tack within two of her overall lengths of a mark . . . she shall give room . . . to a yacht that, by luffing, cannot thereafter avoid establishing a late inside overlap."

A final port-starboard situation at the windward mark occurs when a starboard tacker bears off around the windward mark onto the run. Rule 35(b)(ii) allows that boat to bear off to its proper course, even though it may be bearing

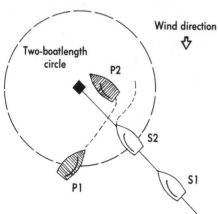

Figure 4.44 *Even though Boat P tacks to starboard within the two-boatlength circle, Boat S is not entitled to establish an overlap and get room. Boat S must luff and stay outside or behind P.*

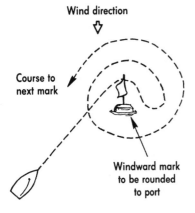

Wind direction

Course to next mark

Windward mark to be rounded to port

Figure 4.45 *This boat rounded the mark to starboard and then realized that the mark had to be rounded to port. To round correctly, it has to turn around and unwind its mistake before rounding the mark correctly.*

off in front of a port-tack boat still heading for the windward mark. According to the rule, the port-tack boat must anticipate the starboard boat's course change and keep clear. In this case the port boat cannot require the starboard tacker to hold its course.

Rule 52.2, states that a boat that hits a mark "May exonerate herself by sailing well clear of all other yachts as soon as possible after the incident, and remaining clear while she makes two complete 360-degree turns (720 degrees) in the same direction, including two tacks and two jibes." No longer does one re-round a mark after hitting it.

For some reason there are two rules that cover hitting a mark. Rule 45 deals with keeping clear after hitting a mark. The first part of the rule says that you not only have to keep clear while exonerating yourself, but you must also keep clear of all other boats until you are on your proper course to the next mark. The second part of the rule states that you have all your rights over other boats until it is obvious that you are exonerating yourself.

If you go around the windward mark (or any mark) the wrong way, Rule 51.2 says that you must retrace your course—unwind your mistake—before rounding the mark correctly. (See figure 4.45.) Rule 51.2 states, "A yacht shall sail the course so as to round or pass each mark on the required side in correct sequence, and so that a string representing her wake, from the time she starts until she finishes, would, when drawn taut, lie on the required side of each mark."

chapter 5

Downwind Tactics

Most sailors relax when they round the windward mark, since the boat becomes level and the apparent wind drops considerably. This chapter will make clear that the reaching and running legs are no place to ease off. There are plenty of places to be gained—or lost—off the wind. So stop thinking about lunch, and we'll start off with getting around the windward mark.

The Rounding

Turning the rudder as little as possible is the fastest way to make all mark roundings, because your rudder works as a brake in that it creates drag. The farther you turn off centerline, the more it will slow you down. Skippers who steer boats with huge spade rudders will attest to this. Therefore, one of the keys to fast mark roundings is reducing rudder drag. To avoid making major course changes, bear off gradually around the mark. Overstanding the mark by a boatlength not only ensures that you won't have to make two extra tacks near the mark, but also makes your turn around the mark more gradual.

Another way you can cut down on rudder drag is to ease the mainsail as you fall off around the mark. If your boat is heeling, ease the main and let it luff in order to get the boat back on its lines before trying to turn. Dumping the main while keeping the jib tight will spin the boat with hardly any rudder movement. Another reason to keep the jib tight is that the spinnaker won't be as hard to raise because the spinnaker won't be rubbing against the jib.

In dinghies, you can minimize rudder drag by hiking hard and heeling the boat to windward. Only heel the boat to windward when you're sure the mark's anchor line descends at a steep angle. Heeling your boat to windward makes your centerboard "reach out" toward the mark's ground tackle. By definition, the ground tackle is not part of a mark; therefore, you can hit it without taking a penalty. But if you catch the anchor line of a mark, and that drags the mark into your boat, you'll have to do a 720-degree turn.

Since it's impossible to get an anchor to hold when the anchor line goes straight down, race committees can make things easier on the racers by hanging a 10-to-15-pound weight on a tether from the bottom of the mark and then attaching the mark's anchor line to the bottom of the weight. Unless you are sure the race committee anchors marks by using this procedure, make a point of overstanding the windward mark the first time you go around. If the current is going in the same the direction as the wind, you might have to overstand the mark by two to three boatlengths if there is loose ground tackle floating on the surface.

In any boat with more than two crew members, only one person should work on getting the spinnaker ready to go up, while the others must keep hiking and concentrating on sailing the boat fast. When rounding the windward mark to port, have the foredeck person start rigging the spinnaker while on your final port-tack approach to the mark. This way, he can clip the spinnaker bag to the lifelines and attach the halyard and sheets, while keeping his weight on the windward rail. When you tack to starboard, the foredeck person can get the pole ready while keeping his weight to windward. If any rigging has to be done at the bow, the bowman should plan out moves ahead of time so that the least amount of time possible is spent on the bow; for example, if sheets have to be led around the forestay, he should have the cockpit crew make sure the sheets are untangled so that they'll run when he pulls on them. That person's weight, no matter how light, disturbs the helm. During the actual rounding, it is better to concentrate on speed than to worry about getting the spinnaker up, pulling the board up, or making minor adjustments to things like the outhaul and cunningham.

Hiking

When sailing a dinghy, it is impossible to hike straight out all the time. Even if you had the superhuman strength to do so, your knees aren't tough enough to hold your body horizontal for long periods. That's why it's important to ration your bursts of maximum hiking. In maximum hiking in a dinghy, the crew straight-leg hikes with the backs of their knees over the gunwale, while those hanging on a trapeze wire fully extend their bodies with their arms past their heads. On a big boat, the crew inches out so far on the rail that the tips of their tailbones and the lower lifeline are the only things holding them on the boat. The extra speed gained from maximum hiking is needed right before the start, just after the start, when approaching marks, or when crossing other boats. Don't interpret this to mean you don't have to hike during the rest of the race; we're telling you to exert your strength to the fullest only at these crucial points in a race.

Raising the Spinnaker

As you round the mark, the tactician should give the helmsman the new course to steer. Provide either the course to the next mark or the course to steer that will get the boat to the mark the fastest. Frequently in light air, or if the reach is too broad, the fastest course will not be directly to the mark. If you are in the midst of traffic, tell the helmsman to stay high with the rest of the boats until you can pick a path through the mess.

Because the position of your competition influences the point at which you raise the spinnaker, the tactician should call the hoist. A great trick in a dinghy is to postpone your set to get past a leading boat. Appear passive during the rounding by staying right behind the other boat. Rig your spinnaker pole, but don't raise your spinnaker. When the skipper of the boat ahead bends over to reach for the spinnaker halyard, make your move by heading up and driving over him. The skipper of the leading boat won't be able to match your course change since he'll most likely have his head in the bilge and the tiller between his legs, while pulling up the spinnaker. Even if he did see you in time, he'd lose a lot of speed in making a sharp turn to windward with his spinnaker halfway up and luffing. So, when his rear end goes up, you go up.

In big boats you can do the same. Just delay your aggressive move to windward until the leading boat is committed to raising its spinnaker. Once

▼

the chute is going up, you'll be able to make your move to windward uncontested.

In light air on big boats, you can make gains by delaying your spinnaker set. As you round the mark onto the reach, your apparent wind strength will drop faster than your boatspeed. Until your speed falls, your apparent wind angle will be too close to fly a spinnaker. So, instead of rushing to put up your chute, only to have it luff against the stays, bear off around the mark and bleed off some speed. In heavy boats, it can take a minute or more to burn off speed from the beat. When you do finally go for a set, the less your crew jumps around, the less momentum your boat will lose. "We learned this lesson the hard way during the America's Cup defenders' trials in 1977," Gary says. "On *Courageous*, we had a slim lead over *Enterprise* as we rounded the windward mark in light air. We set right away. The chute went up and wouldn't fill because the apparent wind was so far forward. The crew of *Enterprise* delayed their set as they slid over us with all their excess speed. (See figure 5.1.) Once they got by us, they raised their chute. That one move cost us the race, since we never got an opportunity to pass in the remaining 20 miles."

Another light-air rounding trick is to bear away slowly in a wide arc around the mark. Not only does this reduce rudder drag, but this way the apparent wind angle will stay constant as you turn. Thus you will keep the wind at a fast angle forward as you come onto the reach, until your boat speed slows down. (See figure 5.2.)

According to Tom, raising the spinnaker is actually easier during a jibe set. As long as the chute is stopped well, you can raise it on the windward side before you jibe. Going up to windward, the man on the halyard won't have the friction of the chute being pulled against the leeward side of the jib. Also, you will be able to check visually whether the spinnaker is up all the way. When you jibe around, the pole can be set and the stops broken.

Wind direction

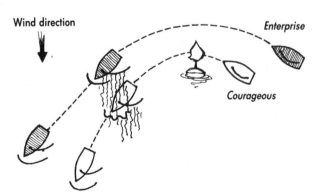

Enterprise

Courageous

Figure 5.1 *During a light-air race in the 1977 America's Cup defender's trials* Enterprise *passed* Courageous *by delaying her spinnaker set.*

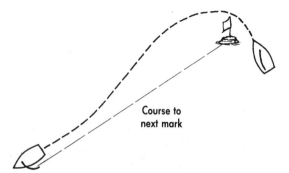

Course to next mark

Figure 5.2 *Avoid sharp rudder movements in light air, which slow you down; make your turn around the windward mark gradually.*

The Getaway

Once around the mark, make a fast getaway. Your tactics for all downwind legs should be to go for speed during the first half of the leg, while on the second half of the leg you need to work into a position that will get you buoy room at the next mark. On your getaway from the windward mark, haul up the spinnaker, adjust your sails, and settle in for pure speed. Often, sailors work hard on the windward legs, only to relax downwind. But this is the opportunity to make ground on the leaders, or to get away from the fleet. When in doubt, the fastest reaching (as opposed to running) course between two marks is a straight line. As a matter of fact, if the wind does not shift noticeably while you're sailing a reaching leg, the fastest course is the rhumb line between the two marks. But there are plenty of times when strategic tactical concerns require you to deviate from the rhumb line on a reach. When planning a strategy for the reach, you have to consider (1) whether you can carry a spinnaker, (2) whether the wind will shift as you go down the leg, (3) whether the wind strength will change, and (4) whether the current is a factor. Your tactical concerns are (1) where the competition is, (2) what course will keep your air clear, and (3) what position you need to be in while going around the next mark.

General Rules for Deviating from the Rhumb Line

1. If you think you are going to be lifted as you go down the course, sail low in the beginning of the leg, so that when you approach the next mark,

▼

you will be sailing at a faster wind angle than those who automatically sailed high. With better speed, you'll be able to get an inside overlap on the slower boats.

2. If you think you are going to be headed, go high early in the leg to generate better speed. The header should bring you down to the mark. This way you will have sailed the whole leg with the wind at a faster reaching angle. This is truly a case of having your cake and eating it too.

3. If you think the wind is going to increase and the reach is tight already, sail high when you can. As the wind blows harder, the apparent wind will shift farther forward, making it harder to lay the mark.

4. If you think the wind is going to decrease, sail low while you've got the fresh breeze. Then, when the wind dies, you will be able to head up to the mark and generate stronger apparent wind.

5. If you think the current is going to force you above the mark, aim your boat below the mark so that you don't have to end up on a slow dead run, pitted head-on against an adverse current. Likewise, if the current is pushing you below the mark, sail higher so that you don't get stuck so far below the mark that you have to take down your spinnaker to beat to the reaching mark.

Whether to Carry a Spinnaker

The two considerations for carrying a spinnaker are windspeed and wind direction. When it's howling, you might not be able to set the spinnaker on a beam reach, but if it's light, you might be able to carry a flat spinnaker up to a 50-degree apparent wind angle.

In many races, you'll find that the fastest strategy for close reaching legs is to sail a few degrees high of the rhumb line with a jib for half of the leg, and then sail down to the mark with a spinnaker. The half-and-half approach is fast because there isn't a smooth speed transition from a spinnaker to a jib. There is about a 10-degree zone in you boat's performance where your speed will be worse with either sail.

Dinghy sailors, in particular know from experience about the speed drop-off between the extreme ranges of the spinnaker and the jib. By sailing 5 or 10 degrees below the highest course possible with the spinnaker, dinghies come to life, popping up onto a plane instead of going dog-slow with the spinnaker strapped tight and the pole aganst the forestay. A dinghy won't plane if you head too high with a spinnaker. If you strap the chute in tight and head too high, the boat just starts to heel and takes water over the side. On a tight reach, dinghy sailors know to sail off for speed and to head up in the lulls. Dinghy sailors are sensitive to performance changes, because they are close to the water, where they can judge the difference in speed from the sound of the boat going through the water, and from the pressure exerted on the rudder. In racing one-designs, you know right away if you are sailing off the pace, since all the boats have the same speed potential.

Hence, if calculation or experience tells you that you'll barely be able to carry a spinnaker, sail high without the spinnaker first, instead of sailing down the rhumb line with the spinnaker strapped tight. By going high, you'll get into the passing lane and get over boats that automatically raised their chutes without thinking first. Once you have rolled over them to windward, pop your chute and sail down to the mark on a broader and faster reach.

If it's early in a race or a series, and you're not concerned with beating a particular boat, it's hard to get into trouble by going for speed on a reach. Even if you have to sail below the mark to pop your boat up onto plane, you'll gain on the boats that sailed high and slow. At the end of the leg, you can take the chute down and blast up to the mark on a jib reach for the last bit of the leg. Dousing the chute might not hurt you, even if you need to carry it on the next leg, because in high winds you won't have to worry about jibing the sail. In dinghies you'll have taken the spinnaker down to windward, making it easy to raise on the leeward side after you jibe around the reach mark.

But if you are worried about staying ahead of a single competitor, stay between him and the mark—always. That is the number-one rule. If he starts going high, you go high, and if he goes low, you go low. Especially on a reach, don't ever let him get on your wind.

Passing Lanes

On the first reach of a triangular course the passing lane is to windward of boats during the first half of the leg, and to leeward toward the end of the leg.

▼

By sailing high and getting to windward of other boats, you'll go faster as you sail closer to the wind, and by getting to leeward at the end of the leg, you'll establish an inside overlap that will give you buoy room.

To be in the passing lane early in the first reach, you have to sail high enough over your competition so that they can't luff you before you establish mast abeam. It's even better to be high enough so that they won't even challenge. The sooner you go up to get in the passing lane, the less likely it is that the boat ahead will defend against you. For instance, if you head up to pass when you're one boatlength away, the leader will feel threatened and match your course change to windward. But if you are six boatlengths behind and head up for the passing lane, you'll most likely be too far behind for the leading boat to feel threatened. If you're two or three boatlengths to windward of him when you get into his neighborhood, it will be too late for him to defend against your passing him.

"That's how we passed *Australia II* on the second reach of the first race of the 1983 America's Cup," says Tom. "*Liberty* got up on their hip, and then we put the staysail up and charged on by. Since they didn't follow the cardinal rule of staying between their competition and the mark, they were in no position stop us. They did try to head up to us, but it was too little too late. Heading up sharply only slowed them down more and helped us get mast abeam quicker."

If you only need to get around one boat, and you've figured that getting too high on the reach could cause problems, you can minimize your time in the passing lane by lying in wait for the right puff or set of waves to surf by on. Keep an eye out behind and to windward for favorable conditions; then establish yourself in a position to windward to take off in the passing lane once the puff comes through.

A good time to pass is when other boats are having problems. Be ruthless, and sense when the other guy is hurting. Crews dealing with a ripped sail, an override around a winch, or a jammed halyard are less apt to pay attention to you as you go up and get in the passing lane. They've stopped concentrating on winning, and are dealing with survival. And even if they do see you go up to pass, they're in no shape to stop you.

After you have established yourself in the passing lane, you have to work your boat to get over boats below you but on a parallel course. To get extra speed out of your boat, pay attention to the waves and puffs of wind. The IYRU rules have become increasingly strict on working your boat to stimulate acceleration. Rewritten Rule 54 prohibits pumping, ooching, rocking, sculling, and repeated tacks or jibes. (See Rule 54.2 for exact definitions of these terms.) Rule 54.3 does allow one pump of a sheet per wave or gust of wind, to promote surfing or planing. To minimize the effect of pumping the mainsheet, Rule 54.3(b) states that you can no longer pump with part of the mainsheet tackle. The new wording reads, "The mainsail may be pumped using only that part of the sheet between the crew member handling the sheet and the first block on the boom." Pumping spinnaker guys is expressly prohibited. Check your class rules on pumping, because the new Rule 54.3(c) states that class rules may alter or add to Rule 54.3(b).

Big-boat sailors are just as entitled as dinghy sailors to pump their sails as long as they do not infringe Rule 54.3(b). When you do get a wave to surf on, or a puff to plane with, pump the chute and the main together for better acceleration. On a big boat it's a little harder because it requires more winch-power. On a big boat you can pump the main more easily if your mainsheet system has coarse- and fine-tuning capabilities. Pump the 2:1 coarse part of the system.

Never pump a sheet right as it comes off the sail. Make sure the line goes through a block anchored to the boat. If you pump by pulling directly on the sail, your arm will act as a shock absorber, sapping the sail's ability to pull the boat. If you really want to get the most pull from the sails, you can use low-stretch lines like Kevlar or Spectra for sheets. Also, if you have ratchet blocks on your sheets, make sure the ratchet is engaged during all conditions to reduce any loss of power from the sail. On big boats, sheets should always have at least one wrap around a winch to avoid any loss of pull from the sail. Trimmers tend to turn the ratchet off or take sheets off winches so that they can feel a sail better, but if they remove this source of friction, they will be the only one feeling the power of the sail—the boat will get none.

How to Avoid Being Passed

The racing rules endow the boat to leeward with a strong defense against boats trying to pass to windward. Rule 38 (Luffing Rights) allows a leeward boat to alter its course to windward as fast as it wants, and it can make this move without announcement or warning. If the windward boat fails to keep clear during the luff, it must retire or take a prescribed penalty, such as a 720-degree turn (two full revolutions).

▼

So, if a boat is threatening and has unwisely left itself in striking distance, think nothing of picking it off by cranking the rudder over. The rules allow you to go all the way to head-to-wind at your discretion. Don't worry about the spinnaker collapsing; you can always get it flying again when the other boat retires or does his 720. In a dinghy, you can make your luff more effective by having your crew trim the main hard as you jam the tiller over. Lower your centerboard without being noticed before your sneak-attack. If a racer to windward isn't expecting a sharp luff, its board will be up and (a) its crew won't have time to lower it, which means their boat will sideslip into yours as they try to head up, or (b) they'll drop it too fast, which will slow them down.

Gaining mast abeam doesn't entitle the windward boat to force you to sail directly at the next mark. The rule book defines *proper course* as "any course that a yacht might sail after the starting signal, in the absence of the other yacht or yachts affected, to finish as quickly as possible. The course sailed before luffing or bearing away is presumably, but not necessarily, that yacht's proper course." In other words, a leeward boat's proper course is the fastest course to the next mark—the one it would sail if no other boats were around. Therefore, even if the windward boat had mast abeam, the leeward boat can still luff because its proper course could be higher to catch a wave or to head toward a breeze line.

When it is inevitable that a bigger boat is going to pass you, encourage him to pass to leeward. Yell over to him that you're a small boat and you won't hurt his speed much. If that doesn't work, luff up sharply while he's still deciding which side to pass you on. Show him that you will make the high road as uncomfortable as possible. Even though he may be in a different class, he is still susceptible to being protested by you. Let him roll over you only if there are no others following him. You could end up dead in the water for minutes on end as the fleet rolls by. Without any wind, you'll be helpless to prevent more boats from rolling by. You'll feel like a driver on the highway who got forced out of the passing lane by someone flashing his lights, only to get stuck behind a slow truck for the next five miles because there were no gaps to get back in the fast lane.

"If a bigger boat is determined to pass you to windward," says Tom, "bait a trap by getting him to pass as close as possible. When he's in striking range, nail him with a sharp luff and teach him a lesson. It will be a while before he tries to pass close to windward again. It's like fighting guerrilla warfare. The smaller force never wins in open-field combat, but it can win by attrition."

During a luffing duel with another boat, it's easy to lose track of the rest of the fleet. To prevent getting into an extended luffing confrontation that allows other boats to pass to leeward of you, give the aggressor a sharp luff as soon as he makes his first move to go high. Make it clear right away that you're not going to let him pass you to windward. It doesn't hurt to yell over to the other boat that you'll take him to Portugal if necessary to keep him from going over you. A sharp luff and a verbal reinforcement will make your intentions crystal clear. Then tell him that he is more than welcome to pass to leeward. If you head up slowly to match the moves of a boat trying to go over you, the two of you will find yourselves off the course while the rest of the fleet sails by.

There are times in a fleet race when it might be more expedient to let a boat ride over you than to risk getting involved in a costly luffing duel. When there are many boats nearby, and you think that you'll lose too many of them while you go high with the one other boat, then it's time to consider letting the one boat by. A businessman would call this thinking about his five-year business plan instead of just about his one-year plan. What ever you do, don't let emotions get in your way. Don't let yourself get obsessed with beating your archenemy or old friend. Your goal should be finishing as high as you can, not just in front of a particular boat. Before you let that boat roll over you, however, make sure that the whole Red Army isn't going to follow through the hole he creates.

If a skipper makes it clear that he won't let you ride over him, avoid a luffing match that could cost you places by sailing through his lee. Rule 39 protects you by stating, "A yacht that is on a free leg of the course shall not sail below her proper course when she is clearly within three of her overall lengths of a leeward yacht or a yacht clear astern that is steering a course to leeward of her own." A protest under Rule 39 is hard to prove, but if you inform the offending skipper, he'll usually stop.

The way to minimize the effect of the windward boat's wind shadow as you try to pass to leeward is to sail low, keeping your apparent wind aft of his wind shadow. Do this by making sure his masthead fly is pointing in front of you. When his masthead fly points at you, harden up to a reach so that you cross through his shadow quickly. Heading up will increase your apparent wind, which should give you enough speed to get through the windward boat's shadow. Once you are through his wind shadow, bear off and resume your course down the leg. (See figure 5.3.)

Points to consider when passing to leeward: the closer you pass to leeward, the greater the wind loss you will suffer, but the briefer the affliction. The

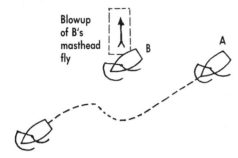

Blowup of B's masthead fly

B

A

Figure 5.3 *When passing to leeward of a slower boat, remember that your wind will not be disturbed until the windward boat's masthead fly is pointing directly at your boat. At that point, head up to bring your apparent wind forward.*

wind shadow radiates to leeward of a boat in a conical shape with the boat at the apex of the cone; that is, the shadow gets broader in proportion to its distance from the boat. (See figure 5.4.) It can become ten boatlengths wide at ten boatlengths to leeward. The shadow begins to disperse at some point, but the point of dispersion depends on the strength of the wind. What we do know is that in light air the wind shadow disperses more slowly. In heavy air, a wind shadow is not as important because the cone stays closer to the boat. In extremely light air you should worry about a boat 20 boatlengths to windward, while in very heavy air you can pass four boatlengths to leeward without a problem.

If you do try to pass to leeward, remember that you are protected by Rule 39. If the windward boat tries to come down, immediately hail, telling it not to come down on you.

The Low Road

On the reaches, fleets typically bow to windward of the rhumb line, since everyone is protecting his own wind. With the fleet sailing high, boats have a chance to make gains on the low route. The low road can be treacherous if you are not far enough below the fleet. In large fleets, all the boats on the high road will create a wind block that will disturb the wind to leeward for over ten mastlengths. Tactically, the low route works best when the leaders head high while in a luffing match of their own or, occasionally, because they are sailing toward the wrong mark and the fleet acts like rats following the Pied Piper. To make the low road pay, don't come up and sail to the mark

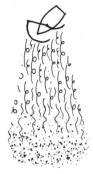

Figure 5.4 *Wind shadows radiate to leeward in a conical shape.*

until you are making your final approach. This way, you've kept your wind clear for the longest period of time. If you get tempted and come up too soon, you'll waste your burst of speed and be blanketed coming into the mark by all the boats that sailed high.

The main advantage of choosing the low road on the first reach is that you will be able to sail a higher angle and consequently have a lot of speed coming into the reaching mark, but Tom says, "It's all relative. A lot of speed? What did you give up in the beginning to get that opportunity?"

Your strategy on the low road will vary depending on whether you are sailing a match race or a fleet race. The whole low-road idea in a match race can be summed up this way: When your competitor is not right on you, start off by sailing a bit below the mark. Therefore, if you become lifted as you go down the leg, you can come up to the mark still sailing a fast apparent wind angle. If you get a header, you'll still be able to hold off the boat behind you, because you'll have increased apparent wind strength as you head up to the mark.

In a fleet race the decision is relatively the same, except you'll have to worry about more boats. At no time should you pick the low road if you're in danger of being passed. The other reason for picking the low road is to maintain your inside overlap at the reach mark.

Catching a Tow

Catching a tow, or drafting, is a slower boat's revenge. If you're entered in a long race in a mixed fleet, it can be a powerful tool. By positioning your boat in the trough between the bigger boat's quarter wave and its first stern wave, you can get pulled along at the same speed as the bigger boat, because those waves are being pulled by the boat ahead of you. The distance between the waves relates to the length of the leading boat, and by getting caught between those waves, you fool the water into thinking your boat is the same length as the leading boat.

"I remember catching a tow off the 62-footer *Thunderhead* while sailing *Love Machine IV*, a 42-footer, during the 1982 Stamford–Vineyard Race [Stamford, Connecticut, to Martha's Vineyard and back]," Tom says. "I'll always remember Charlie Hoffman standing on the stern of *Thunderhead*, yelling at us to get away. They pulled us right through our whole class. To get rid of us, they zigzagged down Long Island Sound, trying to shake us off, but we just matched their course changes. The only way they could have ditched us would have been to take down their chute and sail upwind, but since that would have taken them so far from the mark, they were reluctant to do it. Charlie is a very big, strong guy who can be pretty intimidating when he's mad, but I just had to laugh as we hung on to their stern wave for over an hour. We just drove them crazy. Thanks to that tow, we won our class."

"Keep your bow as close to the faster boat's transom as you can without worrying about hitting him," says Tom. "It takes masterful steering to keep so close without hitting the other boat. Remember that the first wave pulls you along better than the second wave, the second wave better than the third, the third better than the fourth, and after the fourth there is hardly any pull left."

Big, draftable stern waves are only produced when a boat is charging along at hull speed on a power reach—when the apparent wind is between 70 and 120 degrees in relatively flat water. You can draft off a boat's windward or leeward wave. "When you are close-reaching with jibs instead of spinnakers, it's better to be on the windward wave to keep out of the pulling boat's backwind," says Tom. "As the reach squares up [as the apparent wind moves aft of the beam], it always seems better to be on the leeward wave. It's not uncommon to see five boats towing behind one much bigger boat. It looks like a group of geese flying south."

The defense against a slower boat drafting off you is to make fast course alterations. If it's on your windward quarter, use your luffing rights. Another way to shake off a pest is to slow down so that your boat stops producing a sizable stern wave. You can lose speed by heading up to a close reach or falling off to a dead run. When you're jib reaching, just head up and beat; the other boat will go right out the back door as it falls into your bad air. Once you stop producing a wave, you'll waterline the slower boat to death. But by all means get rid of a boat drafting on you if it's in your race. Rating rules work under the assumption that bigger boats go faster than smaller ones, and if a smaller one keeps up, you will be beaten on corrected time.

Approaching the Reach Mark

Getting the inside position at the jibe mark is paramount. No matter how great or small the overlap, an inside boat will pass outside boats every time while rounding the reach mark. The inside boat will also be the windward boat exiting the mark; therefore, the windward boat will be on everyone else's wind while no one will hurt its wind. The inside boat not only extends its lead by being the only boat to come away from the mark with clear air, but pulls away from those that rounded outside of it, since it turns a shorter distance. The distance an outside boat loses increases exponentially with the number of boats inside of it, since it has to give the inside boats room to jibe. In dinghies with long booms, such as Thistles, the farthest-outside boat in a group of five could end up well removed from the center of the action.

The one time out of ten when the inside position is not paramount is when the second reach turns out to be a run. In that case it's better to stay on the outside of the fleet at the reach mark, so that you'll be the windward boat as the fleet bears off around the mark instead of jibing.

Since getting buoy room, or denying another boat buoy room, is so important, let's go through several ways to make and break overlaps. To get buoy room, you need to establish an inside overlap with the boat ahead of you before the leading boat is two boatlengths away from the mark. An overlap is established when any part of your boat's hull, sails, or other equipment, in its normal position, crosses an imaginary line passing through the aftermost point of the leading boat, and perpendicular to its centerline. (See figure 5.5.)

Start planning your approach to the reach mark halfway down the first reach, so that you can size up where other boats are in relation to you. Then think of how you can get the inside position on them. When trailing a boat, slow it down by continually changing course. First threaten to pass to windward and then bear off and threaten to pass to leeward. As the leader attempts to

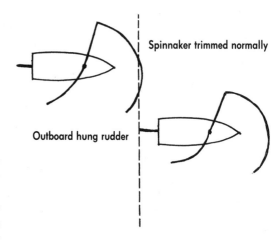

Spinnaker trimmed normally

Outboard hung rudder

Figure 5.5 *Even though the hulls of these two boats are not next to each other, the boats are overlapped. An overlap occurs when any part of a boat's hull, sails, or other equipment in its normal position crosses an imaginary line passing through the aftermost point of the leading boat, and perpendicular to its centerline.*

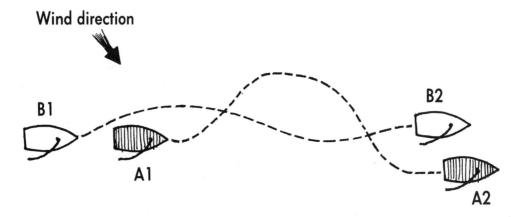

Wind direction

B1

A1

B2

A2

Figure 5.6 *Sailing downwind, the trailing boat has the advantage since the helmsperson and crew don't have to look around to keep an eye on the other boat. Being on the attack, the trailing boat makes a lot of distance by timing its moves to take advantage of waves and puffs of wind.*

match your course, you'll gain about a half-boatlength in every exchange because your course changes can be timed to take advantage of the wave and wind conditions—head up gently in the lulls, fall off in the puffs, and ride down the faces of waves. The leader loses because his course changes are solely a reaction to your new course. Since the skipper of the leading boat is reacting to a surprise change you've already made, his course and trim changes will be made more abruptly, which slows his boat down even more. Constantly turning around and watching you does little to help make his boat go faster. The more ground he loses to you, the more poorly he'll sail. (See figure 5.6.)

Another way to attack leading boats involves creating a chain reaction that earns you buoy room on more than one opponent. Do this by heading up and threatening the boat ahead of you. As he goes up, the boat in front of him will go up, as will others in front of him. Keep the group sailing high above the layline so that when you all finally go down for the mark, you'll have an inside overlap. (See figure 5.7.)

The closer you get to the mark, the more of a mistake it becomes to attempt to drive over a boat ahead. If the skipper of the boat ahead is smart, he'll let you go over him, knowing that you won't be able to get clear ahead by the time you get to the two-boatlength circle; therefore, you'll have to give him room at the jibe mark and he'll leave you behind. The only time to attempt passing to windward of a boat ahead of you, when you are within 15 boatlengths of the reach mark, is when you're on a plane and the other boat is not.

Pulling within a boatlength of a leading boat is the hardest part when you're seeking an overlap. Remember that you are not trying to pass the boat; to get an inside overlap, all you need to do is to get the minutest part of your hull, equipment, or sails to overlap the boat ahead. You can create an overlap by staying right on the leader's transom as you both approach the reach mark. Even if the reach is not broad enough for you to blanket the boat ahead of you with your wind shadow, you will pick up some speed by sailing in its wake. The reason is that you'll catch a tow.

If the boat ahead tries to sail below the mark to prevent you from sailing down to get an overlap, yell at its skipper not to sail below his proper course (Rule 39). Then wait for a good puff or a wave that you can ride to establish an overlap. Your bow doesn't need to cross an imaginary line extending from her transom to create an overlap. In dinghies, you can overlap the boat's rudder with your spinnaker. Note that in big boats, where spinnakers are much larger,

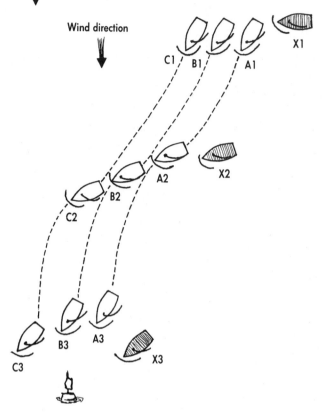

Wind direction

C1 B1 A1 X1

A2 X2

B2

C2

B3 A3

C3 X3

Figure 5.7 As A *heads up to*
protect its wind, a chain reaction
is created with boats B and C.
After sailing past the layline to the
reaching mark, X falls off to the
mark. As the boats turn toward
the mark, X has the inside overlap.

it's not uncommon for spinnakers to fly anywhere from 10 to 15 feet in front of a boat's bow.

The value of an inside overlap increases with the number of boats you overlap simultaneously. It's not uncommon to pass four boats at once while going around the jibe mark. Also, the overlap rule creates a chain reaction; that is, if you overlap a boat that overlaps another boat, you are overlapped with the other boat down the line. In figure 5.8, Boat A is overlapped with Boat C even though no part of A is overlapped with C, because both overlap Boat B. Therefore, Boat C has to give both A and B buoy room.

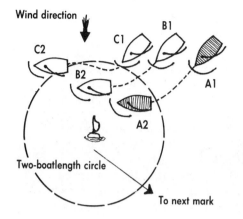

Figure 5.8 *Boat C must give room to both Boat B and Boat A. Even though none of A's hull, sails or equipment overlapped C when C entered the two-boatlength circle, A is entitled to room because it overlaps B, which overlaps C.*

On the other hand, if you are an outside boat, you'll want to work hard at preventing others from getting an inside overlap on you. Let's go through some ways of preventing boats from getting an overlap, and some ways to break existing overlaps.

Defending Against an Inside Overlap

During close situations when you are not sure if a trailing boat has an overlap or not, it's in your interest to go to the stern of the boat and sight across the aftermost part of your vessel. By sighting from the back of your boat, your better perspective gives your side of the story in a protest more weight than that of the skipper of the trailing boat.

If, after looking, you see that the inside boat has only just established an overlap, a simple way to break it is to head up. Your transom will swing around, leaving the other boat clear astern. (See figure 5.9.) With a flick of the tiller, the inside boat becomes a boat clear astern. The trick is to enter the two-boatlength circle while the overlap is still broken. Once your boat crosses the two-boatlength circle, you can head down to the mark. Even though this will re-establish the overlap, the leeward boat will not be entitled to room. But if the other boat contests this move and you don't have a witness to say

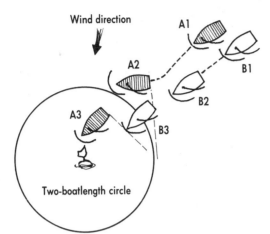

Wind direction

A1

A2

B1

A3

B2

B3

Two-boatlength circle

Figure 5.9 *Before reaching the two-boatlength circle, Boats A and B are overlapped. To prevent B from getting buoy room, A heads up and breaks the overlap (A2). When A crosses the two-boatlength circle with the overlap broken, B is not entitled to room at the mark, even though when A falls off to the mark the overlap is re-established (A3).*

that the overlap was broken before you crossed the perimeter of the two-boatlength circle, it's in your interest to give the inside boat room and then protest. Rule 42.1(c) says that when an overlap between two boats exists, the outside boat must prove to a protest committee not only that it broke the overlap, but that it became clear ahead before it reached the two-boatlength circle. If you can trim your sails in such a way as to acutely backwind the boat that heads down to get the overlap, you will also stand a chance of keeping your opponent at bay.

Since the surest way to lose boats is to round outside of others while going around the jibe mark, you need an alternate plan in case you don't end up with an overlap or are stuck outside of other boats. When all your attempts to gain the favored inside position fail, Plan B calls for a little bit of patience and a little bit of playing possum. Slow down and fall behind the group of boats you failed to get inside of, then round behind the innermost boat of that group. By slowing down and following the inside boat around the mark, you'll pass all those that were forced to the outside in the group ahead of you. By hanging back and then rounding next to the mark, you'll prevent yourself from being passed by boats coming up from astern. (See figure 5.10.)

Another asset of Plan B—slowing down so that you can round next to the jibe mark—is that you'll be in a position to pounce on any boats in front of you that have problems while rounding. If the leader flubs his turn and goes wide, or if his spinnaker gets tangled around the headstay, you'll be able to squeeze in and get above him. The golden opportunity occurs when the inside

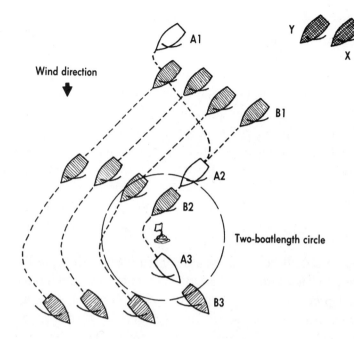

Figure 5.10 *Caught outside a group of boats, Boat A jibes around in order to follow Boat B, the inside most boat, around the mark. If A didn't jibe to the inside and round outside of the group, A would end up getting passed by boats X and Y. Also notice that by rounding behind B, A insures itself clear air after rounding.*

boat ahead of you goes around the mark without its centerboard down far enough. Before he realizes why he's going sideways to leeward, he'll jam his rudder over, which will stop his forward progress altogether, leaving a hole big enough to drive the Staten Island Ferry through. The only thing better would be if he sideslipped into boats to leeward of him.

Even if a hole doesn't open up, by slowing down and following the inside boat around the reaching mark, you'll be able to sail over those boats forced outside, because they'll be wallowing in bad air while you'll have clear air.

Different ways to slow down on the first reach include heading up and luffing, trimming your main into the boat's centerline, putting down your centerboard all the way, turning your rudder sharply from one side to the other, or pulling your spinnaker behind the mainsail.

The Rounding

When rounding with no other boats nearby, you can make a nice wide rounding so that you don't lose speed and so that your crew can easily fly the spinnaker

▼

through the jibe. One word of caution: beware of jibing in lulls, since the wind usually returns to full strength at the least opportune times. In traffic, it's important to get your chute around to the other side of the headstay quickly so that it doesn't backwind and slow you down. Even if your crew just muscles the spinnaker to the other side without trying to fly it, a spinnaker luffing to leeward is a lot faster than one backwinded against the headstay.

Since jibing a big boat requires sailing downwind for approximately two boatlengths, incorporate this downwind distance into a smooth rounding when the first reach is broader than the second. Depending on how close other boats are, head for a point one to two boatlengths directly to windward of the reach mark. By jibing before you round the mark, you'll be squared away before rounding the mark, allowing you to be on a close reach as you pass the jibe mark. (See figure 5.11.)

Ideally, you should head above the mark at least ten boatlengths from the mark, so that your turn to windward is gradual. But if other boats are attempting to get an inside overlap on you, you'll have to postpone your course change until you've crossed the perimeter of the two-boatlength circle. As long as you stay within the two-boatlength circle, the other boats must round outside of you. Use your luffing rights to take up boats to windward of you when you head up to initiate this rounding technique.

In heavy air, the most critical steering job during a jibe is to keep the boat under the sails to avoid capsizing or broaching once the boom slams across. The S-jibe is a technique that reduces the force of the boom and helps keep

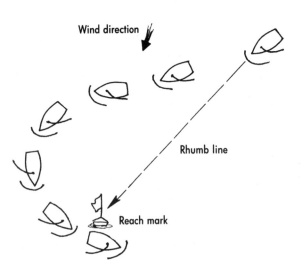

Wind direction

Rhumb line

Reach mark

Figure 5.11 *Make a better rounding by heading a boatlength or two above the mark so that you've completed your jibe before rounding the mark. If there were boats above you, you could justify taking them high of the mark under the proper course provision, which says on a free leg of the course (when you are not beating to windward) a boat's proper course is any course that a boat might sail in the absence of other boats, to finish as quickly as possible.*

Wind direction

Reach mark

To next mark

Figure 5.12 *The S-Jibe is a heavy air jibing technique that helps keep the boat under control by reducing the force of the boom.*

the boat on its lines. To do an S-jibe, bear off until the boat is slightly by the lee. Then trim the main in for a tight reach and choke the spinnaker down slightly by overtrimming the guy and sheet. Now steer into the jibe, but as the mainsail comes across, steer back toward the old course (in the direction in which the main is going). The change of course breaks the power of the boom's swing and keeps the boat from rounding up into the wind. (See figure 5.12.) Then ease the main out as you fall off to your new course. If something goes wrong with the spinnaker in the middle of the jibe, hold the boat dead downwind to reduce the pressure on the spinnaker pole. During an end-for-end jibe, for instance, filling the chute on the new tack, before the inboard end of the pole is attached to the mast, may oblige your bowman to ask for assistance at the mast.

The Second Reach

Even though the buoy-room rule so heavily favors inside boats, outside boats have their chance for revenge immediately after rounding the mark. After jibing around the mark, an outside boat becomes the leeward boat with luffing

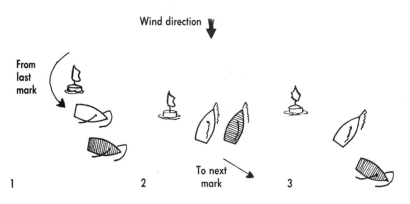

Figure 5.13 *After rounding the reaching mark, a leeward boat should luff a windward boat to get rid of the threat to its wind. Most times the leeward boat will catch the windward boat unaware.*

rights if the inside boat does not have mast abeam. Unless you are a masochist, luff the windward boat sharply as soon as you finish rounding the mark. Normally, the crew of the inside boat will be busy trying to sort themselves out after doing a tight turn around the mark, so try to catch them off guard. As long as you don't make the other boat hit the mark, you are not violating the buoy-room rule. Even if the skipper sees your luff and heads up to avoid you, his spinnaker will collapse if his crew is concentrating on getting squared away on the new jibe instead of paying attention to the boats around them. Once you get clear ahead, fall off and leave the other boat in your dust. (See figure 5.13.)

It pays to sail high on the second reach. Your strategic goal of sailing high and fast coincides with your tactical goal of sailing high to be the inside boat at the leeward mark. Once you've completed your jibe around the reach mark, start your getaway by planning your approach to the leeward mark. If you are one of the first boats around the mark, you can discourage other skippers from going high by sailing high for a length or two, and then coming off to your proper course before other boats round the reaching mark. This way they will round and stay under you. (See figure 5.14.)

Just as on the first reach, it is bad practice on the second reach to get caught in a continuous luffing match. If a boat tries to go over you, give it one sharp luff to send it a message that you won't let it do so. One sharp luff is infinitely

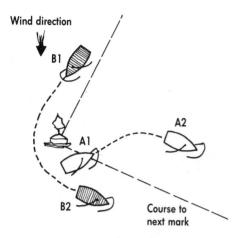

Wind direction

B1

A2

A1

B2

Course to
next mark

Figure 5.14 *To discourage a trailing boat from starting a luffing match, sail high after rounding the mark and then head down toward the next mark.*

better than a series of short and continuous luffs. If a faster boat is going to sail over you no matter what you do, don't take it up unless you are trying to get out of the main stream of traffic before you get rolled. By going high to get above the rest of the fleet, you'll avoid getting trampled by everyone and their friends. Above the fleet, you'll have clear air with which to get your speed back up. Until you get your speed back up, you're as vulnerable as a newborn babe.

If the fleet is heading too high on the second reach, opt for the low route, especially if the leg is a very broad reach. The boats that go high will have good speed initially, but they will end up on a slow dead run coming into the leeward mark. And as they come down to the leeward mark, they will be stuck in each other's wind shadows. By going low first, you'll be free to sail wind shifts and play waves without worrying about how to stay out of other boats' wind shadows. When you approach the mark, you'll be able to head up and sail faster than those coming down from on high.

But most of us find ourselves being forced high after rounding the reaching mark, as boats in front and behind head up to clear their air. In this case you have to head up with them to keep your air clear. To salvage a bad situation, keep close to the rhumb line by encouraging the boats around you to fall off by sailing down in the puffs or riding waves to leeward when you can.

Those lucky enough to be leading the fleet by a few boatlengths can stretch their lead safely by not sailing as high as the trailing boats scrapping for clear air. However, even though the leader could gain more distance

▼

on those heading higher by sailing straight down the rhumb line, it would be too risky to ignore the competition totally. If the wind builds or heads, the boats to windward will be able to sail right down over him. To hedge his bet, the skipper of the leading boat in this situation should steer a course that splits the difference between the course of the group behind him going high and the course to the leeward mark. This way he'll continue to make gains, but if the boats astern start gaining because of a wind shift or an increase in wind strength, he can head up and match their course to prevent them from sailing by.

"We did something like this on the second reach of the last race of the 1987 America's Cup challenger finals against *Kiwi Magic*," says Tom. "We pulled the perfect sucker move on them. That was when gennakers, or asymmetrical spinnakers, had become the rage as the newest loophole in the 12-meter class rules. Gennakers were particularly fast if you went high on a reach. So we developed a tactic for sailing against a boat that was flying a gennaker when we weren't. We lulled the Kiwis into a false sense of security by playing their game. We spent our lead by slowly heading up higher and higher. Of course they kept gaining on us, but our plan was to stay up as high as we could until they were just about to pass. Then we headed down to the mark and squared our spinnaker pole back. Downwind they were very slow, since the 12-meter rules don't allow gennakers to be flown from a pole because they are measured as jib. With our pole back from the headstay, we walked away from them. Our gain grew as they tried to change from their gennaker to a spinnaker, only to get both sails spliced together."

When a leeward boat has run out of moves to break a windward boat's inside overlap coming into a leeward mark, the move of last resort is to take the windward boat to the wrong side of the mark. When done correctly, the leeward boat luffs the windward boat past the mark and then jibes back to the mark, leaving the other boat clear astern with no rights to buoy room. (See figure 5.15.)

Carrying a boat to the wrong side of the mark used to be a heavily regulated maneuver, but under the new rules, only Rule 38 (Luffing Rights) applies until the two boats are about to round or pass the mark—at that point Rule 42 (Buoy Room) overrides the leeward boat's luffing rights. When making this move, take care to keep out of the two-boatlength circle. If you get too close to the mark and cross into the two boatlength circle, Rule 42 will kick in, and you'll have to fall off and give buoy room to the other boat if it still has an overlap.

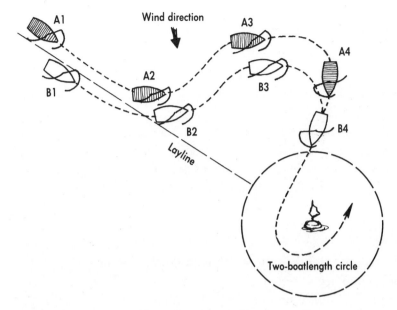

Figure 5.15 *Taking a boat to the wrong side of a mark is a maneuver of last resort to break an inside boat's overlap.*

"Save this move for a 'really good friend,' particularly those who have been offering heated remarks throughout the race," says Tom. "In 1983 we did it to Tom Blackaller during the America's Cup defender trials. Going to the wrong side of the mark makes a real mess since no one is ever ready for it. Both crews worked like crazy getting the chutes down while we jibed to the mark. We came out of that controlled crash clear ahead, and turned what would have been a sure win for them into a sure win for us."

This option only makes sense when you are match racing or if you're fleet racing and must beat a particular boat. Figure the scores carefully before you try this move, since you will lose a lot of time and places to other boats that go straight to the mark. Trying to control the effects of this move is like trying to contain a nuclear explosion. Leeward mark roundings can be difficult enough in the best circumstances, but throwing in extra tacks and jibes in close quarters, while the crew is stripping the chute and hoisting the jib, raises the disaster coefficient exponentially. Calling this move a controlled crash might a bit optimistic.

The Run

The common question from the foredeck when approaching the windward mark before the run is, "Which side do you want the pole rigged on?" The foredeck man needs to know what jibe the boat will be on after rounding the windward mark. To make that decision, a tactician needs the answers to a lot of questions. Which jibe is favored? What wind-shift pattern are you sailing in? How close is the competition? On which side will the geographical conditions, such as current, be favored? How long will the leg be? Will there be faster or slower boats around at the start of the leg? The tactician must grapple with these questions long before the boat starts turning around the windward mark. He should have time to think these through during the calmer period of the beat that comes after the boat is sailing well on the favored side of the course and before the hectic period when boats converge at the approaches to the windward mark. The decision has to made early so that the crew can get the spinnaker set up while hiking out on the windward rail.

To determine which jibe is favored, insist that your navigator calculate the compass courses between all marks when you get the course from the race committee. Most crews simply record the marks and which way to round them. The courses between marks have to be computed and given to the person calling tactics, because that person has to decide which side the spinnaker should set before figuring out the final approach to the windward mark. (It's also helpful to know the courses between marks, so that you don't get led astray by lost leaders.)

Knowing the rhumb line for the next leg allows you to compute which jibe you'll be on. If the wind is blowing to the right side of the rhumb line, you'll be on starboard jibe. If the wind blows from the left side of the line, you'll be on port jibe. (See figure 5.16.)

A quick method for figuring out the favored jibe is to remember which tack you sailed more during the beat; the favored jibe is the tack you sailed least during the beat. For example, if you sailed on starboard tack more during the beat, then the wind must be blowing from the right side of the rhumb line (looking upwind); therefore, port jibe will be favored on the run. (See figure 5.17.) If you didn't time how long you were on each tack, look at your log of compass headings and find the average between your mean heading on each tack.

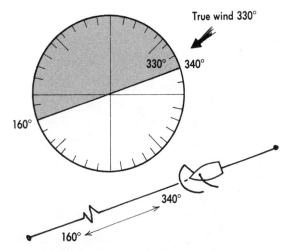

Figure 5.16 *The compass course for the next leg of the course is the most important piece of information in figuring out which side of the boat to set the spinnaker on. Compare that course line to the true wind direction. If the wind is blowing to the right side of the line, then you'll be on starboard jibe. If the wind blows to the left side of the line, you'll be on port jibe.*

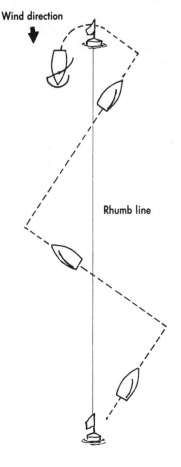

Figure 5.17 *Since the boat spends almost twice as much time on port tack than starboard going upwind, starboard jibe on the run is favored.*

Even though your calculations indicate that a bear-away set is favored, the proper rounding move could be a jibe set just to protect the inside overlap at the next mark from the boats close behind you. Also, windspeed will influence whether you do a bear-away set or a jibe set. A jibe set is slow in light air because you lose so much speed making the 180-degree turn. The tighter the turn, the more speed you lose. Unless you are match racing, jibe sets are to be avoided unless the opposite jibe is favored by more than 20 degrees. But when the competition is hot on your heels, it's better to trade some of your lead for insurance toward keeping the inside position at the next mark by doing a jibe set. In most fleet-racing situations a bear-away set followed by a jibe is more effective than a jibe set because you won't lose as much speed.

When developing your game plan for sailing the run, you'll have to use all the information you've collected on the behavior of the wind thus far in the race. When sailing an Olympic course (windward leg, reach, reach, windward, leeward, windward), you'll have sailed two beats before you start the run. This is where your compass log continues to be valuable. After sailing four legs of the course, you should have a very good idea of how the wind is shifting over the racing area. By looking around and recording what the wind has done throughout the race, you'll know whether the wind is oscillating or persistently shifting; you'll know if the shore or any other geographic feature is bending the wind; and you'll have an idea of whether the wind is dying or strengthening.

In an oscillating breeze, you can predict the first shift downwind before going around the windward mark by consulting your compass log. If you were last lifted on starboard, begin the run on port. In other words, if the wind last went right (while looking upwind), go left looking downwind. By jibing on the shifts, you'll keep from getting too far from the center of the course. Going downwind, you should avoid the corners of the course where the laylines from the marks converge, just as you do when going upwind.

When sailing in a persistent shift, sail the lifted tack first. Then when you jibe you'll be on the knocked course all the way to the mark. (See figure 5.18.) Sailing too far away from the shift can cause two problems: first, the wind does not fill in across the course evenly, therefore the boats closer to the new wind will be sailing in higher velocity, enabling them to sail a lower angle with better boatspeed; second, if you go too far on the lifted tack before jibing onto the headed jibe, you'll overstand. In this case, overstanding means that you would be coming into the mark on such a tight reach that those above you would be cracked off and going faster. Hence, in a persistent shift, hedge

Initial wind direction

Wind persistently shifts
to the right

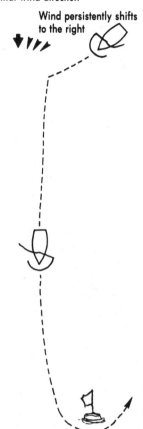

Figure 5.18 *When sailing downwind in a persistent shift, sail the lifted jibe first. When you jibe, you'll be on the headed course all the way to the mark.*

your bet by staying near the fleet and keeping it between you and the new wind as you sail.

When you're not sure which wind-shift pattern you're sailing in, and are looking for some empirical data on what the wind is doing, stand up and look astern. On the run, the new wind will always fill in from behind. So use the boats behind you as telltales. Check how the boats on both sides of the course are trimming their sails to discern where the new wind will be coming from.

In picking which jibe to start the run on, the final consideration is how long the leg will be. The longer the run, the more you can concentrate on playing the shifts, and the less you'll have to worry about protecting the inside overlap.

When the current is running hard, forget about playing the wind shifts on the run. The best strategy is to hook into a strong favorable current or stay out of an adverse current. During the 1987 Newport leg of the Maxi Worlds, Tom, while steering *Kialoa*, broke the cardinal rule of staying between the competition and the next mark to get out of a two-knot adverse current. One race's downwind leg was a run from Brenton Tower into Narragansett Bay, against an ebbing tide. After rounding Brenton Tower, *Kialoa* had a narrow lead over the nine-boat maxi fleet that would be hard to keep on the run. Noticing that the rest of the fleet was set up for a jibe set so that they could head straight down the rhumb line through the middle of Narragansett Bay, Tom had his crew execute a bear-away set and headed toward the east shore of the bay. By hiding behind the Castle Hill shore, *Kialoa* avoided the strong current and kept the rest of the fleet from blanketing their wind. Over previous America's Cup summers, Tom had learned that the current along the shore was much weaker. (See figure 5.19.) "At first we looked like we'd thrown away our lead as we sailed away from the fleet," says Tom. "It was scary, and I started to question the call. But we came offshore near the leeward mark looking like prophets. Our lead was substantial."

Tactics on the Run

Let's preface our discussion of downwind tactics by saying that if two boats started the run neck-and-neck and then split for opposite sides of the course, the boat that sailed inside the rhumb line between the windward and leeward marks would have room when the two boats converged at the mark—that is, if the wind and current were equal over the course. On a course where the leeward mark is rounded to port, the boat that went inside the rhumb line initially will have the added benefit of the starboard-tack advantage when converging with a competitor.

Most boats, whether big boats or dinghies, will get to the leeward mark faster if they tack downwind from broad reach to broad reach than if they head straight for the leeward mark on a dead run. To get the most out of each jibe, the strategy on the run is to jibe on the lifts. When lifted on the run, the apparent wind moves aft and gets lighter, causing the boat to slow down. For example, you have been lifted if you find that you need to trim your pole aft and ease your sails more to sail the same compass course as before. At this point you should consider jibing. Just as you don't tack on every header when

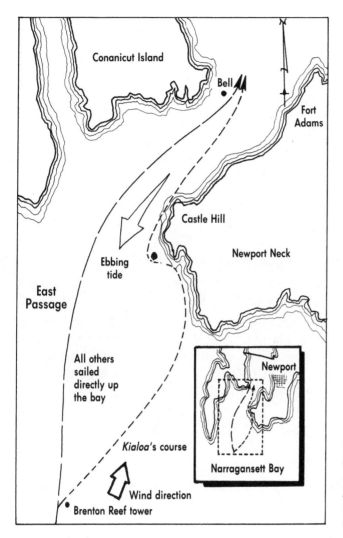

Figure 5.19 *On a run up Narragansett Bay from the Brenton Tower during the 1987 Maxi Worlds, Kialoa pulled away from the fleet by getting out of ebbing tide by sailing up the east shore of the bay.*

going to windward, you have to sail on for a few boatlengths to make sure the lift will last; it could be a temporary velocity shift. (See the discussion of apparent wind on pages 128–132 for more information on velocity shifts.) The more time you spend on the headed jibe, the faster you'll go, since the apparent wind will be farther forward as well as stronger.

The angle that you sail away from the rhumb line varies on the type of boat you sail and the wind strength. The stronger the wind, the closer to the rhumb line you can sail. Dinghy sailors can only find their boat's optimum sailing

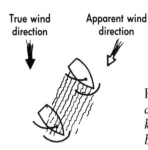

True wind
direction

Apparent wind
direction

Figure 5.20 *Your wind shadow falls in the direction of your apparent wind instead of in the direction of the true wind. To keep out of another boat's wind shadow, never let a windward boat's masthead fly point toward your boat.*

angles through experience in a range of wind conditions, while big-boat sailors have the advantage of electronic instruments, computers, and, most important, Velocity Prediction Programs. (For more specific information on how to find the optimum jibing angles for a big boat, see Chapter 8.)

Whether you're on the offensive or the defensive, the first tactical principle to consider on the run is where your wind shadow is cast. The wind coming off your sails goes to leeward in the direction of the apparent wind, not the true wind. (See figure 5.20.) This is especially important to realize when sailing downwind, because the direction of the apparent wind varies much more than it does when you are sailing upwind. Therefore, when on the defensive, keep an eye on the masthead fly of the boat behind. Don't let yourself get caught with his masthead fly pointing directly at your boat. If the trailing boat's masthead fly is pointing behind your boat, you are ahead of his wind shadow. When its wind indicator begins to move toward you, head up get some speed to pull away from its approaching wind shadow. If the windward boat's masthead fly is pointing in front of your boat, you haven't crossed through its shadow yet. When its fly, which has been pointing in front of you, starts moving toward you, fall off to gain distance to leeward, and slow down so that you don't sail into his shadow.

On the run, it's the trailing boat that has the upper hand, because its wind shadow is projected forward. Since the skipper of the leading boat has to look over his shoulder to protect himself against the trailing boat's onslaught, it's easy to harass him. Let's go through the moves to make on the run.

If your goal is to get by a leading boat and have the inside overlap at the leeward mark, you can't cavalierly head down the course solely with the idea of blanketing any boat in your path. You've got to think several moves ahead so that you can force the other boat into a disadvantageous position. Unless it's windy, the jibing angles for most boats are too wide for a trailing boat to be able to blanket a leading boat's wind on both jibes. Therefore, you have to create a strategy in which you'll blanket the leading boat when it counts— on the longer jibe to the mark.

For instance, say two boats are going down the run on starboard tack toward a leeward mark to be rounded to port. The boat behind not only wants to pass the boat ahead, but also wants to get the inside position at the leeward mark. To slow the leader most effectively, the trailing boat would use its sails to blanket the wind from the leading boat by sitting on the leading boat's windward quarter. But this would force the leading boat to jibe away onto port to get clear air. At that point the trailing boat has gained nothing, since the leader has jibed over to the inside position. (See figure 5.21.)

Figure 5.22 shows how the trailing boat can avoid the problem addressed in figure 5.21. Instead of blanketing the leading boat by getting up on the leader's windward quarter, the trailing boat rides on the leader's leeward quarter and pushes the leader past the layline to the mark. The boat clear ahead is kept from jibing because it would be jibing too close. If the trailing boat is not close enough to prevent the leading boat from jibing, the trailing boat should bear off and sail a lower angle before the leading boat jibes. When the leading boat jibes, the trailing boat will be able to jibe right on the leader's wind and force him to jibe back toward the port layline.

Figure 5.23 takes up where Figure 5.22 left off. Once in the lead, Boat B still needs to fight to protect the inside position. To get back in the race, Boat

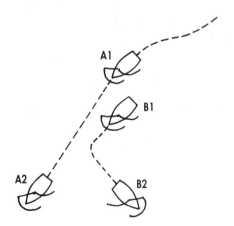

Figure 5.21 *As A sails above B's quarter and blankets B's wind, B jibes away where it will have the inside position coming into the leeward mark.*

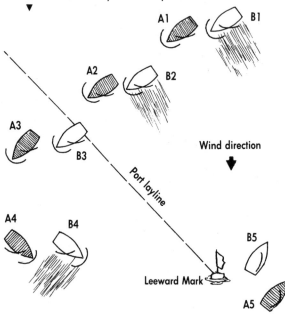

Figure 5.22 *To pass Boat A and get the inside position at the mark, Boat B pushes A past the layline to the mark. By keeping very close and slightly to leeward, B prevents A from jibing. Once past layline, B jibes and heads for the mark.*

Figure 5.23 *In position 1, A is pinned to the outside and has no chance of getting buoy room at the leeward mark. By slowing down and falling behind B (position 2), A is free to sail higher than B. To protect its wind, B simply heads up to a closer reach so that A's wind shadow is not a threat. In position 5, B makes a sharp turn for the mark and breaks any overlap.*

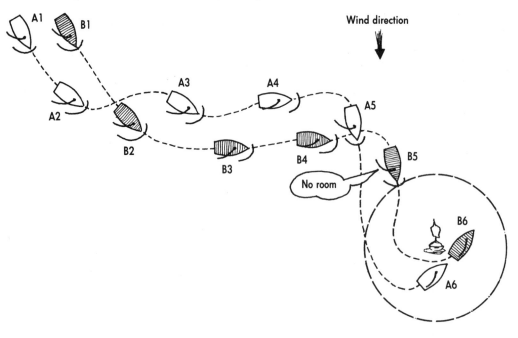

A, the one pinned to the outside, must slow down and fall behind the inside boat so that it can swing around and try to get an inside overlap. But Boat B has three good options. First, B can slow down with A to keep A pinned to the outside. Second, if B doesn't want to slow down because other boats in the fleet are catching up, or if B doesn't want to lose distance on the leaders, B can ignore A's move to windward and attempt to outrun Boat A to the mark. Normally, attempting to outrun Boat A would be risky, but since Boat B made sure to overstand the mark, its apparent wind should be far enough forward that A won't be able to get on B's wind and slow B down. The third option B has is to head higher on port tack to match A's change in course. Sailing high protects B's wind and the inside position at the mark. Just before getting to the two-boatlength circle, B can break any overlap A might have established by falling off sharply and heading to the mark.

Jibing Duels

Just as your goal in a tacking duel upwind is to herd the trailing boat over to the layline so that you can blanket the trailing boat all the way to the windward mark, the same is true in a jibing duel—except it's the trailing boat that herds the leading boat to the layline. On the layline, the trailing boat will pass the leader by slowing it with a continuous stream of bad air. To herd the leading boat to the layline of your choosing, use loose and tight covers. Sail behind the leader so that your shadow is clear of his sails when he's going in the direction you want, and sail up on his windward hip, blanketing him when he tries to escape. When he's blanketed, he'll have no choice but to jibe back and continue in the direction you've chosen.

A fake jibe is the leading boat's defense during a jibing duel. When done right, the leading boat will get the trailing boat off its wind by tricking the trailing boat into jibing away. A fake jibe is easier to make convincing than is a fake tack, and you lose very little speed in the process. To pull off a fake jibe, exchange a few actual jibes with the trailing boat first, then quietly pass the word to your crew that the next jibe will be a fake one. Go through all the motions: get the mast man and bowman in position, have the appropriate people in the cockpit manning the winches, have the pitman at the topping lift—everyone should be looking at the chute. Then yell, "Jibe ho!" or "We're jibing." Fall off and sail dead downwind, pull your main in to the centerline, and to complete your deception, yell "Trip!" for the spinnaker guy to be released from the pole. Since the person who trips the pole knows that you are doing a fake jibe, he won't release the guy from the pole. He can add to the illusion that you're jibing by reaching up and pulling down on the trip line—while being careful that it runs through his fingers.

Another trick that adds to the illusion is to tension the lazy sheet and then let the after guy run so that the spinnaker pole swings forward. (See figure 5.24.) Even though the pole goes forward, the guy is still in the jaw of the pole so that as soon as your competitor jibes, you can pull the pole back into position.

If you've done things right, the other boat, desperate to stay on your wind, will complete his jibe when he hears you yell "Trip." Even if the trailing boat doesn't take the bait, you won't lose much distance since your spinnaker will be full throughout the maneuver. The fake jibe is the perfect escape when a trailing boat pins you to one side of the course.

"The fake jibe is one of my favorite maneuvers," says Gary. "I've done this many times in 12-meters, maxi boats, and a variety of smaller boats. The best time to do one is when sailing side by side with another boat on starboard tack. The key is to have a good communications system with your trimmers and foredeck crew. The standard command for initiating a dip-pole jibe is 'Trip,' which is like saying 'Helm's a lee' when tacking. (Normally when the skipper yells 'Trip,' the mastman releases the guy from the end of the pole so that the pole can swing across to the other side of the boat.) My crew knows that if I yell something like 'Hit it,' or 'Do it now,' they should fake tripping the pole.

"When the other boat jibes in response, then I come back onto my original course, which is starboard tack, while the other boat is now on port. You don't

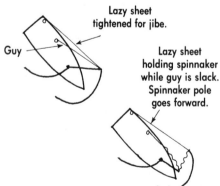

Lazy sheet tightened for jibe.

Guy

Lazy sheet holding spinnaker while guy is slack. Spinnaker pole goes forward.

Figure 5.24 *To make a fake jibe more convincing, tighten the lazy sheet, so that when the skipper yells "Trip," the guy can be released, which lets the pole go forward and makes the hoax look more convincing. Yet with the lazy sheet tight, the spinnaker will stay trimmed.*

even need to hit the other boat to hurt them. The damage gets done as they do a panic jibe to stay out of your way. Their chute collapses and everything gets tangled. It's a great high for your crew to watch a competitor scramble to keep clear. When it works, the fake jibe is a guaranteed way to make two boatlengths."

To keep from being sailed out to the layline, the one possible defense the windward boat could attempt is to slow down and make it too painful for the leeward boat to keep going to the layline. The leeward boat would either have to slow down also, since it wouldn't be able to sail through the windward boat's wind shadow, or the leeward boat would have to jibe away for clear air. If the leeward boat slows down and keeps going to the layline, it will be forced to worry about keeping ahead of other boats in the fleet catching up and passing. Before attempting this defense, the tactician on the windward boat has to figure out the race results. If his boat can afford to let a few boats pass while maintaining its place in the standings, and the leeward boat can't, then the only reasonable option open to the leeward boat would be to jibe away. Obviously this would not work in a match race, since the leeward boat would lose nothing by slowing down.

One defense that a boat clear ahead and to leeward can use that doesn't require slowing down is to sail as fast as possible to the layline. At the layline or even slightly before it, the leading boat must jibe before or at the same time as the trailing boat does, in order to keep the lead from changing hands. After the jibe, the leading boat will be the outside boat; but by jibing before or at the same time as the inside boat, the outside boat (neé the leading boat) will keep its apparent wind forward of the inside boat's wind shadow. To get the inside position at the leeward mark, the outside boat needs to luff the windward boat high of the mark. Not only does this move the outside boat's apparent wind forward—away from the inside boat's wind shadow—but when the outside boat falls off to the mark, it will break the windward boat's overlap.

Sailing by the Lee

You're sailing by the lee when your boat sails downwind with the wind blowing across the boat's leeward quarter. Because of the potential for an unplanned jibe, sailing by the lee should be done with considerable caution. There are many tactical situations where doing so is useful for a short distance to avoid a time- and distance-consuming jibe. Sailing by the lee is fast when going below another boat to get an overlap; when crossing a downwind finish line; when sailing down to the leeward mark to avoid the tangle that would result from a jibe immediately followed by a takedown; or when maneuvering to get out of a trailing boat's wind shadow. Attempt this tactic only in light to medium wind, since boats become unstable when sailing by the lee in heavier winds. Never sail by the lee for a sustained period of time because of the inherent risks; just take little bites to leeward when they can help you the most.

The best time to try this tactic is when the boat is sailing its fastest, because the apparent wind has moved forward. Normally, when sailing downwind, a helmsman will steer the boat to leeward in the puffs, and reach up to gain speed as the puffs dissipate. A helmsman can take a bite to leeward in a puff of wind, or when surfing down a wave; in either case, the apparent wind moves forward as the boat goes faster.

Beware, however, when your boat begins to slow down. It is important to act quickly by heading up to keep the boat under control. In centerboard boats, a skipper can easily sail lower and lower in a puff without realizing he's greatly by the lee. When the puff dies, the apparent wind becomes equal to the true wind, and the boom will jibe with such force that the boat will capsize.

Remain aware of your masthead fly; avoid sailing more than 20 degrees by the lee. If the boat feels out of control because the underwater surfaces are taking over and beginning to steer you, simply head up to regain balance. To balance the helm, experiment with all angles of heel. When sailing by the lee, this will normally be about 10 degrees of windward heel. When sailing by the lee with a spinnaker, stability may be enhanced by strapping the foot of the chute. See that the clews stay on opposite sides of the headstay; having both clews on the same side of the forestay will induce rolling.

Stability is reduced when sailing by the lee because you are forced to trim the spinnaker almost completely on the windward side of the boat. If you don't, the spinnaker will end up blanketed by the mainsail, and will collapse. Therefore, your helmsman has to have an excellent feeling for how the boat is behaving, and the crew should be looking out for puffs or waves approaching from astern that could start the boat rolling out of control.

If the boat gets out of control, your best solution is to head up. You can try overtrimming to stabilize the spinnaker, but overtrimming can cause an unscheduled jibe unless a preventer has been rigged on the boom. A wild, flying boom is dangerous on any boat, particularly on boats with boom vangs that attach to the mast. These vangs allow the boom to swing from side to side while keeping the boom low so that it rakes the deck clear of any crew members standing up. A preventer rigged to a block led forward is the solution.

When sailing with the jib winged out to weather, instead of with a spinnaker, it is best to ease the sail forward until it starts to become blanketed by the mainsail.

Gauging the Fleet

As when sailing to windward, while sailing the run, keep an eye on the rest of the fleet to judge your performance relative to others, and to read the wind. On boats with more than two crew, one person should be responsible for constantly looking aft for new wind, because when sailing downwind, the new wind fills in from astern. Don't just look for cat's-paws on the water, but look at the other boats and use them as wind socks. In dinghies, take note of where other boats are planing if you're not. In big boats, you can pick out the strong puffs coming toward you as boats astern start rolling from side to side. Whatever type of boat you sail, you can pick out wind shifts by the angles at which other boats are sailing.

It's often difficult to determine whether you are ahead or behind on a run, whether you are gaining or losing compared to boats around you. A good way to observe this without a hand-bearing compass is to look at the mainsails of other boats. Mainsails make a good reference, because on a run all the boats in the fleet will have their booms out nearly perpendicular to the centerline of their boats. If you see the forward part of a boat's main, this is an indication that you are ahead. If you see the back side of the other boat's main, it is ahead of you. When you see both the front and back sides of the other boat's main simultaneously, you are even. Should you start seeing more and more of the back side of another boat's main, you are losing ground; if you see more and more of the forward side of another boat's main, you are pulling away.

Gaining and Breaking Overlaps

It is on the run that the greatest variety of headings can be justified as a boat's proper course. Therefore, to increase your tactical options and to control other boats, you have to be adept at making and breaking overlaps. First let's go through gaining and breaking overlaps while sailing down the leg, and then how to do the same while rounding the leeward mark.

A leeward boat is most vulnerable when it loses its luffing rights to a windward boat. On a run, leeward boats have two easy options for getting back their luffing rights. By definition, boats cannot be overlapped when they are on different tacks—except when going around all marks other than the windward mark. Also, Rule 38.2(b) says that for the purpose of Rule 38 (Luffing Rights), a new overlap is created when the windward or leeward boat tacks or jibes. Hence, if you jibe away and then jibe back, you'll regain your luffing rights as long as the windward boat doesn't still have mast abeam.

Jibing to break an overlap can be greatly abbreviated while sailing dead downwind. Because the wind is coming straight across the boat's stern, you can jibe your sails without changing course. By throwing your mainsail from one side of the boat and then back, you'll break the overlap and be fully entitled to luff as you please again, as long as the other boat doesn't have mast abeam. This is especially useful in boats not using spinnakers. Since Rule 64.2 doesn't allow you to fly your spinnaker pole and mainsail on the same side of the mast, you'll have to jibe your spinnaker too—or at least attempt to do so. When jibing, see that your boom or spinnaker does not touch the other boat. A boat tacking or jibing must keep clear of a boat on a tack.

Rule 41.2 keeps you from luffing the windward boat immediately after finishing your second jibe. The rule states that if you tack or jibe into a right-of-way position, you must complete your tack or jibe far enough away that a boat on a tack can keep clear without having to begin altering its course until you have completed your tack or jibe. To satisfy a protest committee that you did not jibe and then start your luff immediately, establish a sense of timing by counting out loud to five. If the other boat hasn't moved to windward by then, you can stuff your boat up to windward as fast as you want, and there isn't a jury that will throw you out for hitting it. Once the other boat alters course to get away from you, it loses its protection under 41.2; at that point, stop counting and start luffing.

You can also use Rule 38.2(b) as a defense when you are sailing down the run with a leeward boat luffing you. You can turn the tables on it by jibing your sails over and claiming right-of-way as a starboard tacker. Be sure to give it room and opportunity to get out of your way. Rule 41.2 states that you can't tack or jibe into a right-of-way position unless the newly burdened boat has time to keep clear. The newly burdened boat does not have to begin altering its course until you've completed your jibe.

Rule 38.2(b) also says that for the purposes of luffing rights only, if two boats become separated by more than two lengths of the longer boat, than the overlap is broken. On a run, it's easy to diverge two boatlengths to leeward without losing distance on the boat to windward. When you re-converge, you'll have regained your luffing rights, provided the windward boat doesn't have mast abeam.

Both of these options for breaking an overlap that pertains to luffing rights can be done on a reach or a beat, but they are much easier to do when running because you are unhampered by the windward boat's wind shadow, and because you can jibe away with little or no change of course.

Your third option for breaking the overlap is to sail clear ahead of the windward boat, but that's hard to do. The overlap is broken when you drop back and are clear astern of the windward boat, but Rule 38.2(a) prevents you from luffing above your proper course "if when the overlap began or at any time during its existence, the windward boat had mast abeam."

Approaching the Leeward Mark

The first rule of approaching the leeward mark is not to approach from the outside layline—i.e., the port layline when the mark is to be rounded to port, or the starboard layline when the mark is to be rounded to starboard. As the outside boat you'll have to give room to everyone and his brothers, cousins, long-lost relatives, and casual acquaintances, because you'll be overlapping

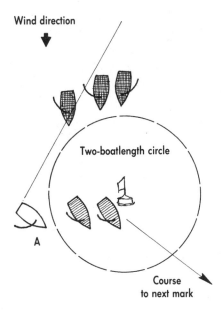

Figure 5.25 *Being the outside-most boat, A must give room to all the boats in the diagram.*

the lot of them. (See figure 5.25.) If you are sure there are going to be no other boats nearby when you round, coming in from the outside layline allows you to make a smooth turn around the mark. Let's go through some safe ways of approaching the mark so that you can execute a smooth rounding.

Once you, or a boat or boats with which you are overlapped, gets to the two-boatlength circle, the buoy-room rule supersedes the most fundamental rule in the book. During the rounding is the only time a starboard-tack boat does not automatically have right-of-way over a port-tack boat. So to avoid getting pushed around by a port tacker, use your rights as a starboard tacker as long as you can—until the first overlapped boat crosses the two-boatlength circle.

When converging with a port tacker at a leeward mark to be rounded to port, pressure the port tacker to sail away from the two-boatlength circle so that you will have as much space as you need to make a wide turn around the mark. Once you enter the two-boatlength circle, the port tacker can demand that you not take too much room. Therefore, start nudging him away from the mark while you are five to seven boatlengths away. Go as far as to force him to jibe to starboard. Unprepared for a last-minute jibe, the outside boat will tie itself in knots. If you push him to the outside far enough, you'll be able to jibe and head to the mark without the other boat overlapping you. With the overlap broken, you can take all the room you want while rounding the mark. (See figure 5.26.) Of course, if you go too far to the outside, other boats can cut inside you—so keep your eyes open!

When behind, you can establish an overlap by blanketing a boat ahead of you. Just before you catch up enough to tap his transom, duck down to leeward and establish the overlap. Or, if the wind is dead aft and you are both approaching the leeward mark on starboard jibe, you can force the leading boat to the outside by setting up off his leeward quarter so that you blanket only half of the leading boat's sail plan. As he begins to slow down, the only way he can keep you from gaining an overlap is to head up to escape your wind shadow. If he falls off to preserve the inside position, he'll be totally blanketed and you'll catch up and take the inside position anyway. The leader's defense would be to head up a bit to get his apparent wind farther forward, and then, once up to speed, jibe and try to sail across your wind shadow to the inside position.

To protect your lead from a group of boats behind you, position your boat so that your sails get wind blowing through a gap in the pack of boats behind

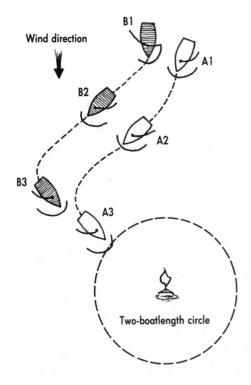

Wind direction

B1

A1

B2

A2

B3

A3

Two-boatlength circle

Figure 5.26 *Since the buoy room rule strips a boat of its starboard tack rights once the boats are in the two-boatlength circle, Boat A uses its rights as a starboard boat before losing its advantage.*

you. The breeze blowing through the gap will be stronger than the normal wind because the wind accelerates through the gap. It's the same principle that creates tide races through constricted channels. So, just when it looks as though you are about to be blanketed, you'll actually be getting stronger wind that will allow you to pull away from the group astern. Be careful that the boats don't close the gap and leave you breathless.

Should you be quiet or noisy when approaching marks? By staying quiet you can make a sneak attack to the inside position, but once you have established an overlap, make your intentions known so that all the boats that must give you room have time to respond.

Getting buoy room on a whole slew off boats can be as easy as stealing candy from a baby; all you have to do is round just behind a large group of boats. If you're to the outside of two or more boats heading toward the leeward mark, slow down five or six lengths from the perimeter of the two-boatlength circle so that you can try to get the inside position. Even if you don't get the inside overlap, you'll pass the outside boats in the group that rounded the mark ahead of you, because when a group of boats goes around the mark, only the three boats closest to the mark have crossed into the two-boatlength circle. All the other boats that go around the mark outside of the three innermost boats round the mark without ever crossing the perimeter of the two-boatlength circle; therefore you'll be able to establish an overlap and claim buoy room from them. As you go around the mark behind a group of boats, get on the windward quarter of the boat farthest inside. This keeps you in clear air, traps leeward boats so they can't tack, and keeps boats approaching from astern from getting inside of you.

It pays to keep your eyes out of your own boat as you approach the mark. Always be on the lookout for a last-minute opportunity, because many times boats will work hard trying to get an inside overlap, only to screw up their boat handling. Keeping a sharp lookout, Gary passed 20 boats at a leeward mark sailing a Finn at CORK (Canadian Olympic Training Regatta at Kingston) in 1972. "Twenty boats fought to get to the leeward mark first. The first boat did a great job getting there, but its skipper forgot to put his centerboard down. I was trailing the group of boats, and I noticed out of the corner of my eye that the inside boat didn't have his board down. Therefore, instead of getting in line to round outside, I shot for the inside position. As the inside boat went around, he started sideslipping, which allowed me to get inside of him. In that one move, I passed 20 boats."

To preserve your inside position for the last four or five boatlengths before reaching the perimeter of the two-boatlength circle, you'll have to ensure that you sail no faster than the outside boat. Slowing down when the outside boat does will prevent him from being able to cross behind in an attempt to get inside of you. You can slow down by overtrimming your main or getting your jib up and taking down your spinnaker early.

A trick that Gary uses to make or break overlaps coming into a leeward mark is to get the other boat to hoist its jib too early. "Before a spinnaker takedown, boats generally raise their jibs when the boats around them hoist. So, whether I'm ahead or behind, I do a fake hoist. Above five lengths from the mark, I'll loudly yell 'Hoist.' My crew has been informed to raise the jib a third of the way. They raise it as fast as possible to convince the other boat's crew that we are raising the jib all the way. Once the other boat's crew gets their jib up, they'll slow down, so you'll be able to come from behind and get an overlap, or you'll be able to squirt away to break an overlap.

"At the Maxi Boat World Championship in Newport in August of 1986," says Gary, "we were having a particularly competitive downwind leg on *Mat-*

ador, sailing against *Ondine* and *Boomerang*. After perfect spinnaker sets, all three of the boats were separated by just a few feet as we sailed downwind. The whole leg was a battle for who would get the inside overlap at the mark, five miles away. Barring crew errors, the boat that could claim the inside position at the mark would win the race because it would have an invincible position on the short beat to the finish line. We used every trick we knew on that run to gain the inside overlap. We slowed them with our sails, either by blanketing them or by channeling turbulent backwind toward them. We inched ahead by jibing to take advantage of wind shifts and to get the starboard tack advantage at crossing situations. With sheer muscle power on the coffee grinders, we pumped the spinnaker so that we could ride waves better. Once ahead, we stayed there by making the others sail in our wake. Smaller boats don't mind sailing in bigger boats' wakes because they can catch a tow, but when you're racing against boats whose hull speed is the same as yours, your stern wave acts like a wall that the other boats have a very hard time getting past. Our final trick was to herd the other two boats together so that they would be forced to battle each other. In the end, *Matador* got the inside overlap. It was one of the greatest moments I've had in maxi-boat sailing; we came from behind two boats, having a clear overlap as we rounded the leeward mark.

"Despite the results, I made a critical tactical mistake. Having been intent on the overlap and running the crew at a pace that left no margin for error, I didn't leave the crew enough time to set up for the spinnaker takedown and the leeward mark rounding. During the battle for the inside position, we were forced to change back and forth between a floater and a leeward spinnaker takedown. Eventually the crew became confused with the rapidly changing calls.

"While it was clear in my mind exactly what circumstances required which takedown, it was not clear to the crew. So while we won the battle to get the inside overlap at the leeward mark, disaster struck. We rounded the leeward mark with the genoa halfway up, the spinnaker dragging in the water, and total chaos on board. However, in the middle of all the confusion I took a quick look around and noticed that *Ondine* and *Boomerang* were also suffering similar 'Chinese fire drills.' Here were three of the world's best racing yachts. Many among the crew had competed in the America's Cup and/or the Olympics, and had dozens of national and world championship credits among them. Yet all three boats had spinnakers in the water, headsails on the deck, and skippers yelling more and more about less and less. It was a real lesson for 75 sailors. In the end, *Ondine* was able to clean up their mess the fastest and deservedly won the race. *Matador* was runner-up, just one second ahead of *Boomerang*."

As you approach the leeward mark, remember to keep your speed up so that you'll be able to get away from the mark quickly. If there are no other boats around, don't simply bear off to a dead run at the end of the leg when you really ought to put in one more jibe. The only way to sail as aggressively as possible is to go out and practice your boat handling so that the crew can quickly do a jibe followed by a takedown.

The Rounding

Make your final approach to a leeward mark so that you change course as little as possible when heading up for the beat. The basic rounding maneuver is to swing wide and cut close to the mark as you leave it behind. This way you avoid losing a lot of speed in going from a dead run to a beat. By cutting close to the leeward mark when leaving it behind, you'll be as far to windward as possible, which allows you the freedom to tack away, because no boat behind you will be able to get on your hip. Practice going around marks to find your boat's optimum turning radius. The optimum turning radius is the closest course you can steer around a mark without losing any speed. Most boats can make this radius within one to one and a half boatlengths of the mark.

Swinging wide and cutting close as you round is called a *tactical rounding*. A tactical rounding may be easy when you are the only boat going around the mark, but it takes a lot of practice to do it right. The rules don't allow an inside boat to take all the room needed for a tactical round, but Rule 42.1(a) does allow for a "seamanlike" rounding.

On the other hand, if you are clear ahead of other boats, you can take as much room as you want within the two-boatlength circle, and if a boat from clear astern tries to get between you and the mark, just slam the door on him. Boats coming from clear astern have no rights to take room if they did not establish an overlap in time. But you've got to be able to slam the door. You can't simply throw someone out for taking room. If you forgot to put your centerboard down and slipped to leeward of the mark, leaving enough room for him to get in, he can take the room. But he's taking a risk. If you get your board back down, you're entitled to squeeze back up to the mark. If you prove that you could have hit the boat that snuck in, he'll be disqualified unless he takes an alternate penalty.

There are several techniques to use when rounding a leeward mark. Make all your adjustments during the approach, so at the mark you can concentrate on rounding. Trim your sheets in as you round up. Never pre-sheet your jib, because this will prevent your boat from rounding up toward the wind. Trimming your main in early will actually help your boat spin toward the wind, to say nothing of saving the arms of the mainsheet trimmer. When trimming, grab the sheet right at the block and make a few long trims on the line instead of a lot of short pulls. The faster you get the sheet in, the sooner you can concentrate on hiking and steering.

Dinghy helmsmen who trim the mainsheet through their teeth will immediately start having better roundings as soon as they cure themselves of this bad habit. Trimming the mainsheet can be done faster and more safely by trimming the mainsheet out to your hand holding the hiking stick. Holding the sheet and the hiking stick with one hand frees your other hand to reach in and continue pulling in the sheet while you are hiking out with your eyes on the boats ahead of you. Other advantages of not using your teeth are that you won't get dead-fish breath, and you won't need dentures prematurely.

As you round up, keep the boat flat; when a boat heels, it makes leeway. By keeping the boat flat, you can stay up on the windward quarter of boats ahead of you. Avoid tacking immediately after rounding. The abrupt change in direction could stop you in your tracks. Also, the wake of the fleet still approaching the mark will meet you head-on for the first few minutes. Let other boats ahead of you tack away and clear out first. If you're the first to tack, and several boats follow, you'll be trapped again by many windward boats. Wait until you are up to full speed before tacking.

Avoid making a short tack to clear your air. The two quick tacks will cost you too much ground, and you risk getting tacked on.

Never dive to leeward of a boat after rounding the mark unless you have a 100-percent chance of breaking through to leeward. Boats often get caught heading too high after rounding. This is your chance to sail low with speed, and push through to leeward.

The Buoy Room Rule

Before we get into the technicalities of room at the jibe mark, let's define some terms. The *two-boatlength circle* is an imaginary circular perimeter around a mark with a radius two overall boatlengths long.

Overall boatlength comprises the boat *and all its equipment in its normal position*. Therefore, if you had a dinghy overhanging the stern of your boat from davits, that would add to the overall length of your boat. When a boat is flying a spinnaker, its overall length is measured from the farthest aft point on the transom to the farthest reaches of the billowing spinnaker. Hence a 40-foot boat could have an overall length of 50 feet when you take the spinnaker into account.

According to the preamble of Section C of Part IV of the rule book (the section of the rules covering passing marks and obstructions), the rules in Section C override those in Section B (Principal Right-of-Way Rules) when there is a conflict. The only exception is Rule 35, which covers limitations on altering course. Therefore, the buoy-room rule gives right-of-way to an inside port-tack boat over an outside starboard tacker; gives an inside windward boat rights over an outside leeward boat; causes leeward boats to lose their luffing rights; and when specifically allowed, the buoy-room rule gives an inside boat room to tack or jibe without having to keep clear of boats on a tack.

This turnaround in the rules does not start until the leading overlapped boat crosses the perimeter of the two-boatlength circle. The radius of the two-boatlength circle is based on the overall length of the leading boat. That means if you are sailing a C&C 34 and are overlapping an 80-foot maxi's stern, the radius of the two-boatlength circle is 160 feet.

Of course, on the water, situations are never this black and white, since there are no sophisticated devices that trigger a signal when a boat enters the two-boatlength circle. Instead, judging the distance is more or less subjective, and is left up to the competitors.

To keep competitors from abusing this situation, the rule makers put the burden of proof on the boat getting the most benefit from a call. Hence, if you are getting closer and closer to another boat, and claim you had an inside overlap as that boat entered the two-boatlength circle, then you must prove to a protest committee that you made the overlap in time (Rule 42.1 [d]).

Normally the only way you can satisfy a jury is to have a witness who was in a position to see the overlap as well as judge when the leading boat crossed into the two boatlength circle. On the other hand, if you've been sailing down the reach with a boat overlapped inside of you, and you claim to have broken the overlap before crossing the two-boatlength circle, then you must prove that you broke the overlap in time (Rule 42.1 [c]). In this case you may win the protest without a witness if you went to the back of your boat and sighted abeam.

Determining who has benefited most from a call becomes murky when the overlap has been intermittent coming down the leg. That's why you should loudly hail the other boat when you're in favored position. As outside boat, break the overlap ten boatlengths from the mark, and shout over to the inside boat, "No overlap." If the skipper of that boat surfs down a wave and re-establishes the overlap, he should yell back, "I've got an overlap." By making your claims loudly, you'll draw the attention of potential witnesses.

When proving your position, whether you are an outside boat claiming you broke the inside boat's overlap, or whether you are a boat approaching from clear astern claiming you established an overlap, don't contest the privileged boat's call and force a foul. Instead, defer to the privileged boat's call and then file a protest. By not forcing a collision, you can go into the protest hearing knowing that you are in a no-lose situation. It is counterproductive to contest an outside boat's claim that no overlap exists by rounding up and hitting it. Rule 42.1(d) states that a boat establishing an overlap from clear astern must prove that it got the overlap before the outside boat got to the two-boatlength circle. Hitting the outside boat may prove that an overlap existed, but it does not tell the committee that you got the overlap in time. Unless you have a witness, you'll be disqualified for hitting the outside boat.

Another reason to keep communicating with the other boat is so that you don't get caught short by Rule 42.3(a)(i), which states, "A yacht that establishes an inside overlap from clear astern is entitled to room . . . only when . . . the outside yacht is able to give room." The intention of this rule is to prevent the chaos that would result when a boat planes in from astern just before a whole group of boats enters the two-boatlength circle. If there is not enough time for all the boats to move and create room for the latecomer, Rule 42.3 says tough luck to the latecomer. So if you're overlapping a group of boats, let them know far in advance of the two-boatlength circle that they are all going to have to give you room.

Next, consider rules that apply as the boats go around. When your boat is clear ahead, you can take as much room as you want to round, as long as you stay within the two-boatlength circle. According to Rule 42.2(a), boats clear astern must keep clear of boats clear ahead going around the mark. Keeping clear doesn't mean the boat behind must round outside of a boat clear ahead. If the first boat rounds too wide and leaves space for another boat to round inside, then the trailing boat is free to take a risk. But the privileged boat, the one that was clear ahead when it entered the two-boatlength circle, is free to luff the opportunist into the mark. Greedy trailing boats should beware of traps like this.

When you round inside another boat, you have to be careful not to take too much room. Rule 42.1(a) states, "Room is the space needed by an inside overlapping yacht, which is handled in a seamanlike manner in the prevailing conditions, to pass in safety between an outside yacht and a mark . . . and includes space to tack or jibe when either is an integral part of the rounding or passing maneuver." Rule 42.1(e) also gives us an idea of how much room an inside boat is entitled to. It states that when an inside boat has to jibe to assume her proper course to the next mark, "she shall jibe at the first reasonable opportunity." Nowhere are exact distances specified. Instead, the rule makers were intentionally vague because varying wind, wave, and crowding conditions create too many variables for a comprehensive ruling. The rule makers' main goal is to ensure that boats are able to round the marks safely. Therefore the phrase "she shall jibe at the first reasonable opportunity," in Rule 422.1(e) could allow a boat to jibe two or three lengths away from a mark in high seas and stormy winds, because the crew was jibing slowly and cautiously.

Faster Finishes

Controlling other boats is the key to sailing the last leg of a race, which is usually a beat. Typically, by the final leg of the race, you're sailing with boats of equal speed and tactical ability. To hold your position, you'll need to think about controlling more than just one boat, which means you'll have to think several moves ahead. In this chapter we'll divide the final beat into three parts: (1) the getaway from the leeward mark; (2) consolidating your position or correcting your mistakes; and (3) concentrating on where to cross the finish line.

Part I: The Getaway

Once you have rounded the leeward mark, you must decide when to make your first tack for a fast getaway. Many people feel that tacking away from the leeward mark immediately is a good thing, but avoid sailing underneath the spinnakers of boats coming downwind or, worse yet, into the waves kicked up by the boats still headed for the leeward mark. Even if a boat is on your wind, it may be better to sail for several boatlengths to gain speed before you tack to clear your wind. You can't build speed while sailing in waves, because the wind is shaken out of your sails, and the rocking motion prevents your boat from building forward momentum. Just as you need to avoid making too many tacks after the start, it is also important not to make too many tacks after rounding the leeward mark. Sailing in bad air for a short time can lose you far less distance to the leaders than would several extra tacks.

Even before you round the leeward mark, you should be thinking about which side of the beat will be favored. Use all the tricks you know for figuring out what the wind is doing. Think back on how the wind has shifted during the day, and consult the log of wind readings that you've kept throughout the race. Keep track of any wind shifts while you sail down the run. Look at the angles that the boats ahead of you on the beat are sailing. Focus your binoculars on the flags on the finish line marks, or on boats anchored on the course. Look for new wind lines. Whatever you do, don't get lazy on the last leg to the finish.

If you lead by a few boatlengths going into the leeward mark, spend some of that distance by tacking soon after you round the leeward mark and then tack back before your competition rounds the mark. (See figure 6.1.) Now you'll have a lot of flexibility because you'll be ahead and to windward of your competition. For instance if you decide that you're on the unfavored tack after your competitor rounds the leeward mark, you can crack off your sails slightly and head off so that you sail down and blanket the trailing boat, forcing it to tack in the direction you want it to go. On the other hand, if the other boat

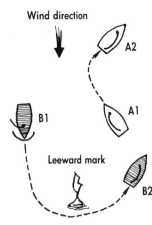

Wind direction

A2

B1   A1

Leeward mark

B2

Figure 6.1 *To insure its lead and preserve its options, Boat A makes two quick tacks after rounding the leeward mark. By getting to windward before Boat B finishes rounding the mark, A is in the no-lose position of being between its competition and the next mark.*

is already going where you want it to, see that you don't affect its wind; maintain a loose cover. By not tacking right on a boat's wind, you can corral your competition out to the layline, where they'll have practically no chance of passing you.

If you need to expand your lead, wipe off a trailing boat on the boats coming down the course with their spinnakers up. For instance, say you are just ahead of "Old Joe," whom you're tied with in the Wednesday-night series. If you beat Joe, you'll be first in the Catalina class, and if he beats you, he'll win. Throughout the race, Joe has hung right on your stern, waiting for you to blunder. It's been distracting, to say the least, having Joe breathing down your neck. It would be nice to get a boat between you, or at least to extend your lead and get some breathing room.

To expand your lead, start by spending some of the lead you already have. If you don't have enough time to get to windward by making two quick tacks, get as high as you can by pinching. By climbing to windward, you'll be able to leave Joe wallowing in your bad air after he rounds the mark. (See figure 6.2.) If he tries pinching too, he'll lose all his speed, since sailboats can't pinch well at all in bad air. Joe's only other option is to tack. But that course will put him into the waves and backwind created by the fleet coming down the course with spinnakers. If he tacks into the fleet, don't follow immediately. The longer you delay your tack, the less bad air and disturbed wake you'll get from the fleet heading toward the leeward mark. (See figure 6.3.) The longer you slow him with your bad air and the bad air and waves of boats on the

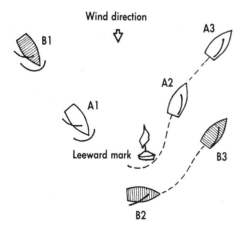

Figure 6.2 *When a trailing boat is hot on your heels, and you don't have time to make two quick tacks before it rounds the mark, spend some of your small lead by pinching until the trailing boat rounds.*

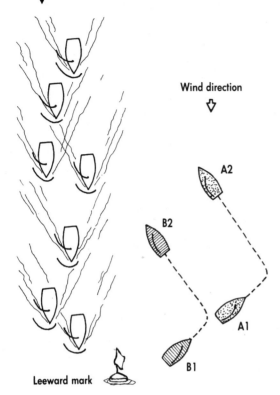

Wind direction

Leeward mark

Figure 6.3 *By being ahead and to windward of Boat B after rounding the leeward mark, Boat A is in great shape. B is faced with either tagging along in A's bad air, or tacking into the disturbed waves and wind of the fleet approaching the mark.*

run, the greater the chance another boat will catch up and get between Joe and you. When that happens you've bought some insurance.

Part II: Consolidate or Catch Up

Once you've figured out which side of the beat you want to be on, and you've gotten away from the mark, then it's time to consolidate or to catch up. If you are clearly behind, your tactics should be to get away from the other boats to get some leverage so that a shift can help you catch up. A shift could hurt you too, but at least the risk-to-reward ratio is better. If you just stay behind the boat ahead of you, or in its bad air, you'll never pass. So the rule is, if you're behind, get leverage; if you're ahead, don't allow leverage. When you're ahead, do everything you can to stay between the trailing boat and the finish.

Covering a trailing boat becomes more important as the laylines converge near the finish line.

If you find you're spending too much time trying to control one other boat, pass off your problem by tangling that boat up with another boat. The more boats on the racecourse, the more opportunities you'll have to get your competition tangled up. Sailboats passing through the course are great weapons you can use to shake off a boat that is tailing you. Simply time your tack so that your foe will tack into the bad air of the cruising boat if he tries tacking with you.

On the other hand, if you're the boat being covered, you can shake off your foe by using other boats on the course. The idea is to tack in a position where the boat covering you won't tack to cover. For instance, if you see a boat on the opposite tack that's ahead of you and ahead of the boat that's covering you, tack just below his wake. By tacking below that boat's wake, you'll be far enough behind that its wind shadow won't reach you, but if the boat covering you tacks, it will be slowed by the other boat's shadow. (See figure 6.4.)

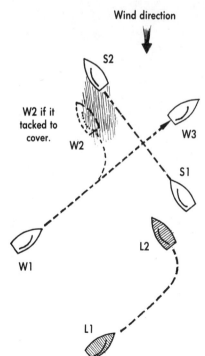

Figure 6.4 *Boat W is applying a loose cover on Boat L. In attempt to get away from W, Boat L plans its tack so that if W tacks to cover, W will be in the bad air of Boat S. Seeing S, W is left with no other choice but to keep sailing on port to get beyond S's wind shadow.*

If the other boat doesn't tack to cover you, you'll not only get out from under it, but you'll be able to generate some leverage as well. Gaining leverage on a boat that has been tenaciously covering you will put you in a position to gain from a wind shift.

"That's exactly what we did during the last race of the 1989 50-footers' world qualifying regatta in Tortola," says Tom. "In that incident Gary Weisman, steering *Champosa V*, had a loose cover on *Springbok*, the boat I was steering. *Champosa* had to beat us to maintain fifth place in the regatta. About a mile from the finish, we were both on port tack nearing the starboard layline, with *Champosa* on our beam six lengths to windward. When I saw *Windquest* coming across on starboard tack, I recognized our chance to escape. I tacked when we still had clear air ahead and to leeward of *Windquest*'s wind shadow, but if *Champosa* had tacked to cover us, Gary would have been in *Windquest*'s bad air. [See figure 6.5.] But Gary was smarter than that and kept sailing another ten boatlengths on port to clear his wind on *Windquest*. The ten

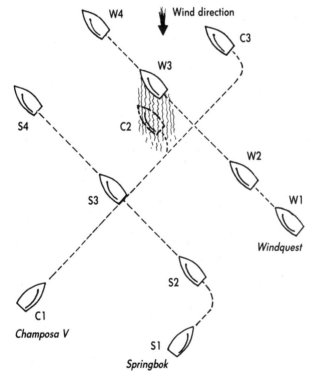

Figure 6.5 *Sailing* Springbok *at a 50-footer regatta, Tom used* Windquest *to scrape off* Champosa V, *which was covering him.*

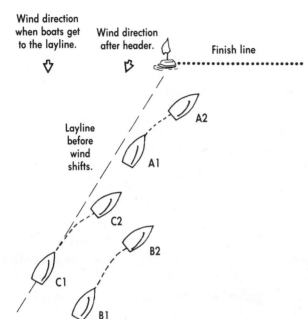

Wind direction when boats get to the layline.

Wind direction after header.

Finish line

Layline before wind shifts.

A2

A1

C2

B2

C1

B1

Figure 6.6 *Boat A has corralled boats B and C to the port tack layline of the pin-end of the finish line. Boat A is in a no-lose position. In a lift, all boats simply ease their sails and hold their course. In a header, A gains distance on both boats.*

boatlengths of separation was enough to close the gap between us, but at the finish line Gary still beat us—but only by a half a boatlength. If *Champosa* had tacked to cover us in *Windquest*'s bad air, we would have had an excellent opportunity to pass them. But Gary was calm in the situation; he played it right by going for clear air. He also preserved the starboard tack advantage by sailing to the right of us."

As mentioned in Chapter 4, the way to neutralize a foe or foes is to corral them to the long layline to the finish. On the layline, there are no passing lanes because on the laylines wind shifts won't help your competition. If a lift comes, you and the others simply crack off your sails and reach to the line— you keep your lead. If a header materializes, none of you will make the mark, but the boat ahead gains on the boats behind. (See figure 6.6.) Therefore, when you are being covered, keep away from the laylines. Try to stay in the middle of the course, where you can gain from wind shifts and find boats to scrape off the boat that's covering you.

If you're not being covered, but you're having problems finding clear air because there are constantly boats on your wind, "then you're pretty well committed to go all the way to a layline, because your chance of getting dirty air there is much reduced," says Tom. You'll find clear air on the laylines because most people try to avoid sailing out to them, since they are practically a no-win deal. The disadvantage of going to a layline is that if the wind shifts, either you'll overstand or the boats on the other side of the course will gain on you. But if you're behind, going to a layline will minimize the bad air you get, since the smart sailors will avoid the laylines. If you do commit to a layline, make sure you know which side of the course is favored, because you want to go to the layline that gives you the most chance to gain.

As the race draws toward its end, the more resolutely a smart leader will cover a boat just behind him. But if you're being covered simply because you're the closest boat around, you might be able to shake the boat covering you by ducking a boat sailing by on the other tack. Passing behind the boat on the other tack might persuade the leader to perceive the other boat as a greater threat than you. If you're lucky, the leader will tack on the boat you ducked. This only works if the leader is covering you simply because you're the closest threat. Expect to be covered tenaciously if he needs to beat you to maintain his standing in the regatta.

Part III: Approaching the Finish Line

Just as you should have an idea of which side of the last beat is favored before you round the leeward mark, you should be thinking about the favored end of the finish line long before you get to it. In this section we'll discuss how to approach the finish line before you can tell which end of the line is favored, how to determine the favored end, and then how to cross the line.

Approaching the Line Before You Know the Favored End

"If you are close to another boat, and there's a question of which side of the line is favored, always save the starboard tack advantage for the finish," says Tom. "Stay to the right of your competitor, because whoever gets the last shot at being to the right without overstanding is going to win. The boat on the left will have to come back toward the line on port tack sometime, and it will be forced to duck the starboard tacker, who stuck to the right. [See figure 6.7.] So when in doubt, stay to the right of your competitor."

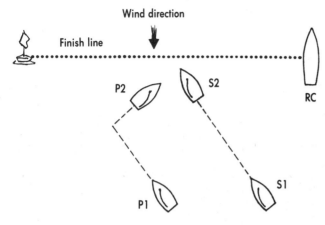

Wind direction

Finish line

P2   S2

RC

P1   S1

Figure 6.7 *Not knowing which side of the finish line is favored, Boat S stays to the right of Boat P. As the boats approach the line bow-to-bow on opposite tacks, S is guaranteed the win simply because it's on starboard tack.*

"This advice might seem contradictory to how we sailed the finish of our race against Tom Blackaller in the first round of the America's Cup challengers' elimination trials in Australia. In that race we came in from the left and crossed *USA* by inches. "In that race, Blackaller was staying to the right, and was on starboard tack. We came across on port, and he thought that we couldn't cross him. But we just made it across. In fact, Blackaller went wrong in a few races by trying to slam-dunk us near the finish. If you think about what happens in a slam-dunk, you see that it's the wrong move to make. He slam-dunked us several times, but each time we got through his wind shadow. Once we got by him to leeward, we gassed him and forced him to tack off. As soon as he tacked away, we were to the right and inherited the starboard tack advantage. [See figure 6.8.]

"If it's a sure bet that the slam-dunk is going to work, you'll never lose by doing it. But if it doesn't work, you're taking a risk. The risk-to-reward ratio is not perfect there. A better risk would have been for Blackaller to tack just under our bow. We never would have passed him. Even though we were ducking, he still should have tacked on our bow or our lee bow. That way he could have pushed us back with his backwind."

Another way to increase your chances of beating your competitors is to head for the middle of the line until the favored end becomes apparent. Tom says that he will never forget this lesson after losing a race to *Courageous* in the 1983 America's Cup defenders' selection trials. "I was the tactician on *Liberty*, and in that race we led *Courageous*, skippered by John Kolius, all the way around the 24-mile course. As we sailed on port tack toward the pin end's

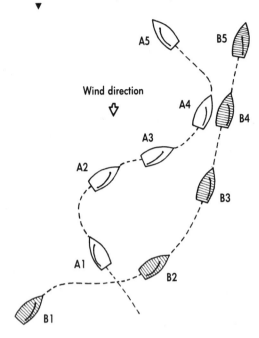

Wind direction

Figure 6.8 *Boat B on starboard tack is narrowly ahead of Boat A, but B loses its advantage by attempting to slam dunk A. Since A built up extra speed by cracking its sheets as it ducked, A gets through B's wind shadow before B accelerates to speed. In Position 4, A gasses B with backwind forcing B to tack off. Being to the right, A now has the starboard tack advantage coming into the finish line.*

starboard-tack layline, the responsibility for calling the final tack fell on me. While still on port, we had *Courageous* up on our hip, about a boatlength and a half behind us. [See figure 6.9.] In making the call as to when to tack, I ran two scenarios through my mind. If we tacked to starboard too early, we would miss the line, while Kolius would go behind us on port and then tack when *Courageous* could fetch the finish. But if we tacked too late, Kolius would tack inside of us and make a big gain on us. I called for the tack on what I thought was the layline, but the wind got a little lighter as we sailed toward the line, so that we couldn't sail as high. We ended up being unable to lay the mark. Kolius won the race because he had sailed past our wake on port before tacking for the line. Up by the line, we had to tack to port to reach the finish line. The extra tack cost us. When we came together at the finish line, both boats shot the line and *Courageous* won by a few seconds. When judging when to tack for the line, I made a common mistake, thinking we should aim for the pin rather than for the middle of the line. I had miscalculated the risk-to-reward ratio. That's a case where there is nobody to blame except the tactician.

"At the end of the day, Dennis didn't chew me out; he made a good observation, though. He said that since the line was pretty square, we should

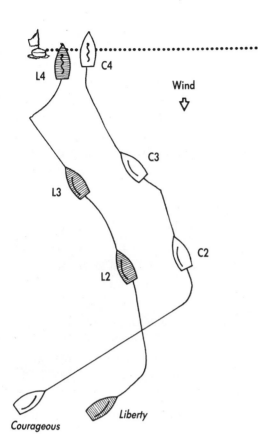

Wind

RC

Courageous

Liberty

Figure 6.9 *During the 1983 America's Cup Defenders' trials, Tom learned to add a little cushion of safety when calling the final tack to the finish line. In this example* Liberty, *the boat he was calling tactics on, got beat by* Courageous. *After tacking on the layline, the wind got lighter, which meant* Liberty *couldn't point high enough to make the finish line.* Courageous *on the other hand delayed its tack to the finish line, and when the wind went light,* Courageous *could still make the line.*

have aimed for the middle of the line so that we would have had a little more latitude to play the wind shifts. So unless you think the line is very favored on one end, plan to sail toward the middle."

Sailing toward the middle of the line until you're able to determine which end of the line is favored is a high-percentage move. In two out of three cases you'll have done the right thing. In the third case you'll have overstood the finish, but overstanding is not always fatal. To simplify matters, in the following three instances, assume you are on starboard tack approaching the line. (When approaching the finish line on port tack, reverse the final two situations.)

In the first instance, say the line is set perfectly square to the wind. In that case, where you finish on the line doesn't matter. If you are even with another boat coming up the course, it doesn't matter which side of the line either of you sails to; if your boats are even in speed, you'll finish at the same time.

When the line is square, it really pays to shoot the line by heading into the wind before crossing the finish line. Shooting will get you across the line faster, since the shortest distance to the line from any point below the line is a course that crosses the line perpendicularly. People who sail light centerboard boats will not be able to shoot as effectively as those sailing heavier keel boats. For instance, a Laser may be able to coast to windward without losing speed for a half a boatlength—that's six feet. On the other hand, a heavy boat like a 12-meter can coast to windward without losing an appreciable amount of speed for two or three boatlengths—that's 130 to 195 feet. (For more information on shooting the finish line, see pages 253–257.)

The second instance in which aiming for the middle of the finish line is a high-percentage play is where the right side of the line is favored. As you aim for the middle of the line on starboard tack, you'll notice that you are sailing almost parallel to the line. So as soon as you can tack and clear the mark or the committee boat at the right end of the line, do so and you'll make the perfect finish. (See figure 6.10.)

The one instance in which heading for the middle of the line on starboard tack won't help you is where the left side of the line is favored. In that case you'll overstand the favored end of the line, but that isn't necessarily fatal; if the line is only a few lengths long, you won't overstand much. But if the line is ten boatlengths long, and you are finishing in the middle of the line, you will sail at least five boatlengths too far on port tack. That's quite a bit to give up, especially if a boat five lengths behind you tacked right onto the starboard layline to the left side of the line.

Once you get close enough to the line to determine that the pin end is favored, you can minimize your loss from overstanding by cracking off your

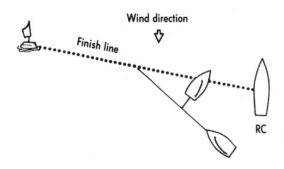

Figure 6.10 *When heading toward the middle of the line on starboard tack, you'll know the right side of the finish line is favored because you'll be sailing almost parallel to the line.*

sails and footing off to the favored end. With the extra speed you'll get from freeing up your course, you should be able to drive over any boats that are close-hauled on the layline to the favored end.

Tricks for Determining the Favored End

It's easiest to assess the favored end when the same line is used for both starting and finishing. You'll have accumulated a lot of solid information before the race and at the start. For instance, the opposite side of the line will be favored at the finish, because the favored end at the start was the end farthest upwind, while the opposite is true at the finish. The end of the line that is farther downwind is favored, since it is closer to the leeward mark.

If the wind shifts during the race, however, you won't automatically know the favored end by simply finishing at the opposite side from that which was favored at the start. To be able to figure out which end is favored after a wind shift, get a bearing on the line before the start. You can do this by sailing down the line and reading your compass. Write down the bearing so that you can compare it to the latest wind direction when you are on the last beat of the race.

If the race committee sets a different finish line after the start, there are plenty of other tricks you can use. When the new finish line is set between the windward and leeward marks, have one crewmember keep an eye on the line as you sail by it on the final run. When the two finish-line marks line up, have the person take a bearing on the line with a hand-bearing compass or by sighting over the deck compass. Then compare the line's bearing to the direction of the true wind to figure out which end of the line is farther downwind. (See figure 6.11.) You can get the true wind direction from an electronic instrument system, or you can figure it out on the final beat by computing the average of your upwind headings on port and starboard tack.

You can also determine the favored end of the line by watching where and how the boats ahead of you are finishing. After a while it will become very evident which end of the line is favored. For instance, if a majority of the fleet finishes at the pin end, then it's a pretty good guess that the pin end is favored. You can double-check this hypothesis by noting the angle at which the boats ahead of you cross the line. Remember, the shortest distance to the line from any point below the line is a perpendicular course across the line.

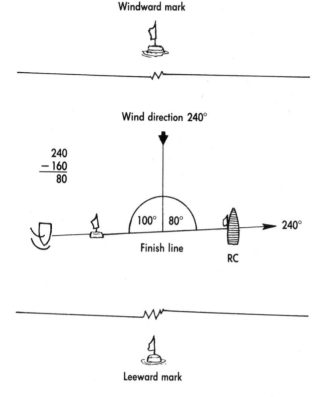

Windward mark

Wind direction 240°

240
− 160
———
80

100° 80°

Finish line

RC

240°

Figure 6.11 *When the finish line is between the windward and leeward marks, take a bearing on the finish line with a hand-bearing compass or with your deck compass as you sail by. Calculate which end of the line is farther downwind by comparing the bearing of the finish line to the direction of the wind. The end of the line that creates an angle greater than 90 degrees to the true wind direction is the favored end.*

Leeward mark

Thus, you should cross the line on the tack that takes you over it closest to a 90-degree angle. Thus, if boats cross the line on starboard tack, then the left side of the line is favored. If boats on either tack shoot the line, then the line is even. And if boats cross the line on port tack, then the right side of the line is favored. Not everyone will be sharp enough to pick the favored end of the line before getting to it, but once the line is in front of them, most skippers will cross the line on a perpendicular course, which tells you what end is favored.

If you're in the lead, there won't be boats finishing ahead of you that you can study. In that case, the prudent thing to do is to stay in the middle of the course and to the right of your competition until you figure out which end of the line is favored.

Shooting the Finish Line

Most sailors only think of shooting the finish line when they are neck-and-neck with another boat. But since most race committees set square finish lines, sailors should be shooting the line at almost every finish. Again, the fastest course across the line from any point to leeward of the line is a perpendicular course.

One point to keep in mind about shooting the line is that the heavier the boat, the greater its momentum, and the farther it will coast into the wind while the sails are luffing. Lightweight dinghies carry the least momentum, while small keel boats like E-22s and J/24s carry more way, and heavier boats like maxis and 12-meters carry enough momentum to carry them six to eight lengths directly upwind. Therefore, the shooting techniques we're about to cover are primarily for big-boat sailors.

The common fear of shooting the finish line is that you'll shoot too soon and end up losing too much speed before you cross the line. That's a legitimate fear; if you shoot too soon, you might have been better off holding your course and simply sailing across the line. To maximize your gains when shooting the line, you need to know the velocity made good (VMG) that you were making before you luffed up into the wind. Get your VMG from your instrument system, if it displays VMG, or from a polar diagram for your boat or a sister ship.

Velocity made good is the speed you are making to a point directly into the wind as a result of your current course and speed. For instance, if your boat goes 6.5 knots when sailing 45 degrees to the wind, then your speed into the wind, or VMG, is 4.6 knots. (See figure 6.12.) The following is a description of how to finish faster by shooting the line using VMG:

As you approach the line, note the present VMG reading from your instrument system, or get the VMG you should be making from your boat's polar diagram. Then shoot head-to-wind, letting the boat's inertia carry you across the line. Once you are moving directly into the wind, your VMG reading will equal your boatspeed.

To maximize your gain, your boat should coast across the line at exactly the same speed as your VMG before you shot the line. Therefore, if you're sailing at 6.5 knots while making 4.6 knots VMG, you'll want to head up into the wind, coast, and poke your bow across the line just as the boat slows down

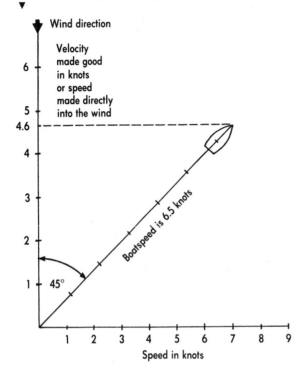

Figure 6.12 *This graph shows that if a boat moves 6.5 knots through the water when sailing 45-degrees to the wind, then it's Velocity Made Good, or speed to a point directly upwind, is 4.6 knots. If the boat sailed 6.5 knots while on a course 90 degrees off the wind, then it's VMG would be zero since the boat would not be moving toward the wind at all. Only when sailing directly into the wind does its VMG equal its speed through the water.*

to 4.6 knots. If you cross the line at four knots, you'll have shot too soon, and if the speedometer reads 5.4 knots as you cross the line, you shot too late. If you shoot too soon, you'll still gain over a boat that didn't shoot, but after you lose enough races by a couple of seconds on handicap, it will be worth it to go out and practice shooting the line.

Another way to get a little more speed and a bit more carry when shooting the line is to drop the jib to keep it from luffing against the mast and the shrouds. Dropping the jib eliminates drag, letting you coast upwind faster and farther. "Probably in the next few years the majority of the fleet will cross the finish line with their genoas on the deck," says Jim Marshall of Ockam Instruments.

Tom points out that sometimes it will hurt you more to have crew on the bow getting the jib down. He says that detriment can be reduced if you practice dropping the jib quickly and efficiently.

To optimize your technique for shooting the line, you need to experiment in different wind and wave conditions and record how far and how fast your boat will carry directly upwind.

Downwind Finishes

On a downwind finish, boats will cross the line the opposite way from the way they would cross on an upwind finish. If boats bear off to dead downwind to cross the line, the line is square. If boats finish on port tack or jibe onto port before crossing the line, the left-hand end of the line is favored. You'll know the right side of the line is favored if boats cross the line on starboard, or jibe to starboard just before crossing the line.

Just as you can lose distance by shooting the line too early when you're finishing upwind, you can lose distance by shooting the line too early going downwind. A common mistake many sailors make when finishing on a run is that they sail dead downwind to the line too soon. If you've been jibing downwind to build better speed, you should maintain your jibing angles until you're four or five boatlengths from the line. Only when you are that close should you bear off to the line and cross it perpendicularly. Going downwind, you can shoot earlier, since your boat won't coast to a stop if you shoot too soon, as it would if you shot too soon at an upwind finish.

Another reason not to fall off to a dead run too early is that the higher you sail, the farther forward your apparent wind will be. Keeping your apparent wind forward is a defense against boats behind you trying to steal your wind. So don't get greedy. Stay alert, and don't leave yourself open for attack on downwind finishes, because the boats behind you are the ones in control.

Rules at the Finish Line

According to the definition of "Finishing" on page 10 of the International Yacht Racing Union's rule book for 1989–92, "a yacht finishes when any part of her hull, or of her crew or equipment in normal position, crosses the finishing line in the direction of the course from the last mark, after fulfilling her penalty obligations, if any, under Rule 52.2(b), Touching a Mark." Thus, if your boat has a bowsprit, you've finished when the front tip of the bowsprit crosses the line, or if you're finishing downwind, you have finished when the forwardmost edge of your spinnaker crosses the line—as long as you're flying it in its normal position.

Rule 52.2(b), referred to in the above definition of "Finishing," clearly states, "When a yacht touches a finishing mark, she shall not rank as having finished until she first completes her turns and thereafter finishes." Rule 52.2(a) goes into detail about penalty turns. It says that when a boat hits any mark of the course, "she may exonerate herself by sailing well clear of all other yachts as soon as possible after the incident, and remaining clear while she makes two complete 360-degree turns (720 degrees) in the same direction, including two tacks and two jibes." In the text of the 720 Rule, paragraph 1.2 states, "When the infringement occurs at the finishing line, [a boat] shall make her turns on the course side of the line before she will be recorded as having finished." The meaning of all these rules is that if you hit a finish mark—the pin or the committee boat—you have to sail to a point below the line or its extensions, where you will not interfere with any boats still racing, and then make two complete circles before attempting to re-cross the finish line. (See figure 6.13.) To have completed two circles, you must end up on the same tack you were on when you hit the mark—before crossing the line.

Once you have poked your bow across the line and finished, you must not hit either the pin or the committee boat until you've cleared the finish line. But if you are in danger of colliding with one of the marks or another boat, you do not have to sail all the way across the line to finish. Rule 51.5 states, "It is not necessary for a yacht to cross the finishing line completely; after finishing, she may clear it in either direction." So if a foul tide is running, all you have to do is poke part of the boat across the line, then you can fall off and go with the current to get away from the line. Once you have cleared the line, you can turn on your engine and head for the barn.

"Clearing the line" goes undefined in the rule book, but if you look at the

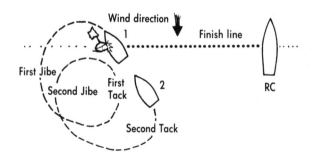

Figure 6.13 *When you hit a finishing mark, you must do a 720 on the course side of the line. Rule 52.2(b) states that you must do two tacks and two jibes before attempting to finish. You've completed two circles if you end up on the same tack that you were on when you hit the mark.*

definition of "racing," you can get a better idea of when you can crank up the old engine. This definition says, "A yacht is racing . . . until she has . . . finished and cleared the finishing line and finishing marks." We'd define clearing the line and finishing marks as the point at which you are in no danger of hitting another boat or any of the finishing marks. Therefore, if there is plenty of wind and no current, and no other boats are around, you'd be safe in turning on your engine after your boat crossed the line. But if you crossed the line with a group of boats, you shouldn't turn on your engine until you're outside the finish line.

Also, until you've cleared the finish line you are required to avoid any boats that are still racing. If you cross the line on port tack, you still have to keep clear of starboard tackers until you've cleared the line. If you foul a starboard tacker or any other boats, you'll have to get back to the course side of the line, do your two circles, and then re-finish.

◄ c h a p t e r 7 ►

Steering

Sailing to weather is an art that requires both a kinesthetic sense of the boat and the ability to integrate information from a number of sources. A helmsman's mastery of steering increases the number of tactical options available to him.

On a big boat, every helmsman should steer from the windward side, whether with a wheel or a tiller. You'll find that most top sailors steer from the windward side because from this position they can see the waves, feel the wind in their faces, and gauge the pressure on the rudder and the heel of the boat in relation to the horizon. Sitting to windward also keeps you out of the disturbed air in the slot. You won't improve your tactile ability until you steer from the weather side. Put the boat's instruments as far forward as you can and still be able to read them. This allows you to keep all the steering aids—telltales, waves, angle of heel, instruments, sails—in your field of vision at once, and eliminates the need to look down. If you have to turn your head and change your focus to see the speedometer or compass, you'll have to reorient yourself every time you look up.

When steering either a big boat or a dinghy, you need to develop good steering posture. On a boat with a wheel, it's best to stand to windward of the wheel, with your body parallel to the centerline of the boat. This gets you to windward, where you can see the jib's telltales. By standing, you can see over the crew sitting on the rail, concentrate on the waves and puffs coming down the course, and feel the wind on your face. This position gives you better leverage on the wheel than you would have by standing behind the center of the wheel. On a boat with a big wheel that moves easily, lean against the wheel with your leg to create friction that steadies the steering motion. However, the best position to steer from is the one that is comfortable for you.

On a big boat with a tiller or a hiking stick, it's difficult to steer standing up, because you lose mechanical advantage as you raise it. Just sit wherever you're comfortable and have the best view. A hiking stick gets you farther outboard than a wheel. Since modern boats have such big rudders, it's best to control tiller movement by working the hiking stick with both hands.

When steering a dinghy, posture, weight placement, and comfort are critical. Many times you'll have to compromise the perfect steering position in exchange for better boat balance and boatspeed. Make sure your crew knows that it's their job to balance the boat.

When you find the position on the windward side that allows you to see, steer, and balance the boat, it is important to spread your weight evenly to reduce fatigue from the restriction of blood circulation. If you're using a hiking strap, be sure your weight is evenly distributed between both legs. Adjust the straps so that the inside edge of the deck touches the middle of your calves, the gunwale touches the middle of your thighs, when your knees are bent at a 90-degree angle. On boats with no deck or a wide deck, set up your straps so that the gunwale hits the middle of your thigh.

Use comfort devices when you can. If your class rules allow it, attach pads to the rails as Finn sailors do. Pad your hiking straps with the black neoprene tubing used for insulating air-conditioning pipes—you'll be able to hike much longer with this one change. Hiking pants reduce the pressure against the backs of your thighs. (These are tight-fitting shorts with fiberglass battens stitched into the backs of the legs to keep the boat's gunwale from digging into legs and restricting blood circulation.) If you start to lose circulation in some part of your body, it's time to change positions. Sometimes standing up for a few seconds will get the blood moving again.

Don't hike out so far that you're too low to the water to see waves hitting the bow or wind shifts on the water or telltales on the jib or other boats on the course. Hold the hiking stick with your aft hand across your body like a microphone; this way you get more leverage on the tiller, and your arm will tire less quickly than when holding it behind your body.

Beware of Telltale Hypnosis

Too many helmsmen become mesmerized by telltales. Not that you shouldn't use them, but the less you depend on them, the better off you'll be. On big boats, put telltales about a third of the way up the genoa luff and two feet back from the headstay. On a dinghy, put your telltales six inches behind the headstay. (Typically there are more than one set of telltales on the jib, but those are used by the trimmer, not the helmsman.) Telltales on the shrouds help too. The person who uses many different performance indicators, such as speedometer, waves, the horizon, and the angle of heel, and can compute them while steering, will become a good helmsman.

The Upwind "Gears"

Think of telltale activity representing four distinct gears, as in a car. By turning the boat a degree or two, the helmsman "shifts" gears, depending on wind conditions and speed requirements. As we go through these gears, refer to figure 7.1.

First gear. Leeward telltale stalls for a split second, and windward telltale streams straight aft. This "gear" is used for acceleration from very slow speeds, such as when you need extra power to recover from waves or accelerate after a slow tack.

Second gear. Both telltales stream straight aft. Use this gear for acceleration, also when you are close to full speed and external conditions require that you achieve maximum speed (e.g., approaching waves or a need to foot for clear air).

Third gear. Windward telltale lifts to about 45 degrees, and leeward telltale streams aft. Once you've attained your desired speed, put the boat on the wind into this "point mode." This is the "gear" you should use for most upwind sailing.

Fourth gear. Windward telltale lifts to vertical, and leeward telltale streams aft. The most forward part of the jib begins to lift. This is "super-point mode," used when you need to depower in heavy air, take advantage of a flat spot, or squeeze off a competitor on your windward quarter.

While the helmsman "shifts gears," the sail trimmers must also adjust sail shape. For example, on a boat about to hit waves, the helmsman would head

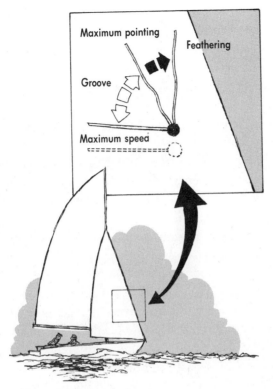

Figure 7.1

off into "second gear" to accelerate, and the trimmers would simultaneously ease the backstay to get fuller, draft-forward sails. As the boat recovered, the helmsman would "shift" from second to third, while the trimmers would tighten the backstay to flatten the sails again. This is when communication between the helmsman and the trimmers is so important.

"Of all the factors that you use while steering a boat upwind," says Gary, "the thing that I study the most is the angle of heel. Whether sailing a dinghy or big boat during day or night, find the correct angle of heel for your boat. You learn this by studying your performance against that of other boats. Once you know what the optimum angle of heel is, strive to obtain it by using your weight, your steering, and your sail trim. Heel is a combination of all three. When sailing any boat to windward, I spend 40 percent of my time worrying about angle of heel, 10 percent looking at my telltales (much of that time is spent looking up at the masthead fly, because the wind changes direction at the top of the mast first)—[see Chapter 8 for an explanation of wind shear and gradient], 20 percent looking around at the approaching waves and wind puffs,

10 percent glancing around to make sure my crew isn't making any mistakes, and the remaining 20 percent thinking about tactics."

When racing, it's difficult for even the best helmsman to look at many instruments; you have to concentrate on a couple of key ones. The two most important instruments are boatspeed and windspeed. Tom says he prefers using true wind, if possible, since it won't be affected by acceleration or deceleration, as a less expensive apparent windspeed indicator. If you have made a performance chart of your boat for a range of wind conditions, or if you have a Velocity Prediction Program for your boat, you will know generally what boatspeed you should be getting at each wind speed. For example, if the skipper sees that the windspeed is 16 true and knows from experience that the best boatspeed is 6.8 knots, then the helmsman should start looking for 6.8 on the speedometer. (Velocity Prediction Programs are available from the United States Yacht Racing Union for all boats with International Measurement System rating certificates. See page 290 for information on how to acquire a VPP for your boat.)

Steering upwind is a continuous trade-off between going higher and slower or going lower and faster. The course that pays off is the one that will get you to the windward mark fastest. Electronic instruments can tell you the precise course to sail for every wind shift (see Chapter 8 for how to use them and how they work); if you are sailing a dinghy or other boat without instruments, you'll have to depend on your own experience.

The optimal sailing angle to windward depends on wind strength and sea conditions. In smooth water, for example, it usually pays off to sail higher than you would through chop. This will give you the best progress upwind, but it also may mean that your speed through the water is actually lower than it might be in waves. "Some helmsmen are confused when I suggest that we try sailing at a slower boatspeed," says Tom. "They can't believe that I want them to go slower. What I'm really saying is, 'Let's head a little higher at the expense of a little speed to see if that doesn't produce better progress to windward.' "

As a rule of thumb, the average sailor steers a boat too fine; that is, too high and too slow. This is because most people are obsessed with pointing when they go upwind. What they don't realize is that pointing is a net effect—it's not just where you point the bow. It involves a boat's speed through the water and how the keel interacts with the sail plan. When the tactician says you're not pointing well, you can't just aim the boat higher, because this means you'll go slower and the keel won't create as much lift.

To point a boat better, the first thing you must do, believe it or not, is bear off and ease your sails slightly; you can't point higher without building speed first. Speed begets more speed. The faster you go, the more apparent wind you will create. The extra speed makes your keel more efficient so that it generates more lift. In fact, if you create more lift from your keel, you'll make a higher course, even though your bow is not pointing closer to the wind as the boat is making less leeway. Once up to speed, you can create more weather helm by heeling more, moving your crew weight back and raking the mast aft, and trimming your sails tighter to move the draft farther back.

Communication

You definitely don't want everyone in the crew trying to communicate at once; that is not good for the helmsman's concentration. Only two or three people should talk to the helmsman: the tactician, the sail trimmer, and possibly the navigator. During a race, the helmsman will concentrate on steering the boat fast; the tactician will report tactics; the navigator will communicate primarily with the tactician; and the sail trimmer will talk directly to the helmsman about speed. The rest of the crew will speak up only if there is something on the course that should be considered. Any ideas from the crew should be filtered through the tactician.

Big-boat sailing is a team sport. The skipper can't do everything when he's driving; he has to delegate responsibility. If he sets up a hierarchy of communication, then he'll hear what's essential and not waste his time being distracted. He'll also free himself from having to tell everyone what to do.

Of course, the helmsman does need to talk with the crew. Information must flow *from* him as well as *to* him. The obvious things he should say are, "Hey, the boat feels sluggish," or "We feel overpowered," or "I can't sail the jib that tight at the target speed." These are all things that have to be felt through the tiller or wheel; anyone else will have a hard time figuring out what's wrong. Tom says he knows that he's better at feeling why the boat is slow when he's on the helm: "Off the helm I can only guess."

A skipper can be helpful in determining sail trim. A mainsheet trimmer, for example, looks at the main all day long and can get mesmerized with his own little problems. It's ironic that a skipper can look up and say, "Hmmm, we need a little more twist." The trimmer may be able to make the sail *look* perfect, but he can't *feel* its effect on the boat. Another thing the skipper can determine better than anyone is the boat's angle of heel. A crew member can look at the inclinometer and see how many degrees the boat is heeling, but the helmsman can say, "I think the boat would go better with a little more heel." Again, what's important is pressure on the helm, or the feel of the boat.

Pressure on the helm is the key to getting the boat "into the groove" (a state where the boat performs well). The first thing to do when sailing a new boat is to mark the wheel or tiller so that you can always tell how many degrees of helm the boat needs. With a tiller, this means starting with a protractor at the rudder post and drawing lines forward on the deck or cockpit sole at 3, 4, and 5 degrees on each side of the boat's centerline. You want the lines to go as far forward as possible, because the small angles show up best farther way from the rudder post.

Marking the rudder angle on a wheel is a two-person job. One person draws the 3-, 4-, and 5-degree lines on the port and starboard sides of the steering quadrant. The second person turns the wheel, and as each mark lines up with the boat's centerline, he marks the top of the wheel with different colors of tape.

The optimal amount of weather helm is probably 3 or 4 degrees. With modern rudders being so big, having a rudder angle greater than 4 or 5 degrees is slow; 3 to 4 degrees will give the boat a little extra lift and provide the helmsman with the opportunity to feel when he's in the groove. This is particularly important with a wheel, which desensitizes the boat's feel much the way a car's power steering filters out the feel of the road.

One of the things that Tom Blackaller's radical 12-meter USA made clear is how much lift the rudder creates. USA's keel created no lift. Her keel was a 40,000-pound lead torpedo slung at the bottom of a narrow strut. The keel's only purpose was to keep the boat upright. All the hydrodynamic lift that kept the boat from sideslipping came from her two high-aspect rudders—one in the bow and one aft. So don't rely solely on your keel for hydrodynamic lift; don't underestimate how critical steering well affects your upwind performance.

Big rudders are a double-edged sword. Kept at the correct angle, they will generate lift to windward, but move them around too much and they'll create a lot of drag. The bigger the rudder, the more lift it creates and the more you lose from poor helmsmanship.

Gary says one of the things that helped him with big-boat steering was the time he spent on a training ship while at the State University of New York Maritime College. "We would all steer the 589-foot ship for an hour at a time, and a course recorder would graph our efforts. We steered by a gyrocompass that made a clicking noise every time the boat changed course a fifth of one degree. We tried to keep the rudder turned so the ship would hold its course without the gyrocompass clicking. Well, on a ship that long, yawing in big seas, with winds blowing 35 knots, when it's night and there's no horizon, it's impossible to steam a straight course. So we used to have contests to see who could finish up with the straightest course chart.

"Because it was a competition, we concentrated very hard. Every now and then we'd go wildly off course, by 3 or 4 degrees, and the thing would be clicking like mad. Then we'd overcompensate and go back too far. While this didn't help me steer a sailboat any better, it helped my powers of concentration while maintaining a balanced speed. A good helmsman will sail at one speed, say 6.8 knots. His speed will balance between 6.9 and 6.6, but basically he's going 6.8 knots. An inexperienced helmsman, or someone who is tired and not steering well, will go 7.1, then 5.8, then 7.2—they never get the boat in the groove. So speed is a great reference for how you are steering. The best helmsman stays with a very constant speed that varies no more than two-tenths of a knot from the target speed he's trying to maintain."

If you have only 1 or 2 degrees of weather helm, it's probably not enough to feel like you're in the groove; a small rudder angle won't create the optimal amount of attainable lift. Ways to add pressure would be to heel the boat more, to move your weight forward, or to trim the sails in a manner that will provide more power—ease the halyards; ease the backstay, which then eases the headstay; move the traveler to windward and ease the mainsheet; tighten the runner; ease the outhaul; and move jib leads forward.

For example, if you're sailing along in light air and have a hard time finding the groove, put a few crew members on the leeward rail and heel the boat more. It will give better shape to the sails and a better feel to the rudder.

One of Gary's tricks is to move crew members down below when he doesn't have any helm in light air, because the boat is being slewed about by every wave and ripple. "During the Liberty Cup in New York Harbor, light air is a killer, thanks to all the chop from passing ships. In those conditions I put three of my six-man crew below, on the leeward side of the keel. It's really fast. On a maxi boat I've had 20 people down below, by the keel. When you do this, make sure to rotate crews and give them a pep talk, because they won't be able to see any of the action on the course while they are swimming in sweat."

The Mechanics of Steering

Some course changes are very small, almost unnoticeable, such as when you want to pinch slightly upwind. At other times, as when tacking, you have to turn the boat through a very large course change. Basically, there are three ways to make a boat turn from one course to another:

Rudder. The disadvantage of the rudder is that it can function as a brake. As soon as you turn it slightly, water flow separates and the rudder stalls. In general, the rudder should be used as little as possible to turn the boat. A good way to practice is to try steering a dinghy without the rudder. You'll be amazed at how much steering control you have with just sails and angle of heel.

Sails. How you trim and handle the sails has a great effect on where the boat wants to go. Using the sails to turn works as follows: If you want the bow to head toward the wind, trim the main and ease the jib. If you want the bow to head away from the wind, such as when you are rounding the windward mark, leave the jib trimmed and dump the mainsheet. (See figure 7.2.) You are using the sails to move the center of effort and pivot the boat around the centerboard or keel (center of resistance).

Heel. Changing the angle of heel is another way to turn a boat. When a boat is standing upright, its underwater profile is symmetrical, and it tends to go straight through the water. As soon as the boat heels, however, its underwater

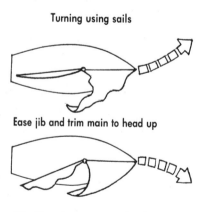

Turning using sails

Ease jib and trim main to head up

Trim jib and ease main to head off

Figure 7.2

profile becomes asymmetrical, and the water flow makes it want to turn. Heel the boat to windward to head away from the wind, and heel it to leeward to head up. This is why more heel produces more windward helm. Small boats respond readily to movement of crew weight, so changing heel angle is very important for turning. Bigger boats are less responsive to weight placement, but you should still move your crew to help make turns, especially in lighter air.

Whenever you are steering, use all of the above methods to make every turn, no matter how slight your course change. This will keep the boat going as fast as possible. On big boats, where weight placement can't control the heel of the boat very much, keep a firm grip on the helm and don't let the boat slew over the course. A light touch is not the right touch.

In the Groove

Every sailor has experienced times when a boat nearly sailed itself, going light-years faster than the competition. Being "in the groove" is a subjective state where the boat feels good and performs well. It's like hitting a tennis ball with the "sweet spot" on your racket. You don't necessarily know exactly where this spot is, but you definitely know when you hit it.

The goal of the helmsman is to keep the boat in the groove as much as possible. You can make the groove wider and easier to find by moving the draft forward to give the genoa a wider leading-edge angle. Ease the backstay and/or increase luff tension by tightening the halyard. This rounds the front of your sail and makes telltale activity more sedate. It also permits the sail to function efficiently over a wider course range.

A wider groove is a good idea when the helmsman is not very experienced and is having a hard time keeping the boat on the wind. A wider groove is also necessary when sailing in waves or puffy winds, where you can't avoid being out of the groove for a certain percentage of the time. When sailing at night, it's also a good idea to sail with a fuller entry jib, because you won't be able to steer the waves, which are invisible.

The disadvantage of a forgiving sail is that you won't point as high as possible. And sometimes the windward telltale will seem insensitive to steering changes. In this case, the luff may be too round for the conditions. By reducing headstay sag, you flatten the jib's entry, which increases your pointing ability. Increase pointing ability on a big boat by tightening the backstay, which reduces headstay sag. On a dinghy, tighten the sidestays, put blocks in the mast partners behind the mast, or tighten the mainsheet—if you can do so without causing the leech telltales to stall. Remember that the more you flatten the front of the jib, the harder it will be to stay in the groove, because you'll need to pay more attention to the boat's angle of attack to the wind.

The leading edge of the jib is too straight when a small course change causes the jib's telltales to swing from sailing too high to sailing too low. In other words, if your windward telltale is standing straight up, indicating you are sailing too high, and you only head off the wind 1 or 2 degrees before the leeward telltale hangs down, indicating you are sailing too low, then the sail has too straight an entry. If you can turn the boat 3 or 4 degrees between windward and leeward telltale flutters, then the entry shape of the jib is probably about right. But if you don't notice any affect on the telltales through a course change of 10 degrees or more, or if the sail luffs when you try to point as high as other boats, then the jib's entry is too round.

Weather and Lee Helm: Finding a Balance

When steering a sailboat to windward, the boat should sail straight ahead with the wheel or tiller turned about 4 or 5 degrees to windward. This little bit of weather helm not only gives the helmsman a feel for the boat, but also creates lift to windward that helps to prevent leeway.

More than 5 degrees of weather helm will slow your boat. To reduce weather helm, usually a problem in heavy winds when the boat is heeling over, you can do the following:

1. Flatten the main (and jib) by tensioning the backstay and outhaul.
2. Move crew weight outboard and aft.
3. Flatten the boat by pinching more and easing the traveler to leeward.
4. Raise the centerboard a bit. If you can, move your board back in the centerboard trunk.
5. Move the mast forward.
6. Reef the main.

If you have lee helm, neutral helm, or less than 3 degrees of weather helm, you can increase pressure on the helm in the following ways:

1. Heel the boat by moving crew weight to leeward.
2. Move crew weight forward.
3. Make the main and jib more powerful by easing the backstay and outhaul.
4. Pull the traveler to windward.
5. Add mast rake, or move the mast back to move the sail plan aft.

To stay in the groove, avoid pinching, especially if the wind is shifty or the seas are choppy. In other words, when in doubt, err on the side of sailing the boat slightly lower. Since the movement of displacement boats is constrained by momentum, once you start going slower the problem accumulates, and it will be harder to get back up to speed. Trying to point high in shifty or choppy conditions is like sailing with a jib that has too flat an entry—the envelope for error is narrow. And when the conditions are variable, it's harder to find the groove again after getting out of it, so if you're in doubt, sail slightly lower.

In San Francisco Bay it's usually very windy, but the water is relatively smooth, so the chance of coming back up to speed quickly after you slow down is good. This means it may work to sail the boat a little higher and therefore a little slower, to net better progress upwind. But if you're sailing in Hawaii or in the Gulf Stream, where the waves are much bigger, it can take forever to get a big boat back up to speed and back in the groove. If you try to point as high as you would in San Francisco Bay, you'll be going slowly. So you have to sail faster boatspeeds.

Sailing in Overpowered Conditions

To keep the boat from making leeway, the key element is to sail the boat flat. In breezy conditions, the way to do this is to hike hard. On a dinghy this comes naturally to the crew, but on big boats the lower lifelines should be kept as loose as the rules allow so the crew can get their rear ends on the edge of the rail. It's uncomfortable but extremely effective.

The next alternative is to depower your sails by flattening them. Tighten the halyards, backstay, outhaul, and cunningham, and ease the checkstay if you have one. The next step is to ease your traveler to leeward to depower the main. On boats with backstays, you can leave the traveler on centerline and ease the mainsheet to twist off the top of the sail. This way, you dump wind out of the top of the sail, where the most heeling force is created. On a dinghy without a backstay, depower the main by lowering the traveler to leeward instead of easing the mainsheet. When you ease the sheet, your mast will straighten and go forward, making the main more powerful and easing forestay tension, which would hurt your boat's pointing ability. All of this happens because sheeting the main in hard pulls down on the boom, which pulls on the mainsail, which in turn pulls the mast back, tightening the forestay.

If easing the traveler to leeward on a dinghy does not get the boat upright again, centerline the traveler and ease the mainsheet to luff the main. As mentioned, easing the mainsheet will reduce forestay tension, and that will diminish your pointing ability. But as the forestay sags, tension will be decreased not only on the jib's luff but also on the jib's leech; this combination flattens the sail and reduces heeling force. The jib can be depowered by moving the sheeting lead aft so that the top part of the sail luffs.

Gary remembers regaining the lead against New Zealand *wunderkind* Chris Dickson in the 1985 Citizen's Cup match-racing series. "We were racing in Auckland Harbor in 20 knots of wind, and Dickson was ahead. Noticing a wicked line squall approaching, I got my crew to move the jib leads back as far as possible. This was not an easy task on these boats, since the crew had to unbolt a shackle and then re-shackle the block to a pad eye farther back. The storm hit, packing an honest 40 knots and driving rain. We were trying to race against a boat we couldn't even see. But our efforts paid off. While the top half of the jib was useless as it luffed, the boat stayed upright and we got around Dickson's boat, which was laid over with its rail in the water."

If the leg is long enough, and you are certain the wind won't die for a while, it is usually much better to depower the sailplan by putting up a smaller jib, or by reefing the main. By reducing sail, you'll not only speed up, but you'll greatly decrease your leeway. Less sail area is fast in strong winds!

There always seems to be one argument after another on many boats concerning whether to reef or not. If you think it's time to reef, instead of arguing about it, simply give it a try. A well-organized reef, where everybody knows his job in advance, doesn't take long, and you won't lose much distance. After a quick and painless reef, it will be easy to compare whether you're performing better against the competition. If you have a long windward leg to go, it's better either to take a reef or at least make the test. If you've only got a mile or less to sail to the next mark, it's probably not worth reefing.

Practice sail changes and reefing procedures so that you can depower and repower your sail plan as well as you tack the boat. In many races, you'll find that one sail-plan configuration is not versatile enough. One of the hardest calls to make is when the start is in blustery conditions a couple of miles offshore, and the windward mark is in the lee of a shore. You ask yourself "Can we hang in early in the leg by flattening the sails and feathering until the wind gets progressively lighter and the seas progressively calmer, closer to shore? Or is the crew good enough to start with a smaller jib and then change to a bigger sail when the wind lightens?" The more you practice, the more options you'll be able to choose from.

Steering Through Waves

In waves, you should sail a big boat up the front side and down the back side. The bigger the sea, the more you have to think about how to sail each wave. When you're going upwind, against the waves, obviously you want to steer the waves so that you are affected as little as possible by their action. Do this by sailing a little high on the face of the wave, and lower on the back of the wave. Sail through the low spots between waves when possible. However, the worst thing you can do is to turn the rudder too much while being hit by a wave. Both the wave and the rudder movement will slow you.

You need to have good peripheral vision and anticipate what's going to happen in wavy conditions. It's like skiing; if you only look at the next mogul, you're not going to be a great skier, but if you get the total picture first and then deal with things as they come, you could become one. When you're steering a sailboat, you want to look five or ten waves ahead, and at the same time handle each wave as it gets to you. Ask your tactician to let you know when a big wave is coming, just in case you've missed seeing it; also ask for input on where the flat spots are.

Another rule of thumb is to keep the amount of weather helm to a minimum in waves. Generally this means using less sail area than you would in flat water. Most people think they have to put up a lot of sail to power through the waves, but this creates a lot of helm. The natural reaction is to try to reduce the weather helm by feathering. But every time you feather in waves, you start going slower and slower. You want the amount of sail area that will let you drive off for speed without overpowering the boat and at the same time steer the boat through the waves without being overwhelmed by weather helm.

If you find that you're in an area where there is an extreme chop, and it's hard to go through, Gary's recommendation is to tack away and go a half-mile from there. Often, places with extreme chop are localized due to current, the bottom, or passing ships. Go for speed, hike hard, and take the waves at an angle to the bow. Don't even think of pinching. Races are won and lost when the fleet goes through this stuff, so grit your teeth and remember that it won't last forever.

If you have to sail in chop, Tom advises not trying to steer through every wave. Just point the boat a little lower than you normally sail, so that you can keep your speed up. In nasty chop, which you find on large, shallow bodies of water like the Chesapeake Bay and Lake Erie, the sail trimmers have a lot to do with your performance. When boatspeed is down, have them ease the sails.

Tacking

A big boat has a lot of momentum, and therefore a lot of shoot. Use your boat's momentum to maximize your gains to windward by tacking slower than in a one-design. By prolonging the turn, you gain distance to windward in the middle of the tack. The heavier the boat, the slower you can tack, but you don't want to take too long, or it will be hard to accelerate coming out of the tack. Generally, the best way to tack a big boat is to swing into the wind slowly and then turn faster after passing through the eye of the wind, to get the sails filled quickly on the new tack. The lighter the wind, the more you should backwind the jib to get down to your new course.

On a dinghy you maximize your gains by roll-tacking, which is an art in itself. Many long articles have been written on this subject, and for a well-illustrated series, see the November 1984 and January 1985 issues of *Sailing World*.

One common question asked by many big-boat helmsman is, "Should I steer through the tack in a way that helps the crew grind the jib in, especially when the wind is blowing at the upper end of the range for the heavy No. 1?" Tom says, "Absolutely not." Gary, on the other hand, says, "Absolutely! Because of equipment, the size of the sails, the strength of the wind and the waves, there is a limit to how fast crew can get the sail in. If the boat isn't tacking well, or if the clew hangs up on the shrouds, I find it's better to just hold high for a second or two to give the grinders and tailers time to get the jib in. As soon as the clew clears the shrouds, hold a high course to allow the crew to trim the jib in. Don't let the clew bang on the shrouds and the mast, because that creates turbulence that slows you down. All that banging also creates wear and tear on the jib. Once the sail is in all the way, bear off and accelerate. This is particularly necessary on smaller boats that are under-winched, and on which there is only one grinder and one tailer. It's another matter on a 12-meter or on boats with coffee grinders that combine the effort of four big guys to grind the sail in—that's power. In that case, I agree with Tom."

When steering through a tack on a big boat, stay in your position on the windward side (as it becomes the leeward side) until you see the jib fill. The windier it is, the sooner you'll have to move to the weather side. When crossing to the new windward side in a dinghy, always face forward so the boat doesn't turn too far. Perhaps the biggest trick when tacking a dinghy is holding both the mainsheet and the hiking stick in one hand behind your back for a split second when you cross.

Before the tack, a big boat tactician should give the compass course for the new tack. Once the jib has filled, jump up to windward and watch everything that can help get the boat back in the groove. Steer up to speed as quickly as possible. In light air, come out of the tack below your optimal close-hauled course, with your sails eased a few inches to build speed. In heavy air, come out of the tack only slightly below, and closer to, your optimal close-hauled course.

Steering Downwind

It takes more latent ability to steer a boat well off the wind on reaches, and especially on runs, than on a beat. One big difference between upwind and downwind is that you feel a lot less breeze when you are driving off the wind. For example, if the true windspeed is 14 knots, you might feel 20 knots of apparent wind on a beat, but on a run you may only feel about seven knots apparent. This means you're sailing in lighter air a majority of the time off the wind, which is why most crews light up their cigarettes or eat their sand-wiches then—because it's a relief from the noise and the wind of beating.

It's difficult to steer downwind well in light to medium air because unlike upwind, you feel the wind less and you don't have a constant angle of heel or pressure on the helm to use as a guide. Downwind sailing almost requires an entirely different mental approach from upwind sailing. Therefore, when you round the weather mark, it is often a good time to change helmsmen.

The breeze doesn't stop shifting when the spinnaker is hoisted, and the helmsman needs to continue to use as many aids as possible—instruments, masthead fly, telltales, waves, other boats, sails, and pressure on the helm.

Where a helmsman stands or sits is important off the wind. You have to be comfortable as well as braced, since you turn the rudder more than you do when going upwind. When the boat isn't heeling, being in the middle of the boat gives you the best leverage possible. But this isn't a fixed rule. With a tiller, you can use the hiking stick to steer from the windward side. As the breeze comes on, you certainly should be in a position where you have as much leverage as possible, so that you won't let the boat broach or wander. This often means sitting on the windward side and holding the tiller with both hands. Brace your feet against something solid, or you won't last long on an overpowered reach.

Try to steer from a position where you can see as much of the waves and sails as possible. Since the helmsman is pretty far aft in the boat, he usually has the best overall view of the sail plan and won't get mesmerized by the luff of the spinnaker, as the trimmer might. Your position is also important for seeing the instruments. These are a little harder to watch downwind than upwind because the crew, instead of being on the rail, is in the center of the boat and moving all over. It always seems as though someone is sitting right in front of the dials.

Going downwind, the instruments you want to use are the same basic ones you use when sailing upwind—boatspeed and true windspeed. Also, you need to use the true wind or apparent wind angle instrument, because your optimum wind angle downwind is a little harder to feel by the seat of the pants. When you're beating, there is a very narrowly defined wind angle where the boat will feel right. But on a run, your wind can be practically anywhere for making your best speed toward the mark. The best sailing angle depends on wind strength and the size of the waves. (See Chapter 8 for information on how to figure out the optimum sailing angles downwind.)

If you are sailing a dinghy, or a boat without instruments, keep watching how you're doing against the other boats. They are your best indicator of relative speed, and you should keep experimenting. On a run, for example, jibe more than you think is right—it won't slow you down too much—and see how you're netting out against the boats around you. "I think it's great to learn how to sail by the seat of your pants," says Tom. "It keeps you from getting too dependent on electronic instruments."

At night, one of the best guides is a lighted Windex at the top of the mast. You don't want to steer looking only at the Windex, but use it as a reference. You'll get a stiff neck if you keep looking up at the Windex all the time. Tom remembers one 1,000-mile heavy-air race down the coast of Mexico with Dennis Conner. "Dennis didn't care about the instruments; all he wanted was for someone to shine a light every now and then on the telltale on the windward shroud so that he could avoid sailing by the lee." Another good place to put a telltale is on the backstay over your head.

As when sailing upwind, the helmsman sailing downwind has to have a good sense of the boat and the wind. Top sailors interpret the breeze on the back of their necks, which helps them anticipate what is going to happen. "Did you ever notice how short Dennis Conner gets his hair cut before a big race?" Tom asks. "He has it trimmed very close in the back, and I hardly ever see him look behind when sailing downwind."

Another way to keep track of everything that's going on is to get some help from your crew. Don't try to do everything yourself. If the tactician is too busy to look back for puffs, appoint someone else to do the job. In heavy air the crew is camped out on the stern anyway, so have one of them keep an eye out for puffs. On boats with running backstays, the person responsible for them is in the best position to look for puffs, because he or she is positioned farthest aft. Puffs will appear as dark spots on the water moving toward you, or you can look for their effect on other boats. Tell the crew to keep an eye out for boats rounding up, broaching, planing, surfing, or just moving faster than others. Make sure you get information on what is going on behind you, because you'll lose your concentration if you have to keep looking back over your shoulder.

The Downwind Groove

On a run, getting the right amount of helm is just as important as it is when sailing upwind, except that your goal is to balance the helm so that it is neutral. In other words, minimize the amount that you have to turn the rudder. Having helm downwind is definitely slow, because you just want the boat to go straight. You're not asking the rudder to produce lift as it does when sailing upwind. Turning the helm only creates drag while sailing downwind.

Moving crew weight around is one of the best ways to balance the helm. If you have leeward helm, move some or all of the crew to leeward. If you have windward helm, move them to windward. The helmsman is the key person in terms of feeling how much helm there is, and what needs to be done to balance the boat. Balancing the helm on a reach is a different story. Even though weather helm is slow, sail area is fast when reaching. Therefore, it pays to put up as much sail as you can control, even though this makes the boat heel and develop helm. While you'd never sail upwind with more than 4 or 5 degrees of weather helm, on a reach you may be fastest with up to 10 degrees of helm.

There is definitely a groove where the trimmer feels as though he's got some pressure on the spinnaker, and the helmsman feels that the boat is going well. Experiment to find the angle at which the boat feels lively and the sheet is pulling, and try it for a while. Watch how you're netting out against the boats around you. "The best drivers can feel a little pressure on the helm once they start cookin'," says Tom. "It's kind of a vibration. Again, the speedo is the key instrument, and the helmsman essentially lives and dies by it. Figure out what speed seems to net out well, and then steer the boat up and down to maintain that speed."

When Tom talks about steering up and down to maintain optimal speed and course downwind, he doesn't mean to give the impression that these changes should be large. "It's the same concept as varying your course a few degrees while going upwind. The problem is that the apparent windspeeds change quicker downwind than they do upwind. So it pays to have a better helmsman downwind than upwind, because the feel of the boat and staying in proper groove is much more difficult when the apparent wind strength is changing so quickly." (See "The Downwind Cliff" on page 308).

What most people have difficulty comprehending is the necessary interrelation between the spinnaker trimmer and the helmsman. Finding the groove requires communication between these two. The spinnaker trimmer should be saying things like, "It feels right here. I've got good pressure. Come up a little now because I'm losing pressure." Or, "Come down a little because I'm gaining pressure." The groove is not as obvious downwind as it is upwind, so the helmsman has to be very sensitive.

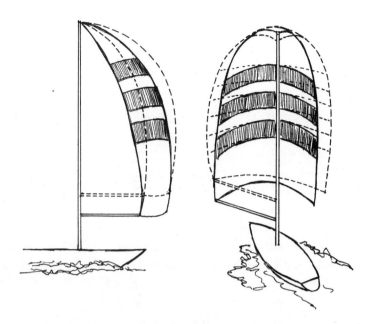

Figure 7.3 *Raising the spinnaker pole opens up the leeches of the sail (dotted lines), but it also flattens the sail. Lowering the pole makes the leeches straighter and makes the cross-section of the sail more full.*

To make the groove easier to find, lower the spinnaker pole and make the spinnaker fuller. (See figure 7.3.) The more open-leeched a spinnaker is, the narrower the steering envelope becomes. In other words, the flatter the spinnaker is, the more attention from both the trimmer and helmsman is required. It's like having a fine-entry jib when you're sailing upwind. One way to make the spinnaker more forgiving is to give it a rounder shape by closing the leeches a little.

When in doubt downwind, another way to make steering easier is to sail higher and faster. It's similar to widening the upwind groove by sailing a smidgin on the full side when beating. Most people err on the lower and slower side downwind, and that's a mistake. You will pay for being low much more than you will pay for being high, because once you start to slow down, the problem accumulates as the apparent wind strength decreases, the apparent wind angle moves back, and the boat loses momentum.

Steering Guides

There are many guides you can employ while steering downwind. Becoming fixated on a compass course, while ignoring the wind on the water, waves, telltales, and instruments, is a mistake. One of the main disadvantages of a compass is that you usually have to look down to see it. When you lower your gaze, you lose track of many other aids.

Current and leeway are also going to affect the course you're steering. The best way to steer a straight course for a mark that you can see is to line up the mark with something on land behind it, and then keep them in line.

If you can steer straight for a mark while sailing your optimal speed, then you can use the compass as a guide. But again, you can't count on only one aid to help you go the fastest possible. The best helmsmen figure out how to steer a compass course and at the same time wiggle the boat down the rhumb line according to the waves, windshifts, puffs, and lulls.

On distance races, digressions from the course can become much greater. On a simple calculator program it is very easy to find out how much faster you need to go for each degree you steer higher. This way you can check to see if the speed you are going by sailing high is fast enough to justify the course change. The longer the leg, the more you have to steer with potential wind shifts in mind. Err on the side of speed. If you can change your course 20 degrees and go two knots faster, don't hesitate—throw the tiller over and get the lead out. Whether the course is 60 miles from San Diego to Ensenada, or 630 miles from Newport to Bermuda, or 2,200 miles from Los Angeles to Honolulu, your course should be determined by the speedo, not by the compass.

Similarly, when sailing an overpowered tight reach in a dinghy, it's better to sail low of the mark to get your boat on a plane, instead of dogging it with the chute strapped too tight.

Use everything possible as a reference when steering at night. If you see a stern light ahead that's on a boat steering the same course you are, nothing keeps you going straighter. It's the same when you can see a lighthouse or mark toward which you're headed. Sometimes you can line up a star in your shrouds, but remember that this will only work for short periods of time since the stars are moving across the sky. The angle of the waves will also help at night, as will sail trim. If your sails are trimmed for the course you want to steer, and suddenly they start luffing, you've either been headed or you're steering high of the course. Pay attention to the wind angle, waves, stars, moon, clouds, stern lights, angle of heel, horizon, a point on land.

Steering Downwind in Overpowered Conditions

In overpowered conditions, the first thing you should do is get good leverage on the wheel or tiller. Second, communicate with your crew. Too many helmsmen just sit there with the tiller up under their necks, and don't say anything. Tell the sail trimmers about the helm. See that they ease the sheets as much as possible in overpowering conditions. The spinnaker is particularly easy to overtrim because it looks good when it's in tight. The best way to keep the boat level is for the helmsman to yell "Dump!" when he feels the helm start to load up. This tells the spinnaker trimmer to quickly ease the spinnaker sheet two feet. Experienced trimmers don't wait for the helmsman's cry for help; they can judge when to dump the sheet based on the strength of the puff and the angle of heel before the puff hits. Better crews tend to lose their spinnaker more often than one might think, because it's eased so much. Use telltales near the spinnaker leeches to help keep the sail eased to the maximum. You read them the same way as the ones on the luff of the jib.

Communicating with the mainsail trimmer is equally important; he's usually right next to the helmsman. There should be a lot of talking back and forth between the trimmers and the helmsman.

Make sure somebody constantly monitors the vang as well. Many dinghy roundups are the result of the boom's tip dragging through the water and not allowing the sail to be eased out enough. When you let the vang off, the boom will rise out of the water, permitting the sail to be eased further. Even if the boom is not dragging in the water, releasing the vang luffs the upper half of the main immediately.

Other mainsail trim for heavy-air reaching includes keeping the outhaul and flattening reef tight to open up the lower leech. If the top of the main luffs consistently, reef it to cut down on windage and drag.

It's usually worth using the spinnaker, even if it means you round up every once in a while. This may make the boat harder to steer than a genoa would, but it's faster. Don't start depowering the rig until you're at the point where you can't steer the boat straight because of excessive weather helm when the rudder is stalled. The main rule for depowering is to start at the back of the sail plan and proceed forward, because that reduces weather helm. The first thing to do, assuming that the spinnaker is eased as much as possible, is to ease the mainsheet and vang. Other ways to depower the main are to bend the mast, put in the flattening reef, or even go to a reef. Next, take a staysail down if you're flying it to reduce heel and therefore lessen weather helm. Finally, you can go to a flatter spinnaker. The helmsman is the only person who can really feel when it's time to make these changes.

When weather helm builds up and the rudder begins to stall (i.e., there's an air bubble around it) before you can depower enough, one technique to reattach flow on the rudder is to give the helm a few quick pumps. Keep an eye out for waves as well, because they can push the boat over enough to lift much of the rudder out of the water. Anticipate big waves by steering a little lower so they won't push the boat on its side so much. As usual, steer higher in the relative lulls and lower in the puffs.

Tom advises helmsmen sailing downwind on a run to compare steering the boat to skiing: "On skis you have to keep your body, and therefore your center of effort, over the skis. You can't lean way uphill or way downhill. In sailing, you have to keep your whole sail plan over the hull. Looking at it another way, you have to steer to keep the hull under the sail plan and prevent the keel from becoming a pendulum. For example, if the boat heels to the right, steer under it to the right. If the boat heels to the left, steer under it that way. These steering corrections should be fairly small; you don't want to oversteer. If you're having a hard time keeping the boat under the sails, perhaps your crew weight is too much to one side. You must balance the helm in windy conditions."

Steering downwind in a breeze is made more difficult by the fact that downwind sails can't be reefed as working sails can. Even if you could reef the main, you'd end up with too much sail on the spinnaker side of the boat. So it's critical to figure out a way to balance the boat with the sails, and this requires working extra hard with the sail trimmers. For example, if the boat wants to round up to windward, ask the person on the guy to square the pole (pull the spinnaker pole back). If the boat wants to fall off to leeward, ask for the pole to be eased forward and the sheet trimmed. A blooper can help to balance the spinnaker, especially on masthead-rigged boats where the mainsail is relatively high-aspect—tall and narrow.

A boat is most vulnerable to broaching and jibe-broaching (uncontrollably jibing and then spinning out) when the rig is loaded up. This usually happens at the bottom of a wave, where the bow digs into the next wave, slowing the hull, and the rig tries to keep on going. Ideally, the helmsman wants to go dead down the back of the wave, and then head up a little in the trough to avoid slowing the boat.

Steering corrections on a run should be as small as possible. The worst thing you can do when you start to round up is to overreact. An inexperienced helmsman will typically crank the helm over as the boat starts to luff up, but when the sails fill and flow reattaches to the rudder, the boat will have so much momentum going the other way that it will jibe-broach. The important thing is to try to get flow back on the rudder without an abrupt move. Give a few quick tugs on the helm to ventilate the rudder and get rid of the stalled air bubble.

If you think the boat is about to round up, have the person trimming the chute dump a foot or two of sheet to unload the rudder. Even if the chute collapses, you will lose less speed than you would if the boat rounded up; at least the boat will still be going straight down the course. If broaching is inevitable, aim for a high-speed rollover and recovery. In general, boatspeed is your friend during a broach; rudder drag and heel are your enemies. If you keep up your boatspeed, your rudder will continue to function and the boat will bear off. As the broach commences, your helm will probably be hard over and stalled. Save the situation by taking the following steps:

1. Straighten the helm quickly to reattach flow. The longer you drag a stalled rudder through the water, the slower you will go. The slower you go, the more the apparent wind moves aft and heels the boat.

2. Collapse the sails to pop the boat upright.

3. When the boat straightens up with the sails luffing, you should still have most of your original speed. Now bear off sharply to a broad reach. Head off far enough to avoid another roundup when the chute refills, but not so far that the boat starts death-rolling. A second broach is difficult to recover from, because you are going so slowly.

4. The first sail that you trim back in should be the spinnaker. Just as you depowered the boat from back to front, you should power up from front to back.

Preventing and Recovering from a Broach

The release sequence to prevent a broach must be perfectly clear to the entire crew. Listed in order, the mainsheet, boom vang, and staysail sheet should be eased; and then the spinnaker sheet should be dumped to ventilate the chute and unload the rudder. If all else fails, steer into the broach and collapse the chute.

Go over your recovery plans before you broach because your crew will be working on a deck that is practically vertical once you've broached.

Jibe-broaches are usually the result of the helmsman trying to sail the boat dead downwind. With mainsail all the way out one side, and the spinnaker almost totally on the other side of the boat's centerline, the boat is prone to death-rolling. As the helmsman makes radical rudder movements to try to get the boat under control, the boat can round up either to windward or leeward. If you are unlucky enough to have flow reattach to the rudder while you are trying to recover from an oscillation to windward, the boat will quickly bear off, jibe, and then broach as the spinnaker pole digs into the water and the mainsail backwinds.

Recovering from a jibe-broach is more difficult than recovering from a normal roundup because the sails will be trimmed on the wrong side of the boat. The boat will lose all her forward speed and lie on her side until the spinnaker halyard and mainsheet are released. If the boat has running backstays, the old windward runner, now the leeward one, will prevent the mainsail from being released. Until a crew member dumps the runner, the main will be held on centerline, causing the boat to stay on her side.

Preventing a jibe-broach is a lot simpler than recovering from one. When the boat starts to oscillate, head up some, ease the pole forward and trim the sheet so that the center of the spinnaker is in line with the headstay, choke the chute down by lowering the pole and sheeting to a block forward of the boom. Don't let the spinnaker trimmer get both spinnaker clews on the same side of the headstay. When sailing dead downwind in heavy air, have one crew member look back for gusts. Just before one hits, head the boat up to avert death-rolling.

Anything you can do to increase your speed will improve the boat's stability and allow more control from the rudder. With the right wind and wave conditions, surfing is a way to add speed. "Mark Soverel is one of the best downwind drivers I've ever sailed with," says Tom. "He's unbelievable, and it's because he's a surfer. Steering a big boat or a dinghy down waves is no different in concept from surfing. What you're trying to do is build up boatspeed and apparent windspeed by steering across the wave. You then use this speed to make progress to leeward by heading off and going down the face of the wave. When your bow is about to dig into the next wave, head up so that the rig doesn't become overloaded. It's definitely not fast to sail in a straight line. My advice is to watch a surfing contest on television, and just study those guys going across a wave."

In surfing conditions, the tactician or helmsman should look for troughs on the windward side of the boat and also watch the bow wave. If you see the bow wave starting to get bigger, it's time for the helmsman to head up a little. You want to pick the biggest waves to surf on, and this is where looking behind can really help. Every third wave or so is bigger than the others. Spend most of your time going down the big waves, rather than trying to go down the little waves and missing the big ones. You have to discriminate. Steering by the lee can be very fast when you're on a wave.

Another trick that some helmsmen use for catching waves is to wiggle the tiller just as a wave starts to lift the stern. I think this breaks up the suction that is created when a boat is moving fast through the water, and stops the boat from being sucked into the wave.

Steering Through a Jibe

You lose very little by jibing downwind as long as your crew can execute a jibe properly. One basic rule is that the helmsman ought to jibe at a speed that's good for the crew. It's no good to spin the boat quickly if the spinnaker ends up inside the headstay. If you jibe only for the benefit of the crew, you'll usually be steering through the jibe too slowly. The problem with turning too slowly is that you don't have apparent wind building fast enough on the new jibe. As a result, your speed stays in the low range, and it may take a long time to get it back up again. Almost always turn more sharply than you think is right.

By and large, you want to come out of the jibe a little high, and then fall off to your optimal course as the apparent wind builds. Your goal is to load up with apparent wind on the new jibe as quickly as possible. If you don't come up fairly sharply just after the jibe, you'll lose too much momentum. Your course should be up and then down; that's the ideal jibe. A tack looks the same in reverse—go down to build speed and then head up for better pointing. The only exception to this is when sailing downwind in heavy air: then you don't need to sail high to get back up to speed.

During the first half of the dip-pole jibe, the helmsman should keep his eyes on the spinnaker, so that he can direct when the pole is tripped. He should yell "Trip" when the pole is fully squared and the boat is dead downwind. This is the moment when he wants to start turning the boat a little faster.

During the second half of the turn, use the angle of the Windex and the compass to help determine what heading you should be on for the new jibe. Try to end up with the Windex a little farther forward on the new jibe than it was on the old jibe to keep speed up. "If I'm sailing with the Windex about 25 degrees forward of dead aft," says Tom, "I'll say, 'Let's jibe through 35 degrees, keep good speed, and then bear down to our optimum angle.' As we come out of the jibe, I'm looking for a rough compass course and Windex angle."

Tactical Instruments

In the age of microchips and computers, sailing with the aid of electronic instruments has become increasingly popular. Tom and Gary grew up in the age when the instruments racing sailors depended on were the compass, masthead fly, and telltales. Now they find themselves sailing with sophisticated computers and electronic instruments. Ockam Instruments is at the forefront of performance electronics development and the novel concepts and techniques they've spawned. Jim Marshall is director of sales at Ockam Instruments and is the director of the Ockam U. Seminar series. We asked him, as one of the best in the field, to write the following chapter about the leading edge of "new age" sailing:

As you might imagine, at Ockam we have learned a great deal about how a boat sails and how to sail a boat faster, based on our extensive experience with the last four America's Cup campaigns. Instruments have given us the tools to apply physics to the problems we have seen in this arena. The results often confirm the techniques many sailors naturally practice. Surprisingly, however, many of the results are counter-intuitive. When we've seen an apparent contradiction, we've delved into the data and the math modeling to prove to ourselves why the opposite is so. From that we have opened up an entirely new series of techniques to performance sailing. We've dubbed this new age sailing. Therefore, this chapter will not only benefit those who sail with electronic instruments, but also those sailing the smallest of dinghies. The physics apply to all boats equally. In this chapter I'll go through what various instruments can do for you, which instruments and techniques to follow on short and long courses, and how to analyze whether your instruments are giving you good numbers and what causes them to produce erroneous information.

Most sailors reduce their potential by being too dependent on their sense of sight in judging their boat's performance. Helmsmen's addiction to sailing by telltales is a manifestation of this dependency. I would call these helmsmen "telltale automatons." In fact, as we grow older the sense of sight is responsible for most of our sensory input.

Almost all top sailors started sailing when they were very young, while all their senses were open and receptive to the inputs of the sailing environment. While they learned to use their senses equally, they also realized that "feel" was the key to performance. The feel of the boat is the cumulative result of all the factors involved in a boat sailing in its environment. Helmsmen with a refined sense of feel have an almost innate and simultaneous knowledge of everything happening around them. Some people seem to have the knack, some don't.

As Tom inferred in the previous chapter, the best helmsman steer from a position where none of their senses are compromised. So remember to sit or stand to windward, where you can feel the wind on your face, see the wind on the water, and sense small changes in the balance of the boat.

In a way, top helmsman use their senses as their own personal instruments. The fastest and most responsive instruments in the world cannot perceive and respond to changes in the boat or the surrounding environment as quickly as a well-developed sense of feel. Sailing instruments will never replace the human body, but they can help. Their purpose is, first, to reinforce, develop, and confirm our senses, and second, to give us the confidence to trust those senses. Instruments are a means to an end.

If you aren't lucky enough to have started sailing when you were five or six, the good news is that as an adult you have a much greater ability to hone that sense than you might think. You have the intelligence and objectivity to make a logical correlation between what you feel is going on and what the instruments are telling you. Just like learning anything new, at first it's difficult to discern the minute differences. Only the big ones hit you between the eyes. But with concentration and time, your feel for the subtle changes will improve markedly.

There are times when instruments do a much larger portion of the work. They can be very helpful when there aren't any other boats around to use as performance guides, or at night, when people are just plain tired. They can pick up small but significant shifts downwind when there isn't a horizon to provide a reference heading.

Instruments are also useful in performing complex functions where information comes from a variety of sources and the mathematics can become difficult. This is where the power of integrated instrument systems is a tremendous benefit. Microprocessors do those multidimensional equations, which would take much longer by hand or with a calculator, in fractions of a second. Mostly these functions involve mathematical solutions to tactical and navigational problems.

Keep in mind that instruments are only tools. Knowing how to use the tools is just as important as having them in the first place. Instruments alone can't be expected to make a boat go fast or in the right direction, but they can provide you with the confidence to trust your senses, and give you data to make sound decisions. Sailors, not instruments, win races.

The Basics

Instruments have greatly refined sailboat racing strategies and tactics over the years. Sailors have almost universally embraced as standard equipment the compass, boatspeed, apparent-windspeed, and apparent-wind-angle instruments. The information displayed by these instruments comes almost directly from the sensors. They supply the raw data that is used in more complex instrument functions. Almost every other instrument readout you can buy uses these basic four inputs in different combinations to solve other mathematical problems.

Most elementary instrument systems on the market offer limited integration, which produces the functions of true windspeed and true wind angle. These functions are computed with the inputs of boatspeed, apparent wind angle, and apparent windspeed. True windspeed and true wind angle can be computed with a hand calculator after dredging up some long-lost trigonometry; the beauty of the microprocessor in the instrument system is that it can do these calculations quickly and continuously.

True-wind readouts are valuable, since the apparent wind can be deceptive when one is trying to make correct sail selections. Sailing upwind, the breeze feels stronger than it actually is, and often one chooses too heavy a spinnaker for the downwind leg. The converse is also true. Sailing downwind, the wind always seems lighter than it really is, and the natural tendency is to set too light a headsail for the ensuing upwind work. By contrast, a true-windspeed readout is an excellent reference for making the correct sail call, especially when approaching a mark. Unlike apparent windspeed, true windspeed does not change as the boat changes course.

How many times have you been in a situation where you're sailing downwind and the apparent windspeed is about 8 knots, while your boatspeed is 6½ knots? Since you are not sailing directly downwind, you can't add the two speeds together to get the true wind, but you know the true wind is somewhere around 14½ knots. So you say, "Let's subtract 15 or 20 percent." Now you decide that the true wind is blowing 12 knots. But now you're faced with a new problem. If the wind is truly blowing 12 knots, your fastest sail is the light No. 1. But if the wind is blowing 13 knots, your fastest sail is the medium No. 1. As the apparent windspeed readout fluctuates, you keep the foredeck crew running around, rigging the different jibs. All these efforts are a waste of concentration and energy that can be avoided by having a true-windspeed instrument. Instead of spending all your time making your best guess as to what sail to use, you could spend that energy trying to gain an inside overlap at the leeward mark.

Many helmsmen still try to sail upwind by steering a certain apparent wind angle. Since the apparent wind angle changes with every change in windspeed, wind direction, and boatspeed, the helmsman is bound to sail a drunkard's path. A small change in true windspeed, for example, creates a "velocity lift" or "velocity header." A velocity shift has a dramatic effect on apparent wind angle. Thus, the true-wind-angle and true-windspeed functions give crews steadier and more accurate numbers to work with.

The next step up in instrument sophistication integrates the compass. Only the top tier of instrument packages do this. The main benefit derived from integrating the compass is magnetic wind direction (usually called "true wind direction"). Besides boatspeed, *magnetic wind direction is probably the most important instrument system function you can have on a boat*. (Boatspeed, apparent wind angle, apparent windspeed, and compass bearings are fed into an equation to create magnetic wind direction). The wind direction display tells you immediately where and how fast the wind is shifting. You can change your course or boatspeed, but the magnetic wind display will not change unless the wind shifts. With a true wind direction readout, you can get a bearing on the wind without slowing to a stop and luffing into the wind. Instead of being content with knowing that the wind is blowing out of the southwest, the instrument system says the wind is from 226 degrees. Therefore, from a tactical viewpoint, this instrument is essential. Wind direction gives you enormous value for the amount of money it costs.

How Sensitive Are You?

To judge how sensitive to wind shifts you are, let's divide a test into four categories: upwind and downwind during the day and night. Most good sailors during the day can detect a five-degree shift upwind without instruments by noticing how their boats are heading relative to others, watching their compasses or looking at the shore. Sailing upwind at night is a little more dicey, since you can't see other boats, but you can still use your compass. So let's say most sailors can pick up a 10-degree shift at night without wind instruments.

Downwind during the day? If you stay on top of things, you should be able to pick out a 10-degree shift by looking at other boats around you.

Downwind at night is a whole other category. How many 20-degree shifts have gone by you? A lot, right?

Target Boatspeed

Target boatspeed is the magic number to sail when tacking upwind and jibing downwind. Before we can discuss how these magic numbers are derived, we'll have to lay some basic foundations. You'll see that target boatspeed works well as a servomechanism that helps crews maximize their boat's performance upwind and downwind. It tells them how to trim the sails and where to point the boat. There are many instruments that crews monitor, but boatspeed is the steadiest—it's less likely to change over the short term. Therefore, we'll concentrate on the target boatspeed concept.

For any wind strength, an electronic instrument or a graph will tell you what speed you should sail upwind or downwind. The optimal speeds are produced by computer software called a Velocity Prediction Program (VPP), which analyzes a boat's hull lines, keel and rudder design, mast section size, and in-the-water measurements. Then the VPP brings into equilibrium sail forces, hull resistance, and heeling moment to create speed predictions. After a computer crunches up all the various inputs, the VPP results are expressed on a graph called a *polar diagram*. (See figure 8.1.)

There are three different sources for polar information: Design Systems & Services; an International Measurement System (IMS) certificate available from USYRU; and your own testing and data collection. Design System offers a full Velocity Prediction Program done on a custom basis for a boat. The information is quite detailed, and very accurate. Write to Design Systems & Services, 105 Eastern Avenue, Annapolis, MD 21403. USYRU offers a performance package for any boat with an IMS rating. The IMS information is not quite as detailed for the full range of polars, but it does highlight the upwind and downwind targets. Write USYRU at P.O. Box 209, Newport, RI 02840, or phone 1-800-327-0303. To make your own polar diagram take careful notes of wind speed, wind angle and boatspeed each time you sail. Once you get enough data points for a given wind strength, you can connect them to draw the curve. But as a practical matter, few people have the time to mount such a major technical effort. Homemade polars will only provide a rough estimate at best, especially in the reaching wind angles, since most of your data points will be generated while beating or running.

Figure 8.1 A *Polar Diagram is a graphic representation of the speeds a boat should obtain sailing at any wind angle. This diagram gives the speed characteristics of a fictional "Fast 35" at windspeeds of 3, 4, 6, 8, 10, 12, 14, 16, 20, 24, 28, and 32 knots. To determine this boat's predicted speed in 32 knots of wind while the boat is sailing 120° off the wind, go to the 120° line and find where it intersects the outermost ear-shaped curve, which represents 32 knots of wind. That intersection occurs just shy of the semi-circular scale that represents 12 knots.*

The term "polar" refers to circular nature of the graph where all measurements start at one point—the origin or the pole. A point on a polar diagram is found by moving from the origin in a specific direction (the wind angle) for a specific distance (the boatspeed).

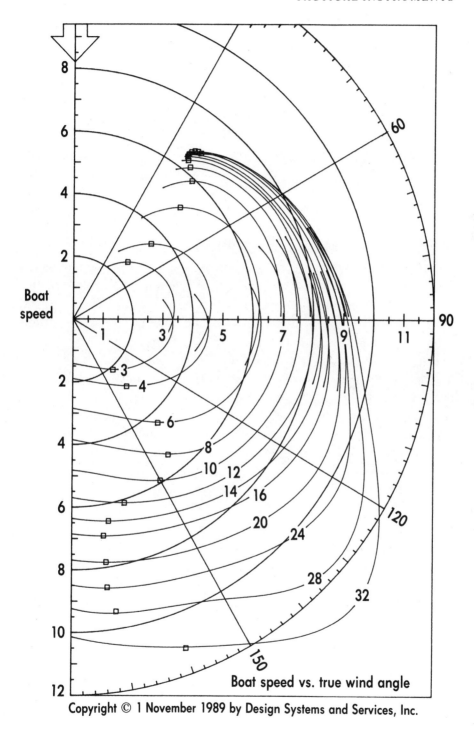

Boat
speed

60

90

120

150

Boat speed vs. true wind angle

At Ockam Instruments, we take the polar information and put it onto a computer chip that can be integrated into our instrument packages. In an integrated system, the true windspeed and true wind angle are processed with the boat's polar predictions, and the exact polar speed is displayed continually.

Polar diagrams may be bit intimidating at first, so let's break them down into manageable chunks. The concentric semicircles are simply measurement scales for boatspeed, as are the horizontal and vertical axes. The wind blows down from the top of the diagram. True wind angle is measured clockwise from the vertical axis, starting from 0° on the vertical axis and increasing through 60°, 90°, 120°, 150° to 180°. The ear-shaped curve drawn on the graph in figure 8.2 represents the boat's predicted speeds at a particular windspeed—in this case 10 knots true windspeed. The curve represents all the boatspeeds from about 36 degrees to 180 degrees true wind angle.

Now go back to figure 8.1. It has many ear-shaped curves that represent a Fast 35's predicted speeds at many different true wind strengths. On this diagram there are boatspeed curves for 3, 4, 6, 8, 10, 12, 16, 20, 24, 28, and 32 knots of true wind. (For this diagram and all other polar diagrams in this chapter, true windspeeds and true wind angles are used.)

Now see figure 8.2. I have singled out the 10-knot true windspeed curve for simplification. To find your predicted boatspeed in any set of conditions, draw a line from the origin (the intersection of the horizontal and vertical axes) marking the true wind angle that you're sailing. The intersection of the wind-angle line and the ear-shaped curve identifies a point for your boatspeed. The length of the line joining the origin of the diagram to that point is your predicted boatspeed. To find your speed in knots, measure that line against the scale marked on either of the axes.

For example, in figure 8.2 sailing with the true wind 60 degrees off the bow, the Fast 35's predicted boatspeed would be 7.13 knots. Or if the true wind angle was 150 degrees, the Fast 35 would be going six knots.

In this simplified graph you can see that the curve is actually made up of two overlapping curves. That's because the top part of the curve shows the Fast 35's performance with a main and jib up, and the bottom part of the curve is with the main and spinnaker. On the polar diagrams supplied by

Figure 8.2 *This is a simplified version of Figure 8.1. It only shows the predicted boatspeeds for the "Fast 35" in 10 knots of wind.*

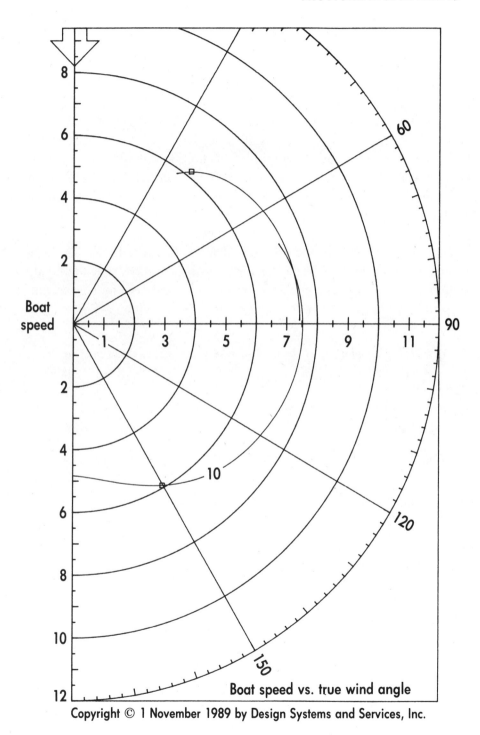

Boat
speed

8

6

4

2

2

4

6

8

10

12

1   3   5   7   9   11

90

60

120

150

10

Boat speed vs. true wind angle

USYRU in their IMS Performance Package for boats with IMS certificates, the graph smooths over the junction between the spinnaker and jib to make a continuous curve.

Thus far we've discussed how a polar diagram can give speed predictions for every true wind angle. Target boatspeeds, on the other hand, are the speeds a boat should maintain for optimal progress upwind or downwind. To get a better idea about the concept of target speed, let's zoom in on a portion of figure 8.2. Figure 8.3 shows the speed predictions for a Fast 35 sailing in 10 knots of wind at true wind angles between 0 and 90 degrees. Notice the small square near the top end of the curve; it marks the optimal velocity made good (VMG) to windward. VMG is the speed your boat makes into the wind, i.e., boatspeed is a vector made up of the components of speed into the wind and speed across the wind. In the full polar diagram (figure 8.1), you'll see the squares not only toward the top of each ear-shaped curve, but toward the bottom of each curve. The lower squares mark the boatspeed for a given wind strength that will get your boat downwind the fastest.

Figure 8.3 *This is a blow up of the upper half of figure 8.2. It shows that no other course nets out higher on the vertical scale, which measures speed directly into the wind,* VMG.

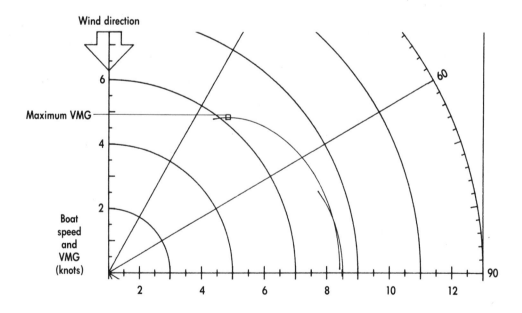

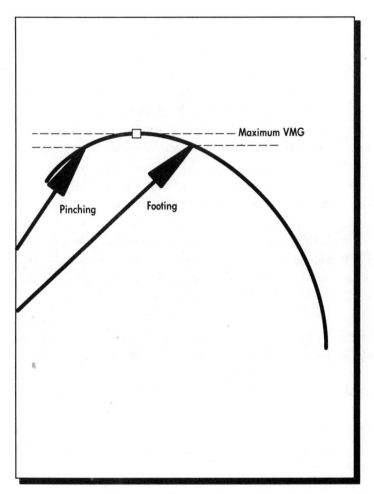

Figure 8.4 *VMG decreases when pinching or footing. There is only one unique wind angle and boatspeed that you can sail at to reach your maximum VMG in any given wind strength.*

In figure 8.4 notice that VMG decreases when a boat sails higher or lower than the point of maximum VMG. On either side of your optimum sailing angle, you lose valuable distance. Upwind when you're pinching you may go closer to the wind, but you're going slower, and when you foot off, your speed increases, but your progress upwind is less.

When tacking upwind or jibing downwind, you should always try to maintain the speed that maximizes VMG. Some crews try to steer by VMG alone, but that's a *serious* mistake! Steering to the VMG read out upwind causes you to pinch excessively because VMG is a function of both true wind angle and boatspeed. Since inertia keeps boatspeed from changing as soon as you alter course, you can improve VMG by simply heading closer to the wind. The closer you head to the wind, the greater your VMG reading. This gain is fool's gold, because as your sails go light you lose driving force and slow down. And as your speed drops, your VMG will plummet (Ockam Instruments originally wasn't going to make a VMG readout, but at the time the company was founded, VMG was a relatively new-found function that everybody thought was a godsend. We looked at it as something that could be harmful when used in an attempt to maximize performance. Yet we manufactured it and sold it anyway because of marketing pressure. If we hadn't sold it, people would have thought we couldn't produce it. Now we've weaned people off it.)

Since VMG as an instrument function is detrimental to your performance, the target boatspeed function is the tool to use to maintain maximum VMG. Target boatspeed is an elegant function, since it eliminates the wind-angle component of VMG. In figure 8.4, notice that the boatspeed at which you achieve maximum VMG for a given wind strength is unique. Upwind, if you are slower than the target boatspeed the polar diagram indicates that you are sailing too narrow a wind angle, and VMG is less than optimum. Likewise, if you are faster than the target boatspeed, you are sailing too large a wind angle, and similarly VMG will be less then optimum. In fact, there is only one point on the ear-shaped performance curve where you'll find the one speed that achieves maximum VMG.

On each curve of a polar diagram, the target boatspeed is indicated by the small black box. When sailing upwind, there is only one unique target boatspeed for each windspeed. Target boatspeed doesn't change if you alter course; it only changes when the windspeed changes—you've jumped to another curve.

Let's take this a step further: When you are slower than the target boatspeed, the polars are telling you to bear off, ease sheets, and get the boatspeed up to target. Likewise, if you are faster than target, head up and slow down. It is as detrimental to performance to go too fast as it is to go too slow.

The relationship between what the polar diagram indicates as target boatspeed and actual boatspeed promotes excellent teamwork between the sail trimmer and the helmsman. It provides both with the proper course of action to keep the boat at maximum performance, and helps them work in concert.

For example, if you were too slow, the communication between the helmsman and sail trimmer should go as follows:

SAIL TRIMMER: Two-tenths slow of target. I feel the need for speed.

HELMSMAN: Okay coming off slightly. Ease with me.

TRIMMER: Easing sheets slightly. Jib lead forward one inch. Speed coming on.

HELM: Speed accelerating nicely. Coming back on the wind.

TRIMMER: Lead coming back. I'm trimming as you come up.

HELM: Speed at target. Return to normal upwind trim.

When you're too fast, the interchange should go like this:

TRIMMER: Two-tenths fast. Let's bleed off that speed to windward.

HELM: Okay coming up. Sheet on a little harder.

TRIMMER: Lead back one inch. Trimming with you. Speed starting to slow.

HELM: Coming back down. Normal upwind trim.

TRIMMER: Coming in on target nicely. Lead forward. Genoa at max upwind trim.

HELM: Boatspeed at target. Full upwind trim.

TRIMMER: Sails look good. Gained a quarter of a boatlength to windward with that excess speed.

The undoing of many boats is lack of communication between the trimmers and the helmsman. If the helmsman is steering by the telltales—and we telltale automatons know who we are—then the trimmer is actually steering the boat. Every time he adjusts the sail, the helmsman will have to change course to chase the telltales. Sailing by target boatspeed forces the helmsman and the trimmer to work together to meet a common goal.

The tactician can also use targets to judge the speed potential of the boat in close tactical situations. If you are presently slow, it could be a disaster for the tactician to have the helmsman pinch up to prevent a boat passing to windward. When slow of your target, you'll only slow your boat further by coming up, and there is a very good chance that the windward boat will roll over you. In the same situation, however, you can build some excess speed before the windward boat gets too close. Then you will have plenty of speed to sail your boat high and pinch off the boat to windward.

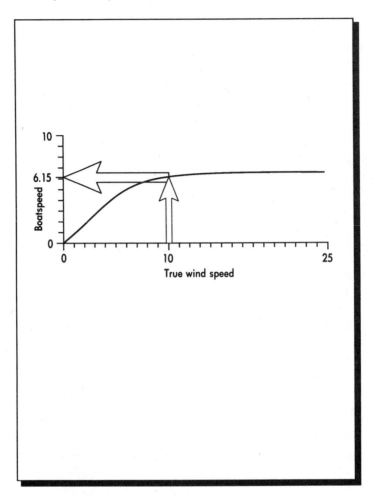

Figure 8.5 *The graph shows that when sailing upwind when the wind blows between 0 and 9 knots a Fast 35's boatspeed increases rapidly as the windspeed increases. After nine knots, more wind does not mean that the boat will go that much faster.*

Figure 8.5 is a graph of target boatspeeds as a function of true windspeed. Notice that on this graph, prepared for a Fast 35, from 3 knots true windspeed to about 9 knots, the graph is very steep. For each knot of change in true windspeed the VPP is telling us that boatspeed should differ by .6 knots! However, from 9 knots on the graph flattens out and we expect only .04 knots of boatspeed change for each knot of change in true windspeed. Thus, there are two very distinct true-windspeed/target-boatspeed ranges in upwind sailing.

Where do you see the greatest difference in performance between similar boats? When the wind blows over 12 to 13 knots, most boats are sailed very close to their optimum, and they usually arrive at the weather mark in order of their rating. But what about the six- to -eight-knot true-windspeed range? It's certainly not unusual to see great differences in performance in the lighter air. We've all witnessed that.

The problem is not so much being able to maintain the correct boatspeed for each true windspeed, but rather *to have the most efficient technique for accelerating or decelerating to the new target boatspeed!* When the true windspeed is less than 9 knots for the Fast 35, small changes in windspeed create a correspondingly large change in boatspeed. The difference between the proper and improper response to windspeed changes has a tremendous impact on overall performance in the transition range between light and heavy air. In terms of apparent wind angle, a puff creates a velocity lift, because for the initial period when the puff hits, the apparent wind goes aft. Likewise, a lull in true windspeed creates a velocity header, with the apparent wind suddenly going forward. (You can review velocity shifts on page 130.) Let's explore the correct response to each of these conditions, using target boatspeeds.

True Wind Speed Increase

When you sail into a puff, the apparent wind angle increases. The telltale sailor will respond by heading up immediately—chasing the telltales. The use of target boatspeeds dictates a different approach. Assume that the true windspeed is 6 knots. The Fast 35's target boatspeed is 4.98 knots. (See table 1.) When the puff hits, the true windspeed increases to eight knots. Our *new* target boatspeed is 5.86 knots. For the new windspeed, we're almost one knot too slow! Thus we need to take the most efficient approach to increasing our boatspeed. *Steer the boat straight, or bear off slightly, easing the sails at the same time.* As the boat nears the new target boatspeed, steer up slightly to capture the new target at close-hauled sail trim. This is finesse—the ability to maintain top-level efficiency through all the fluctuations of the wind on the course.

Contrast the two responses. Which will accelerate the boat the fastest? Certainly, easing the sails to the velocity lift and steering straight or bearing off slightly promotes acceleration much more rapidly than keeping the sails trimmed in and chasing the telltales.

	TABLE 1
True Windspeed	Upwind Target Boatspeed
3	2.52
4	3.49
6	4.98
8	5.86
10	6.15
12	6.29
14	6.37
16	6.45
20	6.56
24	6.65
28	6.70
32	6.72

True Windspeed Decrease

When you sail into a lull, the apparent wind shifts forward and the telltales tell you to bear off. Is this the correct response? Absolutely not! Again, assume that the true wind is 6 knots; target boatspeed is 4.98. In the lull, the true windspeed is 4 knots, which makes the *new* target boatspeed 3.49 knots. For the new wind, you're 1.5 knots fast. *Sailing by targets tells you to head up if you're going too fast.* The conservative response is to steer straight—but don't bear off to follow the telltales! The most efficient way to burn off the excess speed when the windspeed drops is to head up slightly. Use that excess boatspeed to gain valuable distance to windward. As the boatspeed starts to near the new target, fall off to a close-hauled course.

If you are having trouble envisioning the rationale, imagine a binary wind condition in which you have an 8-knot wind that intermittently drops to zero. In the "off" mode, the apparent wind comes dead ahead—it's purely a product of the boat's forward motion. If you were to follow the telltales, you would ultimately complete one or more circles until your 5.9 knots of boatspeed eroded to zero. Instead, the proper response would be to point the boat in the direction you wanted to go. Ultimately, your boatspeed would still fall to zero, but you'd be a lot closer to where you wanted to go in the first place.

Telltales are useful, but don't let them dominate your sailing technique—especially in light air. They're only a part of the picture, whereas target boatspeed gives the entire perspective on the overall performance of the boat. Thus the two techniques, sailing by telltales and sailing by boatspeed, are 180 degrees opposed—only one can be correct.

In the true wind range above 9 knots, the concept of targets still applies, but the response is much closer to what you've always done before, sailing to the telltales. This is because, in the higher wind ranges, the expected boatspeed differential doesn't change dramatically with changes in windspeed. For example, the change in target boatspeed between 14 and 16 knots of true wind is only a tenth of a knot. (See table 1.) The boat responds almost instantaneously to the change in wind velocity. The physics and mathematics are exactly the same, but the *time* required for the boat to accelerate or decelerate to the new target is minimal. Steer by feel and, especially in the higher wind velocities, by heel.

Target boatspeeds will give you the ability to respond to the dynamics of each of these situations in the most aggressive, positive, and efficient manner. It's important to remember that these responses are long in duration for the lower wind range, and short for the higher wind range. However, it's the cumulative gains of proper responses for each change of windspeed that add up to significant boatlength gains on the racecourse.

The world's least expensive instrument for displaying target speeds is a piece of duct tape stuck next to the speedometer, with the boat's targets for different wind strengths written on it. That way you can quickly tell how fast you should be going. Make one strip for your upwind and another for your downwind targets.

Target Boatspeed Downwind

Most racing sailors would agree that sailing downwind is much more difficult than sailing upwind. Trying to sustain maximum performance in light and medium conditions can be downright frustrating. Some days we catch only fleeting glimpses of top-flight performance, never quite focusing on the correct combination of course and sail trim. As often as the boat springs to life, it feels glued to the surface of the water. The subtle changes necessary to sustain a winning combination are elusive. Equally frustrating is that as soon as we lose our edge, the effects of our speed loss are immediately apparent in the success of the boats around us. However, as difficult as sailing downwind is substantially larger gains can be made off the wind than in upwind sailing.

There are five important factors that change radically when turning from upwind to downwind:

1. The apparent windspeed drops considerably.
2. The inputs to your sense of feel are greatly diminished.
3. The range of likely sailing angles increases dramatically.
4. Telltale usefulness becomes practically nil.
5. The number of correct sailing angles for different types of boats increase substantially.

Upwind, the apparent windspeed is much greater than it is downwind. The stronger apparent wind produces much greater sensory feedback—especially since you feel the wind in your face. Downwind, however, the changes have to be felt on the back of your neck. Another way you get less sensory feedback downwind is that when you sail upwind, the boat responds to changes in apparent windspeed with heel. Downwind, the boat hardly heels.

Consider this example: In six knots of true windspeed, the apparent windspeed for our Fast 35 (the model we've been using) is about 10 knots upwind, but only about 4 knots downwind. If the true windspeed increases to 8 knots, upwind the apparent windspeed would increase to 13 knots, but downwind the increase would only be to 5 knots. How well can you feel an increase of 1 knot of apparent wind on your neck? Clearly, this makes it tough to feel the puffs and lulls. Our sensory perceptions are generally not fine-tuned enough to recognize these subtle wind-pressure differences.

Similarly, feedback through other means is diminished. For example, where you once had noticeable pressure on the helm, now there should be hardly any. Minute differences in helm pressure are indicative of reasonably significant changes in wind conditions. Where the loading on the genoa and mainsail sheets was strong upwind, in light to moderate conditions downwind, hand-trimming the spinnaker and mainsail is common.

The sailing angles upwind have a much more defined "groove." There is simply a much smaller range of sailing angles that are obviously correct for maximum upwind performance. If you sail too high, the sails luff and the boat slows or stops. If you sail too low, your speed increases but your VMG is reduced. By trial and error, we naturally home in on the narrow range of sailing angles that produce optimum performance. The breadth of this range from light air to heavy would be only about 10 degrees.

Downwind, the opposite is true. The range of sailing angles is considerably greater, and it is not so obvious which is correct. We can aim farther downwind to take us closer to the mark, but at the expense of boatspeed. Or we may reach up a bit, giving away angle to the mark in the quest for more boatspeed. Or we can reach quite hard, building substantial boatspeed but losing angle downwind. The available choices fall into a range as large as 45 degrees.

Given the difficulties of downwind sailing, the use of target boatspeeds becomes even more effective in heightening our responses to the minute changes in wind conditions, and in keeping the crew's efforts channeled to maximum performance.

For each true windspeed there is a unique target boatspeed that produces maximum VMG downwind (the component of your speed measured directly downwind). (See figure 8.6.) If you are slower than the target boatspeed for a specific true windspeed, the Velocity Prediction Program will tell you to head up, build speed, and get your boatspeed back up to target. (See table 2.)

T A B L E 2

True Windspeed	Downwind Target	True Wind Angle
3	2.15	141°
4	2.85	141°
6	4.41	141°
8	5.42	144°
10	5.97	150°
12	6.17	164°
14	6.62	170°
16	7.05	172°
20	7.90	172°
24	8.70	172°
28	9.50	172°
32	11.21	172°

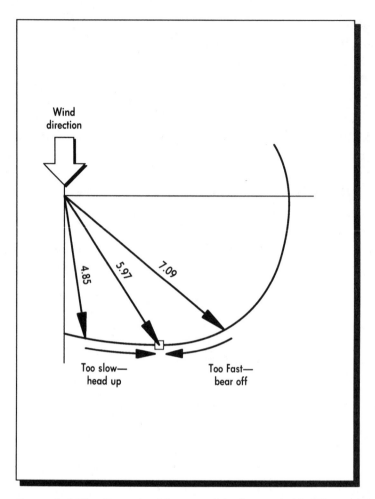

Figure 8.6 *This figure is a blow up of the bottom half of Figure 8.2. It represents the predicated speeds for a Fast 35 in 10 knots of wind for wind angles between 90 and 180 degrees. It also shows that by sailing at 5.97 knots, the Fast 35 will make its best progess downwind.*

Likewise, if you are faster than the target boatspeed, you are sailing too high. Your speed through the water may be good, but your VMG will be less than optimum. When you are sailing faster than the target, the program is telling you to bear off and slow down. Bleed off the extra speed by heading toward the mark.

Coordination between helmsman and sail trimmer is critical downwind. The strongest link for sensory feedback is through the spinnaker sheet, so it becomes the sail trimmer's responsibility to keep track of the boatspeed relative to the target, and to help the helmsman maintain the pressure on the spinnaker. Communicating this information to the helmsman provides both with the proper course of action to take to maintain top flight performance. The target boatspeed provides the focal point from which both the trimmer and the helmsman can work in concert. This teamwork is a significant factor in the difference between being fast or slow. If you are too slow, the conversation between the sail trimmer and the helmsman should go something like the following:

TRIMMER: Two-tenths slow of target. Spinnaker is going soft. We need to build speed.
HELM: Coming up slightly. Tell me when you've got good pressure.
TRIMMER: Pole forward slightly. Pressure starting to come on. Speed starting to build.
HELM: Sliding down. Speed at target.
TRIMMER: Easing sheet with you. That's a good angle for pressure. Speed holding at target.

When you are too fast, the conversation should be similar to the following:

TRIMMER: Two-tenths faster than target. Let's burn that speed off by heading downwind.
HELM: Okay, coming off. Ease with me.
TRIMMER: Squaring the pole. Easing the sheet. Nice bleed-off of speed. Still holding plenty of pressure.
HELM: Tell me when you're losing pressure.
TRIMMER: All right, speed slowing. Pressure coming off. Let's roll back up slightly. Stand by on the pole.
HELM: Coming up slightly.
TRIMMER: Pole forward three inches. That's a good angle for pressure. Speed at target.

Figure 8.7 is a graph of target boatspeeds as a function of true windspeed. There are three discernible ranges: 3 to 9 knots true windspeed, 9 to 13, and

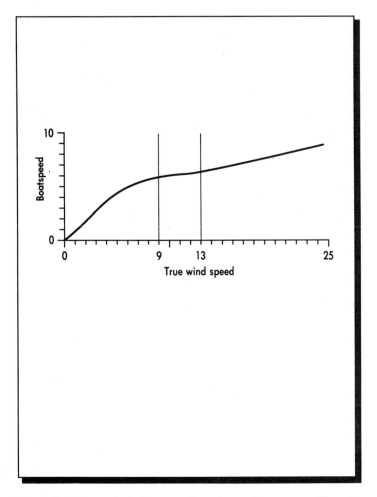

Figure 8.7 *Downwind there are three discernible ranges of how boatspeed changes with increased windspeed.*

13 and above. As in our upwind graph, the downwind graph in the low range shows that a significant rate of increase in target boatspeed occurs for each knot of true-windspeed increase. About .6 knots per knot of true windspeed. At about 9 knots true windspeed, the graph flattens out and the rate of increase in target boatspeed decreases to less than .2 knots per knot of true windspeed. Above 13 knots, target boatspeed continues to increase, but you pay more attention to wave sailing and control than to wind angle.

As in the upwind discussion, one of the most powerful uses of target boat-speeds is in developing the most efficient technique in accelerating or decel-erating to the new target boatspeed as the windspeed changes. Just as in the upwind case, the most discernible differences in sailing technique are in the low windspeed range. The difference between proper and improper response to velocity changes in the low windspeed range has a tremendous impact on overall performance. Just as in the upwind cases, in terms of apparent wind angle, a puff creates a short-term lift, called a *velocity lift*, and a lull creates a short-term header, called a *velocity header*.

True Windspeed Increase

In the first range, 3 to 9 knots true windspeed, the true wind angle remains nearly constant at about 141 degrees. (See figures 8.1 and 8.8) When you sail into a puff, what is the correct response? Somewhere in our early training, someone gave us a basic rule: "Head down in the puffs and head up in the lulls." However, in this first range, that response can be devastatingly slow. Sailing by target boatspeeds dictates the opposite.

Assume that the true windspeed is 6 knots. Our target boatspeed is 4.41. (See table 2.) When the puff hits, the true wind increases to 8 knots. Our new target is 5.42 knots. For the new wind we are 1 knot too slow! We need to build speed in the most efficient manner. Certainly that is not by bearing off, especially as the puff created a velocity lift, moving the apparent wind angle aft. *Steer the boat straight or come up slightly*, keeping pressure on the spinnaker sheet, and accelerate quickly. As you near the new target, slide the boat back down to the correct wind angle for the new windspeed. There will be little difference in the sailing angle, but if your technique is good, the difference in acceleration will be phenomenal. Use true wind angle as a reference to keep you in touch with the correct sailing angle, but *not* as the key to how to respond to a change in true windspeed. Sailing by targets enhances your finesse.

True Windspeed Decrease

Undoubtedly the trickiest condition occurs when you get a lull in the 3-to-9-knot true wind range. Sailing by targets in this low wind range dictates that as you sail into a lull, you should *steer straight or bear off to bleed off your excess speed*. The conservative move is to go straight, as it can be a trap to get caught sailing too low and slow. In a lull from 6 knots to 4 knots of true wind, your target changes from 4.41 knots to 2.85. You have 1.55 knots of excess speed, so make good use of it by bearing off and getting valuable distance downwind, or at least go straight. The worst thing you can do is waste that excess speed by heading up away from the mark. Your spinnaker trimmer is the key here. As soon as the trimmer starts feeling the spinnaker go soft, head back up to reestablish your proper sailing angle.

The Downwind Cliff

In the second range 9 to 13 knots of true wind, there is a much smaller incremental change in target boatspeed—about .2 knots of boatspeed per knot of wind speed change. In this range the largest change in sailing angle is necessary. There is about a 5-degree change in the true wind angle per knot of true windspeed difference to maintain target boatspeeds. Figure 8.8 is a graph of the true wind angle at which the target boatspeed is achieved as a function of true windspeed. In the 9- to-13-knot range we call this rapid change in true wind angle the "downwind cliff." While sailing on the downwind cliff, your response to puffs and lulls should be much closer to the old adage—head down in the puffs, up in the lulls. This is because the boat quickly accelerates to the new target in the puffs and decelerates to the new target in the lulls.

For the Fast 35 model that we've been using, a 2-knot puff from 10 to 12 knots would cause our target speed to increase only .2 knots, but our true wind angle needs to change a little more than 10 degrees. That's a 10-degree change for only 2-knot puff! It's important to bear off quickly as you're accelerating, otherwise you'll end up going too fast—faster than your new target. In a lull, steer straight until your boatspeed starts to drop, then come up sharply to capture your new target at the correct sailing angle.

The "cliff" is steep; therefore, a significant alteration of the spinnaker pole and spinnaker trim is important. Communication with your spinnaker trimmer is vital to achieve this. A 3-knot change in true windspeed for our Fast 35 can mean as much as an 18-degree course change. Knowing where you should be on the "cliff," and how high or low you should be sailing, especially in puffy conditions, provides the opportunity to make large gains downwind.

Surfing

In the third range, 13 knots and above, wave sailing dominates the technique. It's important to be at target when trying to surf a wave. Attempting to

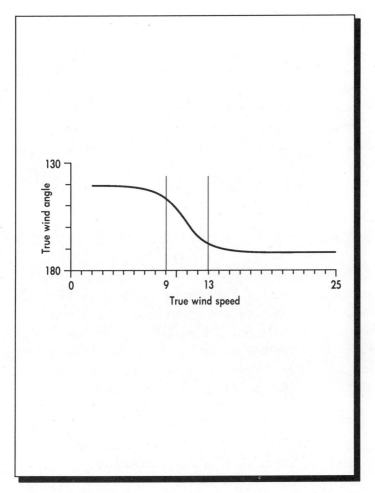

Figure 8.8 *This graph shows the true wind angle that a Fast 35 has to sail to make target speed changes as the windspeed increases. The small area between 9 and 13 knots where the true wind angle changes greatly is nicknamed the "Downward Cliff."*

surf with too little speed leaves you wallowing in a wave's trough instead of surfing down its crest. As a puff hits, the expected increase in target speed is small, and acceleration comes quickly. Pick the next wave to surf out on. Likewise, in a lull, build speed before trying to hook a wave. The true wind angle remains fairly constant above 15 knots, between 170 and 172 degrees.

The primary concern, especially as it blows harder, is control. Sail as low an angle as possible, but one that still allows you to keep the boat on its feet.

Downwind sailing can be the most frustrating or rewarding part of a race. There are certainly opportunities to make big gains, especially in the light and medium ranges. Learn the target boatspeeds for your boat, and make sure your crew knows the speeds and angles that you should be sailing in different windspeeds. You'll find that targets provide a valuable focal point for performance. Practice using them, just as you would practice spinnaker sets. With a concerted approach, targets will tie together the intricacies of sail trim and helmsmanship in what used to be trying conditions.

When Not To Use Target Boatspeed

Sailing by target boatspeeds to maximize your boat's performance is mainly a short-course technique for beating and running. On a reach, the fastest course between marks is a straight line to the next mark. You can sail faster by heading higher, but at the end of the leg you'll have to sail down to the mark at a slower rate. The extra distance at a slow speed nets out to a slower way to sail the leg. Therefore, when you don't expect the wind to change a lot in direction or strength, use the short-course strategy of heading straight for the mark.

How do you define a reach, as opposed to a run? A reach is a leg of the course where you can sail straight to a mark while sailing higher than the true wind angles at which you achieved your downwind target boatspeeds. Table 2 shows that in wind strengths between zero and 8 knots, a reach for a Fast 35 is any course where the boat has to sail higher than 141 degrees off the wind. If the mark were at a broader wind angle in that wind range, it would necessitate jibing downwind to achieve optimum speed toward the mark. From 9 to 13 knots true windspeed, that angle changes from roughly 141 to 162 degrees. Any time it's blowing more than 13 knots, a Fast 35 can sail practically dead downwind—changing its course only to play the waves and to keep the boat stable. In heavy air, the downwind leg is sailed like a reach because you can head wherever you want to go, only changing course for tactical considerations rather than for performance considerations.

When the course is around 155 degrees off the wind, but the breeze is going up and down between 9, 10, 11, 12, and 13 knots, it's hard to know whether you should be jibing downwind or just sailing right to the mark, or whether you should sail low of the mark in the puffs, so that you can come up and sail a higher course in the lulls. This is the most difficult case—the one where you have to do the most balancing of expected changes in true windspeed against the course of the boat.

Anytime you're jibing downwind, you snap into sailing target boatspeeds. Anytime you're on a reaching leg, the concept of target boatspeeds goes by the wayside and you're purely trying to optimize boatspeed in a straight line. This calls for sailing to your polar boatspeed. Polar boatspeed is the predicted maximum boatspeed for any given true wind angle and true windspeed. Polar speeds are used as a trim goal; they are to make sure your crew is working as hard as they should be, and haven't started thinking about significant others or beer.

Downwind is not the time to eat lunch. Lowell North has always said—and I agree with him—that the running legs are really the ones where you can make the biggest gains. The downwind legs have the biggest potential differences in boatspeeds. They are the ones where you have to work hardest. The problem is that sailing upwind is wet, so the crew usually eat their sandwiches on downwind legs.

Velocity Made Good on Course (VMC)

The key factor that determines when to change from short-course strategy to long-course strategy is that in a long-course race we know that the wind direction will shift—either in a known way or in an unpredictable way. Although being a long distance from the mark certainly increases the likelihood that you should use long-course strategy, it is no guarantee. For example, in the TransPac Race, the last 1,200 miles or so to Hawaii are in trade winds. Short-course strategy applies there because the wind won't shift more than a few degrees the whole time.

On the other hand, you can probably recall a day-racing situation in which the wind was behaving in a completely random manner. In that situation you should have used long-course strategy even though the next mark was only a couple of miles away. This leads us to two rules of long-course racing:

1. Select the course that reduces your distance to the mark as fast as possible.

2. Consolidate between the fleet and the mark when the opportunity presents itself.

These two rules seem deceptively simple. Upon hearing them, everybody says, "Of course. That's not difficult." Let's explore how to improve your perfor-

Figure 8.9 *To figure out maximum VMC, draw the rhumb line course and then draw a line perpendicular to the rhumb line that is tangent to the polar curve for the wind strength you're sailing in. The tangent point marks the wind angle to sail that gets you toward the next mark the fastest.*

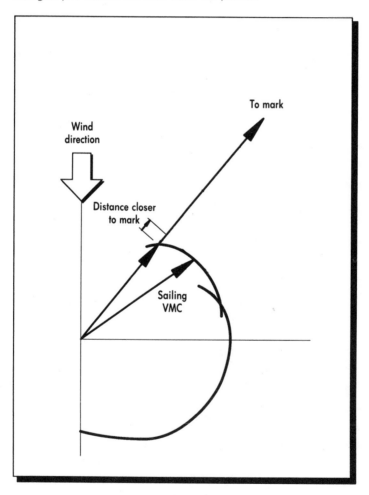

mance in long-course sailing, using velocity made good on course (VMC).

As VMG is the component of our boatspeed measured against the wind direction, VMC is the component of our boatspeed in the direction of the mark. Even though sailing to maximum VMC takes you away from the rhumb-line course, you won't need to sail down to the mark at a slower speed, since you can predict that the wind will shift before you get to the next mark. When the wind shifts, you'll change course to maximize VMC for the new wind.

Figure 8.9 provides an example of how to choose the fastest course with long-course strategy. (For purposes of illustration, a Fast 35's polar curve for 10 knots of wind has been singled out from the complete set of polar curves.) The figure assumes that for the time being, the wind is from the north at 10 knots. The rhumb line course is 45 degrees. To find the fastest course, first plot the rhumb line course on the polar diagram with your present position at the origin of the diagram. Then construct a perpendicular to the rhumb line that is tangent to the boatspeed curve. The point at which the tangent intersects the boatspeed curve identifies a new true wind angle that maximizes your speed in the direction of the mark. In this case, the new true wind angle is about 57 degrees, and therefore you should sail a course that is 12 degrees lower than the rhumb line. The gain in speed in the direction of the mark is impressive. Sailing the rhumb line produces a boatspeed of about 6.6 knots. Reaching off and sailing 12 degrees lower produces a boatspeed of about 7.2 knots, which equates to a VMC of about 7 knots!

Too much emphasis is placed on sailing the rhumb line. The rhumb line is useful before the start in knowing where the mark is, and it's useful after the finish so you can tell your friends how far to one side or the other of it you went in winning the race. During the race, your primary concern should be where the mark is in reference to where you are *now*.

VMC is best explained graphically, for which purpose we've constructed several diagrams. Figure 8.10 shows a mark 60 miles from a starting line. Now let's draw some concentric circles around the mark. No matter where boats are, as long as they're on the same ring, they're the same distance from the mark. Therefore, to get to the mark most quickly, you need to sail a course that gets you across the rings as fast as possible—no matter where your course takes you.

When the mark is a long way off, zooming in on your position makes the visible parts of the circles around the mark look almost like straight lines. (See figure 8.11.) Call these lines "ladder rungs," because you've got to "climb"

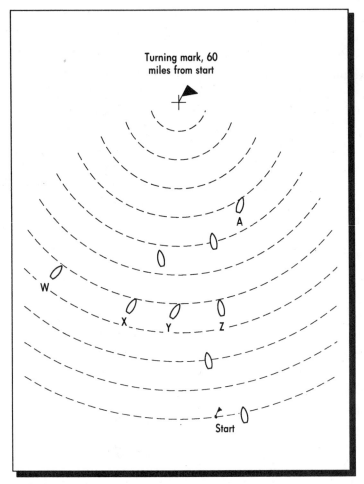

Turning mark, 60
miles from start

W

A

X   Y   Z

Start

Figure 8.10 *Boats W, X, Y, and Z are on the same ring and therefore are the same distance from the mark, while Boat A is clearly in the lead.*

them to reach the mark. The faster you climb the ladder rungs, the faster you'll reach the mark. The skipper of the boat in this diagram has two course possibilities to choose from. The first option is to sail directly at the mark, which happens to be the upwind target speed. The other option is to sail at maximum VMC. The lengths of the arrows represent the speeds the boat will go at either option. The diagram clearly shows that even though the footing course takes the boat farther from the rhumb line, the footing course gets the boat up the ladder rungs the fastest.

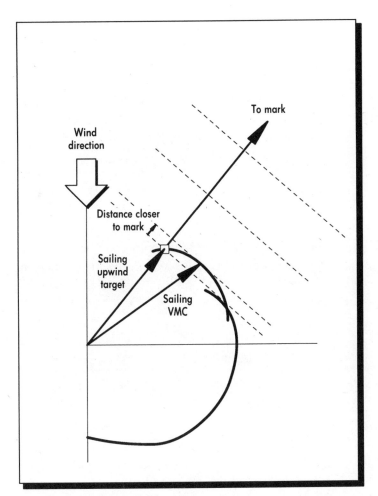

Figure 8.11 *Zooming in on a section of figure 8.10 makes the visible part of the concentric circles look almost like straight lines. Call these lines "ladder rungs" because you've got to "climb" them to reach the mark. The arrows represents a boat's speeds at the indicated wind angles. Notice how the course where the boat sails further off the wind gets the boat up the ladder rungs the fastest.*

What's the lesson for long-distance racing? When in doubt, reach more. This is true on both upwind and downwind legs, and is particularly useful when the wind and the course are about 45 degrees apart—that is, when you're just fetching the mark on a close-hauled course or when on a broad reach. Looking at a polar curve for a given wind strength at both of the sailing angles just mentioned, you can see that speed greatly increases when you sail more of a reach.

The following table gives you an idea of how much steering to VMC will help you on different points of sail. The table is based on the sailing characteristics of a Fast 35 in 10 knots of breeze. Even though you may not sail a Fast 35, the polar curves of most fin-keel boats have the same general shape. Your speeds will differ, but the table will give you an idea of the percentage change you'll get. (See figure 8.12 and table 3.)

In each case, except when sailing down the rhumb line with the true wind angle at 93 degrees, a Fast 35 makes better progress toward the mark by deviating from the rhumb line and sailing to optimized VMC. At 93 degrees, the optimum is found by sailing directly at the mark. Also notice that the percentage of increase in VMC is much greater when you are on a close or very broad reach. Notice also that 75 percent of the gain is made in the first 50 percent of the course deviation. Therefore, if you are sailing close-hauled, separating slightly will still reap huge gains.

T A B L E   3

VMG GAINS MADE BY FAST 35S IN 10 KNOTS TRUE WIND

TWA* When Heading to Mark	Boatspeed Heading at Mark	Optimum TWA to Sail	New Boatspeed	VMG
45°	6.6 kts.	57°	7.2 kts.	7.0 kts.
60°	7.2 kts.	67°	7.4 kts.	7.3 kts.
93°	7.5 kts.	93°	7.5 kts.	7.5 kts.
130°	6.8 kts.	119°	7.2 kts.	7.0 kts.
170°	5.0 kts.	145°	6.2 kts.	5.6 kts.

*True wind angle

Figure 8.12 *This figure is a graphic representation of Table 3. The polar curve is made up of speed predictions at every wind angle for a Fast 35 sailing in 10 knots of wind—the same curve from figure 8.2. Notice that your gains from sailing the VMC course are greatest when you are on a close reach or a very broad reach.*

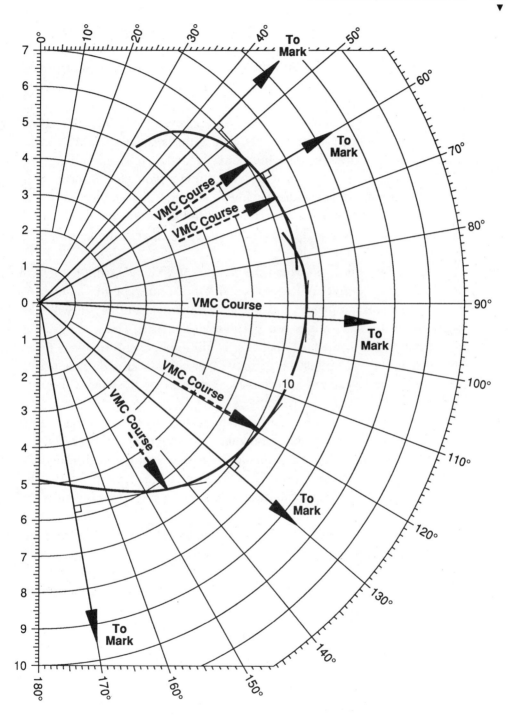

You can figure out whether your deviation from the rhumb line is paying off by calculating your VMC and comparing it to the speed you were making on the rhumb line. To solve for your VMC, multiply your new boatspeed by the cosine of the angle between the rhumb line and your new course. With a calculator, this is simple to do.

Always bring plenty of photocopies of your polars on long-distance races so that you can use them for finding the course that maximizes VMC. Make sure it is oriented to the wind direction correctly, and then have your navigator plot the rhumb line from the origin. Next, using a protractor or some other tool that can make a perpendicular line, move the tool around until it is perpendicular to the rhumb line and tangent to the polar curve for the wind strength you're sailing in. The tangent point to the curve is the heading that will give you maximum VMC.

The primary element on which the concept of VMC is predicated is that the wind is going to shift. When you're racing a 600-mile point-to-point race, you've got to expect a major wind shift in the three or four days it will take you to finish the race, unless you're sailing in the trade winds. If the wind doesn't shift, though, the boat that sails the rhumb line will win every time. But whether you are sailing the 630-mile Newport-to-Bermuda race or the 125-mile Newport Beach-to-Ensenada race, chances are the wind will shift a lot.

The second rule of thumb for the VMC technique is: When the shift is favorable, consolidate your gain. Remember, when in doubt, get between the fleet and the mark. Turn back to figure 8.9 and look at the tactical options for this case. By sailing for maximum VMC, you are the leeward boat. Your distance to leeward of the rhumb line is the leverage you have on your competition. Assume the wind shifts 90 degrees to the right. Now you have several choices to make—the most conservative being to tack and reach off hard in order to get down between your competitors and the mark. This consolidates your gain quickly. The second course option is to reorient your polar curve to the new wind and plot out your new course for maximum VMC. The third option is to lay a course directly to the mark from your current position.

How aggressive you want to be is a function of how far away the mark is, how much of the race is left, your position in the race, the likelihood of another shift, and the location of the rest of the fleet. You should become progressively more conservative in the final stages of the leg, because the chances of future shifts decrease as the time remaining to the finish decreases.

An extreme case would be when you are getting random shifts every ten minutes. In that case, the time to get conservative is when less than ten minutes are left in the race.

When I sailed the 1988 Bermuda race on the Hinckley 42 *Dragon Fire,* we VMC'd like a bandit from the start. We ignored the rhumb line from Newport to Bermuda and just sailed the course that produced the maximum VMC for every wind shift. As we got closer to the finish, we became more conservative and started modifying our headings based on where our competition was. With 70 miles left to the finish, we had every indication that the wind was going to settle in to the south-southwest. So we started closing up with the rhumb line by sailing toward the finish line. As it turned out, the wind went southeast. If we had VMC'd right up until 15 miles from the finish line, we would have gained an enormous amount of time because we'd have been reaching instead of sailing close-hauled.

Knowing when to employ a defensive strategy is just as important as using the concept of VMC to reap great gains. The shorter the distance left to the mark, and the lesser the probability of a future shift, the more important defensive strategy becomes. Consolidate your gains while you have the advantage. If you've tracked and plotted the positions of the competition, the determination of when to consolidate becomes much clearer. With the wind direction in your favor, consolidate by getting between the competition and the mark. Getting between the competition and the next mark minimizes your vulnerability if the wind shifts. Once established in a protective position, you have the choice of being conservative or aggressive in your strategy for the rest of the race. Either way, you've positioned yourself for minimum vulnerability in future wind conditions.

Another important aspect of defensive strategy is knowing your danger zone—the range of wind directions that allows your competition to come out ahead. Figure 8.13 shows Boat A just fetching the mark while sailing close-hauled. Boat B is sailing 15 degrees lower, maximizing VMC. After one hour of sailing, assume the wind will shift and then remain at the new direction for the rest of the race. What is Boat B's danger zone?

Case 1. The wind shifts clockwise 19 degrees. At this point the wind direction is perpendicular to a line connecting the bows of both boats. They are now even. In the range from zero degrees to 19 degrees, Boat A is farther upwind and therefore would win. Therefore, there is only a 19-degree danger zone where Boat A comes out ahead.

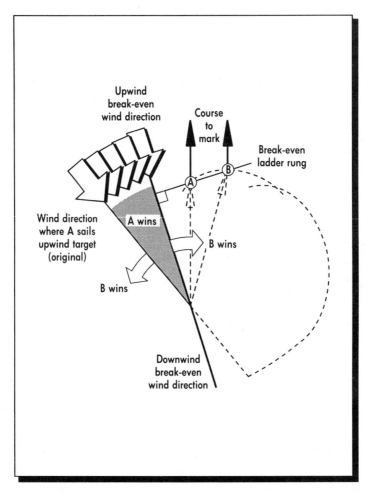

Figure 8.13 *Figuring out the risks of sailing by VMC.*

Case 2. What happens if the wind continues to the right of 19 degrees? Boat B can tack and cross ahead of Boat A. In fact, with the mark still distant, if you keep shifting the wind around clockwise, Boat B's next danger zone is when the wind direction hits 189 degrees. At that point, Boat A is sailing her downwind target directly to the mark, and Boat B must jibe in the future. This danger zone continues between 189 and 204. With the wind direction at 204, both boats must jibe, and now Boat B is to leeward and ahead.

Case 3. With the wind continuing to the right from 204 all the way to north, B wins by virtue of being to leeward and ahead. Therefore, Boat B's danger zones are the two relatively narrow sectors—one upwind and one downwind. This constitutes only 10 percent of the possibilities. In most distance races I will gladly take 90-percent odds.

Notes of Caution

Don't get lulled into using VMC just because you're sailing a distance race. There are plenty of distance races where the wind doesn't shift. In those situations, using VMC would put you in the back of the fleet. For example, as mentioned earlier, once you get in the trade winds during the TransPac, you've got 1,200 miles of short-course downwind tactics to sail because the wind usually doesn't shift more than 20 degrees in the trades. Once in the steady trade winds, the race becomes a series of little downwind jibes on the small shifts to stay in stronger breeze and to guard your position relative to the fleet.

Unless you're racing in an area with a well-established weather system, such as the trade winds, conditions should be expected to change substantially in any 12-hour period. Further, one's ability to predict the rate and extent to which the wind will shift beyond a six-hour period is not great. In these situations, VMC becomes a powerful offshore racing tool.

In areas such as Long Island Sound and the Chesapeake Bay, the geography can prevent you from changing course greatly. Here you must compromise the use of VMC with the area you have to sail in. Remember, proportionally larger gains are made with the first part of the course alteration than with the last.

Using VMC for a tactical advantage is the realm of the new navigator. Ten years ago, the navigator was totally consumed with figuring out where in hell he was and then selling that position to everyone else. These days, anybody who knows the button sequence for the loran can be a navigator. So now the navigator has time to work on strategy. He needs to examine different moves and their results: "If we do this, where will we end up against the competition?"

One last note about using VMC. Be sure you understand the labeling used on your loran. Many loran manufacturers use the label VMC. In our definitions, VMG is wind-relative, and certainly a loran has no understanding of wind direction. Some lorans use SOA—speed of advance—for VMC. I think this is much clearer, but either way, the loran is very useful in showing your velocity toward the waypoint. The limitation of loran is that it provides an average over a long period. This is useful in confirming an average of past performance, but it's not so good in figuring out a solution for the present or future.

Taking Instruments with a Grain of Salt

There are times when the readings from the instruments need to be used cautiously. A large part of the instruments' job is to measure the environment, and certainly that environment can change from weekend to weekend—or even from day to day. When you are not sure that the instruments are giving you the right target boatspeed numbers, use your instruments as a starting point, then go out and sail against similar boats. Tuning up against a sister ship is best. Trust your intuition and sail by what feels fast. Then go back and compare the boatspeed that felt fast—that was equal to or better than that of your sister ship—against what the target boatspeed instrument told you to sail.

On some days you'll find that the target boatspeeds don't feel right. Say you go out to practice and find that the boat feels right going to weather at 5.4 knots, but your target for that wind strength is 5.7 knots. What does this tell you? Are your instruments malfunctioning? Possibly, but if they've been accurate in the past, the first suspect should be a change in the environment. One of the normal changes in the environment is wind gradient. Wind gradient is the change in wind strength with altitude. If the wind at the top of the mast, where your windspeed sensor is located, is stronger than the average wind over the sail plan, then your target speed will be off. Consult Table 1 on page 300 to see how a 2-knot windspeed difference from 6 to 8 knots makes a big difference in target speeds.

Also, if your instruments normally read equal wind angles on opposite tacks when going upwind except on some days, the reason for the inconsistency could be wind shear—the change of wind direction with altitude. If the wind angle is greater on starboard tack than on port, then you know that the upper-level wind is blowing further from the right than the wind in the middle of the sails.

Try to qualify the numbers from the instruments by looking at the performance of the boats around you. For instance, if you establish that the wind on the water is blowing a little slower than the instruments are reading, that's a good indication of a high gradient condition. Looking around, you might say to yourself, "This doesn't look like a 14-knot day. It looks more like a 10-knot day."

If you're thinking of ferreting out wind shear and wind gradient by using a handheld anemometer, don't. The masthead unit is an accurate instrument, while the handheld one is guaranteed to be pretty rough. Besides, the wind on the deck is disturbed by the boat's rigging. But if you really want to pursue the idea, do what the Australian America's Cup contenders did. They rigged masts with wind instruments on their tenders that were half the height of a 12-meter's mast. In that way they found the average wind strength and direction over the sail plan. In addition, by comparing the tender's readings to those from the masthead unit on the 12s, they got an accurate picture of whether there was wind gradient and/or wind shear that day.

Wind shear and wind gradient most often go hand in hand; it's unusual to see one without the other. You'll recognize wind shear if your apparent wind angle is smaller on one tack than on the other, or if your telltales at the top of the jib break early on one tack and not the other, while the jib leads are in the same position of both sides of the boat.

It's easy to recognize extreme examples of wind shear and gradient; however, many sailors often miss the subtler effects of the phenomena, which are quite prevalent in most racing areas. The recognition of small amounts of shear and gradient is a powerful tool that can be used advantageously in striving for top-level performance and tactics. First, let's explore the elements that produce wind shear and gradient. Once we understand and learn to expect those conditions, it becomes much easier to recognize the extent to which each is occurring.

Most sailors' vision of the wind is limited to a two-dimensional view of the wind conditions—how hard it's blowing, and from what direction. Understandably, we assume that the masthead instruments are telling us what's happening on the water's surface. But this is misleading. In the relatively short distance our sails are working in, there's a tremendous amount of interaction between the characteristics of the water, the wind, and the surrounding land masses. Even dinghy sailors, whose masts only reach 20 to 30 feet above the water, notice the effect of wind shear and wind gradient. It's up to the sailor to integrate what can be seen and felt near the water with the information coming from the masthead.

Wind shear is often noted when your apparent-wind instrument tells you that you are sailing too narrow a wind angle, yet your jib is full or even stalled down low. Conversely, when you tack, your apparent-wind instrument is indicating a wide angle and you are having difficulty filling the bottom of your genoa. For instance, if the optimal apparent wind angle for your boat sailing to windward is 28 degrees, and your apparent-wind-angle instrument says that you are sailing 35 degrees to the apparent wind while your lower jib telltales are breaking, then you are experiencing wind shear—that is, if your instruments are calibrated correctly. You can confirm your hypothesis about wind shear by tacking. If your apparent wind angle is narrower than normal on the opposite tack and your jib telltales down low are not breaking, you'll know that the wind is blowing at a different direction at the top of the mast.

Detecting wind shear tells you two things: first, that you should expect the wind to be stronger higher above the water, since wind gradient accompanies wind shear; second, if the wind is generally filling in, the wind on the water will shift and follow the wind direction at the top of the mast.

Wind gradient is coupled with wind shear because the wind at the top of the mast flows more smoothly than the wind on the water. Surface friction slows the wind greatly, causing wind gradient. The effect of surface friction is most pronounced closest to the surface. If you took measurements higher than your masthead, you'd find more of the same gradient pattern.

Probably the most evident circumstance of shear and gradient is a filling sea breeze on a warm day in early spring. The key elements are there: warm air aloft and cold water below, producing a large thermal gradient. The water cools the air immediately above it, making it more sluggish than the warm air above. In the northern hemisphere the sea breeze veers to the right as it becomes established. Because the warm air aloft can move more easily, it will precede the cold air below with changes in direction and speed. With the onset of the sea breeze, you'll see the wind at the masthead 15 to 20 degrees to the right of the wind on the water. Coupled with this is a high vertical wind gradient, in which the wind 50 feet off the water may be 40 to 50 percent stronger than the wind on the surface.

As the land heats up, the development of the sea breeze is enhanced. The strengthening breeze is further fortified by wind mixing, in which the turbulent mingling of warm and cold air allows the sea breeze to fill *down* toward the surface. Again, one tends to think of the sea breeze in two-dimensional terms—moving across the water. In three-dimensional terms, the sea breeze fills *down* as well as toward the land, and this aspect of vertical strengthening in the wind is instrumental in qualifying how much more wind speed and change in direction to expect. As the sea breeze becomes fully developed, the amount of shear diminishes to about zero and the gradient lowers to a 15-to-20-percent difference between the windspeed on the surface and the windspeed 50 feet off the water. From the sea-breeze example we can summarize four important rules:

1. Wind shear and wind gradient are almost always found together.

2. In the northern hemisphere, the wind aloft is sheared to the right about 90 percent of the time.

3. The direction of the wind shear is indicative of the direction of future shifts.

4. The presence or absence of shear and gradient is a good indicator of the type of shift to expect—persistent or oscillating, respectively.

Even though your wind instruments and target speeds can be inaccurate because of wind shear and wind gradient, they can still give you tremendous insight into the sails to use and their trim, as well as enhancing your tactics on the racecourse. For instance, the wind instruments may clock the wind at 14 to 15 knots, which is the range for your medium No. 1 genoa, but if you looked at the wind on the surface of the water, you'd realize that the light No. 1 was a more appropriate sail.

When the masthead instruments indicate that the wind up high is more to the right than the wind on the water, your tactics should be to protect the right side of the course aggressively, because the shear to the right is telling you that the wind will be moving to the right. The greater the difference in wind direction between the wind at the masthead and the wind on the surface, the sooner the surface wind will shift and line up with the upper winds.

The problem is that when you sail to the right side of the course on port tack, the boat's performance will feel lousy. But you have to do the hard thing and pay your dues to get to the right, because being the boat farthest to the right in the fleet will all pay off in spades an hour or 45 minutes later, when you are on the inside of the new shift. When sailing in wind-shear conditions, you can improve your performance by trimming both your main and jib differently on each tack. If the wind is shearing to the right, the genoa trimmer will see the top telltales luffing early, and will be frustrated in trying to get the sail to set properly. This is because the top of the sails are seeing a "header" relative to the bottom of the sails. If you go onto starboard tack, the boat feels much better, as the wind aloft is a "lift" relative to the bottom.

On eastern Long Island, short-course racers are faced with the same dilemma all summer long: whether to stay close to shore and out of the strong currents that race through the eastern openings of the Sound to the sea, or whether to go out in the current to get the sea breeze before it reaches the shore. If you take a chance by going offshore and get the sea breeze before everyone else, you look like a hero and win the race, but if you go offshore and the sea breeze doesn't fill in, the current will sweep you into last place. In this situation, noticing wind shear and wind gradient is an excellent trick for picking up the approach of the sea breeze. If your instruments at the top of the mast tell you that the sea breeze has arrived, but you don't see it on the water, you can be fairly sure that it is going to fill in soon. If you don't see it at the top of the mast, you'll know it's going to take much more energy to push the wind down and across the surface of the water.

Wind shear dictates asymmetrical sail settings for each tack. The genoa leads on one side of the boat will be quite different from those on the other. On starboard tack, where the wind is "lifted" up high, the genoa lead has to be moved aft to open up the top of the sail so that it won't stall in the lifted wind. On port tack the genoa lead will have to go forward to trim the top of the sail tighter and to reduce twist. One note of caution, however: don't exaggerate de-twisting the sails, or the boat will go very slowly. Setting up the boat asymmetrically goes against the great pains taken by many sailors who mark their sheets and lead positions so that they can ensure consistency from one tack to the other.

Likewise, your target boatspeeds will necessarily be different on each tack. You'll have to work hard at establishing good numbers for each tack before the race starts. Similarly, changes in wind gradient from the norm dictate changing your target boatspeeds up or down. Your boat's velocity prediction program is based on a standardized gradient profile and no wind shear.

Another reason for not being able to reach your targets is that the VPP, from which target boatspeeds are derived, presume a sea state that corresponds to the true windspeed. The VPP predicts a target boatspeed for a given ratio of sail-plan lift to hull drag in average conditions. Any deviation from the average will cause a change up or down in target boatspeed. Waves, especially in a confused state, reduce the efficiency of the sail-plan and increase the drag on the hull. Therefore, the target must be lowered in waves and particularly in confused seas. However, expecting that there should be a difference is half of the battle. Common sense and feel is the other half.

I can't overemphasize the importance of the communication between the sail trimmers and the helmsman in wavy conditions. The following conversation demonstrates how I worked with Andreas Josenhans on the J/35 *Rush* when he was trimming the spinnaker and I was steering in one race when the true windspeed was about six to eight knots and the seas were sloppy and confused.

JIM: Andreas, I want to heat it up to build some speed. We're about six-tenths low of target.

ANDREAS: I don't think you're going to get to target without reaching too high. But try a little higher if you want.

JIM: Okay. Let's try some speed building. Tell me when you think you've got good pressure.

ANDREAS: That feels like a good angle. The spinnaker's working better and I've got some pressure. What's the speed like?

JIM: We're still about three-tenths slow of target, but the true wind angle is around 145 degrees. That's the right angle for this windspeed.

ANDREAS: (to the other crew): Let's try the pole down three inches and squared a bit. That will help to stabilize the chute. Snug the twing to keep the clew from bouncing around.

JIM: That's better. It's easier to accelerate in the puffs, and I can hold the speed longer. Three-tenths low feels right. Let me try heading a tad lower . . .

Andreas and I worked on this for about two hours straight, constantly modifying our numbers in relation to the sea state and wind strength.

This brings to mind another race I sailed in which we had to disregard the target boatspeeds. Racing on the Spanish One Tonner *Ramel Dos*, from Barcelona to Minorca, we had a very confused sea left over from a mistral that had blown itself out the day before. The wind was light, and certainly the sea state was way out of proportion to the wind. We tried every conceivable combination of sailing angles downwind, and what amazed me was that running virtually dead downwind was the fastest angle toward the mark. At first I couldn't believe it, but we proved it to ourselves over and over throughout the night.

The analogy that finally made sense was one of effective sail area versus displacement. We know that boats with an extremely high sail-area-to-displacement ratio can achieve much greater speeds by maintaining high reaching angles. In fact the VPP suggests that the true wind angle should not be increased beyond 145 degrees for ultra-light displacement boats (ULDBs) until the wind velocity is over 20 knots or the boat is surfing. If we incrementally decrease sail area and increase displacement, the true wind-speed at which you should steer wider downwind sailing angles decreases. Put another way, heavier, lower-powered boats can sail downwind sooner than lighter, high-powered boats.

The correct true wind angle changes from 145 degrees to 165 degrees in 10 to 14 knots true windspeed for an average production racer/cruiser. Above 15 knots true windspeed, you sail essentially as low as you can while maintaining some semblance of control. If we carry this analysis further, it would suggest that a boat with a disproportionately low sail-area-to-displacement ratio would turn downwind even sooner. In effect, when sailing in light air and big, lumpy seas, the result is a lack of effectiveness of the sail plan (small sail area), and increased hull drag (more displacement). Suddenly it made sense why we did better in *Ramel* heading dead downwind.

So, when your instruments are inexplicably off, the crew must turn to experimentation confirmed by seat-of-the-pants feel to optimize the performance of the boat. To religiously follow the instruments and the VPP could certainly be detrimental to performance. Rather, your use of instruments should be to quantify the speeds and angles that you find produce the best performance. You then have modified the old targets and developed new ones, which apply to the specific conditions at hand. Setting new targets allows you to accelerate and decelerate to target boatspeeds, maintain the best performance achievable, and properly respond to velocity shifts. Just as important, the establishment of new targets gives back to the crew the focal point from which they can work most efficiently.

Instrument Errors

Another reason why your instruments may not be reading correctly is that they truly aren't working right. Let's go through the strengths and weaknesses of the instruments and their sensors to give you an idea of when the instruments are out of whack instead of the wind, and then how to pinpoint problems.

When you first install your instruments, it's critical to get them calibrated correctly. Small calibration problems are magnified in computed functions. For instance, a 1-degree error of apparent wind angle creates about a 2-degree error in true wind angle. That's 2 degrees off on each tack, so when you go from one tack to the other, that skews the wind angle by 4 degrees. Now we are in the range of a perceptible shift for most careful sailors upwind. But even with the error, you are still better off using the wind instruments downwind or at night when it is hard to perceive shifts. But the trick is to locate and eliminate the error.

Just as you spend a lot of time tuning the rig or trimming sails, you have to spend time on the care and feeding of your instruments. When you periodically send someone up the mast to check the rig, have that person check the masthead instruments. The unit shouldn't be bent to either side, it shouldn't be lose, and the bearing surfaces of the anemometer cups and windvane should be clean and lubricated. Below the waterline, make sure that the boatspeed impeller is clean and seated correctly. Take the time to calibrate your speedometer by running the measured mile according to the instructions that came with your unit. Recheck the calibration during the sailing season. Don't try to recalibrate your instruments before every race. A person who calibrates the instruments every time he goes sailing loses any insight on how the environment is changing. By calibrating the instruments to the conditions of the day, you won't be able to tell whether you're sailing in wind shear or gradient. It's much better to get the instruments calibrated once, and then use the relative differences to decipher the wind conditions. Even if your wind angle and windspeed readings are a little off, it's better to make the correction in your head than to retune constantly. This way you'll always have a baseline for comparison. Think of your instruments like the bathroom scale. If you constantly re-zero the scale before you get on, you won't be able to tell whether you gained or lost weight from the last time you weighed yourself. But if you know that the scale reads heavy by a pound, all you have to do is subtract a pound every time you weigh yourself.

This is not the place to discuss the specifics of correcting and calibrating instruments, since all systems come with instructions on how that should be done. But before you purchase an instrument system, remember that not all wind instruments compensate for heel. After all, apparent wind angle changes

4 degrees when a boat goes from 10 degrees of heel to 24 degrees of heel. As a boat heels over more and more, the apparent wind angle gets narrower and narrower. To understand why, imagine a boat that heels over enough so that the mast is parallel to the water. Its instrument would read that the wind was coming from straight ahead. Also, measured apparent windspeed is reduced with heel.

Other calibrations are for different windspeeds and upwash from the sail plan onto the instrument sensors at the top of the mast, and also for symmetry, so that you get the same readings on both tacks. Tuning your instruments is no different from tuning your mast or working out proper sail trim. It's straightforward, but requires time, concentration, and dedication to getting the job done.

Even though most sensors are based on ten-year-old technology, sensor technology is relatively good. Let's start with the compass, of which there are two types: the card compass and the flux-gate compass. If either kind of compass has been swung carefully, and care has been taken to keep interfering equipment clear of the compass, you should have no problem. Which ever compass you use, the greatest errors come from not having the compass swung well. In the old days, when a navigator had only the compass and boatspeed to figure out his position, he guarded the compass with his life. As we've passed out of that era into the loran age, the compass has taken a backseat. But when your instrument system is trying to make calculations that involve the compass, small errors in the compass become very noticeable in the results, e.g., wind direction, opposite tack course, or time to the laylines.

Once you have the compass swung, it will stay accurate unless it is affected by the surrounding environment. After swinging the compass, keep large concentrations of metal or magnets away from it. Boats that are transported by truck or on ships need to have their compasses re-swung after the trip, because they get thrown off by all the metal around them.

Boatspeed Paddle Wheel

The placement of the boatspeed paddle wheel is critical. The rule of thumb at Ockam is that the sensor should be in front of the keel on centerline, a third of the distance from where the leading edge of the keel joins the hull to the waterline at the bow. That keeps it back far enough that it rarely comes out of the water, but most important, it keeps it forward enough that it's not influenced by the water flow around the keel. Flow around the keel is dissimilar to the flow around the hull. Whether you should use one or two boatspeed paddle wheels depends on your boat's hull shape. A flat-bottomed boat, or one with U-shaped sections like an IOR boat only needs one paddlewheel on or close to the centerline. A V-shaped boat with no flat spots needs two sensors. Each should be outboard enough that when the boat heels 15 degrees the leeward one is more or less vertical.

The standard paddlewheel is accurate from 2 to 15 knots. Fortunately that's the range in which most of us sail most of the time. You must remember that at low boatspeeds the paddlewheel's internal friction becomes a significant factor and unacceptably distorts the reading. Therefore, when sailing at low speeds, all the calculated functions that use boatspeed, like true windspeed and magnetic wind direction, are thrown off. For boats that normally sail faster than 15 knots, there are sensors made to perform in the higher ranges.

Sonic speed sensors had a brief vogue, but most people have realized its pitfalls. The strong point of sonic speed was that it gave a very consistent reading. The problem that made the system unworkable was that it measured water flow in one of the worst areas on the boat—right in front of the keel.

Masthead Sensor

Care has to be taken during the installation of a masthead sensor. If the bracket moves, the sensor will fall to leeward and the apparent wind angle will be narrower. If the post on which the vane is mounted is not straight up and down, when you heel you'll get changes in angle, and the cups monitoring the windspeed will be off, since they'll be tilted. Most faults with masthead units can be traced to mechanical problems of installation or maintenance.

Undoubtedly, the two most important elements to successful racing are top-flight performance and tactics. I can think of moments when other ingredients may ruin the feast, but by and large, winning or losing boils down to these two basics. In car racing, I can have bigger wheels and a more powerful engine, but if I can't see the turns, ultimately I will end up in the grass. Similarly, if I understand the tactics of the track, but don't know how to use my engine,

I'll be left in the dust. Having one without the other can only lead to mediocrity—you've got to use both appropriately.

Technology in instrumentation has always been oriented around better and more responsive solutions to these two problems. At the same time, many other useful instrument system functions have been created. And while there are specific instances in which these newer functions are helpful, the majority of our racing still revolves around the basics. The good news is that great gains have been made in advancing the state of the art of these basics. Instrumentation is available that provides the answers. The second part of the equation is in the correct employment of the available tools. Just remember, instruments don't win races—you do.

Putting It All Together

In this chapter, we'll discuss how to organize your thoughts and goals in a notebook. By doing so, you'll be able to learn and improve in an organized manner. Minimizing mistakes is the way to win sailboat races; you'll avoid repeating mistakes by having a written record of what works and what doesn't. As George Santayana said, "Those who cannot remember the past are condemned to repeat it." The key is to isolate problems and examine them step by step. So get yourself a notebook and we'll go over how to fill it up. Use a loose-leaf notebook, because you'll want to be able to add information to many different sections. Headings should include your goals, notes on practice sessions, race postmortems, new tactics, boat maintenance, notes on different venues, boatspeeds, and crews.

"By compiling a record of how your boat should be tuned and set up in varying wind and wave conditions, you won't have to spend the whole race working to get your boat up to speed," says Tom. "Most people don't even get to tactics because they're too busy staying out of trouble on the racecourse or trying to make their boat go faster. All their time is taken up with deciding where to lead their genoa, how tight the backstay should be, how far the boat should be heeling, what jib should be up, and whether or not to take a reef. When you spend so much time on boatspeed, you never get to the subtleties of yacht racing."

Learn to keep track of how the boat was tuned and the sails were trimmed for each race you sail. Being able to recall how far off the spreader the jib was, how much backstay pressure you had, where the jib leads were, what the halyard tension was, and how much bend you carried in the mast you will be able to figure out what settings proved fastest in various conditions. Once you have recorded enough information, dialing in top boatspeed becomes as easy as looking in the notebook.

"As far as tactics are concerned," Tom says, "I've kept a notebook forever. But I probably haven't been as organized as I should have been, because after all the time I've spent on the water, a lot of moves have become automatic. Weekend sailors have to learn with fewer days. They should become students of the game by studying, reading, and memorizing."

In fact, you'll learn faster by taking notes on four or five subjects in this book before your next race. By writing them in the section of your notebook dedicated to new tactics, you'll prioritize what you've just finished reading. We've covered many tactics that will work on a given day, but it's hard to remember all of them—especially during the frenzy of a race. To entrench new tactics in your long-term memory, write down five or six moves you want to try, and use them if the occasion permits. Keep adding to the list after these moves become automatic.

Pre-race Notebook Entries

Top-priority tactics you should write down in your notebook include saving the starboard tack for your final approach to the finish line, and what to do if you're in a crossing situation with a starboard tacker you're not sure you can cross, near the starboard-tack layline.

Taking notes before the race can be just as important as a detailed post-mortem. Reexamining tactical moves to make and then pulling them off is more rewarding than learning from mistakes. If you aspire to be a better sailboat racer, you ought to make every hour on the water productive by maximizing your preparation.

Post-race Notebook Entries

To learn most effectively from your racing experiences, make sure you write down all the hard data of a race: date, wind direction, windspeed, number of races, course configuration, general area it was sailed in, strength and direction of current, sea conditions, crew weight, and results. A record of your successes and failures in a race won't mean anything unless you know the variables that you were up against. For instance, looking back over your notebook, you might decide that you've mastered the art of starting at the leeward end of the line, since you've always gotten good starts at the pin. Such a conclusion could lead to trouble if you've always started in small fleets or if you've never started on a crowded line. To evaluate your starting technique, record what your plan for the start was, where you ended up starting, the number of boats that started, whether you started in a crowd, whether or not you started at the favored end.

After recording all the hard data in a postmortem entry, Tom jots down some notes on how the racing went. "I usually write down three areas: the start, the first beat, and then the race in general. In the section on the start, I write about what happened and how I could learn from it. Then I bring out any key moments in the race that made the difference between winning and losing. If I couldn't implement a tactic as planned, I note what went wrong —what happened that I didn't foresee. Make some comments on your key competitors' tactics. Most important, ask yourself what you learned, and what you could have done better. Dennis and I always talk on the way in from the course about what we could have improved, even if we sailed a great race. If you aren't hard on yourself and don't try to learn from your experiences, you'll never improve."

You don't have to make elaborate notes; just jot down the key points. If you want, create a separate diary section where you can record nonessential events. You can even add diagrams.

During a weekend or week-long series, it pays to record your compass logs from each race in your notebook. If you don't have a true-wind-direction instrument, keep track of your headings on each tack. Recording your compass logs enables you to discover patterns in the wind's behavior from one day to the next, which will help you create a game plan for the remaining races in the series. As long as a front hasn't passed through, chances are that the patterns of the wind's behavior will repeat from one day to the next. Try graphing the wind direction and the windspeed over the course of the day. Any patterns that become evident from the two graphs will help you prepare for the next day's race.

"The prevailing summer breeze for Newport, Rhode Island, and nearby Block Island is southerly," says Tom. "By keeping track of my compass logs, I was able to find out some interesting things about the southerly breeze. If the prevailing sea breeze fills in fairly early to the right of 210 degrees, you can almost count on it going to 230. But if it doesn't blow to the right of 210 or 205, then you can almost count on the wind going left. That's a perfect example of how to learn from writing down what you're seeing. If I hadn't kept track of the wind shifts, I'm not sure I would've caught on to what was happening. It may sound easy, but it's not easy while you're out on the racecourse, trying to assess which way the wind is going to shift."

Tom's notebook helped him greatly when he was calling tactics aboard *Stars & Stripes* during the America's Cup in Australia. "To tell the truth, it's surprising how long it took us to learn that the left side of the course was dominant when the sea breeze filled in," Tom says. "As time went by, we learned that the left side was better. In match racing, it usually pays to start to the right of the other boat, because this means you're automatically ahead with a starboard tack advantage, which allows you to control the first crossing situation. In Fremantle, however, if both boats started on starboard tack, the wind would shift to the left enough so the boat that started to the left could tack and cross the windward boat.

"The sea breeze's shift to the left was something that my notebook helped us learn. Each day I wrote down that starting to the left of the other boat seemed to work, although at the beginning of the race our position didn't look good. After a couple of weeks of noticing the shift to the left, we did a study and found out that the shore was affecting the direction of the breeze. We determined that near the shore the wind shifted more perpendicular to the shoreline, while the farther offshore we sailed, the less perpendicular the wind became."

Organizing Your Practice Time

There are three general areas in which you have to become proficient in order to be a winning sailor. These are boatspeed, boat handling, and "sailing smart" on the racecourse. Boatspeed covers anything that can be done mechanically: fairing and cleaning the bottom, tuning the rig, trimming the sails, and keeping the boat light. Boat handling includes training the crew so that tacks, jibes, and sail changes are not only flawless, but done quickly enough to take advantage of fleeting tactical opportunities. Sailing smart covers steering the boat fast, starting well, going to the right marks, sailing the favored side of the course, playing the current correctly, making the right tactical moves, and not fouling out. You can't do well without mastering all three of these areas. Without boatspeed you might be lucky and win an occasional race by grabbing a good wind shift, but slow boats don't generally win races. And you cannot win races without good crew work. How many times have you approached a leeward mark in a good position, only to have boats leave you in the dust as you tried to sail upwind with your spinnaker in the water? Finally, even if you have the best possible crew work and a fast boat, you won't win races if you're not pointed in the right direction. As Larks Harmoniously had a good chance of winning its 11-boat IMS division at the 1989 Buzzards Bay Race, but ended up second after failing to honor a government mark on the first beat of the third race. After returning to round the mark that she had passed on the wrong side, As Larks was in last place. Determined crew work and a never-say-die attitude got the fast boat back to third place by race's end. However, the impressive comeback did not make up for the tactical error, and the boat that As Larks had to beat finished second and won the regatta.

So keep your priorities in line by tracking your progress in a notebook. Then rearrange your practice efforts as you master boat speed, boat handling and sailing smart. You can even develop a grading system for the key areas you want to work on.

Practice Races

Most sailors use a notebook simply to record their racing experiences, but that's only one way to use such a valuable resource. "One of the first reasons to have a notebook is to organize your goals," says Gary. "Your goals aren't just to win sailboat races. You ought to plan out which races are the most important ones of the season. Having a major championship that you're working toward is a motivating tool. Once you develop a short list of regattas that you want to do well at, develop a much longer list of regattas and races that you'll then use for practice. The more regattas you consider important, the more practice racing you'll have to do."

There is only so much you can learn without actually getting out on the course and racing. People learning how to fly can learn a great deal from a flight simulator, but until they log hundreds of hours of flying time, they won't be qualified pilots. Therefore, to learn sailboat racing, you have to go out and race. However, you have to go out on the course with the right attitude. If you go out feeling pressured to win, you won't have the attitude you need to learn. Sail the course without the fear of failing. Of course, there may be times when you get heat from friends for losing the lead by not covering the fleet, but it's better to make that mistake in a Wednesday-night club race than at your district championship. When sailing races in the practice mode, try different tactics, sails, and sail-handling techniques. Otherwise you'll get stuck in a safe rut and not know if there are better ways to work the boat. Experiment by being aggressive at the start and fighting for the favored position. Or try disciplining yourself to a specific game plan, even though you'll have to dip a bunch of transoms to get to the other side of the course. Consider passing boats to leeward on the reaches, or make a point of passing boats one at a time, even though you have the opportunity to pass groups of boats. Practice crossing the finish line perpendicularly.

Errors etch a lasting impression on your brain. "One of the really painful lessons I learned sailing the SORC came the first time I steered a boat in the Miami–Fort Lauderdale race," says Gary. "Since Fort Lauderdale is a little over 20 miles north of Miami, it seemed to me that the way to go was straight up the beach. I found out how much it pays to sail offshore to get a three-knot boost from the northerly-flowing Gulf Stream when I ended up in last place, about three miles behind the fleet that went offshore. Sometimes, getting burned badly is the way to learn the lesson."

Besides sailing many races, the best practice comes from sailing races in different areas. Traveling to regattas raises your learning curve, since you are stripped of crutches you may have developed by sailing in home waters. At new venues, you'll be forced to get out on the course early and use all your skills to predict what the wind will do. When you sail against the same group of sailors, you begin to learn their tricks and tactical savvy. It doesn't pay to become a big fish in a small pond; your ability will seek the level of those you're competing against.

Go to regattas and sail against tougher competition. Talk to them after races. Most guys who do it right like to brag about what makes them fast. If another boat pulls away from you going downwind, study the boat to see what the crew is doing differently. Watch where their crew weight is, how the sails are trimmed, how far up their centerboard is, how their skipper steers through the waves, and how the crew trims the sails. However, before talking to other sailors who did better than you, analyze your own race. Even if it proved wrong, write down what your game plan was and why you developed it. Then find out the game plans from those who finished in the top five places. Figure out what they saw that you missed seeing.

During the national championships, the Thistle class organizes an "experts roundtable" after each day's racing, where the top three finishers in each race describe their game plans and how they set up their boat and their tactics; then the rest of the sailors are free to ask questions. Try to organize similar discussions in your class for as many regattas as you can.

Another way to improve your racing ability is to sail other types of boats occasionally. Small boats put you in tune with the wind and the waves. Gary feels that Laser sailing makes him a better big-boat sailor. On bigger boats you learn how much you need to depend on organization and teamwork. Even if you just get a spot sitting on the rail of a big boat, you'll be able to look for wind on the water, study how the other boats attack the course, and listen to the decision-making process on your own boat. Things happen more slowly on big boats, since boat-handling jobs that are covered by one person on a dinghy are divided up among many people on a big boat. Thus, yacht racing on big boats is more of a thinking man's game compared to dinghy sailing, which is a test of agility. Therefore, by sailing on different-sized boats, you'll become a well-rounded sailor.

Previsualization

A good way to practice when not on the water is to run through moves in your mind. If you become familiar with a maneuver in your mind, when you actually perform that maneuver on the water, it will be easier. This is a proven technique used to train Olympic athletes. For instance, if you're having problems getting from one side of your dinghy to the other smoothly during a roll tack, think through the proper moves while driving to work, or when taking a break at the office, or when you're lying in bed trying to get to sleep. Imagine yourself leaning out and turning the tiller slowly until the boat's bow comes through the eye of the wind. As soon as your rear end gets wet, lean in and

▼

cross the boat with your aft leg first, so that you face forward during the tack. Pass the hiking stick behind your back to your hand holding the mainsheet. As you sit down on the new windward side, reach for the mainsheet with your free hand and ease the sail some. Then lift up the hiking strap with your forward foot. Get both feet under the strap and hike out to flatten the boat. In a multistep maneuver like tacking, you'll improve by familiarizing yourself with the moves first. Get your crew to practice previsualizing their duties too.

"One thing that helps me before a big regatta," Gary says, "is to sit down and picture what's going to happen. When the actual event happens, I'm more relaxed. For instance, going into the last race of the 1986 Liberty Cup, Chris Dickson was the only competitor standing between me and winning the regatta. To get ready, I mentally pictured what Dickson looked like. I thought back to past races against him, and went over what I did right and what I did wrong. Then I pictured what the sailing conditions would be for the next day's race. I even figured out which side of the course would be favored, based on how I thought the wind would blow.

"Next, I created a game plan of what moves to use against Dickson. He likes to mix it up at the starting line by turning tight circles to force a foul. So my plan was to avoid circling altogether by luffing to kill time. I also remembered that he likes the leeward position coming up to the line, and when he's stuck to windward he normally tacks away. So my plan was to anticipate his move by tacking with him and preventing him from heading back toward the line. And that's exactly what happened. I didn't circle; I went into the luffing mode. I anticipated his tack when he was above me, and I tacked at the same time he did. That way I was able to trap him, and he wasn't able to get back to the line. I had prepared the whole plan mentally the night before, and it all paid off. I beat Dickson in that race and I collected my Liberty Cup win."

The Smile Factor

"I believe that you can improve your sailing by sailing alone," says Gary. "One of the things I do is sail my Laser hard. During the summer of 1989, I kept my Laser on the beach in front of the house I rented on Block Island. I had fun introducing non-sailors to the sport, as well as going out for wild rides in big blows. For four days a week I sailed anywhere from one to three hours a day. During that time I took each of my three kids for rides, and anyone else who wanted to go. Then I sailed as hard as I could while doing drills. My drills not only got my heart pumping hard, but included tacking, jibing, boat handling, mark roundings, and 720s. Typical drills included sailing figure-eights around two buoys or pilings close together, seeing how many times I could tack in 60 seconds, and spinning the boat in four consecutive circles first in one direction and then in the other."

Do some sailing with your crew that isn't race-oriented. Use your boat to day-sail in a relaxed atmosphere. Invite the crew out for a picnic or cruise. Your team spirit will increase, and the crew will be more relaxed on racing days.

"The problem with sailing with an America's Cup team is that practice gets repetitious," Gary says. "Every day you're out with the same crew on the same boat, doing basically the same things. To prevent the crew from burning out, it's good to change the momentum every now and then. That's one of the things Ted Turner did well. One morning when we were racing against *Independence*, they had to go in for the rest of the day to repair some problem gear. Instead of going in or practicing by ourselves, Turner headed *Courageous* to Block Island for lunch. The crew was ecstatic as we sailed the 12-meter through the narrow channel of Great Salt Pond. Going for a ride on the boat changed the atmosphere from another tedious day of practice to something special and exciting. Having a huge lobster lunch didn't hurt our spirits, either!"

Glossary

Angle of Attack: The angle between the centerline of a boat and the direction of the wind.

Apparent Wind Direction: The wind direction you feel when the boat is moving.

Apparent Wind Speed: The wind speed you feel when moving.

Aspect Ratio: The height of a sail, keel, or rudder divided by its width.

Back: A counter-clockwise wind shift. *Also see* Veer.

Backwind: Disturbed wind deflected to windward off the back of a boat's sails.

Backwinding the Jib: A way to help turn the boat by not freeing the jib sheet during a tack. Thus, the wind blows against the jib, forcing the boat to turn onto the new course.

Backwinding the Main: Deflected wind off the back edge of the jib that makes the forward section of the mainsail luff.

Bad Air (Dirty Air, Gas): Disturbed wind coming off another boat's sails. Boats sailing in bad air will go slower than those in clear air. Bad air can refer to a boat's backwind or its blanket zone. *See* Backwind *and* Blanket Zone.

Bald-headed: Sailing under main without a jib.

Barging: Passing between a close-hauled leeward boat and a starting mark. Rule 42.4, referred to as the "Anti-Barging Rule," states: "When approaching the starting line to start . . . a leeward yacht shall be under no obligation to give any windward yacht room to pass to leeward of a starting mark. . . ."

Bear off: To change your current course away from the wind.

Bear-away Set: A maneuver for rounding a mark and hoisting the spinnaker without jibing.

Black Flag Rule: A provision that can be included in a race's sailing instructions that disqualifies any boat over the starting line within a minute of the start. Under the rule, once a boat is disqualified, it is barred from all remaining attempts to start that race.

Blanket Zone: The area to leeward and behind a boat where the wind is totally blocked. *See* Backwind *and* Bad Air.

Blanketing: Using your sails to block the wind from another boat.

Broach: When a keel boat sailing on a run capsizes from a blast of wind or gets knocked over by a wave. This is not uncommon when flying a spinnaker in high winds.

Center of Effort: An imaginary point in a boat's rig that represents the center of the driving forces of the main sail and the jib—somewhat analogous to the expression "center of gravity."

Coffee Grinder: A cranking mechanism for turning a winch made up of a pedestal with cranks on top similar to bicycle pedals that crew turn with their hands.

Crack Off: Easing your sheets and steering slightly below your current course.

Current Sheer: A line of foam and flotsam in the water formed by the meeting of two currents of differing strength.

Dirty Air: *See* Bad air.

Draft: 1. The deepest part of the curve in a sail.

2. The distance from the water line to the bottom of a boat's keel.

Ducking a Boat: Altering course to pass *behind* a boat on the opposite tack.

Ebb Tide: The outgoing tide. *Also see* Slack Tide *and* Flood Tide.

Feathering: Sailing closer to the wind for a few moments when beating. Feathering de-powers the boat in strong winds. When sailing "too close" to the wind while beating, the sails luff slightly, which reduces the boat's heel.

Fetching: When a boat's course allows it to round a mark without tacking.

Flattening Reef: A sail control that flattens the bottom part of the mainsail. The control line passes through a grommet on the leech of the sail about a foot above the boom. When the line is tightened the grommet is pulled down to the boom and out as far as the sail can stretch. Also called Flattener.

Floater Takedown: Dousing the spinnaker by taking the pole down early and then jibing the main sail so that the spinnaker comes down in the lee of the main. Normally done when a boat must jibe to get around a leeward mark.

Flood Tide: The incoming tide. *Also see* Ebb Tide *and* Slack Tide.

Foot (Footing, Foot off): To head lower then your best upwind course. By falling off slightly and easing your sails accordingly; your speed will increase. Footing will help you keep your speed when sailing through a set of large waves. *Also see* Pinching.

Geographic Wind: Wind flow that is affected by local topography, including mountains, islands and buildings.

Groove, In the: The feeling of speed when the sails are trimmed correctly and the person on the helm steers well.

Hand-bearing Compass: A small hand-held compass that you can hold up to your eye to get a bearing on objects like boats, buoys, or points of land. Hand-bearing compasses are also referred to as "hockey pucks" because of their round shape and black rubber protective cover.

Header: A wind shift that brings the wind direction closer to your bow. The usual response to a header is to bear off or trim your sails. When sailing downwind, a header is helpful since you will be able to trim your sails tighter and go faster without a change in course. Also called a knock or knocker.

Headstay Sag: The curve, or sag, to leeward in the headstay caused by the force of wind on the sail.

Heavy/Light: Terms having to do with how the person on the helm is steering. You are steering a heavy course (or "footing") when the boat's angle to the wind is too great. This is indicated by the leeward telltale on the leading edge of the jib hanging limp. Sailing a light course (or "pinching") is when the boat's angle to the wind is too small. You're sailing light when the windward telltale on the leading edge of the jib hangs down straight.

Hole: An area where the wind is weaker then the surrounding environs.

IMS: International Measurement System. A system that handicaps boats based on the boat's hull lines and sail plan. The heart of the program is a computer driven velocity prediction program that determines a boat's optimal performance in different wind strengths and sailing angles. Thus, a boat does not have only one rating under IMS. A boat's rating changes with the wind strength and course configuration. The IMS rule encourages duel-use racer-cruisers once again. *Also see* IOR, MORC, *and* PHRF.

IOR: International Offshore Rule. A handicap system that takes measurements at different locations along a boat's hull. Thus, designers have created hulls with flat spots and "bumps" to get measurement credits. The IOR handicap rule came into its own in the early 1970s and was once used extensively for big boat racing. Now the rule is only being used for a few grand prix events like the Admirals Cup, and racing circuits for the International 50 Class and the International Class A Yachting Association (maxis). *Also see* IMS, MORC, *and* PHRF.

Knock/Knocker: *See* Header.

Layline: The point when you can sail a close-hauled course and fetch an upwind mark; or the fastest downwind sailing angle to a leeward mark. In each case there is a port and starboard layline. *Also see* Long Layline.

Lazy Guy/Lazy Sheet: Lines used on big boats for jibing the spinnaker. Each clue of the spinnaker has a guy and sheet attached, the ones not in use are called the lazy guy and lazy sheet.

Lee bow: An advantageous tactical position ahead and to leeward of another close-hauled boat. When the leeward boat is positioned correctly, disturbed wind off the leeward boat's sails slows the windward boat.

Lee Helm or Leeward Helm: The tendency of a boat to bear off when the helm is released. Lee helm is normally encountered in light air or if your mast is too far forward in the boat.

Lift: A wind shift that allows a boat to sail closer to its destination upwind. When you get a lift, the wind shifts from the bow toward the beam. When sailing downwind a lift slows you since the wind moves toward the stern. (Sailing dead downwind is the slowest point off the wind.)

Loose Cover: A defensive position ahead of a boat or group of boats in which the lead boat does not effect the wind of the trailing boat or boats. *See* Tight Cover.

Long Layline: In the rare instances when the wind blows squarely from the windward mark to the starting line, then both laylines are equally as long. When the course is skewed to the wind, one layline will be longer than the other. The starboard layline, for example, is the longer of the two when the wind blows from the right side of a line running from the windward mark to the starting line and vice versa.

Luff: 1. In the definition section of the racing rules, "luffing" is defined as altering course toward the wind. Luffing is the defense the rule makers give a leeward boat to protect its wind from a boat passing to windward.
2. The forward edge of a sail.
3. The flapping of a sail caused by the boat heading too close to the wind or because the sail is not trimmed tight enough.

Lull: A temporary decrease in wind strength. *See* Puff.

Mast Abeam: The hail made by the helmsman of a windward boat that stops a leeward boat from luffing. Racing Rule 38.2(a) defines mast abeam as when the helmsman of the windward boat sitting in his normal position and when his boat is sailing no higher than the leeward boat, is abreast or forward of the mainmast of the leeward boat.

Maxi (Maxi Boat): A boat designed to the maximum rating allowed under the International Offshore Rule. Most maxis are about 80-feet long and are sailed by a crew of 26. Maxis are also called "70-raters" since 70 is the maximum rating under IOR. The owners of these monsters have created their own class organization called the International Class A Racing Association.

Mid-line Sag: When boats toward the middle of the starting line misjudge where the line is and end up too far behind the line at the start.

MORC: Midget Ocean Racing Club. A measurement handicap rule specifically designed for boats that are 30 feet and under. *Also see* IMS, IOR, and PHRF.

One-Minute Rule: Racing Rule 51.1(c), which requires boats over the starting line within a minute of the start to sail around an end of the line before restarting. The rule is also referred to as "The Round the Ends Rule."

Oscillating Wind Shift: When the wind shifts back and forth. *Also see* Persistent Shift.

Overpowered/Underpowered: A boat is overpowered when it heels too much from having too much sail up. Underpowered is when a boat is slowed because it does not have enough sail up to power the boat to its potential.

Overstand: To sail beyond a layline.

PHRF: Performance Handicap Racing Fleet. The ratings under PHRF are assigned based on how boats perform instead of on a measurement rule. Ratings are assigned by regional committees. Therefore, a boat that does well in light winds like a Schock 35 can owe time to a heavy Baltic 38 in Southern California where the wind is light. But the Baltic owes the Schock time in Massachusetts's blustery Buzzards Bay. *Also see* IMS, IOR and MORC.

Persistent Wind Shift: When the wind keeps shifting in the same direction over time. *Also see* Oscillating Shift.

Pinching Off a Boat: Sailing high of your optimum windward course to slow a boat to windward with backwind off your sails.

Pinching: Heading closer to the wind than your optimum course while sailing upwind. Pinching slows you down, but you can trade that speed for a better tactical position. Also see "Footing."

Polar Diagram: A graph showing a boat's predicted speed at every wind angle over a range of wind speeds. A polar diagram tells you the optimum speeds your boat should achieve.

Preventer: A line or block and tackle that pulls the boom forward, preventing the boom from unexpectedly crossing to the other side of the boat. A preventer is normally rigged sailing dead downwind, when accidental jibes can occur.

Puff: A temporary increase in wind strength. *See* Lull.

Reacher: A high-clued genoa used when close reaching in heavy winds. Also know as "blast reacher."

Rolled: Slang for getting passed to windward.

Roll Tack: A maneuver that minimizes the loss of speed while the boat turns through the eye of the wind. It involves keeping crew weight on the windward rail through the tack to help the boat heel over onto the new tack.

720 Rule: An alternate penalty that allows a competitor to absolve him or herself of a foul on the race course by turning his or her boat in two consecutive 360-degree turns. The 720 is an option open to race committees; therefore, it may or may not be included in a race's sailing instructions—be sure to check. For more details see Appendix 3 of the International Yacht Racing Rules.

Slack Tide: The period midway between high and low tide when the tidal currents are significantly diminished.

Slam Dunk: A maneuver on a windward leg involving boats on opposite tacks. A boat crossing ahead tacks right on the wind of a boat crossing behind, just as the latter passes by the leading boat's transom.

Square the Pole: Tightening the spinnaker guy, which pulls the outboard end of spinnaker pole back.

Stall: When the flow of air around the sails or flow of water around the rudder and keel breaks away causing the loss of lift.

Starboard Tack Advantage: The boat that is on the right side of another going upwind has the advantage of being on starboard tack during a crossing situation. On a run, the boat on the left has the starboard tack advantage.

Tack Change: A method for changing head sails with a double-grooved headstay. The new jib is raised on the windward side of the current jib before tacking. After the boat tacks, the old jib, now on the windward side of the new sail, is dropped.

Tacking Angle: The angle between a boat's headings on port and starboard tack.

Target Speed: Boatspeeds that are used as guidelines for attaining a boat's maximum performance upwind and downwind. The targets for any boat vary with true wind strength.

Tight Cover: A defensive position in which the leader matches the maneuvers of the trailing boat tack for tack, and even slows the trailing boat by using its sails to block or disturb the trailing boat's wind. *See* Loose Cover.

True Wind Direction: The compass heading that the wind is blowing from. The true wind direction is not affected by boatspeed or the boat's heading. *Also see* Apparent Wind Direction.

True Wind Speed: The velocity that the wind is actually blowing—the speed you'd measure if the boat was standing still.

Two-Boatlength Circle: An imaginary boundary around a racing buoy with a radius two boatlengths long used for determining which boat is entitled to room at the mark. If two boats of different length approach a mark, the radius of the circle is twice the length of the leading boat.

Two-Tack the Beat: Getting to the windward mark by only tacking once. To two-tack a beat, a sailor would sail on one tack until reaching the layline to the windward mark, and then tack to fetch the mark.

Veer: A clockwise wind shift. *Also see* Back.

Velocity Made Good on Course (VMC): Component of boatspeed in the direction of a mark. Or, more simply put, how fast you're getting to where you want to go. VMC may well be different from the boat speed measured on a knot meter because one often does not sail on the rhumb (direct) line to a mark (see Chapter 8).

Velocity Made Good (VMG): The component of boatspeed measured against wind direction. That is, how fast you're heading to or from the direction from which the wind is coming (see Chapter 8).

Velocity Prediction Program (VPP): A computer program that analyzes a boat's hull form, weight, and sail plan to calculate a boat's sailing performance.

Velocity Shift: A temporary shift in apparent wind angle caused by a gust or lull in true wind speed. *See* Apparent Wind.

Weather or Windward Helm: The tendency of a boat to head up when the helm is released. Measured in degrees of rudder angle required to steer a straight course.

Working Sails: The sails used for going to windward, e.g. on a sloop, the working sails are the main and genoa or jib.

Index